THE WRITINGS OF
Elliott Carter

Elliott Carter at Lincoln Center.

Photo courtesy of Nancy Crampton.

THE WRITINGS OF
Elliott Carter

An American Composer
Looks at Modern Music

COMPILED, EDITED, AND ANNOTATED BY
Else Stone and Kurt Stone

INDIANA UNIVERSITY PRESS
Bloomington & London

Published in Canada by Fitzhenry & Whiteside Limited, Don Mills, Ontario

Manufactured in the United States of America

Library of Congress Cataloging in Publication Data

Carter, Elliott Cook, 1908–
The writings of Elliott Carter.

1. Music—Addresses, essays, lectures.   2. Music—
History and criticism—20th century.   I. Stone, Else,
1912–   II. Stone, Kurt.   III. Title.
ML60.C22   780'.904   76–48539
ISBN 0–253–36720–4

Contents

Acknowledgments

Grateful acknowledgment is made to the following for the use of articles and musical excerpts reprinted in this collection. Detailed bibliographical information will be found at the head of each article and/or in footnotes.

The American Academy of Arts and Letters, for "Igor Stravinsky, 1882–1971," *Proceedings of the American Academy of Arts and Letters and the National Institute of Arts and Letters*.

American Composers Alliance, for "Wallingford Riegger," *ACA Bulletin*.

Elliott Carter, for "An American Destiny [Charles Edward Ives]," *Listen*; "Introduction to a Poetry Reading Session by W. H. Auden"; "*Brass Quintet*"; "The Composer's Choices"; "Documents of a Friendship with Ives," in *Parnassus* and *Tempo*; "Gabriel Fauré," *Listen*; "The Function of the Composer," in *Bulletin of the Society for Music in the Liberal Arts College*; "A Further Step/(1958)," in *The American Composer Speaks—1770–1965*, ed. Gilbert Chase; "Charles Ives Remembered," in Vivian Perlis, *Charles Ives Remembered: An Oral History*; "Music Criticism"; program notes for *String Quartet No. 2, String Quartet No. 3, Variations for Orchestra*.

The College Music Society, for " 'The Composer Is a University Commodity,' " in *College Music Symposium*.

John Kirkpatrick for his explanatory footnote on page 100.

The Music Journal, for "The Time Dimension in Music."

The Music Library Association and Minna Lederman for all articles originally published in *Modern Music*: "The New York Season, 1937," "Late Winter, New York, 1937," "The Sleeping Beauty," "Season's End in New York, 1937," "More about Balanchine," "Opening Notes, New York, 1937," "In the Theatre, 1937," "With the Dancers, 1937," "Homage to Ravel, 1875–1937," "Vacation Novelties," "With the Dancers, 1938," "Musical Reactions—Bold and Otherwise," "Orchestras and Audiences; Winter, 1938," "Recent Festival in Rochester, 1938," "Season's End, New York, Spring, 1938," "Coolidge Crusade; WPA; New York Season, 1938," "Once Again Swing; Also 'American Music,' " "The Case of Mr. Ives," "Further Notes on the Winter Season, 1938/9," "O Fair World of Music!" "At the Hall of Music," "Season of Hindemith and Americans, 1939," "The New York Season Opens, 1939," "American Music in the New York Scene, 1940," "Stravinsky and Other Moderns in 1940," "The Changing Scene, New York, 1940," "Films and Theatre, 1942," "American Figure, with Landscape," "Theatre and Films, 1943 [May–June]," "Theatre and Films, 1943 [November]," "Ives Today: His Vision and Challenge," "Music as a Liberal Art," "Scores for Graham; Festival at Columbia, 1946," "Fallacy of the Mechanistic Approach." Copyrighted © 1937, 1938, 1939, 1940, 1941, 1942, 1943, 1944, 1945, 1946 by The League of Composers, Inc., and Renewed 1965, 1966, 1967, 1968, 1969, 1970, 1971, 1972, 1973 by The League of Composers/I.S.C.M.U.S. Chapter.

The Musical Quarterly, for "Walter Piston," "Current Chronicle: New York [Roger Sessions]," "Current Chronicle: Italy [ISCM Festival in Rome]," "Shop Talk by an American Composer," "Current Chronicle: Germany, 1960," "Current Chronicle: New York [Edward Steuermann]."

The National Institute of Arts and Letters, for all Ives writings and musical excerpts contained in this collection; specifically, the Ives writings in "Documents of a Friendship with Ives," © 1975 by The National Institute of Arts and Letters.

National Music Council, for "The Composer's Viewpoint," in *Music Council Bulletin*.

The New York Times, for "Sixty Staves to Read," © 1960 by The New York Times Company. Reprinted by permission.

Nonesuch Records, for record-liner notes on *Double Concerto for Harpsichord and Piano with Two Chamber Orchestras* and *Duo for Violin and Piano* (H–71314); *Sonata for Cello and Piano* and *Sonata for Flute, Oboe, Cello, and Harpsichord* (H–71234); and *String Quartets No. 1 and No. 2* (H–71249): © 1975, 1969, and 1970, respectively, by Nonesuch Records, a division of Warner Communications, Inc. Used by Permission of Nonesuch Records.

University of Oklahoma Press, for "Elliott Carter" in *The Composer's Point of View: Essays on Twentieth-Century Music by Those Who Wrote It*, ed. Robert Stephan Hines. Copyright © 1970 by University of Oklahoma Press.

Perspectives of New Music, for "The Milieu of the American Composer," "Letter from Europe," "Expressionism and American Music," an untitled commemorative article on Stravinsky [1971], "In Memoriam: Stefan Wolpe 1902–1972."

The Philharmonic-Symphony Society of New York, for program note for *A Symphony of Three Orchestras*.

Saturday Review, Inc., for "New Publications of Music."

Kraus Reprint, a division of Kraus-Thomson Organization Ltd, on behalf of *The Score*, for "The Rhythmic Basis of American Music."

Tempo (Boosey & Hawkes Music Publishers Ltd), for "Documents of a Friendship with Ives." (See also The National Institute of Arts and Letters for all Ives writings contained in this article: © 1975 by The National Institute of Arts and Letters.)

University of Texas Press, for "Music and the Time Screen," in *Current Thoughts in Musicology*, ed. John Grubbs.

INTRODUCTORY NOTE

Elliott Carter began to write for publication in 1937. At the age of twenty-eight, after graduation from Harvard University and three years at the École Normale de Musique and with Nadia Boulanger, he became a regular reviewer for Minna Lederman's remarkable magazine, *Modern Music*. He chiefly covered recitals of new music in New York, with occasional excursions to Boston, Philadelphia, and Washington, D.C., but he also reviewed opera, ballet, motion pictures, and the theater. In addition, he wrote articles on individuals—Charles Ives, Henry F. Gilbert, Walter Piston, and Roger Sessions, for example—and on more general subjects, such as the delightfully sarcastic description of the 1939 New York World's Fair, "O Fair World of Music!"

All the *Modern Music* articles reveal their author to be a youthful, musically sensitive and knowledgeable, well-educated, idealistic, and occasionally somewhat rash rebel in search of a more perfect musical world in which a truly American new music, free from the thrall of European influences, could flourish unhampered by a conservative American Establishment. Carter's literary activity slowed down considerably when he left New York in 1940 to teach at St. John's College in Annapolis, Maryland, and later when he became music consultant to the Office of War Information.

When he returned to New York in 1945, Carter resumed his writings, but he had become a more relaxed and circumspect observer (though no less rebellious). Besides, he was no longer required to review concerts and meet deadlines, so from then on he wrote only when he himself felt the need, except for a number of occasional pieces produced upon request—testimonials, eulogies, and the like—some of which had to be omitted from this collection because of space limitations (see the list of omitted material at the end of the book). He has continued to resort to verbal expressions of his ideas, on and off, to this day, with a gradual shift of focus toward his own music and its underlying esthetic philosophy.

When we began to prepare Carter's writings for this collection it seemed desirable to group the articles according to certain topics, such as:

1. Elliott Carter on his own music;
2. Elliott Carter on the music of others;
3. Elliott Carter on Charles Ives;
4. Elliott Carter on other individual composers;
5. Elliott Carter on the musical scene in America and Europe;
6. Elliott Carter on dance, opera, theater, movies, and literature;
7. Elliott Carter on music education;
8. Elliott Carter on subjects not covered above.

Obviously, such groupings present problems, particularly with a writer like Carter, whose characteristic approach is to see things in context both musical and socioeconomic in order to discover links and influences, draw parallels, and compare opposites.

Moreover, the impact of Charles Ives on Carter—not only as a composer but also as a philosopher and a human being—has been so profound and continuous throughout Carter's career that it would be unrealistic and artificial to separate the few articles that happen to focus specifically on Ives. Taking these articles out of their chronological context would leave unexplained many of the reasons for Carter's changing attitudes toward Ives's ideas, changes that were due to general as well as personal developments on the part of Carter and to his ever-deeper penetration of Ives's musical aims and the music of other commanding creative personalities, such as Schoenberg and Stravinsky (who would have to be dealt with in *different* topical groups). The same dilemma, to a greater or lesser degree, would of course arise with respect to a good many other subjects.

We therefore abandoned, regretfully, the idea of grouping the articles and decided, instead, on chronological order. And to compensate for the lack of topicality, we have supplied a very detailed index, annotated where it seemed helpful. The chronological presentation, however, has the advantage of providing a *continuous* history of the American musical, cultural, and arts-related socioeconomic development of an especially interesting period in American music, the early thirties to the mid-seventies. During this time an indigenous American serious music emerged, as American composers gradually freed themselves from their traditional dependence on European models. This development—unique in the history of American music—coincided, oddly, with the arrival in the United States of the very Europeans who personified those dominating models: Bartók, Hindemith, Schoenberg, and Stravinsky, and to a slightly lesser extent, Milhaud, Toch, and Wolpe.

Subsequently, this historical panorama traces the ensuing, inevitable reversal of influences, when the newcomers began to absorb the impact of their new environment (or failed to do so), resulting eventually in a conglomerate and synthesis of all these many complex interactions. All of this is reported as seen and heard by one of America's most sensitive, erudite, and keen musicians, who performs the double role of observer and involved composer.

This chronological presentation, naturally, also traces the development of Carter's own personality, as a critical observer as well as a composer. There are the two prophetic early articles "The Case of Mr. Ives" (1939) and "Ives Today: His Vision and Challenge" (1944), which not only show Carter's changing attitude toward the music of Ives but also mark the beginning of the dominant influence of Ives's ideas on Carter's own approach to composition throughout his career. This influence, however, was never more than a basic attitude; in detail and in actual execution, Carter has always been deeply interested in *all* the trends that together make up our uniquely diversified era, and in his early works he tried out whichever style and approach seemed worthy of his attention. He gradually grew more self-assured, gained in independence, and eventually began to develop a musical language all his own. This done, he began to explore its capabilities: each work represented a new challenge he set himself, to test the validity and versatility of his new idiom, a process that has never ceased.

His new approach found its first, still quite cautious expression in the *Cello Sonata* of 1948, and was further tested in a succession of works, each a little farther from traditional methods of composition. Descriptions of his new ways and discoveries were at first limited to program notes, until he found that the time had come for more comprehensive verbal expression in articles such as "The Time Dimension in Music" (1965), which is still linked to Ives in many ways; "The Orchestral Composer's Point of View" (1970), a virtual travelogue into Carter's manifold experiments to isolate and re-order formerly unrecognized musical forces and ingredients; and "Music and the Time Screen" (1976), which constitutes Carter's most profound disquisition so far on the various philosophical concepts of "time" and their "translation" into equivalent musical phenomena and structures in his own works.

In addition to this personal musical development, which naturally threads its way through all the articles, Carter covers his musical environment in much greater diversity than most writing musicians have done, and always in a refreshingly non-routine way: his interests are boundless, but he relates them all to music. He deals with the role of the serious musician, and especially the "advanced" composer, in today's anti-cultural atmosphere, in the university as well as in "real life"; government support of the arts in Europe versus foundation support in the United States; the various avant-gardes, old and new, here and abroad, true and phony; the influences of Schoenberg/Webern, Ives, Stravinsky, etc., on his own music and on that of others; and so forth. There are uncommonly perceptive analyses of the music of many of his contemporaries (including a fascinating glimpse into Stravinsky's working methods); exciting descriptions of music festivals everywhere (and inside views of the juries that select the programs); bitter denunciations of America's cultural Establishment; noteworthy suggestions for radical changes in musical education; and of course a large selection of program notes for his own works, notes that often go far beyond mere descriptions of the compositions. We have occasionally included more than one program note for the same piece because it is interesting to see how Carter viewed a given work years after its composition and how he compared it to other pieces that had not yet been written at the time of the earlier program. note.

In his most recent articles, Ives regains prominence, but now Carter is able to view his Ivesian years with greater detachment, and he does so from two different angles. He collected his personal reminiscences in his contribution to Vivian Perlis's book *Charles Ives Remembered: An Oral History* (1969) and followed it with "Documents of a Friendship with Ives" (1975/6), in which the significance of the two early *Modern Music* articles on Ives is elaborated with remarkable candor.

Elliott Carter belongs to the comparatively small number of composers who throughout their careers have supplemented their purely musical output with literary essays and descriptions to formulate their thoughts and observations and explain their works—composers whose spectrum of interests is broader and more urgent than could be satisfied with "mere" composing.

Else Stone
Kurt Stone

New York
March 1977

ELLIOTT CARTER
Biographical Sketch and Major Compositions

To help the reader place Carter's articles in the context of his life—to relate them to the compositions he was concerned with at the time he wrote a given article, or to find out where he happened to be living or what work he was engaged in at the time of writing—we have compiled the following chronological sketch of Carter's life and career.

1908   Born December 11, New York.

1926   Graduated from Horace Mann High School, New York; went to Cambridge, Mass., to attend Harvard University (majoring in English literature) and Longy School of Music; joined Harvard Glee Club; played chamber music.

1930   B.A. from Harvard University; graduate work in music (with Walter Piston, harmony and counterpoint; A. T. Davison, choral composition; Edward B. Hill, music history; and Gustav Holst, composition).

1932   M.A. from Harvard University; went to Paris to study at École Normale de Musique and privately with Nadia Boulanger; member of madrigal group (Henri Expert); conducted own choral group.

1935   Graduated from École Normale with a *Licence de contrepoint*; returned to Cambridge.

1936   Returned to New York; began to write for *Modern Music*.

1937   Music director of Lincoln Kirstein's Ballet Caravan (until 1939).

        Tarantella (poem by Ovid), arrangement for men's chorus and piano four-hands of the Prologue to Carter's Incidental Music for Plautus's *Mostellaria* of 1936 (commissioned by the Harvard Glee Club).

1938   *To Music* (Herrick), for mixed chorus a cappella (WPA Music Division prize).

1939   *Pocahontas*, ballet music (commissioned by the Ballet Caravan); board member of the League of Composers (until 1952); board member of the American Composers Alliance (ACA) (until 1950); married Helen Frost-Jones, sculptor and art critic.

1940   Left Ballet Caravan to teach music, Greek, and mathematics at St. John's College, Annapolis, Md. (until 1944; there developed a new teaching approach together with philosopher Scott Buchanan—see pp. 105, 155–56 of the present collection).

1941   *Pocahontas Suite*, for orchestra (Juilliard Publication Award); *The De-*

fence of Corinth (Rabelais), for speaker, men's voices, and piano four-hands.

1942   *Symphony No. 1.*

1942/3 *Voyage* (Hart Crane), for medium voice and piano.

1943   Music consultant to the Office of War Information (until 1945); *Three Poems by Robert Frost*, for medium voice and piano; *Warble for Lilac Time* (Whitman), for soprano and piano (later arranged for soprano and small orchestra).

1944   *The Harmony of Morning* (Mark Van Doren), for women's voices and small orchestra (commissioned by Temple Emanu-El); *Holiday Overture*, for orchestra (first prize at the Independent Music Publishers Contest, 1945).

1945   Guggenheim Fellowship.

1946   *Piano Sonata*; board member of the International Society for Contemporary Music (ISCM) (until 1952); Professor of Composition at Peabody Conservatory, Baltimore, Md. (until 1948).

1947   *The Minotaur*, ballet music (commissioned by the Ballet Society); *Emblems* (Allen Tate), for men's chorus and piano.

1948   *Woodwind Quintet*; *Sonata for Cello and Piano* (commissioned by Bernard Greenhouse); Professor of Composition at Columbia University (until 1950).

1949   *Six Pieces for Four Timpani (One Player)* (revised 1966).

1950   *Eight Etudes and a Fantasy*, for woodwind quartet; second Guggenheim Fellowship; grant from the National Institute of Arts and Letters; went to Tucson, Ariz., to write *String Quartet No. 1.*

1951   *String Quartet No. 1* (first prize at Concours International de Quatuors à Cordes, 1953, Liège, Belgium).

1952   President of the U.S. section of ISCM; *Sonata for Flute, Oboe, Cello, and Harpsichord* (commissioned by the Harpsichord Quartet; Walter Naumburg Musical Foundation Award, 1956).

1953   Prix de Rome.

1953/4 Fellow of the American Academy, Rome.

1955   *Variations for Orchestra* (commissioned by the Louisville Orchestra through the Ford Foundation).

1955/6 Professor of Composition at Queens College, New York.

1956   Elected to membership in the National Institute of Arts and Letters.

1958   Taught at the Salzburg (Austria) Seminars.

1959   *String Quartet No. 2* (commissioned by the Stanley String Quartet; Pulitzer Prize, 1960; New York Critics' Circle Award 1960; UNESCO Prize 1961; nominated as "best contemporary classical compositions 1961" by the National Academy of Recording Arts and Sciences).

1960   Professor of Composition at Yale University (until 1962).

1961   *Double Concerto for Harpsichord and Piano with Two Chamber Orchestras* (commissioned by the Fromm Foundation; Critics' Circle Award 1961); Sibelius Medal for Music; honorary doctorate, New England Conservatory of Music; American delegate to East-West Encounter, Tokyo.

1963   Composer-in-residence at the American Academy, Rome; elected to membership in the American Academy of Arts and Sciences, Boston.

1964   Composer-in-residence in Berlin (a Ford Foundation project); returned to New York to be Professor of Composition at the Juilliard School of Music.

1965   *Piano Concerto* (commissioned by Jacob Lateiner through the Ford Foundation); honorary doctorate, Swarthmore College; Creative Arts Award, Brandeis University.

1967   Harvard Glee Club Medal; honorary doctorate, Princeton University; Andrew D. White Professor-at-large at Cornell University (until 1968).

1968   Composer-in-residence at the American Academy, Rome; honorary doctorate, Ripon College.

1969   *Concerto for Orchestra* (commissioned by the New York Philharmonic for its 125th Anniversary Year); Premio delle Muse, "Polimnia," awarded by the Associazione Artistico Letteraria Internazionale, Florence; elected to membership in the American Academy of Arts and Letters.

1970   Honorary doctorates from Boston University, Harvard University, Oberlin College, and Yale University.

1971   Gold Medal for Eminence in Music, awarded by the National Institute of Arts and Letters; *String Quartet No. 3* (commissioned by the Juilliard School of Music for the Juilliard Quartet; Pulitzer Prize 1973).

1973/4 Exhibition of sketches and scores in manuscript in the Vincent Astor Gallery of the Library and Museum of the Performing Arts, The New York Public Library at Lincoln Center.

1974   *Duo for Violin and Piano* (commissioned by the McKim Fund in the Library of Congress); *Brass Quintet* (commissioned by the American Brass Quintet).

1976   *A Mirror on Which to Dwell* (Six Poems of Elizabeth Bishop), for soprano and instrumental ensemble (commissioned by Speculum Musicae).

        A Symphony of Three Orchestras (commissioned by the New York Philharmonic in recognition of the Bicentennial with funds from the National Endowment for the Arts).

NOTE: A chronological list of Carter's compositions, including several facsimile reproductions and other photographic illustrations, and a detailed and comprehensive bibliography of writings *about* Carter are contained in *Elliott Carter: Sketches and Scores in Manuscript*, issued in 1973 by The New York Public Library, Astor, Lenox, and Tilden Foundations, and distributed by Readex Books, 101 Fifth Avenue, New York, N.Y.

THE WRITINGS OF
Elliott Carter

The New York Season, 1937

Modern Music, 14,2 (Jan.–Feb. 1937)

If all that an American prize competition can produce for one of our finest orchestras is Philip James's *Bret Harte*, we are indeed doing pretty poorly. Perhaps most of our composers disdain these contests or suspect them from past performance, and so no longer enter. In this case—the recent Philharmonic offering—they may have feared the suggestions on the entry blank—offered as recommendations, and not set out as conditions—that the music have some connection (preferably explicit) with the American scene. Their fears were amply justified when the judges, on making their decision, used non-conformity to the suggestion as a reason for disqualifying much music that, I hope, was better than the *Bret Harte* they singled out for honorable mention.

In the program notes Philip James announced his desire to restore to the Barbary Coast values which Hollywood had besmirched. In his music, he pays tribute to that same Hollywood with a score characteristic of everything we are accustomed to hear in the more luxurious marble halls of Broadway. The same faked dissonance and tricky syncopation superposed on scores reminiscent of Strauss and Tchaikovsky, and the same brass harmonic filler used by the smaller movie orchestras to achieve the prescribed expensive "glamor," padded out a work that lacked convincing direction or general line. Many of the *tutti* passages, and they were frequent, were confused and unskillful, as was the use of the poor tenor banjo that could have been heard above the din only by the radio audience, because it was placed near a microphone. In Hollywood Max Steiner and Alfred Newman turn out better scores.

After the constant loudness and lack of clarity of Philip James's work, Mr. Barbirolli conducted a peaceful, clear, and small orchestration by Anton von Webern of some unpublished Schubert dances.* In these little works, which

* *German Dances* (1824).—Eds.

were very well conceived from the point of view of sonority both for strings and woodwind, Webern made charming use of an antiphonal handling of the two groups. So suave and peaceful were they that some of Schubert's dance-like character was lost—this was the only violence Webern did to him.

Another quiet work played by Barbirolli was Anis Fuleihan's *Symphony*. This was at its best in a first movement that suggested Pizzetti and, in its limpid sober impressionism, the Respighi of the *Metamorphoses*. But later it lost interest, either, as in the fourth movement, through banality of theme and harmony or, as throughout, because it lacked constructive interest. Ideas which should have been followed out to attain their effect were abandoned too soon, direction and position in form were lacking, so that endings came unexpectedly. Nevertheless, in the impressionistic manner this work had a quite unusual quality.

Weinberger's monster extravaganza, *Schwanda* (how this could have failed at the Metropolitan is a bit puzzling) has been making the rounds again. I wish Philip James had succeeded with the *Outcasts of Poker Flat* [Bret Harte] as well as Weinberger did with Smetana's peasants.

[Paul] Stassevitch disappointed me by substituting Roger-Ducasse's *Sarabande* for Bartók's interesting and seldom played *Tanz-Suite*, but he pleased me very much by including Clementi's *Symphony in C Major*, which Casella completed and partly orchestrated from a defective manuscript. It was an excellent and very worthwhile job for Casella, and I trust that now we shall hear it often.

As if to complement this performance, Koussevitzky played Clementi's *D Major Symphony*, also revived through the efforts of Casella. The second work, found in a more complete state, needed less revision than the first, and consequently Casella's hand was not so much in evidence. The *D Major* is charming and gay, while the other tends towards the classic and the dignified. Both exhibited very interesting and piquant handling, delightful Italianate melodies, great conciseness, and surprising modulations.

Koussevitzky also revived Arthur Foote's modest *Suite in E Major* for string orchestra and MacDowell's *Second Piano Concerto*. With the grammar of Brahms but not his feeling, the Foote work showed a pleasant classical clarity and freshness, as well as skill and invention in working out. In taste and in formal interest it was closer to the eighteenth century than MacDowell's frankly romantic *Concerto*. This latter, because of an overhanging lassitude, gives the impression of having been dated even when it was written. Limpness is insupportable when a work aims at drama and brilliance. The musical conception seems to have stimulated MacDowell merely to write a very elaborate piano part, and this is hardly enough.

Milhaud's *Deuxième* and *Troisième Symphonies* from his *Cinq Symphonies* for small orchestra were played by [Hans] Lange in the Philharmonic Chamber Orchestra series. These works show Milhaud's great ability to employ at that time (1921) experimental and apparently "written" effects in a musical and spirited way. Here, better than in his *Cinquième Quatuor*, he uses a many voiced contrapuntal polytonal texture very effectively. Sometimes all seven instruments have as many independent melodic parts to play simultaneously. This might easily produce a tiresome feeling of confusion, but since these movements are very short, the longest being thirty-six measures, their gaiety and freshness do not pall. I like the two simpler ones: the first movement of the second and the third of the third, which were full of verve and good spirits. The slow movements failed because they seemed to require a richer texture than solo strings could give.

Contrasted to Milhaud's unusual procedures, Honegger's *Pastorale d'été,* which preceded Milhaud on Lange's program, seemed uninteresting and unoriginal. Honegger tends to fall down in moods of Mahlerian calm and show his most banal side.

It is unfortunate that both of these composers should be known here mainly by minor works. Will we ever hear *Antigone*, or the first movement of Honegger's *Symphonie*, or Milhaud's *Pan et Syrinx, Mort d'un tyran, Orestie d'Eschyle,* and *Salade;* or has contemporary music lost out completely in the big organizations that could afford to do these works?

Late Winter, New York, 1937

Modern Music, 14,3 (Mar.–Apr. 1937)

An interesting thing to consider about music is the influence of new works on older ones. For instance, Stravinsky's latest, the *Jeu de cartes* (which will be heard in April) by its pointed wit and broad jokes brushes up our appreciation of Rossini and Haydn, making us keenly aware in present-day terms of the great humor that can exist in music, so that we are able to catch more of it in removed periods like the eighteenth and early nineteenth centuries. Chávez's *Tierra Mojada* and *Antigona* do the same for Perotinus and Guillaume de Machaut. New works like these change our perspective and sharpen our delight in some phases of older music.

Besides the change in appreciation there is sure to be a corresponding emphasis on these newly perceived elements in the performance of old music. During the last months we had a unique opportunity for such observation in the direction of the [New York] Philharmonic by three composer–conductors. Each belonged to a different school of music: Enesco to the romantic of Brahms and Franck, Chávez to the impressionist and early Stravinsky, and Stravinsky, of course, to the later Stravinsky.

Each conducted Mozart. Enesco gave him a good, husky, full orchestra and imbued the *G Minor* with a vigorous and expressive atmosphere, doing it so well that it was as convincing, though not so up-to-date, as Stravinsky's performance with Beveridge Webster of the *G Major Concerto*. This Mozart was a good example of the "non-expressive" playing for which Stravinsky makes a plea in his autobiography. Let the notes speak for themselves; no interpretation by the conductor, who sees that all the markings are carried out precisely and indicates the tempo. Yet actually Stravinsky did a great deal of interpreting in another, newer way. Rather than expressive playing and "golden sonorities," his method was to give strong upbeats, treat repeated accompaniment notes in heavy staccato, keep each part clear of the others, lend rhythmic independence to the bass, and play melodies in an even way over a strong unfluctuating rhythm so that tension, instead of dissipating itself at each rise and fall, piles up to burst out at the accents.

Not up Chávez's alley, the *Jupiter Symphony* was made into a prim and pretty historical reconstruction. However, Chávez came into his own with Debussy, Ravel, and especially de Falla, giving sharply colored, well-contrasted, full-blooded performances to music that we are accustomed to hear wrapped in delicate timbres and thus spoiled of some of its true richness.

As one would expect, the attitudes of these composer–conductors toward the production of notes, sonorities, and rhythms in the performance of old music are the raw material out of which each has built his compositions. Enesco's early music is dominated by romantic legato with dramatic explosions and rich textures. His *Symphony in E-flat* is a work remarkably constructed and concentrated in material and working out. His harmony in this early period is conventional but so tastefully handled that it has a genuinely personal quality. It is rare to hear an academic work rising to such imaginative heights. This is even more true of a better work, his *Octet for Strings*. The *Suite for Orchestra, No. 2* is much clearer than the symphony and not altogether successful in the brilliant places. This and the agreeable *Rumanian Rhapsody No. 2* show signs of impressionist influence which is a weakening one in Enesco's music for he does not achieve the harmonic color that makes such works bearable. In his later works it is actually debilitating, in the *Cello Sonata*, for instance (played by [Felix] Salmond), which, despite beautiful places like the cello solo beginning the slow movement, wanders terribly.

Stravinsky has bit by bit worked out a completely individual attitude toward musical raw material, which I have already attempted to describe. He makes very interesting use of these basic effects, which are after all more suited to his own music and its timing than to the more leisurely works of Mozart. We had no opportunity to hear any of his most recent compositions as did the South Americans earlier this fall. But we did hear excellent performances of his older works, so good in fact that they dissipated for the time being the feeling that they had begun to date. What a remarkable musician to have learned at middle age to conduct his own music and play it on the piano better than anyone else.

As a composer Chávez must surprise those who had heard only his direction of other music. His conducting is much more orthodox than his compositions, which, at first knowledge, appear a denial of tradition. Fundamentally, though, the tradition is that of Mussorgsky. But it is one thing to be influenced by the Russian's music and another by his esthetic, as Chávez is. The effect of the first has been fairly sterile here, while the latter is beginning to produce vigorous results. Chávez is least good and original in his evocation of the *Petrouchka*-fair atmosphere as in *H.P.* [*Sinfonia*] and the superior *Sinfonia India*, which, however, have an individual texture deriving almost realistically from the sounds at Indian ceremonies. *H.P.* is a curious mixture of turgidity and thin, nice places joined together none too well at times. The tangos in it are charming. In *Sinfonia India*, the slower parts with their empty two- and three-part writing produce a beautiful effect. His use of percussion in combination with the orchestra is skillful and sounds well. There is too much repetition in these two works as concert pieces, but as background for primitive festival scenes this same repetition might prove evocative.

Antigona, Tierra Mojada, Spirals, and the *Sonatina* for violin and piano are Chávez's best works. They are conceived in a new idiom completely transforming musical speech to its own ends. It is unfamiliar enough to arouse doubts about the effectiveness of certain procedures. For instance, the remarkable point near the beginning of *Antigona* where violins suddenly start a long line in the highest register against wonderful heavy chords in low woodwinds leads one to expect, after these have drifted to their middle registers, something that carries out the tension of this stunning place. But it does not come, and changing its mind, the work subsides into a peaceful atmosphere. In the latter part there are beautiful moments in two contrapuntal sections and a moving ending on an ornamented octave, of great freshness and force. *Tierra Mojada*, sung by a chorus accompanied by an oboe and an English horn, with its linear vocal writing, its dialog between men's voices speaking and the women's high sung answer is brilliantly effective. Certain realistic picturesque details are perhaps questionable, as when the oboe plays a few isolated high staccato notes as if warming his reed, reminiscent of many a bird-call effect in old music. However, the device does add to the primitive improvisational atmosphere. *Spirals* is free from almost all of Chávez's faults and is one of his best pieces.

The outstanding piece of new music this season was Alban Berg's last work, his *Violin Concerto,* played by Krasner under Koussevitzky and the Boston Symphony. In character like the movingly understated last scene of *Wozzeck*, it is quieter and more rhythmically unified than Berg's other instrumental scores. Like them however it has the same combination of consonance and dissonance ordered by a twelve-tone row. As in the best of Berg's music this usually arid system does not cripple him but rather heightens his effects, giving them a beautiful order that, heard and understood, may be compared to Bach's use of imitation. As completely alive in all its details as the best of Bach, this work never has a lapse from taste nor an incongruity, such as one might expect in the place where Berg introduces phrases from Bach's harmonization of *Es ist genug.* On the contrary, this is brought in so naturally as to seem a necessary part of the work. The orchestration, too, is natural and has a beautiful sonority, avoiding the curious and extreme sounds that Berg has so often used to express violence and fright. For this music, very tender and touching, on occasion impressively tragic, is full of restrained power. It is perhaps because of this as well as the wonderfully expressive use of his original technic that the work appears to be not only one of Alban Berg's best but one of the best of our time.

Many other new works have been heard this season. First of all

Malipiero's *Julius Caesar* (Schola Cantorum), which is the best of that composer's recent works. Heroic rather than realistic and dramatic, this music, Italian in emptiness and lack of power, was strangely inadequate in the big assassination scene. However in lesser moments the score was often good. Its best feature was the excellent scansion of the vocal recitatives, as in scenes one and two. Malipiero has developed an effective lyricism for tender places, as in Marc Antony's music, which is rare in his work. But in spite of many interesting things in this score it is scarcely an addition to the repertory of important modern operas—most of which have still to be heard here.

Bernard Wagenaar's *Third Symphony* at the Juilliard was in a clear, conventional form with sure, well-timed effects. Much less dissonant and more romantic than his other works, it is more real emotionally. The generally quiet low-register atmosphere and leisurely pace were pleasant, though I wished that with all his skill in form and orchestration he had tried to do something more interesting.

But not so interesting as Schoenberg's *Fourth Quartet* played by the Kolisch Quartet at the Public Library. This work is noteworthy for it gives the impression that Schoenberg is seeking after greater rhythmic coherence and more natural sentence structure. He has returned to the dissonant, atonal style of his music before the *String Suite*, and to its sudden extreme fluctuations, their tensity, fragility, and negation of rhythmic flow. These make his music a realistic picture of feelings outraged by the impact of modern life, which, though expressed in terms so refined as to be near the point of unintelligibility, are occasionally very poignant. On the other hand, the slow movement is comparatively sustained and not so intensely "interesting" that the listener must give up from sheer exhaustion.

Hindemith's violin *Sonata in E* played by Szigeti is a good compromise in the matter of interest though at times there is a lag in the facile developments. Mozart and Beethoven are beginning to root out the rather mechanical Bachian counterpoint that he has used for some time, and this is well. Bach still influences composers, often with good effect. Paul Nordoff's *Prelude and Three Small Fugues* played by the Philharmonic Chamber Orchestra in the Bennington Series are an example of this. Over-ambitious in chamber orchestra sonority and not adventurous harmonically, these works were however natural and uninhibited. More suited to chamber orchestra were Saminsky's suave but unimpressive *Songs for Three Queens* and Otto Luening's *Prelude to a Hymn Tune* by William Billings, also on the same program. Luening's music was formed of variations which started consonantly, grew successively more dissonant, and then returned to simpler harmonies. This proved to be somewhat crippling, for Luening, at his best in dissonant contrapuntal anguish, could not sustain the interest in the more consonant parts.

Wesley Sontag and the Mozart String Sinfonietta gave an all-American program for every taste. A slightly augmented seventeenth-century piece called *Ukranian Suite* by Quincy Porter began the program, which went on to a romantic song, *Dover Beach* by Samuel Barber, and a modern work, *Homage to Handel* by Goddard Lieberson. Quincy Porter's work was nice and Lieberson's was interesting, especially in the Minuetto and Air-Courante, which showed considerable feeling. The rest of the program, on which there appeared [Russell L.(?)] Danburg, [A. Walter] Kramer, [Marshall] Kernochan, [Wintter] Watts, [George] Van Epps, [William B.] Ebann, Mauro-Cottone, Marki, was of the leveling tastelessness of radio arrangements, Danburg's *Variations on the Hootchy-Kootchy** being the best but never at any moment evoking the rich associations of this tune.

Movie and radio arrangements in France and Russia have a quality rare to our cheap splendours. Khrennikov's *Symphony* [No. 1], played by the Philadelphia under Ormandy, was a work in the style of the best Russian movie backgrounds—appealing and fresh and full of melodic interest. It is better music than Shostakovitch's *First Symphony* with which it has many points in common.

* The *Hootchy-Kootchy* was a popular song written by Lewis and Bear.—Eds.

The Sleeping Beauty

Modern Music, 14,3 (Mar.–Apr. 1937)

Last month Catherine Littlefield produced all of Tchaikovsky's *Sleeping Beauty* with orchestra and for the first time in America. Up to now we have only known the *Mariage d'Aurore*, its last act, which is given repeatedly by the de Basil Russian Ballet.

This work with Petipa's choreography is the great classic of ballet, summing up the tendencies in previous dancing and putting them to a fine score written especially for it. It contains all the ballroom dances and idealized etiquette of the court of Nicholas the First, theatricalized and made brilliant by the traditional ballet technic and enhanced by Tchaikovsky's music. Well done, this ballet should show us the ideal human world of the past in terms of movement, man behaving according to the conventions of a perfectly ordered society which automatically brings out in him the most elegant, most graceful, and most humanly social aspects.

There are two things to consider in a modern performance of this work. The first is the choreography. If re-devised it must translate a contemporary ideal man into more modern ballet terms. The other is its great difficulty. A company needs to be very good indeed to bring out all the implications of a score that almost visually describes the classic ballet gestures.

Miss Littlefield's choreography ignored Petipa's except in the *Mariage d'Aurore*, which was by far her best number. She seemed to have no serious conception beyond that of telling a fairy story in a fairly ornamental way. Had her troupe been better she might have rivaled Radio City Music Hall in sumptuousness and absurdity. As it was, the inadequacy of her company left her intent obscure, assuming that she had any beyond giving the work its American premiere.

The trip to Philadelphia was rewarded chiefly by an opportunity to hear the score; but even here, where precise indications are given, there was so much license taken with the tempi that interest shifted from the total effect to the minutiae of orchestration.

Season's End in New York, 1937

Modern Music, 14,4 (May–June 1937)

The season has just come to a good end with new works by Stravinsky, Hindemith, Chávez, Copland, and Sessions, in short by the best composers of today.

Hindemith's fourth and least successful quartet, introduced at the League of Composers' concert, showed a complexity that he has since fortunately abandoned. The work, nevertheless, has great musical interest. Later his third and best quartet was played by the Pro-Arte, but being well known it needs no comment here. With the Philharmonic this composer played his viola concerto, *Der Schwanendreher*, which is in his new, fairly consonant style. The clarity of this latest work is an astonishing phenomenon. Eliminating many of the poses of modern music, he gets down to an exact expression of what he wants to say. This is true also of the madrigals,* which were first published in a dissonant and unsingable style, but have now been rewritten with a thinning of texture and a use of consonant chords that is easier for choruses to sing.

This healthy attitude, so refreshing in Hindemith, is the opposite of Stravinsky's. Stravinsky is constantly seeking out more récherché embroideries on the obvious. Hearing his ballets in the afternoon and Hindemith's school works at the Greenwich House Music School in the evening made the contrast especially striking. At the former the Philharmonic players were beset with complications, subtleties, and perversities, from which the music emerged in a tortured form, whereas in the evening, works fresh and frank were rendered by students of twelve years or so, with evident delight and little difficulty. (However this should not minimize the importance of Stravinsky, who to this day continues to exert influence, even on Hindemith.) Outstanding among the Hindemith works at Greenwich House were the *Five Pieces for String Orchestra*, especially the Brandenburg-Concerto-like finale, and the delightful first duet for clarinet and violin from the *Plöner Musiktag*, which has a type of thinness often imitated by modern composers but seldom successfully. In the honesty of his musical expression he is in the true Kapellmeister tradition of his great forebear, Bach.

Every new work of Stravinsky's is in some sense a disappointment because it never follows in the expected way. It was so with *Oedipus, Apollo*, the *Capriccio*, the *Violin Concerto*, and *Perséphone*. In time we have come to realize the greatness of *Oedipus* and *Apollo*, and it is possible that this new score for the *Card Party*, on increased familiarity, will come to delight us more. Is this not, perhaps, Stravinsky's *Nutcracker Suite*, music informed with delicate and grotesque humor? It avoids the local color and brilliant effects of *Petrouchka*, or of Auric's *Les Matelots*.

At a recital of the Chamber Music Society of America, which opened with

---

* *Five Songs on Old Texts* for mixed voices, a revised version (1936) with English texts of the original *Liederbuch für mehrere Singstimmen* (1923).—Eds.

a tiresome talk by Roy Harris, the new and important quartet of Roger Sessions was played. Though no single theme is outstanding (as is often the case with Beethoven), every detail, the cadences, the way the themes are brought in, the texture, the flexibility of the bass, were such as to give constant delight, and at times to be genuinely moving. His sense of a large line gave the music a certain roominess without ever being overexpansive.

Aaron Copland's *Symphony* [No. 1], at the League of Composers' Philharmonic concert, was given a very inadequate performance by Rodzinski. His first orchestral work, it shows the great promise which has since been fulfilled. Even here originality is present, in the conception of a first movement that is tenuous and thin, instead of the usual boisterous sonata allegro.

On the same program Honegger's *King David* was also played badly. The piece still suffers from its hurried conception; at the dramatic moments Honegger is adequate, at other times less so. The Pro-Arte played the *Second String Quartet* (a far better work than his first). It was in his usual brutal and grandiose style, when it was not dull. The slow movement with its accented cello chords was particularly effective, even for Honegger.

The Philharmonic also played Strauss's *Elektra* (much in the same vein as it did Honegger). In even less good taste, this much more vital music, so terribly dated, is just beginning to receive general appreciation.

Szymanowski's *Harnasie* was presented on the day of his death [March 28, 1937]. It is the best work of Poland's finest modern composer. Often brutal, often gay, sometimes wistful, the work is full of interesting orchestration which one would like to hear again.

The Philadelphians played Kodály's *Dances of Galanta*, which, agreeable and soothing, should make a pleasant addition to Pops programs.

Among the younger American composers Goddard Lieberson produced a *Tango* for piano and orchestra, which was over-orchestrated and not as good as his *Homage to Handel*, and Israel Citkowitz a setting to a Blake poem [*The Lamb*], for women's voices. This latter was particularly successful in its mingling of sung words and vocalizing. It is unfortunate that we do not hear more music by this man, whose every work reveals loving care in construction and genuine musical ideas.

More about Balanchine

Modern Music, 14,4 (May–June 1937)

In these last months we have had the good fortune to see three excellent examples of George Balanchine's choreography well rehearsed and well presented by the American Ballet troupe.

Most modern American and German dancers return directly to the gestures of primitive ritual or the miming of basic physiological activities. Balanchine treats these matters within the Petipa ballet tradition, a frame that theatricalizes by making everything more objective, and which he revitalizes by bringing it close to our present feelings. This tradition gives coherence and intelligibility to raw material that in itself has little more than ethnological interest. With these elements he has developed a type of choreography singularly poignant and poetic as well as new and original. Though at times resembling it in outward method, it is in direct contrast to modern dance technic.

A great difference between these two types of dancing is in the interrelations of the people on the stage. The modern dance generally shows us individuals in the throes of self-induced emotions, who by their apparent disregard of the looker-on, seem to move within a ritual like that of the church. Groups of individuals also take part in these ritual dances without contact, apparently swayed by a simultaneously experienced emotion. The relationships are not human and emotional; they might exist between schools of small fish. Sometimes we see satirical situations such as the genius–hero being tortured at the hands of a fantastic society conjured up for the occasion without any social validity.

In Balanchine's world relationships are expressed in lyrical terms. Being of our times they often have some trouble, but this makes them the more appealing and immediate.

For Stravinsky's *Baiser de la Fée,* which pays homage to Petipa in its choreography as the music does to Tchaikovsky, Balanchine invented some of the finest *soli* and *pas de deux* since the days of the Imperial Ballet. In the third scene the formal numbers between Gisella Caccialanza and William Dollar, remarkable for their tenderness, brilliance, compactness, and variety, are strictly within the classic tradition. This type of invention is as rare as it is important. For instance, in the Paris performance done by Bronislava Nijinska, the solo variations were boring, dull, and badly planned, so that the whole work was spoiled. Balanchine's worked-out steps were frequently more interesting than the music though he always followed it closely and sensitively.

The *Card Party* (in which William Dollar as the joker danced with brilliance and imagination) has a rather untheatrical libretto, for a pack of cards is a pack of cards and gives little chance for contrast. Balanchine invented a choreography that had to be followed carefully to be appreciated, as all its effects were microscopic. He interpreted the cards as a comic, perverse society and avoided any of the serious implications of the gaming house with its atmosphere of tension and of suicidal anxiety, a suggestion of which might have added body to the work. In the dancing itself there was many a reference to jazz, which is certainly a good way of revivifying ballet technic and skillfully added to the general grotesquerie and cuteness of the ballet.

Apollon Musagète, seen by a few early comers, was Balanchine's masterpiece. Though in part a reprise of his former choreography for Diaghilev, it was less static and had greatly gained in feeling since its Parisian performance. The jerks from one statuesque pose to another were no longer in evidence and in their place was a very beautiful plasticity having both nobility and repose.

No one has ever worked out flow in dancing as well as Balanchine. In *Apollon*, as in his *Serenade*, there was a constant line of movement which bound all the steps together and never ceased until the curtain fell. There was something magical and stirring about this drawing of the invisible lines in the air. The solo variations were very fine creations, especially those of the three muses, showing a highly creative imagination at work in every small detail. Balanchine's greatest successes have been in this lyric and poetic vein, as in *Errante* and *Orpheus*.

Opening Notes, New York, 1937

Modern Music, 15,1 (Nov.–Dec. 1937)

The Philharmonic started the season off bravely with a first performance of Bartók's *Music for Strings, Percussion, and Celesta* and Gardner Read's *Symphony in A minor*, which won the Philharmonic prize contest last year. No two works could be more widely different in character. Bartók's work is the finest of his compositions to be heard in these parts for a long time. It has much greater clarity than his more recent quartets and is less choppy, with greater broadness than the *Dance Suite*. Recently Bartók has learned how to keep to a simple tonal pattern that organizes his counterpoint and gives it a sense of progression. This work has the very definite tonality of A and many reinforcements of that key throughout; it thus avoids the chromatic wandering that so many of his followers slip into when they begin to write in his style. The first movement, a beautiful fugue, has a simple grand plan and a continuity of expression which rank it with the best of recently composed music. The second movement, in a lively, nervously rhythmic vein, has almost the dignity and solidity of a Beethoven scherzo. The system of development is much more free and natural than in Stravinsky, whose music it resembles. The other two movements sustain the general high level of quality. Throughout there is great beauty of sonority and a very elegant kind of writing that is as rare as it is delightful in modern music.

The other work, by twenty-four year-old Gardner Read, seemed as if it had been written before the war rather than last year. It is a sorry thing to see a young man so unadventurous. If, however, he had been bolder he might not have won his prize. The work is a "motif" symphony in four movements with constant developments of undistinguished material. Read never relaxed into a tune for a moment; he was either working up or calming down to "entrances" of little fragments that were weak and did not merit the fuss he made to bring them in. Although the work was empty and unoriginal, it is quite evident that Read has true musical feeling. This showed itself most often in his orchestration. If he had stuck more tenaciously to a unifying expressive conception, instead of to an intellectual one, his work might have had greater coherence. A more personal and challenging style would not be out of place.

Roy Harris and Elie Siegmeister opened the Fall concert series at the Composer's Forum Laboratory. That remarkable organization has been improving steadily. The standard of performance this year is much higher than last, and the concerts promise to be more interesting. It is too bad that because of its isolation the good works discovered by this unit do not reach wider audiences. But that will certainly come.

In the Theatre, 1937

Modern Music, 15,1 (Nov.–Dec. 1937)

America's idea of opera, if you can judge by the excerpts we see in our movies, or by the performances at our opera houses, consists of well-jewelled audiences listening to standard works sung by well-paid prima donnas in front of standard sets doing standard stage business that is the same in all opera houses (so that identical performances can be given with little or no rehearsal here or in Lima, Peru, or anywhere else).

The Salzburg Opera Guild, now on its first visit to the United States, flies in the face of this tradition. The seats are the same price as in an ordinary theatre, the singers as a group sing and act well, the *mise-en-scène* is adequate, the whole is rehearsed, and the repertory is not standard. This program should meet with the approval of anybody interested in opera as a really living form.

The choice of works is decidedly popular, except for Milhaud's *Le Pauvre Matelot* and Monteverdi's *Coronation of Poppea*. For *Così fan Tutte*, Ibert's *Angélique*, and Rossini's *Matrimonial Market* are gay and spirited and have a great deal of appeal when done the way the Salzburg people do them.

Le Pauvre Matelot has an unfortunate history in this country. It was given last year by the Curtis school, with the orchestra too loud, drowning out the singers. The Salzburg performance also was not good, as the performers did not sing their parts accurately and the orchestra, with too small a string section, sounded confused and bare. The score is original and new and its spirit is hard to convey; strong and simple, it uses popular sailor songs in a contrapuntal texture that is often against rather than with the voice. Its fault is that a few places are too greatly developed. But it does have a new quality of grim humor and many beautiful passages. These have to be done really very well to come across.

Angélique, on the other hand, is an operetta that is built on well-known lines. It is always effective, brilliant, ingenious, and is right up the Salzburgers' alley, for they have a greater gift for buffoonery than for serious acting. The good old, rather trashy, slicked-up French rural comedy has made its way from the films to the opera stage. Musically it is an unmelodic string of clever, often amusing effects. Like most movies this operetta is fun to see just once.

Stage music is becoming more and more popular for Broadway plays. Already there are two schools: the incidental sound effects that have great dramatic value but could not be played away from the shows they are written for; and the set-pieces which do have an independent musical life. With the first type Virgil Thomson has reached a high degree of perfection and effectiveness in his scoring for *Injunction Granted* and *Hamlet*. The danger of this kind of writing lies in the fact that it depends so much on the play of which it is an integral part. The new *Antony and Cleopatra* is badly directed, and hence Thomson's music does not come off well, though it helps to point up many an indifferent scene.

Marc Blitzstein has also used this style for the Mercury Theatre's extraordinary *Julius Caesar*, and with great effect. The wonderful roars of the Hammond organ and the sardonic Fascist march are not easily forgotten; they play their roles with great cogency in a marvelous production.

Samuel Barlow with his music for *Amphitryon 38* represents, very ineffectively, the school of set-piece writing. This could have been so good if the score had only underlined the wit of the play. Instead it emits a few faint Debussyian wisps of sounds, altogether out of keeping with the production.

A film made by the former Resettlement Administration, to be released in December, presents Thomson in one of his best phases: that of composer for the movies. In my opinion he has written by far the most distinguished film scores in America. This one is no exception. Along the same lines as the *Plough that Broke the Plains, The River* illustrates a less pastoral and poetic theme in a vigorous, austere, and simple way. The music is never cheap, though at times it has symphonic effects. The roomy treatment of a hymn tune at the conclusion is one of the best pieces of music Thomson has written. It has a large beauty that never appears in the choppy little musiquettes Auric, Shostakovitch, and Honegger write for the movies.

With the Dancers, 1937

Modern Music, 15,1 (Nov.–Dec. 1937)

The dance season began brilliantly with new works by the Littlefield and Russian Ballets, and a revival of some old ones by Joos. Miss Littlefield's troupe revealed great improvement over last year's *Sleeping Beauty* (repeated during the summer at the Stadium with Smallens correcting the tempi). The choreography is more imaginative, and the dancers are better trained; they showed up well in a small hall and danced with verve and sureness. Poulenc's *Aubade* was offered with Alexis Dolinoff's version of Balanchine's original and more piquant choreography, with Dolinoff in the main role. There was also a miniature *Fantastic Symphony* entitled *Poème* to Ravel's *Pavane* and a miniature *Choreartium* to music by Bach. This last was healthy and vigorous and quite decently danced. As always in Miss Littlefield's work there was a powerful touch of the vaudeville troupe doing something pretty swell. You cannot expect much careful and delicate workmanship from her but you can expect good, obvious theatre even if it's pretty cheap. Miss Littlefield played very safe in her choice of ballets, giving imitations of already proven successes. A little original work would be appreciated.

The morose, none too elegant evenings staged at the shabby Metropolitan have already achieved an air of nostalgia befitting the institution which the Ballet Russe has now become. Few surprises can be expected. The freshest of the new works was the *Gods Go A-Begging*, which, with the help of a Handel score, was once a gay little piece. Lichine as choreographer built this up out of scenery, custumes, score, and choreography created for Diaghilev. It is much less delightful now. Danilova and Shabelevsky footed it with such exquisite elegance that they walked away with the show.

Francesca da Rimini, with which Lichine started from scratch, was less successful. The work had plenty of staring and stamping, waving and pointing of the most melodramatic school. While a "neo-romantic" ballet could be done that way, this one was a failure due perhaps to Lichine's lack of expertness. In neither of his ballets did he handle the movement of groups well and his *soli* and *pas de deux* relied too often on that most obvious of formulae, the pirouette at the musical cadence. However Lichine, who has just begun in this difficult type of work, already shows a great sense of the theatre. Oliver Messel's scenes and clothes are like fine-arts examination "spot questions." I recognized Gozzoli, Fra Angelico, Sodoma, Carpaccio, and Rossetti. Aside from this challenge to one's knowledge there was little worth seeing in the work.

Not so with the *Coq d'Or* revived in the "futuristic polychromy," which Goncharova made into a sensation in 1914. You could scarcely see what was going on for the décors, and a good thing too, for the dancing was not much to look at and the extravagant miming was pretty unfunny. Fokine's choreography, which is a break with the Petipa tradition, seems much more antiquated today than his predecessor's and it is likely to remain so. It has much less scope either in humorous or in lyric works. The décors had that fuming kind of sensuality exploited by Russians for their international Tea-Room trade. The success of this *Coq* crowded *The Amorous Lion*, an expected première, off the bills! Next year we will certainly be given *Kikimora* [by Liadov], *Sadko* [by Rimsky-Korsakov], or *Kitège* [*The Legend of the Invisible City of Kitezh and the Maiden Febronia*, also by Rimsky-Korsakov].

Miss Littlefield and the Russian Ballet are the victims of that unfortunate shortsight of the Business Manager, which gives us warmed-over seconds, old successes in new disguises, instead of new works built on new conceptions. Theirs is the easier way; it is always much acclaimed by both the public and the critics alike. But all too soon it will produce that certain tired feeling.

Homage to Ravel, 1875–1937

Modern Music, 15,2 (Jan.–Feb. 1938)

L'Heure Espagnole, the *Trio for Violin, Cello, and Piano, Les Chansons Madécasses*, the *Piano Concerto, Valses Nobles et Sentimentales, Daphnis et Chloé, Le Tombeau de Couperin, Histoires Naturelles, Ma Mère l'Oye* will have no more successors, for the twentieth century has lost one of its best composers. Maurice Ravel was an exponent of that careful, precise workmanship, elegance, and grace he so admired in the music of Mozart, of whom he was not an unworthy descendant. The type seems to grow rarer as this troubled century progresses. His work, however, was a monument to the dignity and precision that even now all worthy musicians should strive for and that French music has at its best always captured. Combined with an extraordinary sense of style and infallible ear was a refinement of taste and a unique inspiration that made every work he wrote right and final in its own category. All his life he shunned cheapness and facility, yet his style and manner of orchestration have already left their mark on all music, from the simplest jazz to the most elaborate works of Stravinsky. His music will always be a great glory to the art he practiced so long and so well.

VACATION NOVELTIES, NEW YORK

No new modern music of importance was played in New York this month. Apparently the vacation season is not considered an appropriate time for accustoming the public to music which requires any effort to understand.

Many innocuous American works in the single performance or novelty class were performed however. In fact "American" has become synonymous with "novelty" in the field of serious music, for there is no American orchestral work past or present that has been permanently included in the symphonic repertory, to which Sibelius and Shostakovitch have recently been added here, and Elgar and Delius in England. (I mention only second rank composers, so there can be no cry that we have no one as good.) MacDowell, [Arthur] Foote, [George W.] Chadwick, [Edward Burlingame]

Hill, [Henry Franklin Belknap] Gilbert, [Horatio] Parker, [John Knowles] Paine are still considered novelties. Will American music always be treated so condescendingly? A first performance and then complete oblivion seem to be the fate of our composers' serious works, even though critics often praise them highly and add the hint that they should be heard again.

The Philharmonic seems to have taken up the American cause and has been giving many first performances at its concerts. We should, I suppose, be thankful even for this little bit, no matter how bad the choice. Hearing the works played at these concerts in the last month, however, I am not surprised at the public apathy toward our music, for it has not shown up well.

Cadman's *Dark Dancers of the Mardi Gras* is without musical interest. It was bad enough to be funny, but the American public is not prepared to appreciate this. Gilbert's *Dance in the Place Congo* [1906] and *Comedy Overture on Negro Themes* [1905] furnished meagre material, just what people used to expect of American music before it went modern: Negro or Indian themes over a polka bass. Cadman's form is not quite as good as Victor Herbert's operetta overtures, and his orchestration is "livened up" with constant use of xylophone and glockenspiel. To bring the music up-to-date he introduces a piano cadenza on the whole-tone scale. I considered hissing the work but found that the dated stupidity of the style amused me. Besides hissing is impolite in Carnegie Hall.

Deliberate use of this dated quality to produce a musical effect is slightly higher in the scale of sophistication, as illustrated in Mason's *A Lincoln Symphony*. With a program as ambitious as an Ives symphony, Mason dealt with all phases of Lincoln's life. His interest was in the picturesque quick-steps and Negro tunes; the symphony disappointed by being small music about a great subject. It had a certain neo-early American charm that put it above the usual run of Mason's music, but it also has a feeble taste of what our music really has achieved.

With the Dancers, 1938

Modern Music, 15,2 (Jan.–Feb. 1938)

When I consider how often large, official artistic ventures miscarry, I must admit that the Dance International (which was held all through the month of December) did a real service in bringing American ballet and the Modern Dance to a larger public than they usually reach. There were, of course, more than a few "society" events of mediocre quality at the Rainbow Room and bad exhibits of costumes and scenery. But the two performances at the Centre Theatre were justly successful in showing where America stood in the two fields. There was a minimum of attempt to play down to the public and a maximum to attain a high artistic standard. The films of exotic dancing were also an excellent feature of this mammoth project.

The ballet, by its very nature and background, is easily led into vulgarization; its evening went farther in that direction than that of the Modern Dance. Especially as three Broadway entertainers, Patricia Bowman, Paul Haakon, and Paul Draper, were on the program. Nevertheless the two men at least showed how remarkable a technical development ballet and tap have reached in the commercial theatre. The ballet groups were more serious.

Catherine Littlefield's troupe, always astonishing for its great number of performers, gave a better performance than usual, probably because the choreography had only the most elementary quadrille steps and contained a great deal of the obvious pantomime in which her troupe is most at home. *Barn Dance* was an amusing piece based on fiddler tunes in conventional arrangements. It caught in a showy way the atmosphere of these social dances and proved a pleasant piece of Americana. José Limón and Felicia Sorel carried the Dance Centre's otherwise uninteresting performance of *El Amor Brujo* with some intense Spanish tantrums of the expected kind.

The Ballet Caravan's *Showpiece*, to a specially commissioned score from Robert McBride, was the only group work with any notable dancing during the evening. It showed in a fresh new way how well each of the members of the small company danced, how able they were despite a certain immaturity. The work has a great deal in its favor. There is little fuss and pretension about it. Straightforward, with no attempt to build up an elaborate atmosphere, it shows young people doing ballet dances in bright costumes before a black curtain. Throughout, the choreography was ingenious and, within the limitations of the classic steps, had imagination. Probably because of a certain formlessness and lack of emphasis in the music, the ballet did not achieve a natural and theatrical articulation. This somewhat clouded the brilliance of the dancing.

The Modern Dance evening of the festival was a summary of what the courageous people in this city have achieved in the last ten years of hard work. It began at the beginning of the movement, Ruth St. Denis coming out of her retirement to perform some of those Oriental numbers that still, as in *White Jade*, retain the beauty and delicacy of gesture for which she is renowned. Like Swinburne's Greece or Rossetti's Middle Ages, Ruth St. Denis's Orient is superficial and false, but it is theatrical.

The remainder of the program was devoted to Martha Graham, Doris Humphrey, Charles Weidman, Tamiris, Hanya Holm, and their groups, dancers who have gained a large and enthusiastic audience and who are supported on every hand. Personally I cannot share this enthusiasm. In making the following attack I believe that I am also voicing the opinions of many who, like myself, are concerned with the future of dancing in this country.

Once Miss St. Denis's pupils, though now in violent reaction against her prettiness, Graham, Humphrey, and Weidman have continued her tendency to falsify. Instead of misrepresenting the Orient, which is pardonable and perhaps necessary to a culture so basically different, they misrepresent our contemporary American life to us. For they show it in the light of a special state of mind, that of the Germans right after the war, suicidal, hysterical, and not typical of the rest of life, then or now. In America, famine, inflation, and complete disillusionment have not existed on a large enough scale to be part of our common background; they remain a matter of speculation to most of those who attend the dance recitals. If these tragic things are to be shown strongly they must reveal a more cogent point of view.

Each performance at the Centre Theatre, after Miss St. Denis's, presented a group of discontented, unhappy, tortured, self-destructive people on the stage. This naturally arouses a feeling of pity and sympathy in the audience and leaves it with little respect or interest in the performers as artists. Instead of giving the audience a dance work to enjoy or be instructed by, [the adherents of] this school present themselves as people acting under an intense emotional strain. And, as if this were not embarrassing enough, they appear to be quarreling with and loathing the audience. Every gesture that might take on a meaning if fitted into a context is quickly frustrated by the succeeding one, the atmosphere is of confusion and uncertainty and hardly conducive to the presentation of an idea. The music is no less frustrated, without line, point of emphasis, natural sequence, or development. Doubtless the dancers believe (and with some justice) that modern life is disintegrated and frustrated. But there have been works—and there are going to be more—that show this strongly and clearly without being so technically submerged by their message that they are weak and ineffective: Berg's *Wozzeck*, Weill and Balanchine's *Seven Deadly Sins*, and Blitzstein's *Cradle Will Rock*.

What the dancers want to say about society may be significant and valuable. It should be said as strongly and with as much conviction as possible in order for the idea itself not to succumb to the very forces they criticize. Moreover, their message is not delivered on the stage, but via their program notes. Shan-Kar has a much less important announcement to make to Western society, and yet out of his performances comes something, remote as the sources may be, that is more true than anything the modern dancers have yet been able to achieve. He deals with certain basic facts about human feeling and gets his results through a very highly developed technic and a thorough muscular control. His discipline is so great that the moment he comes on stage and makes a gesture, no matter how slight, he arouses a feeling of respect toward him, as an artist, and this is maintained throughout the performance. What he does, not what he is, alone must be considered. And what he does has to do with the body and its parts from eye to toe. The modern dancer's body is always used monotonously as a whole, and the lack of disciplined gesture, hence concentration of meaning, dissipates the message.

The theme of revolt against bourgeois society (and I suspect against any form of society) is a recurrent one with artists. But surely the direction should be not toward that of emotional, chaotic conflicts as these dancers seem to maintain but toward greater physical, intellectual, and emotional discipline; that is the only road to liberation from the society they loathe. The single tendency in this direction to be noted at the Centre Theatre was in Hanya Holm's group, which presented a portion of their large work *Trend*, given previously in complete form at Mecca Temple. Here was real beauty and significance of movement though, as so often in these large works, the level of stylization was uncertain. Obvious realistic parody stood side by side with the most abstract and obscure movements. The insect-like machine gestures at the beginning of *Trend* and the remarkable spasmodic convulsions of isolated individuals during the "cataclysm" were quite extraordinary; they showed what this type of dance could be if it were freed from the personal hysteria that now surrounds it and made more straightforward.

As this issue goes to press, I should like to include a note on the all-American evening the Ballet Caravan has just given at the Avery Memorial in Hartford. Virgil Thomson's *Filling Station*, which had its premiere on this occasion, and Paul Bowles's *Yankee Clipper* seem to me to be outstanding American ballets.

Filling Station is a pointed satire on the way Americans think about the different classes of their society. As if in a movie, the characters are all brought together at a gas station, where a hold-up is staged by gangsters. Paul Cadmus has dressed all this with remarkable cleverness and style; in fact his scenery and costumes almost walk away with the work. Lew Christensen's choreography, however, is both expert and witty, and Thomson's score, like old-time pre-sound, film piano-playing, does not underline the action, move by move, but forms a running background that catches the simplicity of character and situation amusingly. His jazz number is one of the best satires of this style that I know.

Bowles's work has the much more usual relation between ballet music and action, for each situation is made into an appropriate dance. It is straightforward and episodic, like all conventional ballets. Nevertheless it is the Caravan's most deeply felt work. Having to do with the old story of the clipper-ship sailor who is gotten by the sea, the dancing and music are at times boisterous and at times tender. Bowles has written some of his best music in the tuneful sailor dances. He manages to retain his own personality while making pastiches of exotica. Loring's choreography is most convincing in its wistful moods, and the whole is worth seeing because of its touching and evocative charm.

Musical Reactions— Bold and Otherwise

Modern Music, 15,3 (Mar.–Apr. 1938)

There is an ever more prevalent opinion abroad that a great American national characteristic is the inability to have definite views on anything but the most practical matters. We are supposed to be people so confused intellectually that we cannot decide on which side of the fence to be, if, indeed, we can discern the fence at all. Now this idea does have a certain truth when we consider the degree to which the large, regimenting organizations of press, radio, and moving pictures control us. These agencies cannot afford to take sides if they want the whole public to be with them. It is therefore refreshing to find a book like Deems Taylor's *Of Men and Music* (Simon and Schuster), which, written to sell to the large radio public, comes out with such definite ideas on important questions in music. He treats of the American composer and the lack of audience for him, royalties, the badness of virtuoso programs, and the general neglect of the new in music with force and intelligence. On these he is very worth reading.

When he comes to the subject of "modern music" he hedges. This tendency he shares with his fellows of the press, perfect Wagnerites all. His taste is for overpowering, colorful music like that of Strauss, Delius, Debussy, Berg, and the early Stravinsky, and, tentatively, Honegger. On the general subject of modern music he can boldly take both sides of the fence in alternate chapters. After the season of 1926–7, Taylor seems to have ceased experiencing contemporary music as anything vital enough to write about it in detail. He is very reluctant to discuss its development from that date, which corresponds roughly to the end of his reviewing career for the *World*. Though interestingly written, and with considerable love for his art, one could wish that Mr. Taylor's taste were a little less dated, a little less well geared to the demands of the radio audience.

Orchestras and Audiences; Winter, 1938

Modern Music, 15,3 (Mar.–Apr. 1938)

There are two ways of listening to music. The most popular is for the listener to give himself up to an evening of reminiscence or revery after having checked his conscious, critical self at the door with his hat. The small spot he has in his heart for music awakens and he evokes personal images and feelings which only remotely correspond with what is striking his ear. Scenes of childhood and adolescence are evoked by the Debussy or Chopin number, heroic justification of acts he could not make up his mind about is found to the tune of Brahms, Beethoven, Sibelius, or Wagner. If he has any room for modern music he thinks over the sad condition of his bank balance or love life to the agitations of Strauss or the hysterical post-war Germans, and finds anxiety for his own future aroused by the proletarian theatre composers. Though by constant repetition he may discover something to hook on to the most diverse styles and thus find a way of not paying attention to them, he generally rejects any music which jars him out of himself and threatens to afford a new experience, giving way to anger as a protection.

There is a more objective though just as enthusiastic kind of listener. He is eager for new ideas and new feelings. When hearing familiar works he always re-evaluates his previous impressions. The style, no matter how difficult or unusual, does not prevent him from trying to find what the music is all about. He follows it attentively for he knows that it is a living message to him from another living man, a serious thought or experience worth considering, one that will help him to understand the people about him. To him, dead, worn-out formulas or non-communicative styles are anathema. Serious composers and musicians have always aimed at this listener and he in turn has shown that he could take his listener's share of responsibility by keeping his mind actively fixed on the music he was hearing.

Of all the symphonic organizations in this part of the country, Koussevitzky and the Boston Symphony have catered most to the part of the public that listens "actively." This excellent society has done a great deal to stimulate the attentive attitude by treating composers as if they were living, worthy men and not as if they were shadowy, unreal figures hovering uncertainly above the real, printed page. A long list of achievements in this direction can be listed. Commissions for the leading contemporary composers on the occasion of the orchestra's fiftieth anniversary, having composers perform or conduct their own works, and giving memorial concerts when the important figures died. Koussevitzky is the only important conductor to have made this a consistent policy with his orchestra. Most of the outstanding composers have had numerous performances of their works in Boston. That part of the public which is "passive" has not always been sympathetic, but it is noticeable now that, as a result of these efforts, Boston audiences are more liberal than others toward what is new.

The Ravel memorial concerts, received enthusiastically in Boston and coldly here, are a good example. The fact that no New York conductor dared to play such a program is quite a reflection on our taste. Hindemith also scored a great success in Boston as violist in his best viola concerto, *Kammermusik No. 5*, and as composer of the *Concert Music for Strings and Brass*, the work commissioned by the Boston Symphony several years ago. At that time the public was quite cool, but now they greet it warmly. Boston audiences have heard enough music by pupils of Nadia Boulanger to have a great respect for her, and so when Koussevitzky asked her to conduct, the public was eager to really discover what this great person would do. She performed the Fauré *Requiem* with the sincerity and simplicity and musicianship that at one time only her pupils could judge and which now are appreciated by a large audience, who as a result of this performance have a greater respect for her teachings, her pupils, and especially for the beauty of the music which she played.

Out of town orchestras are more awake than the New York Philharmonic, for we owe the first concert performance of Stravinsky's *Suite* from *Jeu de cartes* to the Philadelphians. Ormandy showed himself courageous in this regard, for the work was not popular among the music critics when given here as a ballet last year. He could not, however, resist trying to liven up a score that was condemned as dull by taking tempi which misrepresented the work completely. Andantes were played prestissimo and ritardandos were made which greatly disturbed the flow. The work improves greatly on second hearing. It is certainly not sterile, as the daily newspaper critics insist, though it does not contain the blood and thunder that have made them run to their offices to write raves this year. Quiet, and of small proportions, treating the orchestra as if it were a chamber group, Stravinsky keeps the work a delicate, restrained miniature. The *Suite* differs from the ballet only in the matter of a few short cuts, not altogether good ones either, for they break up the line, especially in the vivacious last movement. For this reason, as well as because the music always follows its own interesting logic regardless of what happens on the stage, *Jeu de cartes*, the ballet, deserves to be played in its entirety in concert. It is a piece of finely drawn *drôlerie*, clever, with sharp wit and mysterious charm the like of which has never been heard before.

New York Philharmonic audiences have had scarcely anything to complain about as far as "modern music" goes, for Enesco has played them six well-stereotyped, contemporary impressionistic Roumanian composers of no interest and two revivals of American works, MacDowell's *Launcelot and Elaine* and Piston's *Suite*. The only really new work was Germaine Tailleferre's *Violin Concerto*, a good choice, for it was delightful, gay and unpretentious, with a very fine slow movement.

In this day of complete stylistic disintegration, when Krenek, who once wrote simple, at times Schubertian, music has gone completely over to the extreme Schoenberg camp, and when Prokofiev has left his strident period altogether and is practically entirely consonant, the public that likes dissonance by profession rather than as an expressive necessity is finding itself outmoded. This public (whose very existence I doubt) has little to feed on now, though at one time it was important in the development of music. Today it has either won or lost its point and dwindled into insignificance, even in the universities. The League of Composers, which certainly does not insist that its members use large numbers of sevenths and ninths, gave two chamber concerts, one of Prokofiev's music and one of Krenek's. Prokofiev's *Sonata for Two Violins* and Krenek's song cycle, *O Lacrimosa*, though the best of what was played, were not representative of these two excellent composers of ballet and opera who have been somewhat slighted recently.

For several years Hugh Ross has performed one new choral work each season at the Schola Cantorum. This year he did two: Delius's *Mass of Life* and Dukelsky's *The End of St. Petersburg*. As I find Delius uninteresting I will confine my remarks to the latter work. Dukelsky is a dual personality in music. His standardized popular songs (the "active" listener will remember them) written under the less frightening name of Vernon Duke, have absolutely no connection with his original and imaginative serious music in either style or content. In this he is linear and dissonant and frequently violently rhythmic, fond of a dry, unresonant orchestration somewhat like that of the *Symphonie des psaumes. The End of St. Petersburg* contains some of the best music by this composer since he wrote his exquisite *Zéphyre et Flore* for Diaghilev, especially the two movements describing the city during the exciting revolutionary days and during a strange apprehensive fog. The rest, though original, is confused in intention.

Dukelsky has recently founded the High-Low Concerts, an organization like the Parisian *Sérénade*, to interest socialites in the more amusing sides of modern music scorned at serious concerts. Meant to be reviewed only by society editors, I mention these private soirées to point out that the first program had an almost exact counterpart in the New Masses Benefit Concert. Music by Aaron Copland, Marc Blitzstein, and Paul Bowles made up the main portion of both and both ended with swing bands, the Duke and Count, Ellington and Basie. It seems that these composers want to have their music played more than they want to show their political affiliations. This is only natural, for they are writing for the "active" listener who will follow them up to the Saint Regis Roof and, if he has the price, crash a High-Low Concert; or go down on Broadway to a radical meeting. The distinctions of upper-class public from academic modern music public or proletarian public are only valid for the listener not primarily interested in music, who wants corroboration of his private beliefs. They make little sense to the person out to discover what is happening in the musical world regardless of his own position in the class struggle.

Recent Festival in Rochester, 1938

Modern Music, 15,4 (May–June 1938)

The eighth annual Eastman School Festival of American Music went about its business with considerable effectiveness this year. For instead of the dry impression that most music festivals devoted to one style of music usually give, here one got the feeling that in spite of the depression, the constant threat of a European, perhaps a world, war, and the general intellectual disintegration which many people seem to feel, music was

carrying on in this country not only hopefully but with considerable enthusiasm and a new pulse of life. This, in spite of the generally conservative
choice of the programs, was especially true of the works of the younger
composers, Vladimir Ussachevsky, David Diamond, and Burrill Phillips.
The festival, almost entirely under the untiring baton of Howard Hanson,
rose to a higher level of performance than is customary at the modern music
affairs I have heard abroad.

David Diamond's *Elegy in Memory of Maurice Ravel* was the most
original and daring new piece played. Scored for brass, harps, and percussion, it was in the nature of a slow-moving chorale with several variations.
Diamond's ability to invent new-sounding, logical, strong progressions of
sonorous, dissonant harmony is highly developed, and the listener who is
not antagonized by dissonances that have real meaning would find the music
in a fittingly solemn, tragic, and noble vein with an impressive, dramatic
mood. The *Elegy* is difficult to listen to not only because of the harmony but
also because of the very unusual melodic line of the chorale theme, but
anyone who has heard much contemporary music has heard many less well
sounding dissonant works than this one. It has more personality than any
work of Diamond's yet played.

Much milder, less striking, but excellently done was Vladimir Ussachevsky's *Cantata* for speaker, chorus, and orchestra. This was a very well
planned setting of selections from the Bible, arranged to form an exhortation to youth to have faith in God. From the dramatic and formal point of
view it was unusually effective, with convincing sincerity and musicality.
The orchestration was expert and did not muddy up the choral writing.
Unfortunately the style was quite derivative and not very personal. Much
King David and *Symphonie des psaumes* came through but with this curious
difference: the harmony was more consonant and did not have the bite that
such a forceful rhythmic style as Ussachevsky's seems to demand. The lapses
from general character would have been disturbing if the general line of the
music had not been so compelling. Ussachevsky is young and he may go far.

Among the new works of older composers, Charles Vardell's *Symphony
No. 1* had a considerable individuality about it, in spite of being in a much
more conservative idiom than the music previously mentioned here. There
was a kind of downright simplicity in his treatment of the folk tunes from the
Carolina hills, which was not without character. It is seldom one hears
works from other countries beside Russia, Finland, and Hungary which

have a style that is consistent with the folk themes that composers have often delighted in using. Usually one finds French or Russian harmonizations of Spanish, Brazilian, American, or English folk material. In fact one might go so far as to say that the folk style, except for some notable exceptions, is the least national of styles. At any rate many musically important countries have gotten along famously without an important folklore movement. It is still in the balance whether (begging the jazz question) anyone will come along who can derive great inspiration from American folk music directly, as Mussorgsky did. Vardell is a step in that direction but his symphony is not entirely convincing because, as so often happens in the "nationalist movement," the area where he is original is very small. His slow movements fall back into the ordinary, though the fast, gay ones have considerable character.

Aaron Copland's *Saga of the Prairie* (*Music for Radio*) was reviewed in these pages when it was first performed on the air last summer. It makes a very good concert piece and reaffirms the excellent first impression. In spite of a growing simplicity in Copland's style, his remarkable musical personality is as evident in this work as it was in many of his earlier ones.

The evening of ballet at the festival was notable mainly for the music played rather than for the dancing and choreography, though Evelyn Sabin, Dorothy Tucker, and especially a modern dancer, Marja Born, stood out from the rest of the troupe. Bernard Rogers's *Five Fairy Tales*, reviewed here before, is music whose great delicacy and beautiful characterization make it excellent ballet material though it is not intended for this medium.

The new dance score which made a big impression was Burrill Philips's *Play Ball!* It is written in a witty, sharp, lively, somewhat polytonal style. There is a real dry kind of American humor about the work that hits home. So often in popular American subjects like a baseball or football game composers have a tendency to become vulgar, as was the case with Kay Swift's *Alma Mater*, done several years ago by the American Ballet. Phillips avoided this completely, for his satirical score is imaginatively instrumented and planned; while avoiding all the cliches of the jazz industry it still keeps some of the basic character of this kind of music. Fresh, neat, and amusing in a straightforward way, it should be heard again with a more interesting stage performance.

Season's End,
New York, Spring, 1938

Modern Music, 15,4 (May–June 1938)

It must be very evident to any thoughtful person that a critic of necessity fulfills a very humble role in relation to the art of his time. For lack of perspective his opinions are likely to be wrong and his judgments irrelevant, even destructive. His obvious function is to point out what works are important, which creators are influencing the contemporary scene, and of course to quicken the understanding of the public and intensify its pleasure in what is happening. It is clear that literary, art, and dramatic critics consider this to be one of their chief duties. Unfortunately music critics in the daily press pay no attention to that important phase of their work. A new novel by Thomas Mann, a new picture by Henri Matisse, or any work by a serious thinker and inspired artist command a literate, intelligent review from a writer who can back up his statements with a thorough knowledge not only of the past but also of the present. But in the field of music, it is the fashion to dismiss all contemporary European works as the sterile product of a dying civilization and the American output as either inept or cacophonous, regardless of quality.

Among the many reasons for this peculiar situation is an economic one which is rarely pointed out. Book publishers and art dealers stand to gain or lose a good deal of money on the reviews of new works. Large sums are involved and the writers naturally feel the responsibility of this pressure. They have to make real sense in their articles and the public has come to expect such a fulfillment of duty. This is not to say that the music critic has no economic influence. He does, but, naturally, only where money is made in music, which is in the field of performance, for he can often make or break soloists or other performing groups. Consequently here the music critic is more highly trained and observant, and as music of the past is the raw material for almost all performances, he is as familiar with it as he is with the different tone qualities of singers and instrumentalists.

In the domain of serious modern composition, however, there is little if any money to be gained, at least in this country, though often large amounts of energy as well as money are spent. From an economic point of view therefore the musical arbiter is under no compulsion to show much interest in such an unrewarding field. He can, and he frequently does, condemn every new work as it appears, and no pressure is brought to bear from advertisers or public; the former have nothing to gain and the latter has succumbed to the critic's attitude through constant hammering. The critic need make no effort to understand, or even to be literate in his condemnation. Every one but the composer is pleased to remain lethargic in this economically unexploited field.

Yet despite the hostility of critics, a taste for such works is developing. Recording companies and the broadcasting systems even find it to their advantage to explore if not exploit contemporary music. In the colleges many excellent teachers and composers are awakening the young to an appreciation of new works, and on every hand there are evidences of a growing interest. Already the public responds more enthusiastically than the critics. The tendency could be observed this season when three outstanding new works were performed in New York: Bartók's *Music for Strings, Percussion, and Celesta*, Stravinsky's *Jeu de cartes*, and Malipiero's *Second Symphony*. Each was a superior piece by a composer who has a reputation for great excellence in the musical world. The entire press was hostile, while the public showed considerable enthusiasm.

The Malipiero *Symphony*, played this spring by the New York Philharmonic, is one of the composer's finest works, continuing the general musical direction of his *Julius Caesar*, which was performed here last year. It is contrapuntal with diatonic modal melodic lines of great simplicity, constantly moving harmony over a well-constructed bass, and a straightforward though free rhythm. The texture is transparent to the point of being bare and it is orchestrated with the most severe economy. Malipiero's approach to the symphony is almost a complete denial of the nineteenth-century dramatic form. It is closer to the instrumental works of Monteverdi, such as the *Sonata sopra Sancta Maria*, where there are no dramatic effects, the expressive interest arising solely from the simple beauty of the themes and their linear free development. Many of the restraints unconsciously observed by Monteverdi, such as the avoidance of violent outbursts, constant growth of tension, strong contrasts, piling up of rhythm, chromatic dissonance, and big orchestral crescendi, are to be observed here. But whereas up to now Malipiero seemed to be imitating the moods of sixteenth- and seventeenth-century music, in this symphony, sub-titled

Elegiaca, he has become much more intimate and personal in feeling. All four short movements, though varying in speed, are permeated with the austere, serious sadness which, as the sub-title suggests, is the symphony's main character. It is the best work of Malipiero I have heard, surpassing his early *Sette Canzoni* in seriousness and depth, and avoiding the dead spots which mar not only so much of his more recent music but also so much of contemporary Italian music.

Among the other works played at the Philharmonic were Quincy Porter's *Symphony No. 1.* Dissonant counterpoint, constant use of short melodic motifs, interesting incidental rhythms but no large rhythmic line, and sparing use of the orchestra characterize the musical side of this work. Emotionally it seemed to be not very clear in intention. At best a subjective, tense, bare atmosphere came across, as in the first movement, which is by far the most successful of the three. The other two lacked unifying conception and tended to be repetitious of the first.

Musical humor falls into several categories ranging from the Haydn, Rossini type, where it is an integral part of the music, through the more obviously descriptive kind as in *Till Eulenspiegel,* to the plain cartoon or burlesque which relies on the recognition of familiar themes and the exaggeration of familiar devices. Walton's *Façade* and McBride's *Fugato on a Well-Known Theme* are examples of the last. This is a sure-fire way to get a laugh out of the audience on first hearing. Whether on several repetitions the naivete of the idea does not wear thin depends on whether the composer has merely exploited the effect of recognition. I feel that neither Walton nor McBride has succeeded in doing more than this, though there are many numbers in the Walton which are extremely amusing at first hearing because of the cleverness of their orchestration. Barbirolli did the Walton up to the hilt and Barzin did very well by McBride.

At the Philharmonic Chasins played his *Second Piano Concerto,* a very brilliant and agreeable work in a kind of Brahms–Reger style, which Chasins handles with consummate skill. As it had no pretensions to great originality but aimed to please and to keep the audience interested it succeeded very well. Not so much could be said of the two other reactionary pieces, [Quinto] Maganini's *Tuolumne* and Samuel Barber's *Overture for the School for Scandal,* though in all fairness, Barber's piece, confessedly a student work, was very well done, while Maganini's was cheap and incoherent stylistically; though well orchestrated it fell to pieces at the end of every short-breathed section.

The Boston Symphony played no American music this year and introduced no contemporary music of any but the most famous composers. They did, however, during this spring season do a significant work by Prokofiev, his suite from *Romeo and Juliet*. The work is in line with his *Lieutenant Kije*. Although in a much simpler and more direct style than his *Enfant prodigue* or *Pas d'acier*, the personality of Prokofiev penetrates into his music even when it is completely consonant. One of the most striking things is his wonderful mastery of the orchestra, which is transparent without any fancy effects and sounds completely original. His melodic line retains its individuality even when it is reminiscent of Tchaikovsky, as it so often is in this ballet.

The Philadelphia scored a great success with Bernard Wagenaar's *Triple Concerto for Flute, Cello, and Harp* played by the Barrère-Salzedo-Britt Trio. This work is uncompromisingly in Wagenaar's individual and rather dissonant manner, and its success bodes well for all the other contemporary composers. To begin with it is an excellent integration of a brilliant cadenza-like style for the solo instruments into a symphonic whole. It is in the general period of Wagenaar's excellent *Third Symphony* of last year but it is more adventurous formally. The work is strong and clear intentioned, with a definite personality behind it. Its only fault seemed to me to be that a few of the cadenzas were a little long.

For some time now Harl McDonald's music has had an annual New York performance by the Philadelphia Orchestra. Each work shows no improvement over the preceding one and each is in a different style. Last year it was a feeble impressionism and this year his *Fourth Symphony* was in the student-work manner derived from Tchaikovsky; it included a few of the Jewish themes left over, I suppose, from his *Three Poems on Aramaic Themes*. His music is disconcerting, since there seems to be no personality behind it, and no noticeable musical intention. There might be some excuse for playing him if he had handled his style well, but the ineptitude of the form and harmony of this symphony was surprising, considering that he had such a good model as Tchaikovsky to go by.

McDonald also appeared on the program of Saminsky's Three Choir Festival, when his a capella *Missa de Battale* was performed. In a pre-Palestrina mood that reminded me a great deal of Goudimel's *Mass* in its straight-laced counterpoint, McDonald wrote a work that is almost indistinguishable from his model except for one short passage where the voices sing in octaves. It would be simpler for the critic if McDonald would make up his mind what style he believed in and started from there.

At this festival there were many interesting things played: Florent

Schmitt's *Laudate Nomen Domine*, full of the robust dramatic quality that is so typical of this composer; a very touching setting of *May the Words* by Bloch; and Saminsky's very fine sounding *By the Rivers of Babylon*, which is in the field of religious music, where that composer is at his best.

David Diamond's *Quintet* for flute, piano, and string trio, a League of Composers' commission, was played by the Barrère—Britt ensemble. The work is characteristic for its excellent and strong harmonic pattern and its nervous excitement, with the slow movement the clearest and most beautiful of the three. There is a tendency to overwriting and confusion in its very free contrapuntal texture. This *Quintet* does not have the same originality and strength that Diamond's orchestral works do, but it reveals his great fertility of musical ideas, especially in harmonic progression.

Another young composer, Dante Fiorillo, had two movements of a *Concerto for Piano, Oboe, and Horn* played at the concert of the Society for Professional Musicians. Though very dissonant in style, the work was not original in conception. The confused contrapuntal texture and the static harmonic basis gave it a diffuse and uncertain quality which canceled out the tension caused by the dissonances. If its form had been tighter and clearer the message might have come across better. The composer seems to have a personality but has not learned to express it convincingly.

The Henry Hadley Memorial Society gave an entire evening of their composer's orchestral works, which turned out to be quite interesting. Although Hadley's style is very much in the European late nineteenth-century romantic tradition, two pieces, *The Culprit Fay* and *In Bohemia*, both achieve a real character and a deeply felt quality that in spite of their lack of strong individuality make them worth hearing more often in our orchestral concerts.

Coolidge Crusade;
WPA; New York Season, 1938

Modern Music, 16,1 (Nov.–Dec. 1938)

Despite storms, war scares, and the seeming apathy of the public, Mrs. Elizabeth Sprague Coolidge continues her intelligent and laudable crusade for modern music. Floods prevented many from reaching her Pittsfield festival, and the tragic radio reports of European news interrupted her performances over the air. Nevertheless, still undaunted, she opened the season in New York by bringing those ill-fated programs of new music before the public in two concerts at the Public Library. A characteristic gesture, typical of the conviction and courage which have made her free concerts throughout the country a great success.

As always, her commissions went this year to composers of top rank in their respective countries: Ernst Toch, Anton von Webern, Frank Bridge, Louis Gruenberg, and Frederick Jacobi. Unfortunately, I missed the Bridge [String] Quartet [No. 4], but arrived in time to hear Toch's excellent Quintet [for Piano and Strings, Op. 64]. In this work Toch carries on the line of last year's easy-flowing, transparent *Piano Concerto*.* He has never been among the startling innovators of our time. Since his post-war beginnings he has relaxed into grace and charm, joining the fine line of composers who, like Mendelssohn and Mozart, never startle but rather interest, delight, and move by persuasion instead of force. Yet Toch uses a very distinct, personal style which has grown spiritually with every year. This *Quintet* is a good example of his latest work and deserves wide hearing.

There is a certain similarity in Toch's and Gruenberg's relation to the music of their time. Neither are adventurers along new, striking paths but rather men who follow, consolidating what is new to their own personal use. Gruenberg, too, has a personal style and like Toch seems to have given up his post-war sarcasms, the "jazz-berries" and "indiscretions" that date faster than they are written. Like Toch he has a trivial and obvious side; in his new

---

* Probably his *Symphony for Piano and Orchestra*, Op. 61 (1932).–Eds.

works this has been submerged. The *Quartet* shows what interest and serious music Gruenberg has in him and how skillfully he can use all the brilliant effects of string quartet writing. This is a well-formed and convincing work.

The other American piece on the Coolidge programs was Frederick Jacobi's *Hagiographia*, or musical portraits of Biblical characters. This quintet for piano and strings also showed a trend toward seriousness and meditation, but in spite of manifest conviction, it was too prolix and the intention hard to grasp. It did not seem to me as successful as Jacobi's *Quartet* [*String Quartet* No.2 (1933)] of two* years ago.

Mrs. Coolidge has never been frightened by the atonal school of Schoenberg and has extended plenty of opportunity to hear that tormented master's work. Now she gave us a hearing of Anton von Webern's new [*String*] *Quartet* [Op. 28 (1938)], which is not nearly so hard to understand as those of the later Schoenberg. Formerly everyone thought of Webern as the composer of tiny pieces for huge symphony orchestra that sounded like a hasty visit to the insect house at the zoo, but now we begin to see that his music, though still very tenuous and delicate, has a real and not merely an odd character. This *Quartet* is much larger and more worked out than his previous *Trio* [Op. 20 (1927)], and also is less dissonant and rhythmically more straightforward. A transparency and sensitiveness to sonority distinguish it from other twelve-tone works; they make it absorbing if puzzling listening.

Paul Hindemith's score for *St. Francis*, one of the new ballets the Monte Carlo troupe staged at the Metropolitan in October, deserves comment here as an important musical event. The score is the culmination of a long series of religious works by this composer, starting with the [original (1923) version of the] *Marienleben*, going on through some of the school-music canons and cantatas on pious texts, to the symphonic music for *Mathis der Maler*. It is evidently with knowledge of this latter work that Massine asked Hindemith to write a ballet like it. Ever since the settings of Rilke's *Marienleben*, Hindemith has approached his religious subjects with an archaizing spirit very similar to Rilke's, and in this early score he poured out some of his freshest and most beautiful music. The *Mathis der Maler Symphony* is the best presentation of archaic simplicity which he had achieved on a large scale. This quiet and simple mood has always existed in Hindemith side by side with a more ebullient, dynamic, and arresting spirit.

---

* The "two" obviously refers to a performance, rather than the year of composition.—Eds.

St. Francis is a reworking of many ideas from earlier music. Actual themes are taken over and redeveloped in a new and simpler way. The scoring is very spare, as is fitting for a story about poverty and chastity, and, hence, is for small orchestra. This does not mean that the work is a bore—far from it. There are several points of interest that quite make up for its lack of thematic freshness. The first is of course the wonderful imagination with which constant variety is achieved in a work of constant calmness. It is not only a tour-de-force but a very convincing musical expression. The other is the attack Hindemith makes on the problem of ballet music. *St. Francis* is not in the conventional form of a series of dances, with or without picturesque transitions, startling entrances, and solo and ensemble numbers, shared by works so dissimilar as *Lac des cygnes*, *Petrouchka*, and Auric's *Concurrence*. It is rather a series of large overall symphonic patterns, developing according to their own musical logic as often "against" the stage action as with it. Some sections are definitely dance music, others are clearly background for pantomine, but whatever they are they fit into a large symphonic pattern. This gives the score a dignity and an interest that more illustrative treatments of ballet have to make up for in brilliance. There is a grand scale, an expansiveness, about this music which no other modern composer handles so convincingly.

This summer afforded a chance to hear contemporary works out-of-doors. Surprising results: Copland's *Music for the Theater* for small orchestra, played by Koussevitsky, made fine open-air listening, while Stravinsky's more massive scores for *Les Noces* and *Symphonie des psaumes*, played by Smallens at the [Lewisohn] Stadium, were distinctly disappointing. *Noces* with the Stadium amplifiers at work sounded like a concerto for snare drum and xylophone with accompaniment of off-stage chorus and pianos. Under the conditions obtaining at the Stadium, at least, no idea could be formed of these two extraordinary works unless one were already familiar with the scores. I suspect that this is true of much that is heard in the open, but usually the music is so familiar that listeners automatically fill in harmony and bass when these are inaudible. David Diamond's *Overture*, also played at the Stadium, had the misfortune of being in an unfamiliar idiom whose fragmentary orchestration depends on careful balancing even in the concert hall. Exposed to the mercy of tricky acoustics it becomes almost impossible to judge. The Stadium is clearly not a place for premieres of music in anything but the most familiar and straightforward style. Nevertheless the *Overture* seemed to be a strong and interesting work.

The Westminster Choir School Festival, held too late to be reviewed before the summer, was the ideal all-American festival. Three concerts were devoted to rehearing of at least two important works of each of the following outstanding composers: Roger Sessions, Aaron Copland, Roy Harris, Walter Piston, and Quincy Porter; then, several concerts, well chosen from many younger, less famous men and from older composers like Arthur Farwell and Edgar Stillman Kelley; all performed by the excellent Roth Quartet and the Westminster Choir.

The works of the older men seem to improve vastly on rehearing. As to the younger composers, William Schuman's choral setting of Whitman's *Pioneers* left by far the best impression and fully confirmed Copland's enthusiastic review of it in the last issue. David Diamond's [*String*] *Trio* [in G (1937)] also proved interesting though it suffered from the fault of not being well thought out for the three strings. Alvin Etler, one of the Midwestern "primitives," played the oboe in a fresh little *Quintet* for that instrument and strings. I liked Etler's humor and charm but regret that he seems to share with McBride a contempt for European influences, influences which might help them both.

Schuman, whose *Second Symphony* was played by Schenkman at a WPA concert of the Greenwich Orchestra, suffers from the opposite fault of a too-obvious plan, the plan being filled with ideas often of no very great interest. The symphony, in one fairly short movement, is built of three long orchestral crescendi over three long pedals. It is repetition music gaining its effect by the hammering in of little fragments and tonalities. This plan, so new in the overture to *Rheingold*, now begins to wear thin, whether used with thematic interest as in Wagner or Strauss, or without thematic interest as so often in Sibelius, or with rhythmic interest as in the earlier Stravinsky. The day for discovering a new kind of plasticity and free-moving harmonies and lines seems to be here. Nevertheless, Schuman has worked out the device of repetition with a seriousness and strength which, though derived from Roy Harris, is original. I hope that he will soon write music that has a more convincing form.

The WPA Composers' Forum Laboratory in New York begins its fourth year with a brochure listing the one hundred and fifty-eight composers whose works it has played. Old and young, academic and "modern," ultra-dissonant and ultra-consonant, famous and obscure composers ranging from Mrs. H. H. A. Beach to David Diamond, from George Gershwin to the composition students of Eastman, Juilliard, Westminster, Bennington, Columbia, Sarah Lawrence, and New York University. Slight changes in the organization of the series are noticeable: a complete abandonment of orchestral works and a decrease by half in the number of concerts. All these seem to favor an improvement in the standard of performance, and in the concert of Lazare Saminsky and Charles Haubiel, which I attended, the performances were indeed much better than they have been. But what of the public who ask such pitiless questions of the composers [after the performances]?

There have been no recent rehearings of successful works. Men who have been discovered in these concerts (I suppose there are some) are not played more in other places, nor have publishers rushed forward to print their works. The famous remain famous and the obscure remain obscure. These concerts appear to have done nothing more than to give a small group of friends and others a chance to hear their works. But is this enough after three years' constant work? What I expected was that by now a group of people in the public would know what they wanted in American music and insist on hearing it from WPA organizations and at other concerts. Maybe question-naires to the public would help.

Why not, with the several excellent orchestras and conductors at its disposal, give a series of retrospective programs of music by composers since 1900, both European and American? Or an historical series of American works from John Knowles Paine on, chosen by a good jury? This could happen if enough people wrote letters to the Federal Music Project. There are many who would be only too glad to take steps in that direction.

Once Again Swing;
Also "American Music"

Modern Music, 16,2 (Jan. 1939)

Swing. Most everything has already been said about swing. A good many people get more thrills out of swing than out of "classical music," though some say it is a kind of dope—lots of kick that puts your mind to sleep. Some call it non-indigenous and African, though it was really invented by whites.

Others call it entertainment music having no emotional or intellectual appeal, with the same relation to "art music" that *Saturday Evening Post* illustrations or comic strips have to the works by [Pavel] Tchelitchev or Dali. Some say the future of American music lies here. Still others, hating its illiteracy and routine formulas predict it will shortly die of emotional and intellectual starvation. Foreigners recall that gypsy orchestras used to play with the same kind of abandoned improvisation, and historians report that the "polka mania" was just the same sort of craze in the last century. All our lives we have been hearing this astonishing and vigorous music develop. It makes the money, it gets the performances, its popularity exceeds the wildest dreams of serious composers. It has set the feet of the whole world stamping in four-four time.

At Carnegie Hall, during the holidays, the intellectuals of swing organized a fascinating historical concert. Starting with African records, they traced its development through the spiritual, jazz, boogie-woogie on up to Count Basie. Performers from little churches in the deep South who had never traveled before were brought out on Carnegie Hall stage, and in this spacious and, perhaps, specious atmosphere attempted to project the charm they exhibited back home. Negroes, probably because of their social history, have always been a race of entertainers like the gypsies in Europe. Theatrically their tradition is outside that of serious music. But this concert, since it was given in Carnegie Hall, challenged comparisons. Certainly the main factor is the hall itself. A concert hall performance of the usual kind takes place as a ritual in which public and performer are ultimately subservient to the ideas of a composer who has put his notes on paper. Swing, on the other hand, is the glorification of the performer. All the adulatory swing slang: "a killerdiller beating his chops," "gut-bucket licks," "in the groove," "boogie-woogie," "jitterbug," "a solid sender doin' some tall rug cuttin'" refer to the performer, to the type of performance, to the audience, but never to the actual, composed "paper" or music. It is, as we well know, a performance that stresses the intensity of nervous excitement "sent out" by the performer rather than the stuffed-shirt feeling of the concert hall. In order to make serious music palatable to the swing audience, composers like Bach and Debussy have to be arranged, to eliminate everything but the tune; rhythms, developments, and harmonies which might confound the jitterbug must be straightened out. When played in the appropriate jam style (for the "paper men," or men that can read music, do not play the notes in the classical time values but have a tradition which, from the point of view of the serious musician, distorts or "swings" eighths and quarters into rhythms impossible to notate) this becomes the genuine article and loses its original flavor. Just so, swing tends to lose *its* character and take on another when appropriated by serious composers for the concert hall. In that setting the music will never interest audiences until a serious composer with artistic perspective has been able to stylize and make it express his personal, creative attitude toward American life. Up to now swing still remains, except for a few isolated instances, in the stage of Russian folk song or gypsy music before Glinka, Mussorgsky, Liszt, or Brahms.

"The American composer should. . . ." Here we are back in the middle of a fight with the exponents of American music talking through their hats. The *New York Sunday Times* has, in the last months, published letters and critical articles revealing not only how wide a variety of opinions exists on this subject but also how little real information its steamy exponents have about what has been and is being done by American composers. The question was not whether Samuel Barber's *Adagio for Strings* (so typical of Toscanini's choice in contemporary music) was good or bad in its reactionary style, or whether it was better, say, than Barber's or Roy Harris's *Symphony* and if so why; no, the question was, rather, whether *all* American music should be "reactionary" or *all* should be "modern." This furor disregards the fact that a composer is good not because he is reactionary (like Brahms) or advanced (like Beethoven), but because he has imagination, vitality, and the other qualities which are always encountered regardless of school or nationality. In fact, I believe, none would be more disappointed than these critics and correspondents who so glibly tell the composers what to do, if musicians followed them and wrote scores in strict accord with their ideas. Certainly neither Henry James nor Walt Whitman ever fulfilled a previous "should," and no important composer past, present, or future may be expected to do the same.

The critics are not well informed about American music. How could they be? They do not cover concerts devoted to it, such as, for example, the WPA Composers' Forum Laboratory, or that of the Musical Art Quartet, which this month presented four American quartets by Daniel Gregory Mason, Quincy Porter, Mark Wessel, and Rudolph Forst. Two of these men have considerable reputations and yet only the [*New York*] *Times* and [the *New York Herald*] *Tribune* bothered to send even their second-string reviewers, who were perfunctory enough to come late or leave early. Other papers made the kind of passing mention accorded to third-rate artists. Paul Henry Lang describes this critical situation brilliantly in his penetrating article "Ecce Criticus" appearing in *The American Scholar*, Autumn, 1938.

The four first performances by the Musical Art Quartet were chosen to give a picture of the studious and serious side of American chamber music. Mason's *Intermezzo* for string quartet is one of the best pieces of this academic composer from the point of view of musical interest, though it lacked the personal quality of his *A Lincoln Symphony* played here last year. Quincy Porter's *Sixth Quartet* is one more Porter quartet with his usual smoothness, excellence of string writing, and transparency. There is a lighter touch here than in some of his others, but nothing is told that we don't already know about his music. Rudolph Forst's *Quartet*, as might be expected from an NBC award, was a fireworks piece, all the tricks of impressionistic quartet writing, form stunts from Brahms and Strauss, ideas having no stylistic or emotional relation to each other, and a lack of musical conviction. Mark Wessel's *Quartet* was the surprise of the evening. It was not altogether easy flowing nor free from reminiscences of Hindemith, but it had a kind of suffused passion and excitement which left one anxious to know his other music.

When Aaron Copland has two premieres in one short month, it is an event of considerable musical importance. Again the critics revealed their lack of information and interest. In reviewing Koussevitzky's excellent performance of *El Salón México*, these probers gave no evidence of ever having heard works by Copland before and hence failed completely to discuss the important change in style made evident in this piece. *El Salón México* is clearly a milestone in the composer's development, for it represents a change from the introspective attitude shown in its immediate predecessor, *Statements for Orchestra*, and in almost all his previous works. Beginning with the Mexican piece, Copland's music has become more relaxed and free, more ascetic in texture, more tonal, more consonant, and much more straightforward and melodic. He has discovered a kind of beautiful simplicity which bears a definite spiritual relationship to the simple, direct, and honest people of this continent. Characteristically, *El Salón México* is a musical description of the liveliness of a Mexican "hot spot," and it is done with gaiety and abandon. The clear orchestration—no trick doublings and messy textures, strong and free—is very typical of its composer. The style is much more accessible to the average public than in his earlier work, yet it is marked at every point with Copland's personality. In the *Symphonic Ode* there are the same breathless rhythms, insistence on brilliant triads, and crescendi of excitement, but here there is a jubilance that is new.

If the critics did not do justice to this work, they scarcely even mentioned Copland's most recent *An Outdoor Overture*, sensibly written for high school orchestra, commissioned and performed by the New York City High School of Music and Art. These orchestras, far less bound by tradition than our more impressive institutions, will unquestionably play a very great role in developing the appreciation of American music. The score is cleverly suited to the needs of young musical performers and serves them especially well as it makes them sound like an orchestra of professionals. Since *El Salón México*, Copland's music has become clearer and more sharply defined in feeling and character. *An Outdoor Overture* is a more impressive piece than the high-school opera, *The Second Hurricane*, for it contains some of his finest and most personal music. Its opening is as lofty and beautiful as any passage that has been written by a contemporary. It is Copland in his "prophetic" vein, a vein which runs through all his work, the slow pages of *Vitebsk*, the opening of the *Ode*, the conclusion of the *Piano Variations*, the "prophetic" movement of the *Statements*, and the beginning and end of his new ballet, *Billy the Kid*. Never before, though, has he expressed it so simply and directly. The rest of the overture with its changes of pace, like the *Music for Radio*, develops very naturally with lots of charm and variety. Each new work of Copland only goes further to prove that he is one of the most important, original, and inspiring figures in contemporary music either here or in Europe. But it is useless to expect the critics to hail him so, for they do not bother to hear or study his works.

During this season Barbirolli trotted forth only two new pieces, both undistinguished, Arnold Bax's tedious *Fourth Symphony* and Haubiel's pedantic-fancy *Passacaglia*. The effort to find new works that will not disturb the ancient and venerable trustees of the New York Philharmonic proves too great, and new music is now almost completely eliminated from their programs.

The Lives of St. Cyril and St. Methodius, by the Yugslav composer [Božidar] Širola, conducted by Hugh Ross at an *a cappella* Schola Cantorum concert, proved a great success. Justly so, for this work, in archaistic style, is both effective and stirring. Let us hope that some day we may hear the whole, instead of only one quarter.

The Case of Mr. Ives

Modern Music, 16,3 (Mar. 1939)

To tell the full story of the first and second New York performances of Charles E. Ives's *Concord Sonata* at Town Hall, January 20th and February 24th [1939] is not my purpose here, for that deserves a whole article. In tabloid form, however, it would read as follows:

> First performance: very small house.
>
> In the next ten days: enthusiastic reviews cribbed from Ives's prefaces by critics most of whom had not been at the concert.
>
> Second performance: packed house and disappointment of critics on hearing work, obviously for the first time.

For a good long while now many of us have been puzzled about the musical merits of the *Concord Sonata* and other of Ives's longer pieces. I came to know the sonata in the years when Stravinsky first scandalized America in person and Whiteman gave the Carnegie premiere of the *Rhapsody in Blue*. A keen time with lots of enthusiasm and lots of performances of new music to which I sometimes went with Ives himself. Sunday afternoons, after these concerts, a few of us would go down to Gramercy Park, where Ives then lived, or later uptown when he had moved to [East] Seventy-Fourth Street, to discuss the music in the calm atmosphere of his living-room, a Henry James, old New York interior. They were lively talks; new music was new and very "modern" and Ives was much interested. Often he would poke fun, sit down at the piano to play from memory bits of a piece just heard, like *Daphnis and Chloé* or the *Sacre*, taking off the Ravel major seventh chords and obvious rhythms, or the primitive repeated dissonances of Stravinsky, and calling them "too easy." "Anybody can do that" he would exclaim, playing *My Country 'Tis Of Thee*, the right hand in one key and the left in another. His main love, however, was for Bach, Brahms, and Franck, for he found in them spiritual elevation and nobility, which, like many a critic of his generation, he felt contemporary music had simplified away. To start the day fresh, he would often play a fugue from the *Well-Tempered Clavier* before breakfast and long hours at the office. Not that he needed much cheering up, for, being a good sturdy Yankee with plenty of vitality, he poured lots of pep, salty humor, and good spirits into everything he did.

During these afternoons we would coax him to try some of his own music, and as he saw we were sincere and not merely polite he would jump to the piano and play. Then the respectable, quiet, Puritan atmosphere was oddly disturbed, a gleam would come into his eyes as fiery excitement seized him, and he would smash out a fragment of *Emerson*, singing loudly and exclaiming with burning enthusiasm. Once the captain of the football team at Yale, he put the same punch into his music. It was a dynamic, staggering experience, which is hard even now to think of clearly. He hated composers who played their works objectively "as if they didn't like them." This strong, wiry Yankee vitality, humor, and transcendental seriousness were very much to our taste and we always came away from Ives full of life's glad new wine and a thousand projects for the future.

In those days Ives was practically never played. Once, in 1927 at a Pro-Musica concert, two movements of his *Fourth Symphony* were given under the direction of [Eugene] Goossens, who sat up all one night with a towel around his head trying to figure out how to keep the orchestra together in the places where the bar lines do not coincide. Ives had the percussion to his house to teach them the rhythms. It is no wonder the work didn't go any too well, for the score of the "lively movement," later published by *New Music*, has complexities well nigh insurmountable. At the time we asked why he didn't write his work more practically, so that performers could play it more accurately. He would reply that it was written as simply as possible, and then play over precisely what was written indicating that it was not as hard as all that. We remarked that certain very complicated textures would never sound, but he countered that he had already tried them out when he conducted a theatre orchestra at Yale. Then we asked why the notation of the *Concord Sonata* was so vague, why every time he played it, he did something different, sometimes changing the harmonies, the dynamic scheme, the degree of dissonance, the pace. He even made a transcription of *Emerson* with many notes changed and the dynamic plan completely altered. He said that he intended to give only a general indication to the pianist, who should, in his turn, recreate the work for himself. In a footnote to *Hawthorne*, he writes: "If the score itself, the preface, or an interest in Hawthorne suggest nothing, marks (of tempo, expression, etc.) will only make things worse."

This improvisational attitude toward music, so familiar in swing, affects all of Ives's more mature work. It affects his conception of performance and of composing. Unlike Chopin and Liszt, who wrote out very accurately in note values what they improvised, Ives leaves a great deal to the mercy of the performer. In his compositions, the notation of a work is only the basis for further improvisation, and the notation itself, frequently of music first conceived many years before, is a kind of snapshot of the way he played it at a certain period in his life.

The improvisation often consists in adding dissonances, harmonies, and complicated rhythms to a fundamentally simple work. This is obvious in many songs, and especially in a comparison of *Hawthorne* with the scherzo of the *Fourth Symphony*, which contain much identical material, greatly overladen with extra harmonies and complicated rhythms. The fuss that critics make about Ives's innovations is, I think, greatly exaggerated, for he has rewritten his works so many times, adding dissonances and polyrhythms, that it is probably impossible to tell just at what date the works assumed the surprising form we now know. The accepted dates of publication are most likely those of the compositions in their final state. Anyhow, the question is not important. Ives himself has said that he prefers people to judge his music not for when it was written but for what it is.

Up to the time [John] Kirkpatrick gave his performances no one had heard the *Concord Sonata* in its entirety in a concert hall. Some of us came wanting to see in the whole work what we saw in fragments. We found ourselves sadly disappointed. Kirkpatrick's extraordinary feat of interpretation did make a great deal of the music assume a shape through clever dynamic planning. But all the ingenious interpreting in the world could not dispel the fact that the sonata is formally weak. Kirkpatrick played the work with more finesse and less breadth and grandeur than Ives does, but this is understandable as Ives rarely ever played the whole work through but stuck to little fragments which he particularly loved; the whole work as a piece seemed to interest him less.

To turn to the music itself. In form and esthetic it is basically conventional, not unlike the Liszt *Sonata*, full of the paraphernalia of the overdressy sonata school, cyclical themes, contrapuntal development sections that lead nowhere, constant harmonic movement which does not clarify the form, and dramatic rather than rhythmical effects. Because of the impressionistic intent of most of the music, the conventional form seems to hamper rather than aid, resulting in unnecessary, redundant repetitions of themes, mechanical transitions uncertain in their direction; unconvincing entrances of material; dynamics which have no relation to the progress of the piece. Behind all this confused texture there is a lack of logic which repeated hearings can never clarify, as they do for instance in the works of Bartók or Berg. The rhythms are vague and give no relief to the more expressive sections, and the much touted dissonant harmonies are helter-skelter, without great musical sense or definite progression. The esthetic is naive, often too naive to express serious thoughts, frequently depending on quotation of well-known American tunes, with little comment, possibly charming, but certainly trivial. As a whole, the work cannot be said to fill out the broad, elevated design forecast in the composer's prefaces.

However, there is also much good in the sonata. Usually the statement of themes is beautiful: in *Emerson*, the beginning, the first "verse" section, the allegro, and the coda; in *Hawthorne*, pages 27 to 32, which lead up to the "pilgrim's song" and the funny parody of *Hail, Columbia*; though less characteristic of Ives's best, the *Alcotts* maintains a consistent level; and *Thoreau*, with its lovely beginning and its beautiful "walking theme," is in the best Ives manner, though it too has a long redundant section which might be relieved by cutting pages 65 and 66.

While his music is more often original than good, the good is really very personal and beautiful. Unlike that of Charles Griffes, here is a fresh and touching impressionism, different from anyone else's. With Griffes, Ives shares many formal weaknesses as well as a similar sensitivity to curious chord formations, but though he has more scope, he is less able to realize his musical purpose. Despite all the problems about music and American culture which form the interesting context of the Ives case, it is not possible on the basis of the music we know to rank him among the great originals of American art, with, for instance, [Albert P.] Ryder and Whitman. Unlike theirs his work, though original, falls short of his intentions. In any case, it is not until we have had a much greater opportunity to examine and hear his music that Ives's position as a composer can be determined. The present canonization is a little premature.

FURTHER NOTES ON THE WINTER SEASON, 1938/9

Nothing could be a greater jump than from Ives to Nadia Boulanger, who during the winter conducted the Philharmonic in performances of great precision, clarity, and understanding. While the Concord school was at its height, Poe was inaugurating the idea: "take care of the manner and the matter will take care of itself." Now we have an exponent of that principle in music, living, and functioning among us. Mlle. Boulanger conducted several new works by [Antoni] Szalowski and Françaix, which clearly reflected this approach and which, though completely realized musically, were not very important. Each new piece by Jean Françaix is so much like its predecessor that it is very hard to think of something new to say about the *Piano Concerto*, performed by himself at this concert. It was a little longer and a little duller than his more amusing *Concertino* for piano and orchestra, but it had the same trivial, boyish charm, agreeable to hear and not particularly agreeable to think about.

Bartók's new *Rhapsody for Clarinet and Violin* proved that a good new work if played by performers with the reputations of Szigeti and Benny Goodman can have great success. This piece consists of two folk-dances, resembling in atmosphere such older works of Bartók as the *Allegro Barbaro*, but they are done with much greater brilliance and surety of technique. It is a work that is less important than his *Music for Strings, Percussion and Celesta** of last year, but shows the same care in construction and many of the same beauties.

At last we had an opportunity to hear Stravinsky's *Concerto for Two Pianos*, excellently played by Steuermann and Gimpel at a New School concert. It sounds even better than it looks on paper, and proves to be one of Stravinsky's finest works. As this composer comes more and more to grips with the problems of abstract music, he gives us increasingly important scores. For besides being intensely interesting in form and movingly serious in atmosphere, the *Concerto* is a mine of invention in sonorities for two pianos. It is good to know that a work of such great quality and seriousness could have been composed in these recent hectic years.

At this same concert there was also played an excellent quartet** by Janáček, a composer whom we should hear more often.

One of the best musical programs of the year was offered at a Juilliard Alumni concert which included Aaron Copland's *Sextet* for clarinet, piano, and string quartet. This arrangement of his *Short Symphony* gives a good idea of but does not supplant our impression of the very interesting orchestra piece which Copland composed before the *Statements*. It goes the

* Carter had "Harp."—Eds.
** We have no information concerning which of Janáček's two quartets was performed.—Eds.

limit in rhythmic invention and offers occasional hints of his later style, especially in the middle section of the slow movement, which is particularly beautiful. The whole gives further evidence of the strong inventive and imaginative qualities of this individual composer and of his great musical skill.

Sometimes in Hindemith's newer works there appears an academicism disappointing in so original a creator. Rarely has any work of his suffered so much from this fault as the *Symphonic Dances*, played here by Koussevitsky. It did not however prevent the slow section of the second movement from being good Hindemith and good music.

The Boston Orchestra also played an inferior work of Vladimir Dukelsky. In *Dédicaces* Dukelsky makes use of all the old hat modernisms and puts them together in scrappy fashion. Nevertheless, as in the better *End of St. Petersburg*, there is a curious, tortured personality which is apparent in all of his very uneven concert music.

Among the young American composers, Hunter Johnson stood out for his *Andante* for flute and strings played by Carleton Sprague Smith at a WPA concert. It was personal and interesting, as was, in a completely different way, Henry Brant's lyric *Viola Sonata*, also heard at the Composers' Forum Laboratory. Brant's music has taken an unexpected romantic turn that is quite fresh and new. Norman Cazden, who is talented and skillful, had *Three Sonatas*, for clarinet solo, for viola solo, and for the two together, played at the Juilliard Alumni concert. These are effective and musically interesting though they tend to the kind of dryness from which solo instrumental works of this kind often suffer. They make good exercises for performers interested in new music, as they are well written for the instruments.

Prize Philharmonic compromises of [David] Van Vactor and [Robert] Sanders did not prove very new. Van Vactor's *Symphony* [in D (1937)] was the kind of modernism we saw at the Chicago World's Fair—academic plan and idea with a few frills of shiny chromium. Moments in it were good though. Sanders's *Little Symphony*, a flat-footed barn-dance version of the *Classical Symphony*, was neat but humorless.

At the League of Composers' concerts, a group of very young composers performed. Harold Brown's *Experiments* were the most finished if not the most original; Herman Chaloff was the most curious, more curious and surprising than anything heard in a long time. Margaret Purcell adapted the style of the Modern Dance composer to the accordion, with amusing results.

Hunter Johnson's *Serenade for Flute and Clarinet* stood out as the only work having a definite character and personality.

So far it has been a good and interesting season.

Important note: Hendrik Willem van Loon has recently published five very interesting, vituperative *Deliberate Reflections* on the situation of the American musician in *Greenwich Time*, January 10–14, Greenwich, Conn. These are having very far-flung reverberations. Here are a few high spots: "The whole business of music in America, by and of and for Americans, has now reached a point where a few honest observations are an absolute necessity. For unless we hasten to save what can still be saved, no one in this rich and easy-going country will have a chance unless he or she happens to have been born in one of the slums of Bologna, in the attic of a Cracower suburb. . . ." "We are going to have an exhibition in New York this summer. . . . It will feature the World of Tomorrow. But for American musicians, it will once more feature the World of the Never-Never Land."

Of the American critic he remarks: "The American critic is as scrupulously honest as he is dull. But there again we can hardly blame him. He is terribly overworked and everlastingly pestered by the most insidious forms of publicity. Furthermore, he writes for a public that is not very well versed in musical lore."

Calling the managers "music brokers," he says: "That little expression will show you in a general way what is the matter with the 'Music of Today' and why it may lead up to 'No Music of Tomorrow' unless we take a little interest in that particular field which to many of us means more than all the stucco *palazzi* now being raised to high Heaven on the Flushing mudflats. . . . Like every other article that has become a commodity, music has fallen into the hands of a small ring of promoters and brokers, who rule supreme and who can make or break reputations and actually do so with the callousness of gangsters."

About what should be done: "It will take years of bitter fighting on the part of the American artists themselves, for they are the ones who will have to unite for commom action if they do not want this condition to prevail forever. . . . What American music needs just now is a revolt on the part of the concert-going public. . . . Music lovers of America, unite and throw off the shackles of that foreign domination which is destroying the hope of your native musicians."

O Fair World of Music!

Modern Music, 16,4 (May–June 1939)

The first sound I heard at the New York World's Fair came out of the good old-fashioned calliope at the merry-go-round in the Children's World. It set the atmosphere of spring, of gaiety, in fact of a fair. Here was one of the few sounds whose barbaric note rising out of windy pipes was not aggrandized, nor was the keen edge of its tone slithered over by radio amplification. By comparison with the rest of the music in the World of Tomorrow it makes a small noise indeed, in deference perhaps to the size of children, and it is one of the few that catches a human freshness and charm, something which electrified music, no matter how well reproduced, never has. Adults are treated, as befits them, on a bigger scale. At every crossroads there is a loudspeaker dispensing, in the morning, selections from *Scheherezade*, then lots of gumdrops like *Kamennoi Ostrow*; in the late afternoon Strauss waltzes, and in the evening selections from the *L'Arlésienne* suite. Such soupy, amplified music always evokes for me the image of some huge Walt Disney monster pouring out his weepy soul in a slightly inarticulate voice, a ludicrous but inevitable trumpet of doom. This sentimental Gargantua is what we now accept as the expression of jollity and merriment.

At present it is impossible to discover from the Fair announcements what music is being used in the exhibits. There is, however, quite a bit that is interesting, which you can stumble on by poking about in the stucco and plaster. The loudest noises at the Fair are the terrifying, wondrous bolts of man-made lightning at the General Electric Exhibit and the whistle of the locomotive of the future, speeding its furious pace on a treadmill. The strangest noises are in the Westinghouse exhibit, which reproduces an old city street lit by gas. Here there is an electrical sound track of katydids, bird twitters, and the roar of illuminating gas, far louder than any modern traffic and just as persistent.

Digging further you will find an entire show at the Railroad Building, *Railroads on Parade*, complete with speakers, dancers, singers, and—of all things—a most excellent score by Kurt Weill. The pageant has loads of charm with real steaming and smoking locomotives playing the prima-donnas' roles. When the famous halves of the Union Pacific meet, the iron horses sing little songs with toots between phrases. Weill has appropriately used all kinds of American tunes, including one of my favorites, *Fifteen Years on the Erie Canal*, with fine taste, intelligence, and showmanship. All this is played and sung by an orchestra of twenty-six and a chorus of eighteen who are below stage; the music is piped up and amplified to sound above the locomotives' roar.

At the Ford Building, I found not the Symphony Orchestra, which was at the exhibit in the Chicago Fair, but Ferde Grofé and three others at three Hammond Novachords and a Hammond organ, playing plushy arrangements of *Old Folks at Home*, and so on, with arpeggios, and sea-sick swellings and diminishings. They show just what the Novachord can do, how inhuman its breathless flutes and gutless violins can be.

Machines have a pathetic, ludicrous inadequacy when they try to be men. "Pedro, the Voder" at the A. T. and T. pavilion, with its keyboard of audible consonants and vowels, emits the most marvelous garbling of English I have ever heard. It is hilarious and provocative with a suggestion of Joyce in *Finnegans Wake*.

Various serious composers, besides Kurt Weill, have been approached by commercial organizations that have apparently learned something from using serious sculptors, architects, and mural painters. Hanns Eisler has done music for a film to be shown at the Petroleum exhibit. Vittorio Giannini wrote a short symphony commissioned by the International Business Machines for their opening program. William Grant Still was selected by a Fair jury to do the music for the show in the Perisphere. As in everything else here the "popular" note is stressed, the definition of what is popular being grandeur, expensiveness, overpowering, almost primitive emotion about the commonplace.

Giannini's score typified this spirit well. It was a kind of *Heldenleben* that worked in national anthems from every nation including Austria. Official ballyhoo hailed it as the most inspired commissioned work yet to come from a modern composer —with sublime disregard for practically all of Stravinsky's works (which have been ordered by Diaghilev, the Princesse de Polignac, the Boston Symphony, etc.) and many by Hindemith and plenty of other important composers.

What promises much in the way of "Gebrauchsmusik" ordered for these exhibits are two scores by Aaron Copland, one for Ralph Steiner's housing film *The City*, which will be shown continuously at the Science and Education Building, and the second [*From Sorcery to Science*] for Remo Bufano's

marionette show at the Hall of Pharmacy. Other new works still unan-
nounced may be offered by the exhibitors. It is a very important step for our
music to have these commercial, industrial, or public-building orders. All
around the country, at shows like New York's Hayden Planetarium and the
Oceanarium in St. Augustine, Florida, there are permanent exhibits which
have music as a background. At present works like Liszt's *Les Préludes* (for
the fish at the Oceanarium) and Strauss waltzes (for the stars) are constantly
played. The Fair may stimulate special commissions of music which would
considerably enhance their charm.

Among the more exotic exhibitions, such as the Turkish pavilion, I was
disappointed to hear only salon classics. A little native music would liven up
the interest. Exotic atmosphere is always one of the chief attractions of a fair.

In the Lagoon of Nations, some splendid fountains extraordinarily lit
erupt nightly. They are very like the illuminated fountains at the recent Paris
exposition. The music here is not, however, by such originals as Auric and
Milhaud but by that king of Broadway arrangers, Robert Russell Bennett.
Perhaps it was the problem of making music loud enough to be heard above
the rush of waters that determined the choice of this clever orchestrator. As a
matter of fact the noise is itself no great problem; even the buzzing of the
clavichord can, by modern amplification, be made to sound as loud as a
brass band. Bennett has very wisely used a concert band, for when it is
amplified it does not sound unnatural; the score is audible through the
torrents. I only deplore the conscious writing down to popular taste which
has led him in his *George Washington* piece (with red, white, and blue jets of
water) to do up all the national anthems, including *Yankee Doodle* in
Wagnerian style, as if the World of Tomorrow were the Dusk of the Gods.
Fountains are gay, strong, surprising, and beautiful spectacles, like fireworks, and not either pompous, or heroic. Later in the evening in the large
Fountain Lake, I saw a less pretentious play of water while the ubiquitous
loudspeakers played the Carillon number from the *L'Arlésienne* suite. This
seemed to me suitable in spirit at any rate.

One night during the magniloquent fountain display, I saw a large group
of people assemble on a platform not far away. Soon they took form as
chorus and orchestra. Since the loudspeakers were blaring the Bennett music
and later the Strauss waltzes, I couldn't make out what was happening.
Nobody ever went over to them; a few strollers walked across their platform
taking a short-cut to somewhere else. Finally I edged my way next to the
bassoon and discovered that this many-peopled group, lost out in the open
air, was rendering a Haydn symphony! A few feet from the heart of the

orchestra not a note they played could be heard. A phantom concert about which I have never succeeded in finding out anything. This large and sadly futile group of performers—classical music in a modern world—disturbed me. If, dear reader, there is ever a concert of American music at the Fair, it will probably be by this ghostly troupe.

There are, however, lots of real people making sounds at the Fair. The management in the second week decided to introduce an even more popular note (as if lowering the prices would not be the most popular thing). Wandering musicians, comics, and musical clowns are now to be met giving little impromptu shows everywhere. These do indeed relieve the dreary oppressiveness of the loudspeakers. I remember a particularly funny man with a toy trombone like the angelic instrument in Italian primitive paint-ings; he played this brilliantly with all the finesse and humor of the best musical clowns.

The Coldstream Guards' Band at the British pavilion does very straightforward and precise arrangements, and its lusty playing is cheery. Band music in the open air is always charming, and theirs is most expert. The carillon at the Dutch pavilion is gay and fresh too. All this music is so much more suited to out-of-doors than the gushy electrical yawps that fill the air over Flushing Meadows.

For concerts, by far the best place that I have found is the WPA open-air auditorium, which incidentally, also has the best murals. I heard Juanita Hall's Negro Melody Singers in a delightful program of spirituals in this garden-like place, and under excellent acoustical conditions. The chorus sounded as fresh and brilliant as music should under ideal conditions. I hope there will be lots going on here all summer long. WPA "Pops" would be welcome; no one else seems to be giving a regular series of symphonic concerts and no one else has such facilities.

A tremendous range of programs has been announced for the Temple of Religion, which, try as I will, I haven't yet been able to locate. As for television you can witness its primitive beginnings at the RCA and General Electric buildings. So far, newsreels of forest fires and other visually over-active subjects are being shown.

AT THE HALL OF MUSIC

So much for the unofficial music at the Fair. On the whole it is perhaps more varied and progressive than what goes on inside the World's Fair Music Hall, which is in the Amusement Area along with many other attractions—the Hunting Lodge, the Cuban Village, the Artists' Colony, and Victoria Falls—that face more to the world of yesterday than do the great commercial and national exhibits on the other side of the Fair.

But for those who still like music in concert halls, new, interesting works have come to light here. The Polish Concert gave us the late Karol Szymanowski's *Symphonie Concertante*, Opus 60, one of his finest works. [Stanislaw] Wiechowicz's *Polish Wedding Dance* from *Chmiel* was a lively piece of folk-lore. The Rumanian Concert under Enesco presented all the academic numbers familiar to Philharmonic audiences, plus a more interesting, modern sounding piece, *Variations on an Original Theme* by Jonel Perlea; in spite of its longwindedness this had a first, second, and last variation of surprising originality.

The Brazilian evenings with their showy, torrid pieces were the most fun of all. We don't hear much Villa Lobos in this country, and here was a chance at two of his most astounding works, *Chôros No. 8* and *Chôros No. 10*. The verve and originality of these savagely primitive scores with their remarkable instrumental and percussive effects, their dense almost tropical textures, and their curious form, inspire much far-reaching speculation about the music of our hemisphere. I was familiar with several short works by this fiery composer, some uninteresting or unconvincing, and only one, a song *Xango*, which gives any hint of what is contained in these big *Chôros*.

There is also scheduled a Swiss concert with Honegger and the less known Frank Martin, whose works deserve more consideration than they have had here. And speaking of what is to come—where, in all this foreign pageant, are Mexico and Carlos Chávez?

A word about the highly acclaimed acoustics of the Music Hall. They are, to any impartial ear, neither excellent nor bad enough to mar one's enjoyment of the music. By being in the Fair they seem to have taken on that curious metallic and inexpressive quality which I heard all about me from the loudspeakers.

These concerts have made one important contribution: they prove that outside the traditional repertory of our symphony orchestras there are lots of scores worth hearing, both old and new. Never again will we believe our conductors when they return from summer vacations abroad with news that no works of any interest are being written. Every foreign concert at the Fair has proved just the opposite.

Season of Hindemith and Americans, 1939

Modern Music, 16,4 (May–June 1939)

Paul Hindemith has burst like fireworks over New York, scattering performances everywhere. At Carnegie he conducted the Philadelphia in the Suite from *Nobilissima Visione*; at the Juilliard Alumni Concerts his *Flute Sonata* and *Hin und Zurück* (very well done); at the New School for Social Research the Galimir ensemble played his *Fourth Quartet*; finally he appeared both as violist and pianist at a Town Hall evening devoted entirely to his works. So we had plenty of chance to compare the Hindemith of before and after 1930, which date marks the great change in his development. It is beyond the limits of this brief review to make a comparative analysis. Hindemith's style since *Das Unaufhörliche* and the Gebrauchsmusik period has obviously crystallized. The texture is simpler, the rhythms and form begin to suggest Mozart and early Beethoven, and the harmony and counterpoint are more systematized. He is now in command of a musical language which he uses, as did the composers of the eighteenth century, to express a variety of thought and emotion, always with great imagination and flexibility. Unlike Mozart's style, which was general to his time, Hindemith's is very personal. Melodically it is one of the richest and most original in contemporary music.

Of his recent works, the *Quartet for Clarinet, Violin, Cello and Piano* is the most interesting. Like most of his newer music, it is best in the moderate and slow movements. (Exactly the opposite was true in the earlier period.) Here the first movement with its graceful, flowing eighths is in conventional sonata form; the peaceful coda reaches a point of exceptional beauty. The slow movement, with its typically Hindemithian fioriture, is untortured and smooth; while the last, made up of alternate moderate and fast rhythms, is loveliest in those quieter moments which breathe the fresh romantic charm that is the most delightful characteristic of his newest music.

Roy Harris's *Third Symphony*, brought here by Koussevitsky, deserves a little more discussion than it has received. Harris also has undergone quite a change. There has been some yielding of his earlier awkward and jagged construction in favor of a more consolidated form and greater lucidity. This work lacks the new vistas of the first symphony, and those curiously broken phrases of the second, which, by the way, was performed at an All-American Concert given in Carnegie Hall by the Composers' Forum Laboratory and the Federal Symphony Orchestra under Alexander Smallens's direction. The *Second Symphony* is a step in the direction of consolidation but is so economical in material that motifs are excessively repeated. The canonic slow movement has several excellent ideas but its course is too dense and awkward. Many have wondered whether this awkwardness resulted from intent or technical disability. It has always seemed to me the effect of a personal if not thoroughly convincing attempt to solve problems in a new way. The present symphony is better tailored, and its direction clearer, but some of the odd originality is gone. The music still never for a moment could be mistaken for someone else's , but in the weaker parts Harris has come to depend on well-tried effects. Echoes of the romantic and heroic "Grand Symphony" of composers like Dvořák and Sibelius soften its bite. This is especially true of the clap-trap ending with its repeated timpani strokes. Perhaps the renunciation in favor of intelligibility may bring Harris back some day with the stirring inspiration of his earlier works re-captured, but better equipped to pour that into convincing musical shape. Then both he and all of us will have gained enormously. His *Soliloquy for Viola and Piano*, played by Primrose at a Juilliard Alumni concert, was less interesting than the *Symphony*, though the almost impressionistic ending made the work arresting. But in every piece of music by Harris there are some wonderful moments; if only the whole were as good as some of the parts.

The all-American program mentioned above was devoted entirely to the works of Guggenheim Fellows. It included Aaron Copland's *An Outdoor Overture* (reviewed in the last issue), for me the high point of the concert. Walter Piston was represented by his charming *Concertino* for piano and orchestra, an appealing work especially in the lyric sections and in the humorous bassoon passages of the finale. I regret that his more important *Symphony* [No. 1] was not selected; its elegance of craftsmanship and distinction would have added much to the program. Paul Nordoff's *Concerto* for two pianos showed a slight leaning toward Les Six; the slow movement gave us a seriously felt, delicate piece of impressionism. The noisy *Prologue* for chorus and orchestra by William Schuman seems to me an unfortunate step in the direction of pompous works like Gustav Holst's *Hymn of Jesus*. It is less interesting than his *Symphony* [No. 2 (1937?)], heard last year, though it seems to be the type of music approved by critics and audiences. The concert was apparently planned for "popular" appeal. Nevertheless I found it regrettable that selection was not made in favor of such interesting young recipients of the Guggenheim as David Diamond and Robert McBride. And on any representative program limited to these Fellows, certainly neither Roger Sessions nor Randall Thompson would have been out of place.

It took Stokowski to import Shostakovitch's *Fifth Symphony*. This work is as big and popular, as curious a blend of the academic and modern, as the Soviet Pavilion at the New York World's Fair. I had no score with which to follow it; but the orchestration of the *Magic Fire* music and *Night on Bald Mountain*, also on this program, were so doctored that I doubt whether the audience heard the Shostakovitch piece as he himself wrote it. The surprising thing about him is his sequence of musical ideas and thinness of texture. The composer of "schizophrenic mazurkas" has become in all other respects conventional. His themes, harmonies, and rhythms resemble those of Tchaikovsky and Mahler, though his melodious moods (indirectly inspired by Mme. von Meck's railway shares [via Tchaikovsky's music]) register the emotions of a very different social system than theirs.

A model in their performance and selection of contemporary music, the New School Concerts brought us Roger Sessions's *Quartet* and Schoenberg's song cycle, *Das Buch der hängenden Gärten*. The quartet intensified impressions of sturdy, excellent workmanship made two years ago. It was this time interpreted more gently, and the beautiful, lyrical slow movement took on true interest. This is music to be heard many times; it is so meaty and thoroughly worked out that it leaves the hearer musically satisfied. The hysteria and poignant sadness of Schoenberg's prewar song cycle made me want to hear *Pierrot Lunaire* again. *Das Buch der hängenden Gärten* is more fragmentary than the other work, also more sensitive. Like Debussy's *Proses Lyriques*, also sung on these programs, the Schoenberg songs give us a taste of impressionism; though of the tortured, German variety they are just as beautiful.

The Juilliard Alumni Concerts introduced Frederick Jacobi's *Ave Rota*, Three Pieces in Multiple Style, for small orchestra. The title, as the score reveals, should be expanded to read, Hail to the Wheel of Fortune. It divides into three sections: the first, *La Balançoire*, indicates the swing in styles between the eighteenth-century concerto grosso and the modern rhumba; the second, *The Merman*, gives jazz treatment to a quotation from "Sumer is icumen in"; the third is a *May Dance* in popular syncopated time. The interesting instrumentation divides the ensemble into tutti and concertino, the latter consisting of clarinet, trumpet, trombone, and solo violin. The whole is neatly done and sounded well. A frankly programmatic piece, it depends for its humor largely on the juxtaposition of contradictory styles. This device has been exploited before and with more abandon by both Milhaud and Honegger. *Ave Rota*, written with obvious command of his idiom, does not, I think, compare with Jacobi's more interesting and happily conceived pieces, as for example his *Second Quartet*.

The third League of Composers' concert dispelled any lingering impression that young Americans today show less promise than the preceding generation. It offered some delightful songs by Irving Feigen, whose subsequent tragic and fatal accident ended a career that offered us much. Paul Bowles, in his best, gayest, and most flippant manner, parodied old movie and dance music in his funny *Pieces for a Farce*. In view of his extreme youth the very Hindemith-like pieces that introduced Lukas Foss were indeed remarkable. Finally came Robert Palmer's *String Quartet* [No. 1], the most hopeful piece of the whole series. Palmer, a hitherto unheard-from composer, was the big surprise of the whole concert series. His music is firm and definite, its dissonance resembles that of younger Europeans like Henk Badings, whom we never hear in this country. And though he has yet to learn how to construct on a broad line, his quartet showed an impressive seriousness and great musicality.

Mordecai Bauman's recital of leftist songs at the New Masses' Concert deserves mention because of its novelty and also the interesting problem it poses. Songs like these by Hanns Eisler, Marc Blitzstein, Alex North, Goddard Lieberson, and others seem more at home in a cabaret than in Town Hall, where Bauman sang them. For one thing the cabaret provides a better "dramatic" setting for the interpretation that such songs need. Also it brings audience and performer into more intimate conspiracy. In Town Hall the music sounds a little overdone and even insincere. Its essence is theatre, left-wing theatre, with the intellectuals not togged out in evening dress.

The New York Season Opens, 1939

Modern Music, 17,1 (Oct.–Nov. 1939)

Sibelius happens to be the right man in the right place (a far-away, neat little country that pays its war-debts) for a big success in this country. And people here are old friends of the symphonic style, as our concerts now usually consist of a big piece written in that form, surrounded by several "shorts" of varying character. Sibelius, a much less important composer than the brilliant Richard Strauss, like him carries on this style, but with a greater underpinning of philosophy and less music. Unlike Strauss he has adopted all those forms which are now familiar to our audiences, and he has at least one piece for each kind of serious-music public: *Valse Triste* for the "Pops" audience, *Finlandia* for the lovers of the *1812 Overture*, the *First* and *Second Symphonies* for Tchaikovsky-Wagner-and-Brahms-ians, the *Third Symphony* for the "little folk in the hills" (Dvořák fans), and so on to the impressionists and the more advanced connoisseurs who can appreciate the stark and strained wisps of music in the *Fourth* and *Seventh Symphonies*. Probably the lovers of the *Second Symphony* predominate (this was the concluding number of the all-Sibelius evening given at Carnegie in October by the NBC Symphony under the direction of [Gerhard L.] Schnéevoigt); but any symphony concert in a place where all these audiences are present and where each group, educated at least to the point of respect by the piece it likes, will listen to all his works with reasonable attention. No other contemporary composer has written so many orchestral pieces of such an essentially related character, which nevertheless appeal to so many different kinds of people.

Few important contemporaries have been so easy on their audiences. Performances of contemporary ballets and operas, or frequent repetitions of the same work, which might help the public to understand the more varied output of other composers, have not occurred. One kind of new music does not always lead to comprehension of another; usually each is a new attack on a new problem of expression. So, if a composer doesn't compose the same piece, over and over again under different titles, and thus train his audience to get the point, he will have a hard time being understood. He may feel that the Dvořák, Tchaikovsky, Wagner, and even Sibelius brand of romantic heroics sounds hollow, but if he has something new to say and insists on saying it, he will develop faster than his audience; he will leave his public and then his public will leave him. One contemporary composer after another has suffered that fate.

Although this is no place for an extended discussion of the Sibelius success story, I would like to register a reservation about his music. It is not that he is unoriginal (at best he has some new color effects which are one of the minor originalities); not that he is unskillful, although in his rather subconscious style of composing he often falls into the abuse of crude procedures; not that his nationalist point of view is a little belated; but that his whole attitude toward music is deeply reactionary. This inevitably prevents his being really fresh and new. A few pieces sum up his point of view artfully and well. The rest are generally flat. But since audiences well trained in nineteenth-century heroics will stand for a lot of tedium, his music has what it takes to be popular at this time.

The ASCAP Festival of American Music is another perfect illustration of my text—the magniloquent and grandiose symphonic style is the popular, prestige style of today. The week of free advertising which ASCAP gave the public at Carnegie Hall was sensibly planned to win the public over to the Society's side should a legal battle follow the expiration of ASCAP's radio contracts. There were box seats, evening clothes, symphony orchestras, and fancy programs with pictures of President Roosevelt and Victor Herbert on glossy paper. There was an article inside the program on the "Advancement of Culture," written as high-pressure sales promotion, which argued that the more emotion there is, the better the art; concluding that what we need is more and more emotion. To show how emotions operate, the first evening started (as did all of them) with a serious, high-sounding speech expressing the pious hopes that in the future America would devote herself to the arts of peace and stay out of the war. The same evening ended in an orgy of gaiety as the audience joined in singing that old war-time favorite of George M. Cohan's, *Yankee Doodle Boy.*

Of course ASCAP is naturally immune to criticism from this column. It has not only been an excellent collecting agency for "light" music; its festival also demonstrated a shrewd realism in going about the business of impressing the public. A little higher "artistic" (meaning more expensive) level would perhaps have been ludicrous; a little more care in providing a suitable frame for each event might have made for more entertainment; but, as

ASCAP seems to divine, the public, in spite of everything, gets a big kick out of being in Carnegie, with a real symphony orchestra on the stage.

Arrangements were the order of the day. Victor Herbert, who conceived his music in terms of the pre-jazz theatre orchestra, sounded by far the best. All the other popular tunes were magnified beyond recognition into monstrous symphonic poems. Just when one soggy arrangement after another (not excluding the false serious orchestral works by Negro composers which opened the second night) was becoming increasingly tedious and repetitious, something happened. There was a revolt. Performers and audience just couldn't stand the cold, chill air of Carnegie any longer, and the "Crescendo Club of Forty Composers Ranged in Minstrel Style" took matters in their own hands. The second half of the Negro evening, with the semi-circle of prancing men blotting out the background of symphony orchestra, was real fun. Whenever things began to drag, one of the forty rose and did a little impromptu dance number, the others encouraging. In the back of the stage there was a noisy argument between the leader of a swing band and the master of ceremonies as to who should accompany what number, which added to the gaiety of nations. On one side of the stage people fought over who was to play the piano next, while on the other, someone did a shining-eyed cake-walk, and everything ran a little wild. The humor of this scene, its utter lack of self-consciousness, must surely have run up some kind of high-water record in the history of Carnegie Hall.

The two concerts of serious symphonic music exhibited pieces that were all, except for Frederick Jacobi's new *Violin Concerto*, familiar. Commissions might perhaps have added interest, but as it was, the programs gave a fairly good idea of what had happened in the past. Hadley (*In Bohemia*) and MacDowell, whose *Indian Suite* is a pretty piece in the exotic style once current among the lesser German composers, were the musicians representing the old. If Henry Gilbert only had been enough appreciated to be made an ASCAP member, his racy and crude music might have leavened these programs. Ernest Bloch's *Winter-Spring* was the most effective impressionist work, while Harris's *Johnny Comes Marching Home* was the best "modern" work of those already known.

Jacobi's *Violin Concerto* played by Albert Spalding deserved the praise it received in the last issue of *Modern Music*. It is neat, beautifully written for the solo instrument, and well worked out formally. The style is that of Jacobi's *Second String Quartet*, light and tending toward neo-classic rhythmic and expressive structure. Here Jacobi appears to be hesitating between a whole-hearted return to classical models and a move toward a newer style. The work is well contrived though it does at times give off an air of uncertainty in musical intention. The delightful clarify of the whole and a tact in handling the combinations of violin and orchestra betoken great mastery. Throughout there was an engaging charm and lyricism. It is one of Jacobi's best works.

This week of ASCAP underscored other points of interest about American musical life. Mainly that a whole Carnegie Hall full of people can listen very attentively to swing and react very directly to its smallest details. It is also clear that the non-paying audience has as much appreciation of serious music, if not more, as the severer cash customers. Somebody should take note; inexpensive symphony concerts seem to be in order.

This large, less articulate audience is well known to the Federal Music Project, which up to now has supplied its demand. At the World's Fair, all during the summer when every other serious musical enterprise had collapsed, the WPA carried on. Now that the government appropriations have been cut, many of the Project's important activities seem to be on the way out—either through curtailment or complete liquidation. But the Composers' Forum Laboratory, which has always interested so many of us, seems instead to have gained stimulus. It will now combine its concerts with those of two very important organizations, the Music Division of The New York Public Library and the Juilliard School. The student programs, to be held at the school, have been wisely separated from the others, which are to be at the Forty-Second Street Library; admission to these concerts is by invitation. The combination of such elements will probably bring about a change of character in the WPA concerts, which have occasionally suffered from a too mechanical effort to show what composers are doing. The first program (at the Library) will be an all-Sessions evening, an excellent way to start the series. The Project also tentatively hopes to arrange for three orchestral concerts at Carnegie Hall after the pattern of the one which was so successful last spring, and that is certainly something to look forward to.

Few new works have as yet made their appearance this season. At the Philharmonic Jaromir Weinberger repeated his *Schwanda* success with *Under the Spreading Chestnut Tree*. The same kind of fugue in the same kind of rhythm topped off the variations, only this time an English tune stuck its incongruous head up through the musical comedy Czech atmosphere.

Of quite different stuff were the two Castelnuovo-Tedesco works, introduced here by the same orchestra. The *Concerto for Piano and Orchestra*

No. 2 is charming; it reveals great sensibility and deftness. This is the work of a man who, though his idiom is to a certain extent reactionary, has revived some of the lightness and humor of Rossini and Bellini, in short of the best recent period of Italian music, and adapted them to his own ends. Castelnuovo-Tedesco, however, like many Italians, is less at home in abstract music than when he is describing something, which is what he did very gracefully in his *Overture to Twelfth Night* (also on the program). Though without the depth of Malipiero or the occasional wit of Casella, his music has the attraction of work well conceived and executed.

American Music in the New York Scene, 1940

Modern Music, 17,2 (Jan.–Feb. 1940)

Critics, performers, and public are making an unprecedented effort these days to evaluate American music. The difficulties of this job have recently been aggravated by bringing into an already acrimonious debate, allusions to other arts more productive and successful here. Although perhaps natural enough, such comparisons lead easily to confusion. Obvious and important distinctions between the arts and their various developments are not kept clearly enough in mind. In America, painting and literature, for instance, have had a good head-start over music and are already in the midst of a kind of Golden Age. Music has been handicapped by certain physical and economic factors: not only must a work be written, it must be performed before it can be heard. The hazards of the field naturally act as a deterrent to the entries; they limit the number of creations. Moreover, in speaking of an obviously American music, the abstract nature of the art should not be overlooked: it is harder to associate music than painting or literature with the external facts of locale.

America, it is frequently pointed out, has as yet developed no composer of the importance of writers like Whitman or Poe, or indeed of many contemporary painters. But how many other countries have? Germany certainly; perhaps also Italy. The plain facts elsewhere are that now, as in the past, composers have less importance than painters or writers. This concession, however, does not deny the virtues of men like Mussorgsky, Purcell, Couperin, Berlioz, or Debussy—all composers in countries where music is generally overshadowed by the other arts.

Nor do parallels between the cultures of other nations and of America come to much either, for it grows steadily clearer that America cannot and will not follow in Europe's footsteps. We won't have an American Beethoven or an American Mussorgsky, even though we may have composers who work toward the same high musical standards Europe has raised.

Nevertheless, important composers are already with us in America. Ours is a varied musical scene: the music-makers, few as they are in comparison with other artists, write in every kind of style, whether it derives from Europe, is boldly original, extreme, conservative, crude, or highly polished. They make up a complex, interesting picture, as interesting and much more individual than many a European scene. Their quality, competence, and seriousness is on a generally high level. Indeed, the variety of current esthetic attitudes is proof that the question of musical competence is no longer the problem it was. One might almost say that American music was born when these differences began to take convincing shape in works. That happened not so long ago, but it has happened, and all-American concerts like the ones given here by Koussevitzky and the Boston Symphony (whatever the argument for or against them) show how much life there is in our music today.

Of all the new pieces played at these Koussevitzky concerts, Roy Harris's *Third Symphony* stands out as the most striking and thoroughly unusual score. A rehearing of this has overcome many of my previous objections. It now seems to me to be his best orchestral work. Its inspiration is remarkably sustained and eloquent, and that grand expansiveness so often sought by Harris has never been achieved so well as here. Harris's work reveals several important tendencies that deserve consideration at this moment—chiefly the apparent deliberate effort to write "American" music. Toward this end his procedures seem intelligibly recognizable. First of all, he has given musical expression to the challenging, vigorous "strong-arm" movement already well known in our indigenous art and literature. The emphasis is prevailingly on qualities of American pioneer life, physical strength, unflinching courage, strong conviction, and the grand, lonely bleakness of certain stretches of the natural scene. The work is of the school of Dreiser,

Benton, ultimately of Whitman. Sharing this attitude, Harris has not, how-ever, fallen into the naiveté of previous American musical folklorists. He has invented a whole new style to give his point fresh meaning. The themes are not actual quotations of folksongs or hymns although they retain reminis-cent melodic turns. The rhythms are closer to various types of American speech and voice inflection than to the native dance forms. It is much the most sophisticated and intelligent approach yet made in the American treatment of folklore.

Musically, Harris's *Third Symphony* represents a step toward simplifica-tion, so that only the most typical and fundamental characteristics are expressed. It is in five block-like sections, each one with a dominating idea so definite that its character can be grasped at once; within each section very little happens that goes against it. Each of the five is built on clearly stated themes, often of considerable length. The articulation of phrase and of section is always clearly marked; transitional material is almost completely eliminated. Voice leading is arranged to give a contrapuntal impression even in places where harmony predominates; counterpoint with one part well emphasized dominates the entire piece. Themes return formally in different sections but surrounded by such a changed atmosphere that little sense of musical position results. This has always been one of the curious qualities of Harris's work. Here such constant change is saved from giving a sense of wandering by the emphasis each theme receives when it first appears. As a folklore work with literary overtones, it reminds me of the Borodin sym-phonies but, of course, it is in an entirely new idiom.

The other major event of this season was the all-Sessions concert at the Composers' Forum Laboratory. In opposition to Harris, Roger Sessions is, obviously, more austere. His devotion to the purest tradition of his art is such as to eliminate all non-musical, literary elements. Among the latter he would probably include the trivialities of folklore and the cultivation of personality by the indulgence in formulae that give a trade-mark to music. This concert, which included his *Piano Sonata* [No. 1 (1930)], *String Quartet* [No. 1 (1936)], two songs (*On the Beach at Fontana* and *Romual-do's Song*), and two short new piano pieces [from his suite *From My Diary*], was a clear demonstration that Sessions, during his whole life as a composer, has shunned the easy effect and the immediate appeal, has fought to keep his music honest, serious, conscientious to the limit of his power. Slowly over the years he has developed his own style. Though every work has always had great musical qualities, not all have been as original as the more recent ones.

His development has been by conquest and mastery of the whole art rather than by the cultivation of personal manner. While not so insular as the later works of Bartók, Schoenberg, and Berg, Sessions's recent music resembles theirs in thoroughgoing point of view: like theirs also it is open to the criticism of over-intellectualization. Certainly his music is not easy, even for the musician. But no one can fail to be impressed by the strong, stubborn conviction and the musicianship, which have produced this highly developed music. It takes a lot of concentration to penetrate the musical structures of Sessions, and yet one is, I think, amply repaid by the severe, orderly completeness of their expression. Sessions is unique in American music, and yet his intransigent rigor is certainly familiar to us as a native quality: his devotion to high standards and ideals is typical of our best . . . Along with the older works, often mentioned in these columns, there were the two new short piano pieces, *Pages from a Musical Diary*,* which are the kind of music he should bring to light more frequently as preparatory for his longer works. In these few but concentrated measures he has packed an extraordinary amount of meat. The slow piece based on ninths is particularly fine in its sudden, violent rise to an abrupt climax. It presents in small form all the power and impressiveness that is Sessions.

Many other figures appeared on the American landscape this month. The Koussevitzky concerts did not stop with the Harris work, nor did the Composers' Forum with the Sessions evening. The former gave us Walter Piston's elegant *Concertino for Piano and Orchestra*, which has been reviewed here before, and William Schuman's new *American Festival Overture*, written for the occasion. Schuman's work is frankly in a lighter vein than his better *Second Symphony*, but it has vitality and conviction behind it. Unfortunately he begins here with his weakest foot—a long "motivic" introduction based on the minor third "wee-awk-ee" street cry that supplies a certain amount of material for the ensuing fugue. This first section, which returns again later, has not the character of an introduction, being too long and too emphatic and closing with a big "collapse," nor is it integrated as a section in its own right. But when the fugue starts up in the strings, there is, in spite of a redundant repetition of the exposition in the woodwinds, a considerable amount of real musical interest. The overture follows the constant accelerando pattern so familiar among the disciples of Harris, and

---

* Later called *From My Diary*, suite for piano.—Eds.

in the end winds up with lots of good spirits and gaiety. Schuman's gift is undeniable, though so far his musical material has shown a tendency to be slight.

It is always a pleasure to rehear Carpenter's *Skyscrapers*, his best score to date. It was superbly performed at the Boston concert and I mention it now only to say that here is as directly pictorial a work as any critic might want for comparison with other arts in America. In spirit close to the Reginald Marsh and Dos Passos pictures of the American 1920s, it evokes just as keenly as they do that boisterous, brutal era of the mechanical heart.

Among the reactionary pieces played by the Boston orchestra, Howard Hanson's *Third Symphony* proved once again how skillful, fine, and ambitious a composer he is. It rightly won acclaim for its clear, excellent writing and seriousness of mood. While not so advanced as *Pan and the Priest*, it has many a place where the sombre atmosphere reminds one of Sibelius. To me this work compares more than favorably with the best works of the Finnish composer (the *Fourth* and *Seventh Symphonies* and *Tapiola*); it has many more interesting musical events and more meaty material.

The *Violin Concerto* by Edward Burlingame Hill, although its slow movement is sensitive, was not on the level of his more significant works. Randall Thompson's *Second Symphony*, with its charming attempt to bring back the kind of American folklore practised in the 'Nineties, does not bear up under frequent hearings. The conventionality of development undermines the buoyancy of this very lighthearted work, and it is not saved by the suavity and beauty of scoring from growing a little pedestrian. *Americana* and the *Peaceable Kingdom* are much more successful.

David Diamond's *Cello Sonata* received a performance at the Composers' Forum Laboratory which was the subject of considerable debate then and there between the composer and the program arrangers. To me there seemed some justification for Diamond's complaint; everyone knows that it is hard to tell how accurately a new work is being played; composers have suffered, and probably always will, from bad performances. Nevertheless many pages of the *Cello Sonata* did come across very well, the opening of the first movement and the closing of the last; the slow movement seemed particularly effective. In the hands of five Juilliard students his *Quintet for Flute, String Trio, and Piano* was excellently done; its gaiety, strength, and great musical invention were apparent, as they were not in a previous performance reviewed here. Each work of Diamond's (and there are many) seems to have a new point of departure. While there are sensitive musical qualities in most of them and much originality of technique, there does not always seem to be a clear individuality behind the music. However his *Elegy in Memory of Maurice Ravel*, originally composed for brass, harps, and percussion and played last month in a version for strings and percussion by the Orchestrette Classique under Frederique Petrides, is a sincerely touching and moving work, its appeal more direct in the strings than in the brass. In these slow, expressive works, Diamond's originality seems to be most in evidence. Since they are in the dissonant style that conductors and audiences seem to shy away from we do not often hear them.

Lazare Saminsky also had a concert devoted entirely to his music. It suffered from both poor performances and a poor choice of pieces. These were all short, mostly slight compositions, which made it hard to form a definite picture of the various sides of the composer. It was clear, however, that Jewish themes such as in the *Two Chorales*, adapted from ancient chants, and the *Violin Pieces*, adapted from old Eastern melodies, had awakened in Saminsky the most beautiful and delicate treatments. In fact, the whole evening of music demonstrated that a sensitiveness of ear and refinement of sonority seem to be Saminsky's greatest attributes. There was no chance here to judge his more extended works.

When Ralph Kirkpatrick announced a program of twentieth-century music for the harpsichord, no one could fail to wonder what music he would play. Most of it, not surprisingly, was written for the occasion. Otto Luening's *Sonata for Flute and Harpsichord* was the best-conceived work for the instruments; it had a delicate, wistful simplicity, an elegance skillfully "more made for sweetness than for violence." By comparison with Florent Schmitt's *Trio for Harpsichord, Flute, and Clarinet* it seemed more suitable; it avoided the heavy chords and soggy sonorities that filled the latter, mildly humorous work. Other works, by Robert McBride and Ernst Lévy, were equally suited for piano.

The New York Philharmonic goes on quietly, unobtrusively selecting new pieces that never offend or surprise. Occasionally they delight, as did Ibert's *Concertino*, already reviewed in *Modern Music*. Little pleasure was to be derived from Arthur Bliss's *Suite from "Checkmate,"* a well-composed, brilliant score in a style which no longer entertains except when used by its originators—Ravel, Strauss, and the Stravinsky of *Petrouchka*. Weinberger, it seems, is a permanent fixture at these concerts; now we have an appropriate *Christmas*, far less amusing than *Schwanda* or even the *Chestnut Tree*.

Like all other music, that intended for the masses can be good or bad. Effectiveness in putting across a message is no criterion of artistic value. Both

Eisler and Blitzstein have shown that real musical imagination and originality can be of great service to their political points by adding character and
incisiveness. But such music on the recent TAC [Theatre Arts Committee]
evening, gallery-funny pieces like Henry Brant's *Marx Brothers* or Morton
Gould's *Sonatina* [for piano] or *Child Prodigy*, or gallery-serious cantatas
like Kleinsinger's *I Hear America Singing* or Earl Robinson's fresher *Ballad
for Americans*, begin to sound thin and the attitude of the composers
condescending. Their apparent assumption is that the masses don't know
anything about music and never will. I wouldn't be a bit surprised if works
like the Sessions *Quartet* or the Harris *Symphony* were to become more
popular than these self-conscious and restricted compositions ever will be.

Stravinsky and
Other Moderns in 1940

Modern Music, 17,3 (Mar.–Apr. 1940)

The recent performances of Stravinsky's music, inspired by his presence in
America, and particularly the Town Hall benefit for Allied relief, which gave
us a telescoped view of his development from *L'Histoire du soldat* to the
Dumbarton Oaks Concerto, cannot, it seems to me, fail to raise important
questions about his position in our musical life. Here is certainly one of the
great figures of the period. He is now fifty-eight years old and his fame has
been worldwide for more than thirty years. The important fact remains that,
of all his rich and varied output, only two works, both of them early—*Fire
Bird* and *Petrouchka*—have won a definite place in the standard orchestral
repertory. Is this situation the result of certain elements and a development
peculiar to Stravinsky's musical nature, or does it reflect tendencies more
general to the musical life of our time?

In the not so distant past, a work would find its way into the repertory if it
displayed the civilized qualities of imagination, depth, and scope of feeling, a
high degree of craftsmanship, and inspiration (and, of course, if it was

scored for the normal symphonic or chamber combinations). Thus with the music of Brahms and Tchaikovsky. But although most musicians will agree that many twentieth-century works meet all these requirements, very few have been so recognized by the public. The reasons advanced for this increasing resistance—the standard repertory is large enough to fill several subscription seasons, nobody wants to gamble on doubtful items, the taste of conductors and performers is less revered than in the day when Brahms and Wagner could be put over "on faith" until frequent repetition should develop appreciation—are surface apologies. It is much more apparent that there has been a rather conscious "hardening" of attitude, shared and indeed to some extent now fostered by musicians, against "modernism," by which is meant the musical styles and the technical discoveries that are the special innovations of the past thirty years. How permanent this reaction will be is something that only time can tell. At the moment, however, the defection of the various European groups which chiefly nurtured these twentieth-century innovations and the accelerated pace at which American composers are now directing their attention to the native scene have temporarily fixed the attitude of both performers and audiences.

Reviewing his career, it now seems open to question whether Stravinsky could have attained his prestige without the opportunity supplied by Diaghilev. Notwithstanding all his réclame and the tremendous interest of conductors and musical élite in each new work, his music since *Petrouchka* and *Fire Bird* still seems, for the great public, too unusual in sonority and feeling, too disconcerting in its distortions of the familiar. This includes *Les Noces*, and to some extent even *Le Sacre*. His point of view has been rigidly set down as "cerebral" and mathematical, and it has earned the opprobrium of being "neo-classic." To give his all-Stravinsky programs he must include the two old works and add interest by his own appearance as conductor. Thus, assiduously, and by painfully slow steps, introducing newer and more typical compositions one at a time, he attempts to familiarize the public with his recent self. This year the *Jeu de cartes* and the *Capriccio* showed signs of thawing out the audience, although *Apollon*, like the *Symphonie de psaumes*, still remains remote and puzzling.

The Town Hall concert gave us an excellent view of the span of Stravinsky's most significant work. His stage music has always been dense and full enough of musical ideas to stand up in the concert hall. But in *L'Histoire du soldat* and the *Octuor*, we find the beginning of that remarkable series in which he concentrated and purified his musical personality. Both reveal his astonishing intensity, his succinctness, his ability to give a special unity and character to each work. All his music bristles with discoveries, yet in each piece, even in the dance parodies, there is a distinction, a sense of importance, a seriousness of purpose which few composers since the days of the early romantics have so consistently maintained.

These two pieces also mark the direction he was to take in using familiar musical material, a habit which has proved so disturbing to many listeners. From L'Histoire, in which certain violin figures are derived from gypsy music, and the fanfare and other themes from ordinary military marches, down to his Two Piano and Dumbarton Oaks Concertos, he has been building up a large vocabulary of so-called musical commonplaces. Sometimes they have been taken from periods, but so utilized that they spring to new life—as in Pulcinella and Apollon (Italian and French eighteenth century) or as in Baiser de la fée (nineteenth-century ballet). All these melodic, harmonic and rhythmic turns, whether of formal periods or from popular sources—derived from history and from the music of the ordinary man—have been completely transformed by Stravinsky and today are welded into one style, his own.

The Octuor, one of his first important non-theatrical pieces, is also one of the first successful attacks on the problem of creating music whose effect depends chiefly on integration, choice of theme, and development. To this example here with eighteenth-century forms, can be traced the consequent use of dissonant counterpoint, canonic imitations, and motivic construction of melodies, which has characterized nearly all contemporary music since the appearance of the Octuor. From that date on, Stravinsky in his non-theatrical music has been bringing to a condensation point the various atmospheres of his stage works. With each new piece he comes more and more to grips with the problem of concert music.

The qualities which are the result of this process in the Two Piano Concerto were discussed here last year. In the Dumbarton Oaks Concerto, just introduced to New York, we see Stravinsky renewing his approach to the concerto grosso form. This is no easy task today. Since Pulcinella and the Octuor, many contemporaries have set themselves the same goal, and there are now hundreds of modern works of this genre. Unquestionably Dumbarton Oaks goes them all one better. In this piece for small orchestra, so gay and lively in the manner which seems to come most naturally to him, Stravinsky has carried out his ideas on a large scale and with rhythmic amplitude. The transparent second movement is tender and delicate, the remaining two, vivacious and directly attention-compelling. With his newer austerity he avoids the more pointed effects of his earlier music and at the same time brings all the technical innovations of his past together with freedom and ease. Since the *Violin Concerto*, Stravinsky has been developing a single style, and in these new pieces we see it carried to its most refined point.

One of the impressive features of the Ballet Theatre's debut this winter was its revival of certain choreographic and theatrical scores whose very existence may be traced to the influence of Stravinsky's successful "breaking through" via Diaghilev. However accidental that collaboration may have been in inception, the lesson learned was deliberately applied by composers everywhere. Many important musical developments of the contemporary period have been the result of the activity and energy which they transferred from the more limited concert hall to the theatre. Today in America the music-theatre is just beginning to be explored, notably by organizations like the Ballet Caravan. The Ballet Theatre, though it did not give us one of the usual Stravinsky works, revived Milhaud's beautiful *Création du monde* and made quite extraordinary use of Kurt Weill's *Dreigroschenoper*. The experiment was justified in the immediate public reaction. Mossolov's *Iron Foundry* and Honegger's early piano pieces were also utilized, as well as Prokofiev's recent *Peter and the Wolf*. Henry Brant wrote the music commissioned for Saroyan's *Great American Goof* with tact and ingenuity, taking as many precautions as possible not to cover up the extraordinary speech-making going on all over the stage. But in this work the composer apparently had the least say of anyone. Indeed the character of the ballet seems not to have been quite clear in the minds of any of the collaborators; the score had the distinct air of being an afterthought.

A determined and what seems for the moment to be a last stand for modern music is being made by the Contemporary Concerts which Brunswick, Sessions, and Steuermann have organized. Here we have a rare opportunity to hear extraordinary performances of little-known works of the past together with many of the "learned," serious pieces of the last thirty years. Each work is chosen for its excellence alone. The result of these fastidious evenings is a sense of satisfaction and a compulsion toward thought, which, alas, are what very few other concerts of contemporary music now inspire. Hearing again von Webern's *Five Pieces for String Quartet* with their rarefied, delicate atmosphere, and Berg's *Four Pieces for Clarinet and Piano*, or Bartók's *Second Violin Sonata*, we experience not the sterility which is the easy and complacent brand-term now so frequently applied to music of that period, but great beauty of imagination and very special feeling; Bloch's *Quartet* [No. 1 (1916)], though not so curious and individual perhaps, and Brunswick's work* also, maintain the same high level of seriousness which is apparently the basic consideration of these concerts. Because of its special atmosphere and difficulty, such music may never gain very wide popularity. The performance is something all the more welcome in a day when even the specialized audience seems to be precipitately abandoning these works as too tenuous and too precious, and turning with eagerness to broader and more popular forms of expression.

Two Europeans who were among the earliest pioneers of the retreat to a more relaxed style—Prokofiev and Martinu—have been represented here recently. Martinu's *Second Piano Concerto* was performed with great success by Germaine Leroux at the Czecho-Slovak benefit. Martinu's extreme musicality and freshness of expression are directly winning qualities. He does not always give an impression of unity because he juxtaposes all kinds of music in one piece, even in one movement. In this work he seemed to be playing off Hindemith against certain romantic composers, but the effect is somehow natural and convincing. Prokofiev's *Second Violin Concerto* (Heifetz in a surpassing performance with the Boston Symphony) is a more integrated, also a more conscious effort to reach the public. Indeed this intention appears to be the mark of all his recent music. The *Concerto* is one of his slightest works. Has he discovered that for symphony concert habitués new music must be so obvious—or that a text must be supplied, as for *Peter and the Wolf*, or a film plot, as for *Lieutenant Kije?*

Among the Americans who have never retreated from their public to the distant point reached by the composers published in *New Music Quarterly* are Quincy Porter and Walter Piston. Both these men have steered a consistently moderate course. Piston, maintaining a comparatively dissonant, contrapuntal style, reaches his audience essentially through clarity of form and great musical orderliness. His new *Violin Sonata* [1939], performed by the League of Composers, is a step toward more direct communication. It is less dissonant than his earlier works and tonally clearer; the classical forms come through more easily. The last movement is characteristically brilliant, and the first is graceful with a dependence for contrast on the simple juxtaposition of eighth- and sixteenth-note motion. There are many cohesive devices of retrograde, passacaglia, and fugato. In this sonata he returns to the intimate quality of his *Oboe Suite* [1934] and *Flute Sonata* [1930],

* *String Quartet* (1936)?—Eds.

but the scope is greater, the workmanship easier, and there is a pleasant romantic atmosphere about the whole.

Porter, whose *Third Quartet* [1930] was recently performed at the Juilliard Alumni Concert, has written a body of interesting chamber music which fills a special place in American quartet literature. There are now six works in this form; not being hard to play they could be presented by amateurs who are eager for what is new (without too many problems of intonation and fingering) and yet at the same time rewarding. The third, fourth, fifth, and sixth, composed between 1930 and 1936, deserve some consideration as a group. They show many common traits, chiefly in excellent writing for the combination, an easy use of all sonorities, and an avoidance of special effect. The harmony moves placidly and, while sometimes dissonant, is never strident. The themes are often drawn from scales, while the textures are of great variety, reaching from polymodal counterpoint back to a purely harmonic figuration. The third and fourth [1931] quartets show a gradual abandoning of French mannerisms. The third has a dark sonority and in character is singing and flowing; the fourth, more lyrical and contrasted in style, has a brilliant last movement built on shifting accents. In the fifth [1935] and sixth [1937], Porter definitely leaves French influence behind; individual characteristics are to the fore. The fifth has a breathless, excited quality produced by many pedal figures; its slow movement, with contrasts of calm and expressive themes, is one of Porter's best. The sixth, in a much lighter vein, has a first movement which sums up his favorite methods of thematic development: it is simply and lucidly built on variants of a short motif of a descending second and a rising fourth, and a little changing note figure in sixteenths to break the continuous eighth-note flow. The modulations resulting from melodic movements are rarely abrupt. It is this lack of abruptness and of tension that is the chief expressive characteristic of all Porter's quartets.

The Composers' Forum Laboratory introduced Douglas Moore's *Ballad of William Sycamore*, which is scored for the unusual combination of piano, flute, trombone, and bass voice (in this case John Gurney's). A rollicking operetta number, it is written in what is clearly becoming the American folk-style, with cultivated crudity and simple heartiness. This should find a place in our light music; it comes across well and audiences like it immediately. . . . The same program brought out several works by the many-sided Henry Cowell, which represent largely his consonant efforts to meet the audience with diatonic melodies of a lyrical nature. Cowell's work always has some special distinguishing character that is due as a rule to the extremes to which he goes in putting his ideas into practice. The attempt to reach the audience has made his music simpler, more diatonic, and clearer than that of almost any other composer moving in the same direction. However, he does avoid musical obviousness, and there is something fresh and new about his work that is appealing if not world-shaking. . . . At a concert of the New Music Group, Paul Creston played the piano part of his *Sonata* [*Suite?*] *for Violin* and his *Sonata for Alto Saxophone*. While not arresting, these works are well constructed and interesting. The piano submits to the humble role of accompaniment; the soloist bears the full burden of statement and development.

The quartet which the League of Composers commissioned of William Schuman is his third and was performed at Town Hall by the Coolidge Quartet. Schuman's music is always personal in conception, even in its weaker moments. This work reveals a new side of his personality, lyric and elegiac and perhaps not quite so original, with a less extensive range than his more dynamic one. In harmony, texture, and rhythm, the quartet is more conventional than his previous pieces. Being quite long it suffered from a lack of grand plan and variety. Yet it has very sensitive moments. Undoubtedly it would be more convincing if its organization were more coherent.

Ives's *Sonata No. 4 for Violin and Piano*, sub-titled "Children's Day at the Camp Meeting," was heard for the first time at the opening League of Composers' concert. It has terrific, obvious faults of construction. Yet it has such a special American flavor, such a charming feeling for American folk-art, that it cannot easily be dismissed. The weakest registers of the violin are pitted against a full piano part: I think the music would sound better if it had been written for viola. It is not nearly so well made as the first *Violin Sonata*, and it is less interesting.

Many of the recently arrived Europeans now living in the United States were honored at a second, special concert of the League of Composers. Not quite up to the expectations aroused by Nikolai Lopatnikov's other music, heard here in the past, was his *Cello Sonata*, with its cold "Neue Sachlichkeit." Alexander von Zemlinsky's songs,* although expertly done, were of the jumpy school; there was little essential relation between them and works in the same category, but of very different quality, by his former pupil Schoenberg, and by Schoenberg's pupil Berg. Karol Rathaus's *String Quartet*** is serious indeed and contrived with great skill. It left, however, less

---

* No detailed information found.—Eds.

** Rathaus wrote five string quartets. No information has been found as to which one was performed at this concert.—Eds.

of an impression than Paul Dessau's archaistic *Psalm III* for voice and three strings, a work of very direct appeal. Stefan Wolpe's *March and Variations* for two pianos was in my opinion the only work on the program with signs of real originality, an originality which, I am told, has developed greatly since 1931, when this piece was written. The concert gave us a brief view of many of those crosscurrents flowing in Europe's musical streams before the present war, and which for the moment seem to be checked and almost stopped up on both continents.

The Changing Scene, New York, 1940

Modern Music, 17,4 (May–June 1940)

The first half of the spring season has fulfilled the prophecy made at the beginning of the musical year by the all-American concerts of Koussevitzky and ASCAP. War abroad is having its predicted effect, and our musical attention turns increasingly to home-made composition. Some quarters demand a fiercer nationalism, others a perhaps more civilized interest in whatever qualities our composers have to offer. There is a discernible effort to stand by the precarious standards of our time, to maintain them against the brutalizing forces released by Europe's conflict.

From the latter point of view, the premiere of Walter Piston's *Violin Concerto*, played cleanly and with fine feeling by Ruth Posselt, [Leon] Barzin, and the National Orchestral Association, is the new work of the quarter which commands the most attention. Piston's music has gradually been evolving toward a simpler, more diatonic style with greater definiteness of feeling. Since the ballet *The Incredible Flutist* his style has become increasingly melodic; he now avoids the nervous, dynamic motor rhythms of his earlier works and also their harsher dissonant textures. His formal clarity and completeness are never banal and, in this concerto, never long-winded or dry. The finish of his music is impeccable in every apposite detail, and an easy order, illumined by personal romanticism or good-humored vivacity, makes it particularly ingratiating, and not difficult to follow. The writing for the violin is inventive without relying on brilliant stunt passages to divert attention from the total effect; the orchestral fabric is cleverly varied without being too recondite. It is, all in all, a highly successful work, distinguished in feeling, personality, and imagination, excellent in musical handling. The same engaging qualities are also in Piston's *Carnival Song* for men's chorus and brass (Harvard Glee Club New York concert). Less impressive than the *Violin Concerto*, it has considerable interest because of the flexible setting of the Italian text by Lorenzo di Medici and its sure command of form. The instrumental combination is particularly well chosen to underline the poem's virile gaiety, and although at times the orchestration is a little over-refined, the general effect of jollity tempered with wistfulness is convincing.

A completely different order of native music was exhibited by John Kirkpatrick at his perennial all-American concert at Town Hall. Except for Roger Sessions's by now familiar *Piano Sonata* [No. 1 (1930)], all the works appear to have been chosen with an eye to special character rather than for musical perfection, although all demonstrated a high degree of musical mastery. I am glad of the opportunity afforded by this program to say that Aaron Copland's *Variations* seems to me to be one of the finest pieces in contemporary piano literature. The feeling, lofty, serious, and dramatic, is intensified in a remarkable way by unifying form. Every detail of the work is instinct with a personality, original and sincere, which makes a profound impression not because of novelty, but because of the vibrant imaginative power and the strong expressive intention. The music is, of course, percussive, bare, and strongly dissonant, with little singing quality, but these characteristics seem so much a part of the composer's feeling that the absence of a more ingratiating style is amply compensated for by the extraordinary emotional qualities and their distinction of statement.

Like the MacDowell *Woodland Sketches, Fireside Tales,* and *New England Idylls* and Gottschalk's *The Union*, the sonatas of Hunter Johnson and Robert Palmer seemed chosen for their personal quality rather than inherent musical interest. (This was largely true also of the Ives *Concord Sonata* on Kirkpatrick's concert of last year.) Johnson's *Sonata*, written in 1934, reflects many of the traits found in his more mature recent works, although it has less clarity and individuality. It is music of considerable expressive breadth. Shot through with reminiscences of Roy Harris's *First Piano Sonata*, its confused textures and forms reveal musical uncertainty, but these faults do not obscure the many points of personal feeling.

Robert Palmer's *Sonata* [No. 1 (1938)] also indicates a personality, though perhaps not so pronounced as Hunter Johnson's. Last year his *String Quartet* [No. 1 (1939)], played at a Young Composers' Concert given by the League, showed a more definite individuality, partly because formal considerations were not so much in evidence. Now Palmer aims at a more flowing line and apparently tries to integrate the fragmentary character of his earlier student compositions. As so often happens with young composers, form seems to be gained at the expense of some characteristic qualities. Nevertheless, Palmer's music is still full of promise; the *Sonata* may be a passing phase.*

John Charles Thomas also gave an all-American evening, including songs by Ives and Virgil Thomson. I could not attend but I find, by study of the program, that the emphasis was placed, as appears inevitable in a song recital of Americans, on the genre type of music. Indeed very few other kinds of successful songs have as yet been composed in America. Concert songs and serious vocalizing arias are prone to be artificial and cold, difficult to put across; outside of opera, there are few in contemporary literature that have much value.

The League of Composers' program of North and South American music was chosen from such completely different categories of works as to make it impossible to compare our own with that of our Good Neighbors'. The serious instrumental music of the U. S. A. was juxtaposed with light genre songs, including Brazilian folk music of Spanish and Indian derivation, that are (like much folk music) better heard in more informal surroundings. The striking personality of Elsie Houston took more than adequate charge of these and "projected" them so far into the audience that even if many were not of great musical interest, with the exception of those by Villa-Lobos, they were all arresting and made the more impersonal music of our own America sound austere and sedate.

Of Roger Sessions's *Quartet* [No. 1 (1936)] much has already been said in these columns. Of Roy Harris's *Soliloquy* for viola and piano, I wrote last year; its companion piece, a *Dance*, performed for the first time at this concert, seemed to me too long for the limitations of sonority and material which the composer set himself. It is in a morris-dance spirit and so, for Harris, surprisingly un-American. Bernard Wagenaar's *Third String Quartet*, which is, of course, of excellent make, did not impress me as being so

---

* He revised the *Piano Sonata* in 1946!—Eds.

individual as his *Triple Concerto* or his *Third Symphony*. It made good use of the combination but is in a romantic style which the composer does not handle as personally as he does his more striking and dissonant one.

Besides a repetition of Palmer's *Sonata*, the League's first Young Composers' Concert presented several able and interesting works. Rudolf Révil's Parisian night-club songs were emphasized by Elsie Houston's performance but otherwise seemed a bit weak and ordinary in a field already very well known. This was not the case with Harold Shapero's *Three Pieces for Three Pieces* in various contemporary styles, "Classicale, Orientale, and Contrapuntale" for flute, clarinet, and bassoon, which are full of musicality and show excellent mastery, though perhaps no great individuality. Bernhard Heiden's *Sonata for Violin and Piano** is a simplified version of recent Hindemith via Beethoven and Brahms. It was, however, graceful and grateful both in form and material, and moved with such ease that it was very agreeable. Donald Fuller's *Trio for Clarinet, Cello, and Piano*, the most striking music on the program if not the most completely articulate, had plenty of verve, fresh rhythmic vigor, and gaiety. At times it resembled Copland's *Sextet*. Here is a composer who has something to say, even if he has not yet found a very personal style.

The one thing clear from this program is that today young composers seem in closer touch with their audience than was the case ten years ago. Obscure, inarticulate works are not so frequent. The composers now are more relaxed, and at times they manage to strike a mean which retains a personal sincerity in the effort to make things clear and easy to understand, not too bizarre.

Benjamin Britten's *Violin Concerto* is an English work which exhibits these same new tendencies. It was played at the Philharmonic under Barbirolli with Antonio Brosa brilliantly executing a violin part with all the old and new-fashioned fireworks expected of a virtuoso piece. Without demonstrating a very integrated conception, the music makes its chief impression by very skillful, original orchestration, which had many really inventive and striking moments. The intrinsic quality of the music varied enormously. In this it appears to be an English counterpart of recent Prokofiev and Shostakovitch music. A composition of this kind has an autobiographical air about it; its appeal lies, I think, in its disarming frankness. The varying feelings of the composer appear to be projected with such intense directness

---

* Bernhard Heiden has informed us that this was one of three early, unpublished violin sonatas which predate the one written in 1954 and published in 1961.—Eds.

as to make the listener forget the great disparity of styles. Prokofiev succeeds sometimes in creating this effect. Britten's work was a little too artificial and contrived. Yet at almost every moment, nobody could fail to be impressed by the remarkable gifts of the composer, the size and ambition of his talent.

Bernard Herrmann's cantata *Moby Dick* received a barrage of publicity which made its premiere more like a Hollywood opening than a first performance at the Philharmonic, where new works usually creep in unobtrusively and pass away in like manner. Indeed, the Hollywood atmosphere was sustained throughout the music. As radio-arranger-and-composer's work it is uncommonly good, being an elaborate, highly dramatic setting of the usual film version of the Melville action (a version, of course, which leaves out of account the most characteristic parts of the novel with its long philosophical, meditative, and scientific digressions). The music sounded its Americana note in the paraphrase of a New England hymn; the program added local color by a dedication to Charles Ives. The score was stern, vigorous, and highly effective in the illustrative style, utilizing all the panoply of radio "background" effects—the roar of the sea, thunder, calm, etc.— punctuated by choral shouts and recitatives. No great effort was made to work out big numbers, except in a few instances. The style was largely Honegger in the noisy places, Delius in the quiet ones. Since both novel and movie lead up to the great scene of Ahab's chase and fight with the whale, I expected Herrmann would follow suit, especially as all the preceding numbers were either broken up or lightly orchestrated and seemed to demand a grand, vigorous finale, perhaps a big sea-terror number combining the best features of *Horace Victorieux* with *Sea Drift*. This need for a long, overwhelming piece was not satisfied by a few violent exclamations and a choral scream. As for the music itself, effectiveness appeared the main consideration; style, depth, originality, invention, all the qualities of concert music were subordinated thereto.

However, I must say that I enjoyed *Moby Dick* more than Prokofiev's *Cello Concerto* played by Piatigorsky at a Boston Symphony concert. This latter, lacking in the same qualities, was also pretty ineffective, so let's forget it.

Films and Theatre, 1943

Modern Music, 20,3 (Mar.–Apr. 1943)

[After reviews of two Russian war films—*The Siege of Leningrad* and *Moscow Strikes Back*—and the American film *Yankee Doodle Dandy*, all of which deal only incidentally with music, Carter continues with a review of *Commandos Strike at Dawn*.]

For a score that must have been composed after the film was made, Louis Gruenberg's music for the *Commandos Strike at Dawn* solves its problem in a very expert way. There is not too much of it, it is rarely obtrusive, often carrying on an impression of motion during visually static scenes, and sometimes pointing up the psychological excitement implied by the camera. The important thing about this music, which as style goes is not very personal or new, is the way it is orchestrated. The majority of the pieces are for solo instruments with transparent orchestral accompaniments which develop one theme throughout whole scenes. Occasionally there are descriptive numbers, among which is the noteworthy musical double exposure of Paul Muni's fitful sleep just before the commando raid begins.

Two Hollywood films by foreign directors who used to be very careful about their musical backgrounds in the old days proved musically disappointing. *I Married a Witch* by René Clair using a super-fancy, Hollywood score cribbed largely from *L'Apprenti sorcier*, and that of Hitchcock's *Shadow of a Doubt* with its creepy harmonizations of the Merry Widow waltz were both conventional and without character. I don't suppose these films with their unusual plot material could afford to tread further on audiences' toes by employing screwy scores too.

THEATRE

Sidney Kingsley's *The Patriots*, about the American 1780s, used the device of period curtain music to put the audience into an eighteenth-century frame of mind. Played in the pit by what sounded like a quartet of piano, violin, cello, and clarinet doubling with flute, the music by the young

English composer Stanley Bate, and the arrangements of Mozart and the rest were not very telling. Bate's original pieces in an English folk songy vein are charming and well wrought but not particularly suited for the theatre and call for a hearing under more favorable conditions. His stretto piece on *Yankee Doodle*, a tune which probably can't be done without in a play about the early days of the republic, was not very effective.

The Skin of Our Teeth, Thornton Wilder's polyhistoric human circus, also uses special curtain music. Some itinerant musicians appear in the aisle before the show, with accordion, clarinet, and drums, and give a funny slap-dash rendering of familiar circus numbers. It is too bad there is not more room for music in this piece, for at times it seemed to need an imaginative score to point up the fantasy.

American Figure, with Landscape
[Henry Franklin Belknap Gilbert]

Modern Music, 20,4 (May–June 1943)

It has been characteristic of musical life in America to neglect the composers of its own past. Although almost all serious compositions presuppose a future audience whose tastes will be affected by them, in our country the death of a composer generally marks the end of his musical career. Quickly he is supplanted by new men anxious to promote their own works before they, too, shall be forgotten. And music that is easily forgotten by musicians is more easily forgotten by the public. Thus we develop the habit of evaluating each new work as having the same unimportance as its rapidly vanishing predecessor.

It may, of course, be true that many if not all of our previous composers have not produced music of great significance. On the other hand, they have occasionally written works which deserve attention because they mirror and communicate to us certain interesting, lovable aspects of the America of their day. Besides, many of the tendencies they set in motion still direct our musical thought.

At the time when Henry Franklin Belknap Gilbert was making his effort to write, as he put it, "some American music," nationalism was the subject of wide discussion by critics, musicians, and composers, including Gilbert himself. A general historical sequence of periods had been formulated to cover our national musical evolution: first, foreign domination, and imitation of non-native art music; second, collection of and familiarization with indigenous folk songs and dances; third, invention of a style consistent with folk material though without using actual quotations; and fourth, the musical millenium, emergence of the national masterworks written by native composers with a large native background and inheritance. This hypothesis, reflecting the historical doctrines of the late nineteenth century and especially the "millenarianism" so dear to America, had its obvious support in the facts of Russian musical history. True, also, to the thinking of the period in omitting the important influences of speculative thought and of religious music in the concert hall, this thesis gave folk songs a basic position as the root from which each national music culture is to grow. All the elements comprising the "manner": rhythm, melody, harmony, and form, evolve from this germ and generate a style that is to be expressive of our native kind of "matter." To put it another way, in a search for a means of expressing the "matter" of our national consciousness, it was assumed that composers would inevitably follow this historical pattern.

The two interrelated doctrines of historical stages, and the antithesis of matter and manner, combined with our special brands of individualism and of progress, have deeply influenced the thinking of our contemporary composers, particularly those of nationalist intentions. The conflict of opinion over which of the four stages we are now in is the basis of many present arguments; while the manner-matter problem perpetuates itself in questions as to the "abstraction" in contemporary music and its "neo-classicism" or "neo-romanticism."

When these doctrines were being considered at the turn of the century, there was a tendency to minimize America's longing for the refinement of feeling and taste of Europe, which found literary expression in Henry Adams and Henry James. But the founding of our conservatories and of our larger performing organizations had been largely motivated by this longing. They were more concerned with promoting an interest in the classical European repertory than in encouraging native compositions.

Obviously under the circumstances the cards were stacked against those composers who were following nationalist doctrines. At a slightly more advanced stage of musical development, their reception might have been very different. If we had been ready, their ideas might have penetrated our musical life. For at that very time, political and economic nationalism were being aggressively declared by such important Americans as Theodore Roosevelt and A. T. Mahan. It was in this same aggressive spirit that the school of American nationalist composers supported their doctrines. In literature the field had already been well explored by the generation of Whitman and Emerson. But in music, as in politics, these ideas still had the charm of novelty and adventure. Composers led lives and wrote music in conformity with them, and the fourfold historical scheme gave men of Gilbert's generation, who modestly placed themselves in the second and third periods, a bright future to anticipate for their music and, by that token, a deep-seated conviction which helped them carry on under conditions often adverse.

Throughout his fifty-nine years of life, from 1868 to 1928, Gilbert struggled against a physical handicap of an unusual sort, which had to be borne in an almost continuous state of extreme poverty. As he would ruefully explain, he was occasionally invited to medical conventions as "Exhibit A"—the only man to survive his thirties with the heart deformity known to doctors as the tetralogy of Fallot. He had been born with the right ventricle of his heart larger than normal, and therefore an unusual amount of blood flowed through the capillaries of his skin. This gave him the fiery red complexion, which was his most striking physical characteristic, and also made him susceptible to many physical troubles of which he never spoke. To have persisted in a career of musical composition at a time when no money could be derived from it, and when he obviously had talents for several more remunerative occupations, illustrated the power of his faith. Bearing his difficulties in an outwardly carefree way, he courageously led the trying life of a pioneer American composer, and at its culmination ventured on a trip to Frankfort, Germany, in 1927, as a representative from America to the International Society for Contemporary Music Festival where his "uramerikanische" tone poem *Dance in Place Congo* was being performed. Probably as a result of his exertions on the trip, he died in the following year.

Gilbert was one of the very few residents of Cambridge, Massachusetts, who ever attained prominence unaided by some connection with Harvard. In its vicinity he was born, lived, died, and he was buried like a good Cantabrigian in Mt. Auburn Cemetery not far from William and Henry James. Both his parents were musicians and encouraged their son to continue in this path. As a result of their efforts Gilbert had an all-American musical education. At the New England Conservatory he learned to play the violin and studied harmony and counterpoint and finally took lessons in composition from MacDowell, who had just returned from Europe. His violin opened up a source of income as a fiddler in resort hotels from Florida to the White Mountains. But even in his early twenties, Gilbert was interested in being a composer, and this conflicted with his hectic hotel-musician's life. By the age of twenty-four, Gilbert had had enough of this and set out to find a more grateful trade that might pay a little better. For the next ten years he gave up music almost completely and tried many different ways of earning his living. He worked in music publishing houses in Boston as an engraver and as an arranger. Wandering away from home, he even got a job as a pie-cutter in the Chicago World's Fair at the time of the hootchy-kootchy. During this period he learned about a great many sides of life in America, and gained the almost Whitmanesque knowledge and love of his country that so deeply affected his musical development.

At the Chicago Fair he met a Russian who thrilled him with stories of Rimsky-Korsakov, Mussorgsky, and the new kind of music they were writing. To familiarize himself and his friends with this music, Gilbert organized a few concerts of Slavic nationalist music at Harvard. His association with Arthur Farwell in Boston, the discussions they had about American nationalist music, which finally resulted in the Wa-Wan Press publications of American music, all tended to rouse him once more into musical activity.

Finally, Gilbert heard rumors of a new French opera about the common people and, shipping on a cattle-boat, went to Paris in 1901 to hear Charpentier's *Louise*. This opera was the touchstone in his life, for he was so impressed by it that he decided to devote all his time to musical composition, come what may. At thirty-three, Gilbert came back to Cambridge, found a job minding a horse and a cow in a barn at Somerville to pay his board, moved a piano in beside one of the buggies, and started to compose on a breadboard resting on a flour barrel. He was going down to rock bottom to create the true American native music.

From his barn, near Harvard, which was then educating such erudite composers as John Knowles Paine, Arthur Foote, Walter Spaulding, and Edward Burlingame Hill, Gilbert threw down the challenge. American serious music was too imitative "not only of the methods of Europe but of its spirit—a spirit which, at the present day, is decadent—which covers its weakness in genuine inspiration with a wealth of invention; a glittering show-off of ingenious externalities; deceiving the unwary into attributing to it an undue worth and importance. The long arm of Europe still stretches its deadening hand of tradition and authority over our American musico-art developments, so that the true spirit of America is lost sight of, and that great potential spirit which is the birthright of the American composer, as of others in their lines of activity, has been thoughtlessly bartered away for a mess of clever European pottage."

In his struggle to cast off the erudite tradition and yet to surmount a crudeness and amateurishness that sometimes helped to stamp his music with personality and sometimes prevented him from realizing his intentions, Gilbert resembles Mussorgsky and Chabrier. Both these men seem to have impressed him with their vitality and unconventionality, and his music occasionally shows their direct influence. The prevailing tradition of the time was largely German, and the prestige and success of Dvořák's American works served to strengthen it. Like anyone reacting against an accepted custom, Gilbert was searching around for unconventional elements. These he found in American and Celtic folklore. From the Russians he took for his cue the vigorous, simple, and even crude style he needed to express the spirit of the America he loved. Like many composers of his time, he did not escape the influence of the saccharine chromaticism of Grieg, Dvořák, and Mac-Dowell; but as time went on he gradually eliminated their over-ripe harmonies and helped to develop the harmonic style which has become the common currency of most popular music since.

Gilbert composed the greater number of his published works from about 1902 to 1913. During these years, he worked on an opera based on Joel Chandler Harris's *Uncle Remus* stories; but after having nearly completed the score he was finally refused permission to use the material. This was one of his greatest disappointments. The opera still lies in manuscript, unperformed, a somewhat remarkable fact considering the success which its *Comedy Overture on Negro Themes* has had in all the years since its first performance in 1911. Judging from this and from the delightful *American Dances* for piano, four-hands, published by the Boston Music Company, which are also excerpts, and from the comment of those who heard Gilbert run through the opera, it is rich in the particular homey American humor that was one of Gilbert's most engaging characteristics as a musician and as a man.

Another good work dating from this period is the set of five rag-timey piano numbers, *Negro Dances*, written in a style that closely resembles the popular music of its day and yet raises it to the level of concert music without pretence or falsification of its spirit. At his best in gay, humorous, short pieces, Gilbert was often at a loss in the larger forms, where a lack of emphasis at important points, such as the climax or the end, makes his works seem too short. The *Symphonic Prologue: Riders to the Sea* suffers from this weakness, and perhaps all his other orchestral works of the period would be more effective if their proportions had been slightly amplified.

All kinds of Negro music aroused Gilbert's interest—minstrel, spirituals, Creole songs, and dances like the cake-walk—because that music seemed closely related to the spirit of all America. Its national popularity testified to that. He was not attracted to it because of its strangeness, and, though a Northerner, he never sought to play up the exotic element. He wanted to get at its forthright qualities of humor, sentiment, and vitality. This humor he attempted to express in the orchestral *Humoresque on Negro Minstrel Tunes*, with its gay setting of *Zip Coon* and comically sentimental second theme; its vigor and enthusiasm are reflected in the orchestral *Negro Rhapsody*, "*Shout.*" His songs, not of great distinction, reveal the strong dramatic sense which pervades all his works. The *Lament of Deirdre*, the *Pirate Song*, and *Salammbo's Invocation to Tanith* are the best instances of this.

Gilbert's greatest popular success came with *Dance in Place Congo*, a twenty-minute tone poem on Creole tunes. Unlike his earlier works, its form is completely convincing, which is why it was more immediately effective. As in Mussorgsky's *Night on Bald Mountain*, there is the striking of a bell in a macabre night revelry which calls the New Orleans slaves back to their quarters. (In the Russian work the dead are called back to their graves.) Yet, although a very effective piece of its kind, it had somehow lost the simplicity and charm of his earlier music. The composer's preface in the printed score admits modestly that he was using the Creole melodies "much after the manner of Grieg or Tchaikovsky." This is not to say that the work lacks personality, for in spite of his admission (which may have been more to calm the public than to inform the critics) it has his characteristic rhythmic vitality and melodic interest. The score, with a ballet interpretation of its program, was performed at the Metropolitan in 1918 and received many enthusiastic tributes. For Gilbert by this time was a composer whom audiences and critics were discussing. All our important orchestras played his music and he had even received acclaim in Russia. His reputation seemed made, most of his scores were published, and he seemed a fixture in American musical life.

But after the end of the war, "modern music" galvanized our audiences. Sides were taken, arguments raged, and the newer music with its tumultuous energy and the violent opinions it aroused made the cause of "American music" and Gilbert's in particular appear tame and faded. Jazz, too, was gaining over ragtime, and Gilbert's raggy pieces began to sound old-fashioned. Gilbert stuck to his guns and wrote the excellent *Symphonic Piece*, which had all the American qualities of his earlier work. It was performed in 1926 by Dr. Koussevitzky and deserves a rehearing today. But time was pressing on and the music of Gilbert had no publicity appeal. Younger composers were busy blowing their own horns. After the first fine frenzy of the modern music movement had died down and Gilbert was forgotten, a whole group of composers started rediscovering the virtues of simplicity, of ascetic Americanism, and of many other qualities which he had prefigured. They claimed these as their own invention, as if Gilbert and his fellow nationalists had never existed.

It would be unfortunate for our culture if the present generation were as easily swept aside as all previous ones have been, yet this is the lesson which our history seems to indicate.

Theatre and Films, 1943

Modern Music, 20,4 (May–June 1943)

During the past three years the League of Composers has been encouraging composers to write theatrical works for communities with modest resources. Out of this project have come *Paul Bunyan* by W. H. Auden and Benjamin Britten, *Solomon and Balkis* by Randall Thompson, and this year *A Tree on the Plains* by Paul Horgan and Ernst Bacon. Like *Paul Bunyan*, *A Tree on the Plains* was revealed to New York audiences by the enterprising Columbia Theatre Associates in cooperation with the Columbia University Department of Music at Brander Matthews Hall. Milton Smith, the theatrical director, was able in both cases to get together shows which were interesting to people who were not in any sense "community audiences" and hence did not exactly conform to the conditions under which the operas were originally intended to be performed. Professional singers were enlisted for important roles, and professional musicians were added to the university orchestra. The Britten work being conceived in a more formal and intricate style was much better adapted to these conditions than Bacon's, which seemed to cry for more intimacy.

Indeed, the best thing that can be said about *A Tree on the Plains* is that all the performers seemed to be having a good time. This is a result of several factors which must play a certain role in any musico-theatrical work to be given by amateurs. First, there should be nothing difficult, risky, or perplexing in the musical score. Next, the underlying feeling should always be direct and self-evident to both actors and audience. Also, the dramatic situations must be simple and natural and varied enough to afford the composer opportunity for different kinds of music and to give the actor-singers ample chance to display their talents. Besides meeting these requirements, Bacon used a musical style derived from various kinds of Americana that Americans can sing in without seeming to carry on like opera stars.

To mention these things, however, is to suggest the danger of obviousness which a work based on such premises must run. Both the librettist and composer often fell into the trap; Horgan, because his book did not have a clear sense of style but wavered between treating the folksy characters as noble and as quaint; Bacon, because he adopted clichés in the more serious sections, especially in the religious and amatory moments, neither of which rang true. In spite of this, Bacon showed a real flair for the treatment of homely comedy, as in his setting of *A Frog He Would A-Wooing Go*, the big production number of the show. Not an outstanding artistic success, the work should serve its purpose and give many people pleasure.

Paul Bowles's setting of the masque within the last act of F. García Lorca's *Asi que pasen cinco años* and named by him *The Wind Remains* was given with chamber orchestra under the able musical direction of Leonard Bernstein at the Serenade Concerts in the Museum of Modern Art. The few vocal numbers were excellently sung in Spanish and the rest was spoken in English and danced against a musical background. In taking an excerpt from one of Lorca's most fantastic plays and presenting it out of its context, Bowles drew attention to the extreme obliqueness of meaning of his author. As Englished, this "zarzuela" has such a tenuous thread of implications that in spite of the music it fails to maintain the poetic tone and easily becomes a vehicle for such free associations by the audience as to verge on the nonsensical. Like the meanings of words, which tend to evaporate under the scrutiny of semanticists, love, the subject of this play, was atomized to the vanishing point. Bowles wisely covered it all with a pattern of coherent music aimed to hold the disjointed fragments of text in a kind of poetic suspension. His work, as always, is a comment on popular or folk music treated in curious ways to deprive them of their usual feelings.

FILMS

Roy Webb's score for Saroyan's film *The Human Comedy* (it happens to be the centenary of Balzac's work) gave a different slant to the author's writing than has been seen hereabouts before. Saroyan has been treated by composers like Bowles as a commentator on life as it is lived, which helps to evoke a kind of wistful mood that makes the action seem unreal and yet somehow to correspond to our desires. Webb and his collaborators treat this script as if it showed life as it actually is. The score continually quotes parts of the national anthem and in other ways, by the constant use of the usual devices in their usual places, contrives to bring Saroyan down to earth. Nowhere does the music match the land-of-Cockaigne mood which persists in all of Saroyan, except perhaps in the magical scene where two young boys wander in astonishment through the towering stacks of the Public Library, overcome by the vast number of authors. The music here catches and sustains the strangeness in a shimmering dissonant chord on the high strings.

Max Steiner, another proliferator of movie scores, each year sees his name in bigger and bigger letters on the list of credits. For *Mission to Moscow* he has harmonized a lot of national anthems to introduce appearances by Mr. Davies (Walter Huston) in each of the European capitals, Madrid excluded. For once this technique seems justified, although the *Internationale* was adroitly dodged just at the point where you expected it.

Theatre and Films, 1943

Modern Music, 21,1 (Nov. 1943)

Kurt Weill's new score for *One Touch of Venus*, coming after last year's *Lady in the Dark*, reveals his mastery of Broadway technique. Apparently he can turn out one success after another with a sure hand. Weill, who orchestrates and arranges his own work, whose flair for discovering and using the stylistic earmarks of popular music is remarkable, has finally made himself at home in America. Where in pre-Hitler days his music underlined the bold and disillusioned bitterness of economic injustice, now, reflecting his new environment and the New York audiences to which he appeals, his social scene has shrunk to the bedroom and he has become the composer of "sophisticated" scores.

The present one represents quite a piece of research into the phases of American love-life expressed in popular music—the barber-shop ballad, the barroom song dripping with bloody murder, the serious and comic parodies of Cole Porter, an uproarious mock-patriotic *Way Out West in Jersey* in the best college spirit style. Even the orchestration with its numerous piano solos in boogie-woogie and other jazz styles constantly recalls night-club atmosphere. Traces of the mordant composer of *Die Dreigroschenoper* and *Mahagonny* occur rarely and only in places where Weill is not trying to make an impression. Compared to his other American shows, the music is neither as ingenious and as striking as *Johnny Johnson* nor as forced as his made-to-order jobs for *The Eternal Road* and the railroad show at the World's Fair. But in the atmosphere of Broadway, where so much music is unconvincing and dead, Weill's workmanlike care and his refined sense of style make up for whatever spontaneity and freshness his music lacks.

. . .

Aaron Copland and Alexandre Tansman have been chosen by Hollywood to write scores for two new films. The results ought to convince our producers that good symphonic composers have something to offer which the usual Hollywood musician does not. Copland's score for the Samuel Goldwyn production of *North Star* is excellent in a technical way that, for instance, Victor Young's music in *For Whom the Bell Tolls* is not. Young serves up a rich variety of different kinds of Spanish music in the styles of Albéniz, Granados, and others, which seem to have no direct relevance to the characteristics of the plot except to emphasize the locale. Copland, on the other hand, comes to grips with actual particulars of plot, character, and mood of the specific picture and emphasizes the points which author and director make. He does this by using fragments of Russian folk song submitted to a process of development and arrangement, and besides, also makes them sound very much his own.

North Star is about a Russian agricultural community before and after the Nazi invasion. The picture falls into these two parts, but they do not play off against each other with sufficient dramatic meaning. The peaceful first part stresses picturesqueness rather than efficient modern collectivization (as a Soviet film probably would have). The comrades seem to be living in the familiar old Russia of peasant song and dance days in a neat, charming operetta atmosphere. No reference to preparation for war is made and no suspense is built up to prepare the spectator for the catastrophe. In these early sequences Copland has written three delightful songs to words by Ira Gershwin and a big dance scene which catches the Russian warmth and lustiness. This music with its childlike gaiety is often reminiscent of his *Second Hurricane*. The "going to school" and the two quiet sleep scenes are the best of this side of Copland.

Interrupting a song, *No Village Like Mine*, sung by the young people who are the heroes of this picture, Nazi bombs begin to fall, dive-bombers spit fire and death on the town, Nazi troops march in, Russian guerilla bands are formed, and the music has the perennially difficult job of being both background for action and for war noise. One of the most successful musical war sequences so far written, because of its plastic use and intensity of style, it employs music sometimes to join one explosion with another and sometimes to modulate from one mood to another, as in the sequence in which Marina and Damian kiss in great quiet before the latter goes on his perilous mission. The most beautiful and dramatic piece is in the background for the scenes of the women burning their own homes before the Nazis come. At every point the intelligence and the personal elevation of Copland's music is recognizable, even in his arrangement and orchestration of the *Internationale*.

. . .

Alexandre Tansman's score for Duvivier's *Flesh and Fantasy* starts out with a bit of title music surprising for Hollywood. In the vigorous, dissonant, and contrapuntal style of his *Triptyque*, and indeed of many another modern score, the music takes off in a very arresting way. Also excellent and interesting is the long dance-music sequence providing the background for the Mardi Gras episode. After this, the score becomes more and more routine, except for those eerie moments, when by many a strange effect it points up rather ordinary looking scenes with a Freudian significance, notably those on shipboard. But by and large, screwiness has its limits in Hollywood and love-scenes impose certain hallowed musical patterns which even Tansman could not break through. . . .

[The cut material consists of a review of *The Merry Widow*, an announcement of the impending premiere performance of *Carmen Jones*, and reviews of three motion pictures: *We Will Come Back*, *The Constant Nymph*, and *The Great Mr. Handel.*—Eds.]

Ives Today: His Vision and Challenge

Modern Music, 21,4 (May–June 1944)

"No matter how sincere and confidential men are in trying to know or assuming that they do know each other's mood and habits of thought, the net result leaves a feeling that all is left unsaid; for the reason of their incapacity to know each other, though they use the same words. They go on from one explanation to another but things seem to stand about as they did in the beginning because of that vicious assumption. But we would rather believe that music is beyond any analogy to word language and that the time is coming, but not in our life-time, when it will develop possibilities unconceivable now,—a language, so transcendent, that its heights and depths will be common to all mankind."

Few composers in our time have come to grips with the basic problems of musical expression, and certainly few have taken so definite a stand as does Charles Ives in his interesting *Essays Before a Sonata* (1920, now out of print*). Reading them, one cannot help feeling that such a man with such ideas *must* be capable of writing exceptional music. The tone is elevated, the wit brilliant. Here, as in his music, Ives reveals himself a devout believer in transcendental philosophy, in the immanence of God in nature, in the glorious mission of music, which is to be achieved only when freed from the pedestrian ideas of professional musicians, in the ability of man to grasp the divinity behind nature through feeling and not through artificialities of logic. Of American music he says that a composer who believes in the American

---

*The 1920 edition was published by The Knickerbocker Press, New York. The "Essays" were reissued by Howard Boatwright, ed., under the title *Charles Ives, Essays Before a Sonata and Other Writings* (New York: W. W. Norton, 1962). All page references in the present collection are given for both editions: first, for the original (1920) edition; then, in parentheses, for the Boatwright reissue.—Eds.

ideal cannot fail to be American whether he uses folklore or not. Of performing musicians he says that the composer must lead the way, the performer must figure out how to play the music. The book is a little masterpiece; it should be known to all musicians.

The difference between Ives and other mystical composers, Scriabin, for instance, is that he believes neither in ritual nor in the methodical training of the intuition which raises man from one level of consciousness to another, leading to a denial of the physical world. Ives follows Emerson. For him the natural world reflects the spiritual, and so is of great concern. Hence the divergence between the patterned music of the Russian and the free, almost random music of Ives.

Ives's dissonance differs from that of most other composers who use it to express physical excitement, sensations of pleasure and pain, or effects of distortion in the manner of the modern painters, or to reflect spiritual conflict, as in the works of Baudelaire. Ives is always in quest of the transcendental. On the surface of his work, the infinite complexity of nature, the rapidly changing moods of forest and plain, the web of counterbalancing forces appear confused and dissociated. But Ives's involved texture, while mirroring this superficial confusion, at the same time attempts to show the larger harmony of rhythm behind the natural process. Faith in the purpose and goodness of nature rather than concern over its savage conflicts and hostility determines his choice of moods. In his essays he says that Debussy, in works like *La Mer*, appears interested only in the physical aspects and never sees beyond them.

Ives, with his exalted goal for musical expression, believes that composers should be free always to follow their highest instincts. Difficulty of performance is the performer's problem, not his. The quest for performances, for payment for music, for success, are beside the point. Ives himself makes his money in business and so has been as free in his pursuit of music as one of his instrumental parts, whose bar-lines, rhythms, notes, and speed do not tally with the rest of the orchestra. He is as difficult to assimilate into the pattern of the organized musical world as such a part is into an orchestral texture. (He has persistently refused royalties, prefers not to have his music copyrighted so that performers may feel free to take liberties, and usually insists on paying for publication. Thus he strictly preserves his amateur status, while his reputation—based rather on what has been written about him than on the few performances of his music—constitutes a threat to the professional world.)

All who have written about his music, and their number is legion, are convinced that if performed it would meet the expectations aroused by his famous ideals. It probably would—provided the listener made several allowances. He must be ready to grant that the quotation of familiar tunes, with which the music is studded, is a device sufficiently powerful to evoke the particular feelings apostrophized. Then there is also the amount of detail left to the interpreter's discretion. The polyrhythms, which appear to be precisely written, obviously call for an improvisatory technique hard to achieve in ordinary rehearsals. Bernard Herrmann and Nicolas Slonimsky have faced this problem most squarely. Herrmann claims that with the proper rehearsal, everything in Ives is playable. A few years ago he boldly gave an Ives series over C.B.S. and brought to the air several highly effective pieces, among them the *Largo for Strings* and the very affecting first and third movements of the *Fourth Symphony.* Taking advantage of Ives's suggestion that performers should "interpret" the works to suit themselves, Herrmann re-orchestrated part of the first movement and ironed-out some of its rhythmic complexities. But such a procedure, followed without great understanding of the music, could easily rob it of characteristic qualities.

Another artist, John Kirkpatrick, whose performance of the *Concord Sonata* is well known, also following Ives's expressed intentions, takes certain liberties with the polyrhythms. With great care and devotion he molds the music into a very moving auditory experience. That Kirkpatrick's conception can be found in the notes is unquestionably true, but it is also true that a good but unsympathetic musician might give a chaotic and unintelligible account of the same score. It is all a question of whether one can enter into the spirit of this music and then recreate it. Such a challenge is good for the profession: it demands a vision that goes beyond the notes.

A quick glance at Ives's total output—which can now be studied in print or in photostat (eleven volumes of chamber music and six of orchestral scores) in the Library of Congress, the Fleisher Collection, and the American Music Center*—reveals many interesting facts. The music shows a rather

---

* John Kirkpatrick, Ives specialist and compiler, among other Ives items, of the monumental annotated catalogue of Ives's works (New Haven, 1960), kindly supplied the following note: "These photostat volumes of chamber music and orchestral scores, together with the printings available in 1944, hardly represent 'Ives's total output,' but do contain all of what he would have considered his most important work. At the time of his death he had given all such volumes away, keeping none. Consequently the Ives Collection at Yale University has only the two that happened to be in the possession of the curator [i.e., Mr. Kirkpatrick]. But the Collection has all the negative photostats from which these volumes were assembled (unless some set may possibly come to light containing the missing *Clarinet Trio* or the *Autumn Landscapes from Pine Mountain*)."—Eds.

spasmodic development, from the product of a youthful organist with a classical background playing in a Presbyterian church, to the elaborate works most of us are familiar with. There has been, from the start, a preoccupation with hymns, marches, and other native American music. The *First Symphony*, written in the '90s, has a fetching, naive quality; it shows influences of Mozart, Bach, and Beethoven and at the same time some strange harmonic progressions that resemble early Shostakovitch. The *Second Symphony*, following almost immediately, reveals chromatic influences, Franck, Brahms, and Dvořák. It is made up of arrangements of earlier organ works and an older overture. The *Third*, for small orchestra, although written only a little later, is a new departure. It has a slow first and last movement and a folksy middle one that is gentle and full of charm. The first is made up of unusual progressions and the last is quite Franckian. Then comes a complete break: the *Fourth Symphony*, written about the time of the last war. It is full of the surprising effects most musicians associate with Ives, which were not noticeable in his earlier works.

There are two other symphonies, *Holidays in a Connecticut Country Town* (Washington's Birthday, a very solemn and beautiful Decoration Day, an extremely elaborate and wild Fourth of July, and a dithyrambic Forefathers' and Thanksgiving Day) and a *Universal Symphony*, which has remained a rough sketch for the last ten years. *Holidays*, like the *Fourth Symphony*, is in his most advanced style and shows all the facets of Ives's music, as do also the *Second Orchestral Set*, the *Theatre Set, Three Places in New England*, and a few works in the chamber music volumes. In these latter there are, besides, what at least to this writer appear to be parodies of modern music, like his satirical songs about modern life.

The orchestral scores of his later period make use of several devices which deserve more comment than they have received so far. Ives is fond of using a separate instrumental group, playing some kind of ostinato figure and maintaining its own tempo behind a fast movement and even behind a slow one, but in different rhythm. This seems designed to give the natural setting of trees and sky against which he places human events. The transcendental background of faint sounds usually starts and ends a movement which may depict, in rather literal fashion by quotation of themes and in other ways, the noisy or religious or patriotic episodes of everyday life. This latter music is often naively pictorial, while his style verges on impressionism and takes on the most advanced dissonance when it represents the transcendental.

Ives's range is remarkably broad. He offers us the rural, homely qualities of Whittier, the severity of Emerson, the fancy of Hawthorne, and the meditation of Thoreau. These moods return again and again in all his later works. The contrast between the transcendental polyrhythm and polytonality, and the human music of hymns, dance, and march, is always present.

This year, on October 20th, Ives will celebrate his seventieth birthday. Yet real consideration of his music still lies in the future. However fascinating it may be to speculate about, its actual sound will be more enthralling. Let us hope, for our sake, as well as for his, that performances will not be too long in coming. He has waited now for many years. The musical public has known all about him for more than ten. It is about time for a real demonstration.

Music as a Liberal Art

Modern Music, 22,1 (Nov. 1944)

Music, considered less as a practice than as an art with whose nature, history, and present state every educated man should be familiar, has suffered a decline.

On the university campus today the Victorian Gothic library, the Greek revival laboratories, the academic halls, present an imposing bulk behind which, in some out-of-the-way corner, the reticent little music building seeks shelter. Music departments are too often staffed by professionals with little capacity to see their subject in a broader light than the teaching of special techniques demands, who tend to be less articulate than their academic colleagues. The thoughtful student who is no virtuoso finds little to his taste in a department that teaches skill without an appeal to reason, that attempts to demonstrate many styles but fails to take up the basic question of style itself, of philosophic and historic meaning. The purely practical approach is largely responsible for the low estate to which music, as a vital part of our intellectual equipment, has fallen.

In less exalted settings, music as a subject develops growing importance. Wartime propaganda devotes much effort to exploitation of the art. A nation's use of music is offered to prove its advance from barbarism, its degree of culture, refinement, civilization. By way of radio, discussions about music now reach the masses and make a claim on their consideration before the higher academies have done much to raise the subject from its present depressed level.

Historically, of course, music is no poor relation of the arts and sciences. In the golden age of Greece it occupied a post of honor. The Platonic dialogues show music to be never very far from the thoughts of Socrates and his fellow Athenians. Besides offering witty, elegant, and often profound comment on the subject, the dialogues give music an important philosophical role. In the *Timaeus*, Plato tells a "likely story" of a creator who imposed on originally irreconcilable elements the mathematical pattern of the ratios of a musical scale, in order to fashion the soul of the universe. Elsewhere Plato finds that music imposes order on the motions of the body and the soul, teaching gracious and harmonious conduct and giving the young student a knowledge of good and evil. Three years, says Plato, should be devoted to learning how to play the lyre and to kindred musical subjects. Philosophical discussions must be included so that the student will never be deceived by "appearances" and forget the true music of which this earthly music is only a shadow. For a music lover only interested in sounds, the kind that conservatories then as now produced, Plato had contempt. They are "the last persons who would come to anything like a philosophical discussion, if they could help, while they run about at Dionysiac festivals as if they had let out their ears to hear every chorus; in town or country—it makes no difference— they are there."

The moral benefits to be derived from the study as Plato saw it, gave music great importance in the Academy in Athens, where its relation to geometry and astronomy was endlessly discussed. This early association of subjects later played an important part in the plan of the medieval university. Here music, one of the "seven liberal arts," now systematized as a discipline, became a branch of mathematics. As the art of measurement, it was an object of major study for several centuries. Under this alliance with what we today call mathematical physics, our aural art, though occupying a lesser position, was widely cultivated. And in the renaissance, so long as medieval thinking continued to dominate education, no education, according to Thomas Morley, was complete without some actual musical training in playing or singing.

That the practice of musicians was deeply influenced by the liberal arts discipline is written on the pages of every treatise of the period. In turn, the practice of music itself influenced thinking in many different fields, as witness the treatises on architecture by Palladio, on astronomy by Kepler. Kepler in the early seventeenth century drew extended analogies between Copernican heliocentric theory and the art of polyphony of his day, contrasting it to Ptolemy's analogy between Greek music and the geocentric theory. His method enabled him to describe the orbit of the planet Mars, a mathematical mystery before his time.

Aristotle in his *Politics* has another approach to music. He lists it under three headings: education, amusement, and intellectual enjoyment. "Amusement is for the sake of relaxation, and relaxation is of necessity sweet, for it is the remedy of pain caused by toil. . . . In addition to this common pleasure, felt and shared by all . . . may it (music) not also have some influence over the character and soul? . . . Rhythm and melody supply imitations of anger and gentleness, and also of courage and temperance, and of all the qualities contrary to these, and of the other qualities of character, which hardly fall short of the actual affections as we know from our own experience." After describing in detail the effects of various kinds of music and pointing out which are desirable, Aristotle concludes, "Music has a power of forming the character, and should therefore be introduced into the education of the young." Together with the discussion of imitation in the *Poetics*, this and similar passages exerted a powerful influence on the philosophy of music and education even as late as the eighteenth century.

However, music in order to assume its classical position in the hierarchy of studies and bear an intelligible relation to them does not require a particular system of philosophy. From the fourth century B.C. through the seventeenth of our era, there were many changes in philosophy, while music's traditional place remained fairly constant. Most of the great music of the past that we admire and much of the literature have some relation to this tradition of the liberal arts. Its terminology still is used in our discussions of esthetics even though meanings have become vague, and its example is a challenge for us all to think more deeply.

In America today, the objectives of education are being redefined, the plan of studies reworked in an attempt to give men a broader and more understanding view of the world. To expand their knowledge of music a few suggestions might be taken from those periods when the art was an integral part of education and of life.

Several methods have already been tried. One of the most familiar is the historical approach, in which music joins hands with other arts and is studied century by century. Its chronology is synchronized with important historical events, the development of court life, the effect of wars, the influence of one school on another. This is unquestionably useful and in the right direction, but as a method it places too little emphasis on the very ideas which have most deeply shaped the artistic works under consideration.

In at least two centers, the University of Chicago and St. John's College in Annapolis, where drastic reforms of the whole educational system have been put into effect, the relation of music to various philosophies is now stressed. At St. John's music has actually been taken out of the music building. It is no longer the special study of the specialist, of the budding professional. Instead it is examined in the classrooms, seminars, and laboratories, in an effort to give it a working relationship with all other knowledge. Since the St. John's plan is the most familiar to me, I would like to present it as an illustration of how music can be brought back into the general life of a university.

At St. John's all students read a certain number of works, from Homer to Freud, that have been influential in forming our total Western civilization. Some are read in translation, others form the basis for laboratory experiments, still others provide texts for mathematics and language courses; all are discussed in seminars. Included in this study during my stay at St. John's were several works of music—a Gregorian mass, a mass of Palestrina, a work by Bach such as the *Goldberg Variations*; and scheduled for the future were an opera of Mozart, a symphony of Beethoven, and music by Stravinsky and Debussy. These were coordinated chronologically with the rest of the reading. However, the college is not concerned primarily in giving a serial picture of various stages of Western civilization, but in having the student know the problems that have confronted us and learn to evaluate the efforts at solution. So musical works were chosen that not only represent their periods but are still being heard today.

The fundamentals of music were demonstrated in such a way as to clarify the intellectual traditions of the subject. The frequent mention of music in the works of Plato, Aristotle, and St. Augustine was thus made vivid and understandable. Music was examined first in the physics laboratory, so that students learned to distinguish intervals, to recognize, for instance, the fifth, whose effect Galileo says "is to produce a tickling of the ear-drum such that its softness is modified by its sprightliness, giving at the same moment the impression of a gentle kiss and of a bite." Here also simple notation was taught, as well as the formation of modes and scales, key relationships, and chord structure. The students tuned sonometers according to all kinds of systems. In a class on the measurement of time, they found out about rhythm and meter, in another they studied the construction of musical instruments and acoustics. One class, held each month, was a concert, another a lecture dealing with music in its formal aspects.

The main emphasis was on preparation for the hearing and understanding of actual works. Scores and recordings were made available, and, whenever possible, the music studied was performed at concerts. Each work was then discussed on two successive evenings for about two hours, often more because the talk became so lively. One of the most recurrent topics was, naturally, the meaning of music. Did it, like language, refer to something other than itself and if so, what? Or was a work of music an ordered pattern of sounds that awakened feelings and thoughts in us as a by-product of our enjoyment of its beauties? Is listening to music simply a pleasant pastime or is it more? What does music bring to the meaning of the words in Gregorian chant? What relation has notation to what the composer imagines and to what the performer does? And so on through all those profound questions that naturally arise in students' minds but are so lightly, so carelessly, brushed by in most music courses. Here arguments developed, sides were taken, controversy was important. Music became a matter of interest, whether it was approached by the scientific, the literary, or the artistic, and it gave one type of student an understanding of the other.

The introduction of music into such a plan of study, indeed into any general plan, has far-reaching results. It stimulates a consideration of the esthetic problems bound to come up in a course on literature or the other fine arts; it can endow laboratory experiments with a quality of imagination often lacking in the more elementary subjects. When the student sees the interconnection of all these things, his understanding grows in richness. And since today no widely accepted esthetic doctrine unifies our thought on the various aspects of music, such a plan at least conjures up the past to assist us; it helps to raise the various philosophical questions involved. In one way or another these questions must be considered, for it is not enough to devote all our efforts to acquiring the technical skills essential to instrumentalists, composers, and even listeners. There must be good thinking and good talking about music to preserve its noble rank as a fine art for all of us, and the college is one of the logical places for this more considered attitude to be cultivated.

Gabriel Fauré

Listen, 6,1 (May 1945)

There is no better example of the power of persuasion in the music of recent times than in the compositions of Gabriel Fauré. Unlike other musicians writing around the turn of the century, he was not interested in attracting the listener by large dramatic effects or sumptuous orchestration. Neither did he believe in the exploitation of any other of those extremes of musical language which overcome the listener by their violence or strangeness and only too quickly lose their effect. His music has a precision of outline, a marvelous clarity, and an intimacy of expression that differentiates it from that of his younger and more widely known contemporaries, Debussy and Ravel. It is the work of a man both simple and modest whose warmth of feeling and loving kindness reveal themselves in every detail. It is by these rare qualities that Fauré stands out as one of the great figures of French music.

During the seventy-nine years of his life, he saw the passing of Bizet, Saint-Saëns, and César Franck and the rise of Debussy, Ravel, and Stravinsky, and his penetrating criticisms for the newspaper *Le Figaro* show us how well he understood the changing scene. But in spite of the new developments, he followed the highly personal path which led him to the style of his late years. This later style had far more influence on the succeeding generation of Poulenc, Auric, and Milhaud than did the music of the impressionists.

Fauré's music is not widely known outside of France for two reasons. First, since a large part of it is vocal, the French or Latin texts must be clearly understood as the settings follow closely the fluctuations of the literal meaning. Second, because the musical language is reduced to the barest essentials, it is often not striking on first hearing. To appreciate it the listener has to pay strict attention; none of the seemingly secondary details must escape him. Using ordinary chords, scales, and arpeggios, Fauré works miracles in the underlying subtle harmonic progressions. Listeners accustomed to large rhetorical effects emphasizing every expressive detail will have difficulty in orienting themselves in this restrained music, which has often been called perfect "though cold." But once the sobriety of Fauré is appreciated, it becomes obvious that such poignant and beautiful expression could not be achieved by the use of more colorful and dramatic means. Adherents of this music find in its understated romanticism a world of deep feeling that often puts to shame those who carry on with empty grandiloquence.

Fauré's music has its counterpart in the paintings of Edouard Manet, with their rather muted colors but definite outlines. This parallelism is also manifested in the relation to the works of the impressionists as well as to those of their antecedents. Goya, Courbet, and Delacroix demonstrate affinity with Manet; Mendelssohn and Schumann with Fauré. In both, flashbacks to earlier periods appear on closer inspection. In Fauré there is a transparency and an economy that is rather Mozartian at times. In his ability to spin out one pattern and to catch all manner of different inflections in a continuous movement, he resembles Bach. A reminder of Couperin's explorations of the Watteauesque, or of the tender gaiety of the French madrigal school hangs over certain facets of this music. At one time in Fauré's life the modal scales attracted him for their kinship with medieval music. Later, after Reinach and other musicologists deciphered ancient Greek notation and resurrected the *Hymn to Apollo* (published with a harmonization by Fauré), he was enchanted by the new discoveries because of their Attic flavor.

Like Manet, Fauré is particularly successful at characterization, and he is best known by his settings of religious texts or of those by Baudelaire, Verlaine, and other "Parnassians." The tender and resigned beauty of his *Requiem* portrays not the horrors of the grave but the sadness of bereavement, and a human, nostalgic picture of Paradise. Similarly, the charmingly fresh settings of Verlaine's *La Bonne Chanson*, and the Hellenic atmosphere of his two operas, *Prométhée* and *Pénélope*, depict with a sure touch each shade of feeling and capture the special character of the texts in a masterly way. Sometimes by a sudden modulation, by varying the accompaniment imperceptibly, or by a touching inflection of the voice, Fauré achieves more than do many others using complicated means. The love of the classic artistic principles—such as logic, order, and serenity—combined with a highly individual sensibility and a refinement of taste, suffuse his work, so that if it is not comparable to the art and literature of Fifth Century Athens, as some have maintained, at least it is characteristic of one of the best sides of French music.

Like his vocal music, his instrumental works reveal a constant development. Of the same general type as the music of his teacher, Saint-Saëns (a composer who was "rediscovered" by Ravel in his later years), Fauré's *First Violin Sonata* in A and his *First Piano Quartet* in C Minor indicate those personal qualities which became more pronounced later. These are works of a graceful triviality; they possess an elegant lyricism or a humorous lightness that is characteristic.

By the time Fauré had reached his middle period, during which his *Requiem* was written, his music had deepened and had greatly widened its scope. At a time when he was moving on to his last and most unusual style, the incidental music for a London performance of Maeterlinck's *Pelléas et Mélisande* (1898) made its appearance, four years before Debussy's opera. The four movements—two rather light interludes in the middle, a nostalgic prologue, and the tragic final adagio, which reaches a remarkable interior pathos—are entirely different from the Debussy score and have to be appreciated on the basis of quite another conception of the work.

As is evident from this work that uses such simple means, Fauré was not primarily interested in the orchestra. Sometimes he entrusted his orchestration to others, as in the case of his opera *Pénélope*, but in *Pelléas* and the *Requiem* he uses the orchestra with full awareness of its capabilities. Simple harp arpeggios, a soft harmonic background, and a floating singing line suffice to paint the tender joy of Paradise at the conclusion of the latter work. It is the conception of a devout man full of sympathy and hope, forgiving his fellow men with Christian charity.

Gabriel-Urbain Fauré's own life exhibits the same order and modesty present in his music. It was spent in composing, teaching, reviewing concerts, and later in directing the Conservatoire. The one profoundly tragic event was the gradual impairment of his hearing, which began when he was about fifty-eight, as a result of arterio-sclerosis. From his son's biography we learn that Fauré's ears distorted the extreme upper and lower registers of sounds, bringing them each a third nearer the middle. For a highly trained musician, listening to music under these conditions must naturally have been painful in the extreme. He gradually relinquished performing his own music, although until his death at seventy-nine, he remained very prolific as a composer. In keeping with his character, this strange deafness was never mentioned and it was only known to his most intimate colleagues. For during this period, knowing only the profession of music and not living in a society which endowed composers liberally for their efforts, he had to continue in his positions as newspaper critic and director of the Conservatoire. That his opinions of the newer trends represented by Strauss, Ravel, and Dukas should have shown such understanding under this terrible handicap is remarkable. To read his criticisms now is to realize how seldom one may find an intelligent critic of new music and how many, blessed with two healthy ears, hear far less.

Born on May 13, 1845, in a town of southern France situated at the foot of the Pyrenees, the youngest of six children of a country school teacher, Fauré lived at home only five years. Until he was four he lived with a foster mother and at nine was packed off to Paris to study music. This early lack of home life must have played an important part in forming his outlook, though he never lost contact with his family and at his father's death was moved to write the *Requiem*. Boarding at the Ecole Niedermeyer in Paris until he was twenty-one, he learned a great deal about Gregorian chant, music of the Renaissance, and, of course, all the classics, largely through the efforts of Saint-Saëns, who was not only instrumental in raising the money to bring the boy there but in teaching him as well. After graduating, he became an organist in various churches and finally at the Madeleine, his career being interrupted by a short period of active military service in the war of 1870. Although neither a student at the Conservatoire nor a winner of the Prix de Rome, two requisites for important posts in that national institution, he became its director in 1905, and in 1920 retired after having completely renovated its policies. With César Franck, Lalo, and other leading musicians, he helped to form the "Société Nationale" and later the "Société musicale indépendante," both devoted to the performances of new works. At these concerts almost all his songs and chamber music received their first performances. With constant concern for the music under consideration and little for drawing attention to himself, he worked as a reviewer on *Le Figaro*, one of the leading Parisian newspapers of the time.

In 1924, after a long life during which the number of his works mounted to opus 121, he put the finishing touches to his only string quartet and died a much venerated figure whose reputation has increased constantly since his death.

New Publications of Music

The Saturday Review, 29,4 (Jan. 26, 1946)

On the basis of music printed in 1945, it is hard to predict what the dominant post-war trend in contemporary composition will be. As in every other field, people expect a change, and yet nobody seems to be able to guess what is going to happen. The startling "modernists" conquered the concert halls and opera stages after World War I. Some people today expect a similar emergence of a new group that will capture forward-looking imaginations with dramatically novel works and new slogans. This movement might originate in one of three quarters. The ultra-dissonant school, with its mystical or primitive ecstasies, might appear in a new guise. Or a group previously out of step, such as one brand of impressionists or another, may call the tune. We might even have a widespread classical revival, with correctness and order the prime considerations. So far, the trend which began in the thirties to infuse music with greater plasticity and variety of feeling looks as though it will continue to bring about a slow change.

As time goes on it is becoming clearer that the distinguishing characteristic of the period now losing its momentum was a tendency to focus on a particular domain of expression. And the great variety of musical styles, when they were handled in a live way, served mainly to give personal color to a series of emotional attitudes common to most composers. These attitudes are far from dead today. For instance, there was an emphasis on speed and concentration. Chords, motives, short phrases, even individual tones—in fact, all the atoms of musical discourse were endowed with heightened meaning and intensity. Hence compositions had to be short, for the sum of such tensions could easily pile up and result in fatigue in the listener. All the varieties of anger, indignation, terror, fear, dismay, disgust, anguish, and anxiety are still frequently expressed. In last year's scores—for instance, Arnold Schoenberg's *Ode to Napoleon* and Benjamin Britten's opera *Peter Grimes*, such feelings were often the source of inspiration.

Often the emotions cited were expressed obliquely in attitudes of resignation, of irony, or of comic parody. Sadness found its typical expression in the nostalgic contemplation of some state of presumed complete satisfaction which could not be found in the present or future, but only in a past such as that of childhood or of an historical period like that of the American expanding frontier, idealized last year in Aaron Copland's *Appalachian Spring*, or in Lukas Foss's *The Prairie*. Our own time has been sung in terms of sombre machine-like vigor, oppressive melancholy, and (to add a bright note) a dynamic, athletic joyfulness. Nobody was able to adopt the grand "epic" tone or to express any feeling that lived in the certainty of present or future satisfaction without running the risk of becoming epigonous. Naturally, this particular tendency has been quite noticeable among Soviet composers, who share the high hopes of their countrymen and who do not put as high a value on artistic originality as we do. Certainly, they have been partially responsible for instigating the new trend.

What is interesting about the whole picture of recent music is that among a welter of different styles, of different esthetic approaches and nationalities, there has been such a close similarity of feeling. Naturally, many composers, especially young ones, have felt this as a limitation and have been on the lookout for a new repertory of feelings, but as this cannot be had for the mere asking, but can only come by slow evolution and from experience, a sudden change is unlikely at this time.

Benjamin Britten is one of these younger men, and the trend in a new direction is more noticeable in his short settings of old Christmas texts, *A Ceremony of Carols* (Boosey and Hawkes) for treble voices, than in his full-length opera *Peter Grimes*, so successful in London recently. Archaic in a way that has intrigued many English composers, these charming carols are direct, warm, and fresh if not too personal. The opera, on the other hand, deals with a typical contemporary subject, although set in an English fishing village of 1830 and with a plot based on a poem of George Crabbe. It is the story of a fisherman who overworks his boy apprentices and brutalizes them in a way that inevitably recalls the Nazi treatment of drafted slave labor and, like the modern parallel, with catastrophic results. At the outset the court finds the first apprentice's death accidental, although the townsfolk have their suspicions. Grimes, feeling the sting of public disapproval, wants to dispel it by making lots of money, becoming a respected member of the community, and marrying the village schoolmistress. To do this, he plunges into such a fury of work that a similar second disaster occurs, and finally Grimes dies in an effort to escape the law. All the other characters and the chorus of townsfolk discuss the pathological implications. Neuroses are hinted at that have been frequently discussed today in connection with Nazi brutalities. The music is as direct as a film score, dissonant, dark in color, with few rays of redeeming warmth. The scenes are on a symphonic scale, the soloists sing brief, intense phrases while the main continuity is carried by rather extended choral numbers and by an orchestra busy suggesting church bells, storms, foghorns, or village dance music, which help to supply interest to a rather static plot. The general style is more fused and less eclectic than in most of Britten's music, but it seems to display an overdose of dramatic machinery as if to make up for a rather schematic and cold presentation of the characters.

Bernard Rogers's setting of *The Passion* (Elkan-Vogel) tells the Bible story with the rapidity of a radio script. Employing the full quota of soloists to take the different roles, and also a chorus with large orchestra, this cantata plays up the pictorial, the physical, and the dramatic, leaving the spiritual meaning to shine through by implication. Therefore, there are no extended solo, choral, or orchestral numbers and there is none of the usual develop-ment of themes. The continuity is obtained by the careful gauging of dramatic accents, by the natural flow of events in the story. It represents a novel and interesting approach to a religious text and to the oratorio form. There are moments of striking power, which must sound very extraordinary in performance because Rogers is one of the most imaginative and skilful orchestrators in this country.

A similar array of singers and instruments join in Lukas Foss's cantata *The Prairie*, using portions of Carl Sandburg's poem as text. Relying rather heavily on Copland for its material, this work seems to have furnished Foss with an impetus to free himself from his earlier adherence to Hindemith. There is a current of sensitive, rather elegant, intimate lyricism that gives the work distinction, but which is not always too well suited to the text. For the masculine power, the homely eloquence, and the largeness of vision of the poet seem to have eluded the composer, and as a result the music does not rise to enough intensity to justify its considerable length, and the main intent of the poem seems evaded. However, as far as it goes, *The Prairie* reveals a composer of great promise with a finely developed imagination and technique.

An even wider discrepancy between text and music is all too evident in Arnold Schoenberg's setting of Byron's *Ode to Napoleon*. On the purely acoustic level this combination of spoken recitation, with voice inflections and rhythms rigidly indicated in the score, and elaborate string and piano [writing] is very difficult to follow. A tricky problem at best, which has rarely if ever been solved successfully, "melodrama" in order to be clearly intelligible needs a subdued musical background, but Schoenberg has written a most complex and agitated score that tends to cancel out the meaning of the words. Aside from this, the expansive bombast of Byron is quite ill-suited to the fragmentary, concentrated, and explosive expression of Schoenberg. And even though the composer is a little more relaxed than usual, the unity of spoken words and music could only be grasped by the utmost concentration. Certainly the weakness of the text would hardly spur any listener to make this effort. Here and there, where the music steals the show, a glimpse can be had of the force and power of the composer's antifascist sentiments, which this composition was designed to express. They are revealed in a magnificently turbulent eloquence, only to be spoiled a moment later by Byron's rhetoric.

Among other vocal works of the year are Burrill Phillips's three effective and personal *Declaratives* (Elkan-Vogel) for women's voices, also some songs: Marcelle de Manziarly's skilled and witty *Three Fables of La Fontaine* (Associated Music Publishers [AMP]), Paul Bowles's tender moods of reticent sentimentality, *David* and *In the Woods* (AMP), and Elliott Carter's setting of Hart Crane's third *Voyage* (Valley Music Press).

The annual publications of Copland, Piston, Stravinsky, and Hindemith add important new works to an already noteworthy list. Stravinsky's *Sonata for Two Pianos* (AMP) is an important example of his most recent lyrical preoccupation. It rarely uses the vigorous and brilliant effects that many have associated with this composer, but is quiet, chaste, and tender throughout, and has an unusual, solemn grace and beauty. His orchestral *Scènes de Ballet* (AMP) is more a recapitulation of earlier works and concludes, like many of them, with an apotheosis in that vein of noble melancholy that is one of the composer's most memorable moods.

The original material in Paul Hindemith's *Symphonic Metamorphoses of Themes by Carl Maria von Weber* (AMP) has been so reworked that this amounts to an original piece. In it Hindemith has a chance to be humorous and fanciful, which is one of his most attractive sides.

The integrated point of view that permeates the mood and style of Aaron Copland's orchestral suite from *Appalachian Spring* (Boosey and Hawkes), his ballet for Martha Graham, is a distillation of what is most touching in his works that delineate an idealized American scene. There is a keen awareness in the choice of folk material and in their handling that transforms everything into the Coplandesque. Quite in keeping with the pastoral simplicity of this work, Copland has developed a method of restraining the animation of the fast sections that is quite original. In his two-piano *Danzó Cubano* (Boosey and Hawkes), this subdued animation seems a little unmotivated and weakens a work that otherwise has an extremely charming rhythmic structure.

Walter Piston in his *Symphony No. 1* (G. Schirmer), written in 1937, seems to be taking a deep breath before a plunge in a new direction. For the subsequent compositions leading up to his second symphony, reviewed last year, are successive steps toward simplification and clarity. The earlier symphony, just now published, is a triumph of skilled handling of complex ideas and textures. It is a restrained and ordered flowering of the "modern" style with all its moods and many of its manners. Piston's particular contribution to this is his ability to organize it in an imaginative way and to satisfy all the musical expectancies aroused by his material. It is as if he were trying to resolve the frustrations inherent in the style by divining an appropriate logic for it.

The contrast between this symphony and any of the Soviet productions brought out by Leeds Music in miniature score this year is striking. There is a careless ease about them, a discursiveness, a clarity of texture, a simplified use of the orchestra, and a directness that shuns neither the obvious nor the academic. The last comment is particularly true of Kabalevsky's second symphony, despite its very musical feeling, and also of Miaskovsky's twenty-first and twenty-second. By now this composer is such an old hand at symphonic writing that he can be convincing and exuberant with almost any kind of an idea, mediocre or original. The imaginative qualities of Shostakovitch, represented in the scores of his fifth, sixth, and seventh, are much more evident by comparison with those of other Russians than they are when considered in a larger context. As almost everyone will agree by now, he reveals an undeniable wealth of musical talent, which he spends in producing striking dramatic effects. Khrennikov's first symphony is an engagingly fresh work with a good deal more sense of style than any of the other relatively unknown ones. Still, Prokofiev, whose two *Suites from Romeo and Juliet* and *Alexander Nevsky* have also appeared in miniature scores, has the most marked personality and the highest grade of musical imagination of any of the Russians we are familiar with here. With so many Russian symphonies printed here, it would be good to be able to complete the picture by an examination of these excellent ones by Stravinsky, Hindemith, and Milhaud, but so far they are not published.

Of shorter orchestral music by Americans, Samuel Barber's *Capricorn*

Concerto (G. Schirmer) is the most elegant. Its small orchestra is put through neo-classic paces with a coherence and fantasy that are most compelling. David Diamond's brilliant and gay *Rounds* (Elkan-Vogel) is the most original, largely because of a highly personal sense of continuity that remains logical through all sorts of imaginative and inventive inflections, sudden hushes and outbursts, and off-accents. A prize-winner in the contest given by Independent Music Publishers, Elliott Carter's *Holiday Overture* (Arrow Music Press) was also published. . . .

Scores for Graham; Festival at Columbia, 1946

Modern Music, 23,1 (Winter 1946)

Copland's *Appalachian Spring* and Hindemith's *Hérodiade*, to which Martha Graham presented dances in her recent New York season, are the most completely integrated and carefully conceived scores that have yet been written for her. Both can stand alone in concert performances, yet they add to the dances themselves an atmosphere of certainty and directness. The music has a sure sense of the theatre and measures out the steps and timing of the dance patterns with great effect. By calling the tune for the dance with such imperiousness, these works put a limitation on the dancer which she meets with many imaginative touches.

In *Dark Meadow*, to a Chávez score commissioned, like the Hindemith and Copland pieces, by Elizabeth Sprague Coolidge, the musical and choreographic approach contrasts markedly with those of the two other pieces. The central part of the score consists of several extensively developed string quartet movements, in style like the composer's *Piano Concerto*. This would go very well in a chamber music concert; it offers very few clues as to what sort of dancing might accompany it. Introductory and closing woodwind sections, however, set the austere, Indian ritual character represented on the stage by that interesting combination of primitive and Christian symbols found in Mexican religious folk art. The music is almost continuously danced *against* rather than *with*, and this greatly heightens the subjec-

tive tension. Coming after Miss Graham's discoveries in many new directions, *Dark Meadow* returns to the older modern dance idiom with an
increased sense of projection that makes it one of her most perfectly realized
works in this style.

During her late spring season last year two experimental works were
offered, one by Merce Cunningham, called *Mysterious Adventure*, to an
ingenious fancy of John Cage for prepared piano. This score, a maze of
shivery strange and delicate noises, is a play of sound with neutral content
and mood which allowed the dancer great latitude. At the opposite extreme
were the tiny little pieces of Charles Mills, interjected between long speeches,
which served as background for Erick Hawkins's *John Brown*. The composer had the problem of projecting a very precise mood in a very short,
undeveloped moment of music. Thus the whole show rested on the choreography and the speaking, but at times the intense little fragments set the stage
with remarkable surety.

A series of annual festivals of American music at Columbia University was
opened last spring with two evenings of chamber works, excellently performed by the Walden Quartet, and an orchestral concert directed by
Howard Hanson. This suffered from inadequate rehearsal, but Dr. Hanson
has a remarkable ability to put across the salient points of new scores
practically at a first reading. His own *Fourth Symphony* and Walter Piston's
Second Symphony have been reviewed elsewhere in these pages. David
Diamond's brilliant *Rounds* for string orchestra were a little scrambled in
performance, but the composer's idiomatic writing and his highly personal
sense of movement were nonetheless revealed. The many shades of
dynamics, accents, changes of register, and phrase constructions give great
flexibility and vivacity, particularly to the fast movements. The material is
largely diatonic, rather folksy in the Copland manner, and the continuity is
most convincing.

Building one's style on the sentimental commonplaces of our music, not
that of jazz bands or particular ethnic regions, just on the plain, old, trashy
tunes that everyone has known for years, is a procedure analogous to that of
Mahler in Vienna and Poulenc in Paris. This may be the idea Henry Brant
had in writing his *Saxophone Concerto*. But at the same time he was
concerned with brilliant orchestrations, with showing off the saxophone in
all the novel ways that he and Sigurd Rascher, the performer, could think of.
These two different aims do not go together very convincingly, but every
once in a while a sour and sad mushiness or a raucous funniness hit home.

Two works on the chamber music programs praised by this reviewer several years ago in these pages seem today equally deserving of this judgment. Wallingford Riegger's *String Quartet* [No. 1, Op. 30], by far the best work I know of this composer, is full of vigorous and beautiful dissonance. He succeeds in domesticating the twelve-tone system and avoids the special rhetoric of the Viennese. The music is straightforward; tone clusters are hammered out, yet the texture remains transparent. Emotional balance and formal clarity are always maintained. Robert Palmer's *First String Quartet* loses some of its impressive somberness and expressive consistency by the inclusion of an additional movement, but it still has his stamp. The cross-accented counterpoint is a bit more comprehensible than that of some of his more recent works.

William Bergsma's *Second Quartet* is most effective, though the relation of one movement to another is not entirely convincing. It explores the moods and manners of the "middle modern" style with such innate musicality that one is attentive even though no personal adventure or experience seems to emerge. Yet saying what has often been said, only more skillfully, seems to be the goal of many members of the new generation. Frederick Jacobi's familiar *Second Quartet* and Robert Russell Bennett's cutely clever *Water Music* were also performed. An oboe was added to the Walden strings for two rather similar pieces, Robert McBride's *Quintet* and Alvin Etler's *Six from Ohio*, both of which provided some sedate comedy.

Fallacy of the Mechanistic Approach
[The Schillinger System]

Modern Music, 23,3 (Summer 1946)

The Schillinger *System of Musical Composition* will most likely arouse considerable feeling, especially among those who have not seen this type of book before. The point of view comes straight out of middle Europe in the early twenties, when the application of a mechanistically conceived scientific method to the arts was all the rage. In this respect Schillinger's work closely resembles the Bauhaus books and the prose writings of Eisenstein on the movies. An elaborate show of scientific language, of schematic exposition that apes mathematical texts, plenty of graphs and pseudo-algebraic formulas, all do about as much to confuse as to clarify.

For this form of exposition is really a rhetorical method not particularly aimed at careful scientific rigor but at a kind of surprise and shock effect. Violent invective, dogmatic assertion, repetition of ideas and phrases, and a certain megalomania are combined with apparently dispassionate and rigorous analysis. Old-fashioned, "intuitive" methods are ridiculed, mistakes of the great composers are shown up in the light of the "new, objective, and scientific methodology." Any of the subtler forms of persuasion, like those found in regulation scientific treatises, which substantiate generalizations with verifiable facts, are omitted; the reader is browbeaten. Schillinger's book even has a rather hermetic and cultlike quality because of its lack of regard for the reader. The terminology is unfamiliar and musical terms are alphabetized: letter symbols are used which even a generous glossary at the back does not always clarify, because their significance changes from chapter to chapter.

But this is all a bitter coating for a book that makes many interesting contributions. The system aims at the all-inclusive, under the one aspect of mathematical patterning. Within the covers of these two volumes one finds the most comprehensive tabulation of musical elements, devices, and procedures that probably has ever been made, certainly within the limits of such a relatively short work. For a book that is to include a systematization of rhythm, scales, melody, harmony, counterpoint, fugue, composition, orchestration, and musical expression must necessarily be brief on many scores. Although it is presented as comprehensive and self-explanatory, the book seems really a manual to supplement actual lessons in which principles are more elaborately and convincingly expounded. Thus the huge number of tabulations, which Schillinger does not derive from already composed works, but primarily from the permutation, combination, and serial arrangement of the divisions of time and pitch. And he is rarely content to mention possible permutations, even of numbers, without listing them all. This takes up space but, as the editor points out, helps save time for hurried arrangers.

Again, if the book is more than a supplementary manual, how can one account for the rather surprising omissions which occur in almost every chapter? In the first one on rhythm, for instance, the function of the bar line in relation to upbeats and downbeats, and the existence of the additive madrigal type of rhythm (which starts with a unit or a foot as a basis and combines them in changing meters) are never mentioned. But he does hit on the novel idea of deriving temporal divisions and irregularities by combining two regular patterns, such as three notes against four, into one line. The whole chapter is systematized on the claim that all rhythms are portions and groupings of such "resultants" of the "interference" of one set of regular beats by another. This conception of "resultants" of "interference" creeps into every part of the book like a Pythagorean refrain, with not too musical results.

Another chapter shows how to construct melodies after the rise and fall of graphs of various kinds of motion and rhythms of growth. One finds that Beethoven did not always balance things "scientifically" because he relied so much on intuition. But the principles of resistance and climax as presented are quite helpful in classifying melodies. The "Special Theory of Harmony" treats triadic harmonies and their sequences in an unusual way, tabulating at tremendous length each type of bass motion and each possible type of combination. The "General Theory of Harmony (Strata Harmony)" constitutes perhaps the most elaborate treatment of modern dissonant harmony to appear in this country so far, with its list of different chords and their progressions.

All this material is presented with no particular regard for when to use what, for whether it sounds good or bad. It is here that Schillinger's system falls down. The composer is not shown how to use the facts or to select from them. Rigid adherence to the mathematical, which here results in rather uninteresting examples, could in fact very well diminish the young composer's ability to discriminate; this would produce a result just the opposite of the best kind of more "intuitive," less "scientific" teaching. However, for musicians interested in filling up radio time or in writing descriptive background music of a not too original character this system will save a lot of trouble and thought. It is curious that a method which gives such a high place to abstract art (art is classified in terms of its abstractness, the highest place being given to the non-representative or non-symbolic) should be followed by practitioners mostly occupied with the most functional aspect of music.

The basic philosophic fallacy of the Schillinger point of view is of course the assumption that the "correspondences" between patterns of art and patterns of the natural world can be mechanically translated from one to the other by the use of geometry or numbers. When this conception is carried to even greater lengths in the belief that music will stimulate reactions if it follows the graphic projection of geometric patterns of "mechanical and bio-mechanical trajectories," one can only feel that the whole idea is arbitrary in the extreme. It comes from a Pythagoreanism that is quite out of place as a primary consideration in art music. Wherever this system has been successfully used, it has been by composers who were already well trained enough to distinguish the musical results from the non-musical ones.

Walter Piston

The Musical Quarterly, 32,3 (July 1946)

For the past twenty years Walter Piston has devoted himself, with a consistency of purpose and conviction rare in our rapidly changing times, to one of the central problems of purely instrumental composition. From his earliest available work, *Three Pieces for Flute, Clarinet, and Bassoon*, in which he reveals himself already skilled and imaginative in the contemporary idiom, his major concern has been the creation of valid and imaginative concert music in the larger forms. It is hard to think of another composer of importance as prolific as he who has written so few theatrical and vocal works. For those remembered primarily for their instrumental music usually have a considerable list of less abstract and more literary works—operas, ballets, choral or vocal music, or incidental scores for the theatre or the films—to their credit also. But Piston, so far, seems satisfied with his single short choral piece and his one ballet and has focused his energies on a considerable series of pieces with such soberly appropriate titles as "Symphony," "Sonata for Violin and Piano," "Prelude and Fugue," and the like.

Through the years when the "avant-garde" moderns were busy exploring fantastic new sounds and sequences, often under the inspiration of literary and theatrical ideas, through the early thirties when a new wave of nationalism and populism startled many into thinking that the concert hall with its museum atmosphere was finished as a place for living new music, down to the present more conservative situation, Piston went his own way. He stood firmly on his own chosen ground, building up a style that is a synthesis of most of the important characteristics of contemporary music and assimilating into his own manner the various changes as they came along. As a result of this tireless concentration combined with rich native musical gifts, his works have a uniform excellence that seems destined to give them an important position in the musical repertory.

On surveying the course of his life, one is impressed by this quality of integration and direction. Once his particular field was decided on, the rest of his career was organized to suit. The rather speculative enterprise of uniting the different styles of contemporary music into one common style and using this in an ordered and beautiful way needs the peacefulness and sense of long-term continuity nowadays more frequently found in a university than elsewhere. Besides, as is well known, composing large works for the concert hall is one of the most unremunerative, though highly honored, fields of music in this country. It requires, therefore, a fairly steady source of outside income at least during its maturing stages if not afterwards, as well as a considerable amount of uninterrupted time. Few positions outside the academic world offer these advantages, and a university provides a place where long-range consideration of questions of broad scope are the rule rather than the exception. All these considerations must have determined Piston on an academic career. Before he decided, he tried out several alternatives, until he became more aware of his own capabilities as a musician. Once having decided, he took up a modest and quiet life as a composer on Belmont Hill overlooking Cambridge and Harvard, the scene of his teaching career.

His paternal grandfather, the one Italian member of his otherwise typically "down East" family, had died when Piston was born in Rockland, Maine, in 1894. Life in a small community being what it is, the Italian heritage had already been considerably erased. "Pistone" was changed to "Piston," and the composer's father, though half Italian, only knew how to count up to five in the foreign language. Like most Americans, the composer had little or no music at home, although several years after his family moved to Boston in 1905, the father bought young Walter a violin and his brother a piano. Up to this time, his innate musical abilities had had no chance to develop. But while he was teaching himself to play on both the piano and the violin, music began to assert its ascendancy. Engineering, which he was studying in a vocational high school, soon lost its interest. When Piston first played a march among the violins of the school orchestra, he immediately fell in love with music, but could not make up his mind to pursue it professionally until he had more training.

From this time until he was twenty-six, he tried different plans. First he made up his mind to be an artist, giving up the draftsman's position with the Boston Elevated Company he had taken on graduation from high school in 1912. Then he wavered several years between being a painter or a musician. During this time, he studied the violin with various teachers and earned his living playing in cafés, restaurants, and dance halls. In this way he acquired the intimate feeling for popular music that flavors many of his compositions. At twenty-two, still undecided, he went to the Massachusetts Normal Art School, where tuition was free. Here he came in contact with French art through his teachers and began to look towards Paris, where he later went to study.

This inclination towards French culture, which still slightly tinges his compositions, was reinforced by many impressions during Piston's student years. Rabaud and then Monteux succeeded Karl Muck as conductor of the Boston Symphony in 1918 and a great deal more new French music began to be heard. Boston had always been cosmopolitan in its relation to European cultures and France had frequently been favored. Puvis de Chavannes had crossed the Atlantic to paint his frescoes in the Boston Public Library. Edward Burlingame Hill had studied in Paris, and Henry F. Gilbert had made a pilgrimage to France on a cattle boat to hear [G. Charpentier's opera] *Louise*. There was, in fact, considerable precedent for a musician living in Boston to be attracted to the French tradition, and Piston's own personal qualities, his love of proportion and restraint as manifest in his compositions as in his elegantly penned manuscripts, predisposed him to regard this tradition with respect.

When the United States declared war, he volunteered for service in a Navy band; counting on his unusual ability to master an instrument, he claimed he could play the saxophone. Called up, he rushed off to buy an instrument and to borrow a manual from the public library; and in a short time he knew enough to be able to hold his own in a band stationed at the Massachusetts Institute of Technology throughout the war. He was already aware that the saxophone can be learned more quickly than any other of the band instruments. But this is only a trivial indication of a penetrating knowledge of musical instruments gained before and after this time. Indeed, his understanding of the different schools of playing, the different makes of instruments, and all the most practical matters of performance surprised and

delighted his fellow students both at Harvard and later in Paris. His knowledge of the registers of the instruments and their qualities and the type of
writing idiomatic for each is evident on every page of every score. He likes to
give each orchestral player something interesting to do in the course of a
work, no matter how subordinate the part. The pleasure he takes in such
matters is always stimulating to his orchestration classes, and this care and
understanding is a token of the thoroughness and realistic grasp with which
he approaches every aspect of his art, from the type of pen to use in copying
to the construction of a symphonic movement.

After the war, he resumed the study of the violin, hoping eventually to
take a place in the string section of the Boston Symphony Orchestra. But the
prospect of being a professional performer did not attract him as much as
the possibility of entering upon an academic career—a possibility opened up
by his studies in counterpoint with Dr. Davison of the Harvard Music
Department. Davison recognized his unusual abilities and was anxious to
enroll him as a regular student.

Thus, in the fall of 1920, at the age of twenty-six, already married to the
painter Kathryn Nason, Piston became a freshman at Harvard. To support
the newly formed ménage, he continued fiddling for a living and also helped
as an assistant in music classes at the college.

About this time, the placid routine of college music teaching began to be
disturbed by the strangeness of the new music. Few had the vision of Hill,
who kept his annual course in modern French music up to date with the
latest scores from Paris. Almost no theory teacher had yet thought of
renovating his courses to keep pace with contemporary music, which Piston
was later to do. Students were beginning to bring in compositions that
seemed to flout every idea that teachers believed in. No one had ever before
doubted the pedagogical usefulness of the Beethoven sonatas. Yet one pupil
raised a protest on being asked to analyze one, saying that he could not even
bear to play it over. One of Piston's fellow students, Virgil Thomson,
arranged a performance of Erik Satie's *Socrate* that is still talked about. But
Piston was not among the dissidents. He applied himself to his studies so
assiduously that he graduated *summa cum laude*.

It was not only through the ructions of classroom revolutionaries that
Harvard was feeling the impact of the First World War. Several different
trends expressed themselves in books by a few of the professors and give a
deeper insight into the temper of the time. Internationalism was stressed as
an antidote to the narrow isolationism keeping us out of the League of
Nations. Ideas sprouted up here that opened the way for new developments

in music in this country parallel to those taking place abroad. It was a short step to an international style in music, a common, exportable language interesting to musicians all over the Western world and subordinating the national and personal. And this language was to serve the purposes of serious art that does not rest on local color and that aims at universal validity. Such ideas were given particular consideration at this time, although they were not new. Edgar Allan Poe, for instance, had made such statements as: "the world at large" is "the only proper stage" for both reader and writer. It is because Piston's music moves on this stage with such mastery that it is so highly regarded by many Europeans.

Rejection of the Romantic gestures and emotional attitudes of the 19th century also marks the music of the time. This was absorbed by Piston along with other characteristics of modern music, but only in certain respects. He has not been affected by the various types of return to the primitive and childlike, or by the modern methods of pastiche which ape the mannerisms of other styles, past and present. Only occasionally does he follow rhythmic and melodic patterns derived from older music, such as that of Bach in the first movement of the *Concerto for Orchestra*, although this is purely modern in feeling and is not a comment on the older style but a direct expression of a character somewhat akin to that of a *Brandenburg Concerto*. Piston's use of classical forms closely related to those of Bach, Mozart, and Beethoven, as well as his sense of order and propriety, characterize his reaction to this trend.

It is important to realize the power of "anti-Romanticism" in the post-war period both here and abroad. It seemed to many the valid answer to a need to sweep away the grandiose illusions and the vaporous hopes fostered by the Romantics and a way of finding a stronger basis in reality for human conduct. Once more, as before the 19th century, artists wanted to be considered artisans, skilled craftsmen, the opposite of romantically inspired, erratic geniuses, and many of the newer composers took pains to foster this impression in their outward actions. In their music, they did not wish to exaggerate human feelings to titanic proportions but sought the well formed and the logically thought out.

Leaving the intellectually active atmosphere of Harvard, Piston, on graduating, went to Paris on a Paine Fellowship, intending to complete a thorough technical and professional training at the Conservatoire. When he was refused admission because he was thirty years old, he turned to Nadia Boulanger as one of the few outstanding teachers of the time who were sympathetic to contemporary music. By this time he was completely won over to new music, and, following all the performances of recent works, studying scores, he was able to master many of its techniques. His first works were played in Paris, and when in 1926 he returned to Harvard, where he has taught ever since, he brought with him the *Three Pieces for Flute, Clarinet, and Bassoon*, which Paul Dukas had called "Stravinskistes." These impressed many forward-looking musicians at once. Starting as an instructor, he rose to an associate professorship and the chairmanship of the music department. Afterwards, he relinquished the latter office because it interfered with his composing. He became a full professor in 1944. Working at his composition modestly and seriously, he has gradually gained prominence in the quiet way that characterizes all of his actions, so that Slonimsky in 1945 was justified in saying: "In the constellation of modern American composers, Walter Piston has now reached the stardom of the first magnitude. He has not exploded into stellar prominence like a surprising nova, but took his place inconspicuously, without passing through the inevitable stage of musical exhibitionism or futuristic eccentricity." [1]

So far, I have indicated the quality of Piston's native musical gifts, his love of *métier*, his openness to new developments, and his continuous devotion to the high principles of purely instrumental music. His early predilection for French culture, fortified by various trends in Boston and Harvard, led him to study in France, and several ideas that were stressed in the post-war period, such as internationalism and anti-Romanticism, helped to crystallize his relationship to musical tradition. The nature of this relationship, so important a part of his musical personality, becomes apparent when we consider his point of view as a teacher.

The impact on music schools of the contemporary, and of the older periods brought to light by musicologists, demanded a complete revision of courses in music theory. Aims had to be redefined and new means of presentation to be devised. As a progressive new theory teacher, Piston tackled this problem and went to its core, attacking it in much the same analytic way that he applied to the study of contemporary scores. The standardized academic routine, which taught harmony and counterpoint according to outmoded and unimaginative textbooks, insensitive to the beauties of the great composers' use of these materials, seemed more sterile than ever as students came to know many different kinds of music. A thorough analysis of the use of harmony and counterpoint by the great composers particularly of the thorough-bass period seemed indicated as a point from which to branch out. In his books, *Harmony, Principles of*

Harmonic Analysis [1941] and *Counterpoint* (in preparation*), Piston
points out many important factors at work in older music, giving examples
from actual scores and devising exercises to supplement these. He dwells on
the problem of rhythm, especially of the rhythmic change of harmony,
which so often enlivens contrapuntal rhythms without coinciding with
them. He shows the relation of strong and weak progressions to strong and
weak beats. In his own music a wide use of these principles greatly animates
the motion. His plan is to continue this series of writings with a book on
contemporary styles.**

His books, like his articles in magazines such as *Modern Music*, have a
smooth and closely packed, thoughtful style that is in direct contrast to the
dogmatic systematization of older textbooks. It has been said that the latter
sought to organize their subject on the analogy of a book on classical
mechanics, in which propositions are deduced from a series of fundamental
axioms. However, few of the authors had the penetration of Archimedes,
and the axioms as well as the deductions are not generally true. The result is
the reduction of the subject to a routine of formulas divorced from living
practice. Piston adopts a more inductive method, searching out fundamental
principles, and is not interested in formulas that make easy examination
questions and bad music.

His own compositions have been praised as exhibiting a new academicism; they have also been condemned for the same reason. If the academic
method consists in drawing up a system of rules that solve every problem of
musical composition including that of expression, Piston's music as well as
his teaching follows a very different direction. His opposition to facile,
routine solutions is obvious even in the detail of his music. For in it,
frequently repeated figures, static harmonies, and extended parallel motions
are the exception rather than the rule. The broad application of general
principles that give ample chance for freedom attracts him most. As Israel
Citkowitz put it: "His insistence on the purity and definitiveness of musical
pattern links Piston to that current of contemporary thought which has
attempted to re-absorb classical principles into the music of today."[2]

---

  * First published in 1947.—Eds.

  ** Piston did follow up with his *Orchestration* (1951), but never published a book on
contemporary styles. However, in a letter dated September 21, 1976, he wrote to us, "I am . . .
very busy working on a Fourth Edition of my *Harmony* (W. W. Norton). It is supposed to deal
more with the transition from XIX to XX centuries. Most fascinating and I am learning a lot."
Less than two months later, on November 12, he died.—Eds.

This emphasis on principles rather than on codifications enables him to teach student composers without dictating their choice of style. In fact, he is against that contemporary academicism that substitutes a new routine for an older one, his opposition resting on the sensible ground that any style, even a contemporary one, gets out of date and may suddenly no longer suit the needs of the growing composer, who, without a basic training to fall back on, will have trouble starting afresh.

In class, Piston is affable, tolerant, and reserved. Though quiet he is far from the dry professor, because he casts over his subject a penetrating wit or a thoughtful seriousness that comes from a deep concern with the subject at hand. His sly humor is always good natured and so aptly expressed that his words linger in the memory long after they are said. Having an uncommon respect for the art of music, he is fond of quoting the maxim "Life is short and art long," and pointing out how it is the composer's business to keep learning. He is not ashamed of admitting how much he finds out from hearing his own works played. Usually willing to talk about his music to someone who is seriously interested, he is not inclined to talk about himself. When he does, it is with a dignified modesty that sometimes baffles those accustomed to the usual ways of musicians. These traits seldom fail to command the respect and liking of his students, especially those who share his concern for the art.

Because of the number and variety of Piston's compositions, it is hard to discuss them in the detail they deserve without taking a great deal of space. Certain broad points can be made which throw light on them as a whole. Because in his music the "form is the feeling and the feeling formal," some have felt that it is without emotion. It is, on the contrary, particularly rich in variety and scope of expression, and grows more so with the years. In certain of his more recent works—for example, the slow movement of the *Second Symphony*—a romantic expansiveness is noteworthy, paralleling the current trend. Contrast this with the last movements of the *First String Quartet* and the *Sonatina for Violin and Harpsichord*, whose wit and sparkle represent one of his most compelling traits. However, a flexibility of motion and of feeling is the distinguishing mark of Piston's music. Moods are contrasted so skilfully that they seem like a comment one upon the other, like the thoughts of a serious man with a sense of humor who can take up a subject and see it in different perspectives. Sometimes an ironic jazz theme comes to lighten the lyricism of a first section, as in the first movements of the *Sonata for Flute and Piano* or the *Sonatina for Violin and Harpsichord*. In fact, this use of a scherzando second theme in the first movement of a three-movement sonata is fairly frequent and is an interesting way of preparing for a vivacious finale, usually accomplished by a separate scherzo movement in other composers' larger works.

He does not play up his contrasts to the hilt but usually stays on a certain level of sobriety, of modesty, and of elegance; he does not seek out dramatic effects, strange sonorities that contrast very high and low sounds often in unusually spaced chords, or use sudden silences. A standard of decorum is always maintained. The themes, for all their extensions and rhythmic gyrations, behave sensibly. Dissonances, though occasionally extreme, find their resolution in a relaxation of tension (Exx. 6–8 below). Phrases are clearly articulated with natural breaths and the extremes of range or dynamics are rarely touched. Nothing is insisted on at extravagant length. In fact all types of emphasis are used with a restraint that occasionally verges on the prim. Like any composer concerned with architectural clarity and order, he balances section with section using well-planned textures that allow each occurrence in the procession of events to claim its proper attention.

By his convincing and imaginative handling of all these problems of musical form, Piston has begun to occupy a place of great distinction among American composers. As Aaron Copland points out:

> Piston's music, if considered only from a technical viewpoint, constitutes a challenge to every other American composer. It sets a level of craftsmanship that is absolutely first-rate in itself and provides a standard of reference by which every other American's work may be judged. . . . Without men like Piston, without his ease and ability in the handling of normal musical materials, we can never have a full-fledged school of composers in this country.[3]

The normal musical material of the time has been the goal of his search. He brings material from many different sources and purifies it of freakishness. Most of the techniques of modern music are found thoroughly and rather impartially assimilated. There are chromatic and diatonic elements, linear counterpoint (Ex. 6), impressionist harmonies (Ex. 4), twelve-tone techniques (Ex. 14), and asymmetrical rhythms, sometimes combined within a single work. One of his main concerns, of course, as of many other contemporary composers, has been the use of the contrapuntal style within the sonata principle. But this is done with a clear sense of harmonic structure and motion that distinguishes his tendency from that of many others with similar aims.

In spite of the fact that most of his material comes from Europe, certain qualities mark the music as distinguishably American, particularly in more recent works. Since the *Concerto for Violin and Orchestra* (1939), it is no longer possible to say as Copland did, "there is nothing especially 'American' about his work."[4] But even in his *Suite for Orchestra* (1929), he started including phrases and rhythms from our popular music and using rhythms that would have been impossible without a thorough knowledge of jazz. Later this native flavor becomes more pronounced, not so much by actual quotation of American material, as by implication, as in the long-breathed clarinet melody in the slow movement of the *Second Symphony* (Ex. 1),

Ex. 1. Symphony No. 2, second movement.
Copyright 1944 by Associated Music Publishers, Inc.

or the lively second theme of the first movement of the same work (Ex. 2).

Ex. 2. Symphony No. 2, first movement.
Copyright 1944 by Associated Music Publishers, Inc.

Even within the frame of a major scale, Piston here shows his ability to be personal and spontaneous. But his American quality is also apparent, much more subtly and pervasively, in the sonority and texture of his music, which are quite distinct from those of any of the schools of Europe.

The works can be divided into two chronological groups, those written before 1938, the year of the *Carnival Song* and *The Incredible Flutist*, and those written after. If in the first period he is occupied with integrating and assimilating modern techniques, in the second there is an urge towards directness and simplicity. There was scarcely a sudden change of heart between one period and the other. Many tuneful and simple elements do appear in earlier works, as in the last movement of the *Second String*

Quartet, while there are elements in his later works of the complexity and dissonance characteristic of his earlier ones, the difference being more a matter of what is stressed in each.

The first period culminates in the important *First Symphony*, where elements of the twelve-tone technique are integrated into Piston's style. It opens in a somber, poignant mood with one of the few examples of an ostinato in his music. The pizzicato bass contains nine of the twelve chromatic tones and the three others are supplied by the theme sung above it. But first, four measures are devoted to a statement of the ostinato figure with a soft timpani roll on the dominant of C, the tonality of the first and last movements; then a theme is stated above the ostinato (Ex. 3).

Ex. 3. Symphony No. 1, first movement.
Copyright 1945 by G. Schirmer, Inc.

A sonata-allegro movement soon follows whose main theme, drawn from the ostinato figure, is presented in one of Piston's most striking and boldly dissonant contrapuntal passages. Returning at the end of the first movement, the same ostinato figure helps to introduce the F-sharp tonality of the second movement and provides material for its themes. The beginning of that movement illustrates Piston's unusual ability to combine different elements with spontaneous and convincing ease (Ex. 4).

Ex. 4. Symphony No. 1, second movement.
Copyright 1945 by G. Schirmer, Inc.

While one of the episodes of the final rondo comes from the introduction, the main theme with its driving power is built around the opening tones of the pizzicato bass inverted (Ex. 5).

Ex. 5. Symphony No. 1, last movement.
Copyright 1945 by G. Schirmer, Inc.

But quotations can only give an inadequate sample of a work that unfolds with dark and forceful eloquence in a close-knit and dynamic structure.

Its immediate predecessor, the *Concertino for Piano and Chamber Orchestra*, is in complete contrast, representing the witty and charming side of the composer as perfectly as the symphony does the serious side. It is a perfect summation of the lighter elements of Piston's music up to this time. One section contrasts with another with remarkable ease, and the orchestra is treated so as to throw the piano into the spotlight as the leader in an elegant conversation of instruments. In this work the frequent use of biting dissonances like the major seventh sounded in conjunction with the blandest consonances is characteristic of the harmonic sensibility of Piston at this period. Such harmonies began to make their appearance in the *Suite for*

Oboe and Piano, where they were boldly marked in the Prelude (Ex. 6) and in the very Pistonian closing Gigue (Ex. 7). Note similar clashes in the string quartets (Ex. 8).

Ex. 6. Suite for Oboe and Piano, Prelude.
Copyright 1934 by E. C. Schirmer Music Co.

Ex. 7. Suite for Oboe and Piano, Gigue.
Copyright 1934 by E. C. Schirmer Music Co.

Ex. 8.   a. String Quartet No. 1.   b. String Quartet No. 1.
Copyright 1934 by Associated Music Publishers, Inc.

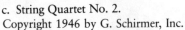

c. String Quartet No. 2.
Copyright 1946 by G. Schirmer, Inc.

d. String Quartet No. 2.

They came to bold elaboration in certain passages of the *Concerto for Orchestra*, where the organization is polytonal. In this last, there is a brilliant and unusual second movement built on the plan of repeating in reverse in the second half the jazzy material of the first half. Piston has frequently used devices like inversion and canonic imitation and other methods derived from the great contrapuntal periods of the past and still used by many composers today.

In the rondo of the *Second String Quartet* a whole section of the theme stated in four parts is recapitulated in inversion, the upper part becoming the bass and so forth (Ex. 9).

Ex. 9.   a. String Quartet No. 2.
Copyright 1946 by G. Schirmer, Inc.

b. String Quartet No. 2.

His use of fugal writing in the course of a sonata movement is particularly effective because he knows how to imply a harmonic background of the same type as that heard in other parts of the movement (Ex. 10).

Ex. 10. Sonata for Violin and Piano.
Copyright 1940 by Associated Music Publishers, Inc.

Of the two excellently written and effective quartets, the second seems more integrated, perhaps because it uses the device of a unifying motif of minor and major thirds that appears in all the movements. It begins with one of Piston's finest and most expressive pieces of two-part writing—a melancholy, tender introduction that establishes not only the tonality of A minor but the mood of the whole work (Ex. 11).

Ex. 11. String Quartet No. 2.
Copyright 1946 by G. Schirmer, Inc.

These two parts are later repeated in double canon, a fragment of which was given in Ex. 8d above.

The figure marked with a cross (in Ex. 11) is later used to form the harmonic background of a lyrical theme, after an allegro first section filled with a variety of different thematic fragments in the fashion of a similar place in the Beethoven E minor Quartet. The second movement suggests the mood of the beginning in a more intense and expressive way, while the last is quite diatonic and has a theme resembling ragtime (see Ex. 9 above). This work moves more freely and expansively than almost any other of Piston's first period.

As I have said, the ballet *The Incredible Flutist* marks a turning point. Being a very effective stage work and a charming concert suite, with its neat manipulation of the familiar dance forms, it is a work of a composer more accustomed to the concert hall than to the theatre, at least as we see the theatre today. Since Stravinsky and the French ballet composers, audiences have demanded of ballet scores the ability both to underline the action and dancing and to set the stage by giving a pronounced sense of environment. This type invariably results in pastiche music that sets the style, the period, and the locale, either taking them seriously or poking fun. Piston's attitude, however, is more like that of composers of Italian operas who leave the Egyptian, Bostonian, Parisian, or Druid backgrounds to the costume and stage designers and concentrate on the foreground of human situations. It is about the circus coming to a village—any village. The only immediately noticeable concession to the circus environment is a short, comic band march. A more modish treatment might have emphasized or parodied the carnival tone and kept it up from beginning to end of the circus's sojourn. It may be that our tastes will change to a less realistic and stylized kind of treatment of theatrical subjects, and if they do, this elegantly written ballet will certainly attract the notice of ballet companies more than it has.

In the next year comes a transitional work of a surprisingly convincing unity, the *Sonata for Violin and Piano*. In this a Mozartean tendency begins to take shape, evidenced by a much more fluid synthesis and a more plastic joining of different materials. There is also a forecast of the melodic sweep that suddenly appears in the next work, the *Concerto for Violin and Orchestra*, written in the same year (1939), for it marks an abrupt change. It is as diatonic as the *Carnival Song* for men's voices and brass but far more tuneful. Its Mendelssohnian charm and facility and its amplitude of form leave one with a sense of completeness not always present in Piston's music. The earlier dissonant sharpness is avoided and the work moves in an atmosphere of warmth and brilliance that makes it an immediate success, although, for some strange reason, it is rarely heard. It ought to appeal to violinists because the orchestra never suffocates the solo part, as it does in most modern concertos. Most of the materials suggest in a very discreet way various kinds of popular music. The first theme has a simple freshness entirely new to Piston (Ex. 12). And the whole movement flows along in this engaging fashion from beginning to end.

Ex. 12. Concerto for Violin and Orchestra, first movement.

A second movement of quiet, peaceful character contrasts a soft background of brass with the fragile voice of the solo instrument in a development that is unusually bland and reflective for this writer of poignant slow music. The finale jokes along gayly, stating its rondo theme against a comically broken-down bassoon figure (middle staff with stems down) changing, later, to more lyric moods (Ex. 13).

Ex. 13. Concerto for Violin and Orchestra, last movement.

Certainly this is a new adventure for Piston, and it anticipates, by his own critical awareness, the criticism of some at that time, which Aaron Copland expressed before knowing the work:

> ... Piston is not adventurous enough. One would like to know less surely what his next piece will be like. One should like to see him try his hand at types of music completely outside the realm of anything he has attempted thus far.[5]

A similar concern for directness and lucidity but on a more serious plane seems to motivate the *Second Symphony*, winner of the New York Music Critics' Circle Award last year. Its beautiful, songful beginning uses the same 6/4 measure and the same type of contrast between lyric and humorous material (Ex. 2 above) as the early *Sonata for Flute and Piano*, but there is a new, greatly intensified eloquence and expressivity. The frankly romantic second movement spins out its theme (Ex. 1 above) somewhat after the fashion of a large figured chorale prelude. Throughout there is a relaxation into grace typical of this second period. Some have complained that they felt the specter of the 19th-century French symphonists lurking here and there, referring perhaps to the heavily doubled theme of the last movement and its rather "heroic" atmosphere. But this feeling is soon dispelled after the statement of the theme by typically Pistonian interplay, with its new, airier character.

The most extreme step in the direction of relaxedness comes in the *Quintet for Flute and String Quartet*, music dominated by the gentle tone of the solo instrument. One feels in this piece, as in the two works with organ, *Prelude and Allegro for Organ and Strings* and *Partita for Violin, Viola, and Organ*, a desire to broaden the scope of his style, to incorporate new moods and methods. Mozartean grace as well as Mozartean combination of all the elements seem to inform the purely contemporary language. For instance, in the latter work, the third movement, "Variations," is built on a twelve-tone row (marked O in the example) and its inverted, retrograde, and retrograde-inverted (marked RI) variants. This material is treated tonally and is imbued with a tender and gentle individuality (Ex. 14).

Ex. 14. Partita for Violin, Viola, and Organ.

Originality of detail, skill in construction, and imagination mark the series of short commissioned works, such as the *Fanfare for the Fighting French* and the *Variation on a Theme by Eugene Goossens*, and all are immediately distinguishable as Piston's. Being a most punctual and methodical worker who can always be counted on to produce music of high quality and imagination, he has received many commissions over the years. The League of Composers heads the long list of commissioning organizations, which include the Coolidge Foundation, the Columbia Broadcasting System, the Alice M. Ditson Fund of Columbia University, and the International Society for Contemporary Music.

Now the composer seems headed in a new direction, for the *Sonatina for Violin and Harpsichord* and the short *Divertimento for Nine Instruments* are written in a fresh vein that returns to the more pointed and terse style of his earlier works. The violin work, particularly, is attractive in its combination of the newly found Mozartean fluency with the older, more acid harmonies and alert rhythms. Both works are organized into large paragraphs containing many contrasting phrases and rhythmic patterns, a most compelling means of avoiding the rather persistent and unrelieved moods by now only too common in recent music. There are a *Third Symphony* and a *Third String Quartet* in preparation that may apply this new-found flexibility to the serious style. But at this point one feels that it is much harder to predict Piston's future than it was in 1940.

One thing is certain, there will be no relaxation of quality or want of imagination, no matter in what line he continues.

In the whole field of contemporary music, Walter Piston occupies an important position. He has summed up the tendencies of the past twenty years both here and in Europe and given them broad and masterful expression. Although living in the time of the "lost generation," he found himself in his devotion to music. His unique contribution is to have done this particular work with outstanding excellence in a country where few have ever made a name for themselves as thoroughly craftsman-like artists. In literature several names come to mind but in music there is hardly one to be found before our time.

To have helped to establish a deep understanding of the value of craftsmanship and taste here and to have given such persuasive exemplification of these in his works is highly important for our future. For, not having as ingrained a respect and love for high artistic ideals as Europeans have had, we have often slipped into the trivial, chaotic, and transitory. Piston's work helps us to keep our mind on the durable and the most satisfying aspects of the art of music and by making them live gives us hope that the qualities of integrity and reason are still with us.

But this sounds like philosophy and Piston once said something about Stravinsky's *Symphonie des psaumes* that could well be applied to his own work:

> Many were the philosophical speculations as to the intent and content of this music after its performance. But the musician must be satisfied that what one gets from any work depends on what one brings to it. In the *Symphonie des psaumes* he will sense unmistakably those elements he seeks in real music.[6]

[A list of Piston's works appended to this article has been omitted here.—Eds.]

NOTES

1. Program notes for a concert of The Civic Symphony Orchestra of Boston, Paul Cherkassy, conductor. April 18, 1945.
2. Israel Citkowitz: "Walter Piston—Classicist," *Modern Music*, 13 (1936).
3. Aaron Copland: *Our New Music*, New York, 1941, p.182.
4. Ibid., p.183.
5. Ibid., p.186.
6. Walter Piston: "Stravinsky as Psalmist—1931," *Modern Music*, 8 (1931).

The Composer's Viewpoint
[The League of Composers]

National Music Council Bulletin, 7,1 (Sept. 1946)

It seems that everything is a problem to the composer. We always seem to be trouble-shooting, trying to explain ourselves to ourselves and to others.

We bother our families with such talk and we get together in meetings to see what can be done to help things, sitting around tables as if we were highly paid executives with big problems of organization on our shoulders. Each of us has already said so much that by now it is hard to know where to begin.

There is, however, just one simple fact, I think, on which all the problems of serious composers hinge. What almost any composer worth his salt would like to write, what all performers and publishers would like to find, what teachers, critics, and audiences agree is what they want to hear, is interesting and durable music. I mean by this, music that stands on its own feet and says what it has to say so well that it can be heard many times with constantly growing interest and understanding. Some cynics have claimed that this cannot be written in our time, that we have lost the knack. But just the same we all seem hopeful, for our clamor about American music and about new music in general really betrays the desire to find and to nurture such durable music.

It is obvious that the world of serious music needs a considerable amount of this music to exist at all. Its public appeal depends on this music and all its operations revolve around it. If we once forget this fact and give the short-lived, the so-called "novelty music" a central position, first, performers will begin to lose their skill for want of mature compositions to call out their best abilities, and then audiences will begin to get bored. The whole profession will run downhill, losing its distinction and prestige on the way.

The kind of music I am talking about does not grow in a desert. It needs encouragement, and the right kind of encouragement. We composers think our desire to write durable music a far-sighted one, though to our performing and publishing friends it often seems very stubborn of us to take things so seriously, turning out sonatas and symphonies that have few chances of performances and fewer of sales. Some of us like to think, perhaps naively, that we can turn out the kind of work that would be immediately successful at once if we wanted to. But many of us feel that a little of this goes a long way. Sometimes what we think is our best work takes with the public, to our own surprise and delight, though in a way this is disturbing too. We have all seen the public go wrong so often in matters of serious music. We think of all those great works, now a part of our repertory, that were complete failures when they were first played. That thought makes us suspicious, especially here in America, where practically none of our great writers and other creative artists were successful during their lifetimes. You can see what I mean when I say that everything is a problem to a composer.

What composers do in this situation is to surround themselves with like-minded people in the hope that if one has not got what it takes to write such music, at least he can help another to do so by providing the encouragement and understanding which one should be able to find among those more in touch with commercial enterprises. Part of the development of a composer comes when he gets the chance to hear his music played before an audience. So, to help each other out, some turn concert managers, publishers, writers, and lecturers—generally, of course, on a non-profit basis, like the poverty-stricken philanthropists they very often are. They start such organizations as the League of Composers, the New Music Editions, the American Music Center, the Eastman Festival of American Music, and the rest, in the hope that durable music will be able to develop unhampered by the disturbing distractions that come with our present economic set-up. They don't want a quick success that results in quick collapse. The results of such organizations prove that composers know their job. For most of our important contemporaries have developed in close contact with such groups.

Composers, as you know, are often men of vision. They are willing to make long-term investments of their own time and their creative effort, believing that only in this way will anything good ever be accomplished. But they are surrounded by a society that insists on quick returns for its money, and in the process is continually meeting with the disappointing fact that successes fostered in this way are transient. When you think of how profitable the durable classics of music have been to everybody concerned, how much more profitable than any passing novelty, then you cannot understand why more performers, publishers, and teachers are not out to foster new music of this level.

Just the opposite is only too often the result of their efforts. Most performers, for instance, treat all works of new music as novelty items, clamoring for first performances as if they did not believe the work could stand a second hearing. Composers are put on the spot by this and have to keep writing music, often more than they should, in order to remain before the public. With the kind of publicity set-up we have in this country, it often seems more important to keep a name, rather than a work, in the limelight because revivals of older works by new composers are among the rarer events in this wasteful quest for novelty.

The destructiveness of this foolish attitude is immediately apparent. It is not confined to performers alone. Publishers are always looking for short, appealing, and easy works, real novelty merchandise, that is intended to sell for a short time and be forgotten for good. In fact they heave long sighs and shake their heads if the misguided music writer shows up at their offices with longer, more important works.

It is silly to take a top-lofty attitude in these matters, for novelties are indeed often the spice of life, if not its meat and drink. But what we composers are worried about is that our musical meat and drink seem so severely rationed at the present time. For its production and distribution are being discouraged by the very ones who stand to make a profit if really good music were uncovered. We tend to look at the situation in terms of the harmful practices of lumberjacks who cut down all the trees in a forest without leaving saplings to grow for another year's lumber. Certainly there are only too few evidences of a long view, a view that would stimulate the best of our talents to mature and be productive.

And so I would like to urge everyone connected with music to consider his responsibility in helping to develop this durable music here in this country. For if a long view is not taken, the short-term stress on novelty may very well crush more lasting efforts and result in a sense of frustration all around. Publishers should be willing to take more risks on works that aim in the right direction, and performers and teachers should be on the look-out for good works whether they have been performed or not.

We must stress and stress again musical quality, looking behind the facade of prestige, of publicity, often such deceptive indications of lasting worth. For it is the achievement of high musical quality that rouses the enthusiasm of each of us, and gives our profession its distinction and power. We must jealously guard it.

An American Destiny
[Charles Edward Ives]

Listen, 9,1 (Nov. 1946)

Charles Edward Ives is one of those outstanding men whose personalities leave their mark on whatever they do. And whatever he does seems to emerge naturally from his own character rather than from some artificially invented plan forced on him from the outside. The bold pattern of his life, evolving in a highly unorthodox manner, reflects a personal logic that assessed the American musical scene of his time and his own capabilities and went its own way regardless of what other composers were doing. And the result is surprising: to be at the same time a highly successful business man, the senior partner in the outstanding New York insurance firm of Ives and Myrick, built up by the two from scratch, and also the composer of a large body of music, much of it not only years ahead of its time but vital and important enough to be hailed by critics here and abroad as an outstanding contribution to the art of music, is certainly the achievement of an extraordinary man.

In many ways Ives stands apart from his time. In our age of specialization, the combination of executive and artistic ability, of originality and personal discipline, of shrewdness and moral integrity, and above all, of relentless energy coupled with religious convictions, fervent patriotism, and a good sense of humor, seems typical of an earlier time. Few men of today can be talked of in superlatives in two different capacities. Ives is probably one of the few. He seems to have floated above the egomania, the pragmatism, and the doubts about the future of Democracy rampant before and after World War I. Indeed, his reaction against these as against the modern music of that time, his hey-day, was violent. In his *Essays Before a Sonata*, and in his political tract advocating a World People's Union (a United States of the World) * sent to President Roosevelt and members of the Congress, he is scornful of many trends of the modern era, while firmly believing that out of the chaos there will be a spiritual affirmation that will sweep away the present troubles. Being the kind of a man he is, he could not fail to assert and to exemplify in his life and his art the noble ideals inherited from his New England background. And these older principles, voiced mainly by the Concord Transcendentalists, form the core around which all the parts of his life are joined.

This typically lean and wiry Yankee is of an exceedingly modest and retiring character. Not unlike many another New Englander, it is hard to get much biographical material from him. Yet before he withdrew from business and finally even from the exertion of receiving any but occasional

---

* Reprinted with annotations in Howard Boatwright, ed., *Charles Ives, Essays Before a Sonata and Other Writings* (New York: W. W. Norton, 1962), pp.215–31.–Eds.

visitors because of grave ill health which began to overtake him in 1930, Ives was not averse to telling jokes on himself. For instance, after a concert conducted in 1927 by Eugene Goossens, on which Debussy shared the program with two movements of Ives's dissonant and complex *Fourth Symphony*, Ives overheard two men talking outside Town Hall. One asked the other if the music was all by contemporaries. On learning that Debussy was no longer alive, he asked if Ives were dead. The answer being, "No," he remarked, "Well, he ought to be."

Ives is against being photographed. One of the few pictures ever taken and the only one ever reproduced shows him sitting outside his house in West Redding in rough summer clothes. It is very much in contrast to the clean-shaven Ives who went to business daily for thirty years looking like any other commercial New Englander, inconspicuously dressed.

With this retiring disposition go many attitudes and opinions typical of one with his background. Often he would express scorn of the cheap and frivolous, of the decadent or lazy, in a sharp, witty phrase. I remember his humorous disgust at hearing of an American composer living in Paris who lay all morning in bed composing. Such behavior would be impossible in the respectable conventionality of *his* home. He deplored the excessive eroticism of late nineteenth-century music in his book as being like "the sad thoughts of a bathtub with the water running out." The one text of Whitman he has used in his songs represents a violent contrast to the generally conventional texts from newspaper poets and standard authors. "Who goes there? hankering, gross, mystical, nude" is the opening of the song which epitomizes the yawpingly physical aspects of the poet—to Ives justifiable, perhaps, as a strongly characterized human picture. But from his point of view, Whitman was hardly to be countenanced as furnishing an outlook on life, which the poet did for so many in this country during the very period when Ives was active.

Rather, the composer inclined to the lofty aspirations of Emerson, the nature moods of Thoreau, the fantastic in Hawthorne, the homely New England cheer of Whittier. His music and his writings reflect this optimistic tone, in their religious, patriotic, or gay moments. The bitter brooding of Melville or the searchings of the conscience of Hawthorne never seem to have moved him to music. And this, too, is characteristic of one aspect of New England Puritanism.

But along with this adherence to many attitudes typical of a slightly older generation than his own, there is a strong streak of originality, which, of course, finds its fullest expression in his music. It also found its way into his business affairs. At the office, he avoided formality; he liked clients to feel that they could come and see him whenever they wished without appointments. He refused to have a secretary and insisted on answering the phone himself. Having a clear mind and a good memory, he followed a personal method of ordering his papers, which meant that his desk usually looked messy. (His curious sense of order is also noticeable in the volume of *114 Songs*, which are, as far as any plan is perceptible, partially in reverse chronological order. Certainly it is not by chance that the song "The Masses," with its huge tone-clusters opens the collection.) He apparently made an important innovation which drew customers by offering, at a time when businesses concealed their inner workings, to let his clients have free access to the books.

In his musical dealings he has persisted since about 1902 in maintaining an "amateur" status, almost consistently refusing any payment for performances or publication. In fact, he has been reluctant to allow his music to be published except at his own expense, and generally will not have it copyrighted unless the publisher insists. On the other hand, he has never paid for performances of his works, letting performers and performing organizations treat him in this respect as they would any other composer, always, however, waiting to be asked for his music. When able to get about he had to be persuaded to go to concerts where his music was played, and he never would take a bow.

This unusual attitude is the application of his idea that music is something more important and more spiritual than the commodities and professional services bought with money. It is the point of view of many non-artists. There is an element of truth in it insofar as we do demand of all artistic products that they seem to proceed from some other kind of love than the love of money. Ives also shunned any attempt to court artistic success, even when it started to come his way, because all of these worldly things probably seemed out of place in the domain of art. But in the end, Ives's life has amply justified adherence to high ideals not only by his business success but more importantly by the unusual quality of his music. Here is one case where pure high-mindedness won out.

This is, however, not to say that Ives always remains on a lofty pinnacle of abstract speculation in his music. On the contrary, all sides of life find their way there as they used to into his insurance office. There is a great love of the concrete—the mistakes townspeople made singing hymns, the way children used to cut up at religious camp meetings in Danbury, the national anthems played by conflicting bands on the Fourth of July, soupy theatre music, the confused sounds of the city heard at night in Central Park. These furnish part of the background of material closely related to the average man he so respected in his office. Continual contact with people prevented him from losing himself in the recondite. The intent of his compositions is usually easy to grasp on first hearing no matter how original and complex the tonal garb. Not only does the deep seriousness of his mature life come through, but also the charming reminiscences of the Danbury of his childhood, of the humor like that of the "Danbury Newsman," who set America to laughing over local cranks and eccentrics, and of the gay holidays.

For Charles Ives was born in that Connecticut country town (now the "Hat City") on October 20, 1874, of a father who was the center of musical activity. George Ives had been a bandleader at sixteen in the Civil War, and his son took after him in musical precocity. He learned harmony, counterpoint, and fugue thoroughly from his father. Along with these subjects went contact with the novel experiments in acoustics worked out in the household. George Ives, like a few other Americans stimulated by such new developments as Karl Rudolph Koenig's tonometric apparatus shown at the Philadelphia Exposition of 1876, that divided four octaves into 670 parts, built instruments that produced quarter and other fractional tones. The effects of acoustical perspective made by placing instruments and even whole bands in antiphonal, opposing position on the village green were also tried. Sometimes one band performing one piece marched in the opposite direction from that performing another piece, and the Iveses enjoyed the fading in and out and the clashing of harmonies and rhythms. This led them to think up many new, dissonant chords. That all this was followed with intense interest by the son is clear, for he made liberal use of these experiments in his own music while inventing many more. What is still shocking conductors today was worked out in the eighties in Danbury.

Seeing how musically gifted his son was, George Ives set him to learning organ playing. By the age of fourteen, young Ives was so good that he became a regular church organist at a salary. To play in his father's band, he picked up drumming from the local barber. Working under his father, who taught him the works of Bach, Beethoven, and Stephen Foster, his talents grew abundantly. Soon he composed a march, which his father decided to play. This touched off another side of Ives, for feeling a certain shyness over his musical activities, he refused to participate. Indeed, at that time, when asked what he played, he would answer, "shortstop"—naming his position on the local baseball team.

In New Haven, at the Hopkins Grammar School and later at Yale, Ives kept up his professional musical activities side by side with a healthy athletic career. He was always an important member of a baseball or football team, even while conducting the Hyperion Theatre Orchestra and furnishing music for the services of the Center Church, one of the beautiful old structures standing on the Green. With his orchestra, he tried many new ideas and gained the practical knowledge of how to attain the unusual effects which appear in his later scores. At the same time he studied with Horatio Parker, an important composer of the period, for whom he wrote a considerable number of conventional works. However, there were glimmerings of what was to come even in his *First Symphony*, which Parker found had too many rapid changes of key.

Coming to New York after graduating from Yale in 1898, Ives had to decide whether to remain a professional musician or to take up a more lucrative activity. His views on the musical profession, expressed in his *Essays Before a Sonata*, suggest that he may have felt that it offered too limited a contact with life and was too narrow for a composer with new ideas. To get a good job in music meant "playing the game," writing music that would enhance his prestige. But he was not the man for expedient maneuvers of this kind. He wanted to lead the life of an ordinary citizen with a wife and child raised in a pleasant home, but saw that much of this might have to be sacrificed if he followed music, and that in turn his compositions would have to be limited by the enforced narrowness of a musician's life. So Ives boldly decided to go into business. Being from Connecticut, whose capital, Hartford, was the insurance city, Ives very naturally got into insurance.

He did not relinquish his performing activities at once. His last position was that of organist at the Central Presbyterian Church in New York (1900–1902). While there he wrote parts of the *Third Symphony*. In business, he first became a clerk for the Mutual Life Insurance Company of New York, where he stayed until 1906. Then, after starting an agency of his own in 1909 with Julian S. Myrick, he formed the firm which later became one of the largest of its kind in the country, Ives and Myrick, managers for the Mutual Life Insurance Company of New York. He retired in 1930 on account of ill health. After 1902, he had retired from the active musical scene, devoting himself quietly at home to composing before and after business hours.

A great body of manuscripts began to appear, most of them hastily scribbled, corrected, and revised frequently, which Ives got into shape from time to time. At his own expense, in 1922 and '23, he published a volume of 114 songs and the *Concord Sonata* for piano, which were sent around to the musical profession, leaving most of them scandalized—except a few who have been instrumental in getting Ives's music before the public since the composer made no effort of his own. But his musical ideas were too many to keep pace with his ability to make clear copies, and today, with his eyesight too bad to do much proofreading, there are many scores which still require patient deciphering before they can be performed. Around 1934, he had eleven volumes of chamber music brought out in photostat, some still in a very unclear state.* But since that time ill health has prevented him from doing any but a very little work on his music, a thing which would have been unthinkable in his active days.

To have combined such different activities in one life and to have done both so well and with such conviction were to Ives perfectly natural and satisfying in a way that would hardly be so to any other musician. In an interview with Henry Bellamann on the subject, Ives said, "My business experience revealed life to me in many aspects that I might otherwise have missed. In it one sees tragedy, mobility, meanness, high aims, low aims, brave hopes, faint hopes, great ideals, no ideals, and one is able to watch these work inevitable destiny. And it has seemed to me that the finer traits were not only in the majority but in the ascendancy. I have seen men fight honorably and to a finish, solely for a matter of conviction or of principle—where expediency, probable loss of business, prestige, or position had no part and threats no effect. It is my impression that there is more open-mindedness and willingness to examine the premises underlying a new and unfamiliar thing, before condemning it, in the world of business than in the world of music. It is not even uncommon in business intercourse to sense a reflection of philosophy—a depth of something fine—akin to a strong beauty in art. To assume that business is a material process, and only that, is to undervalue the average mind and heart. To an insurance man there *is* an 'average man' and he is humanity. I have experienced a great fullness of life in business. The fabric of existence weaves itself into a whole. You cannot set an art off in the corner and hope for it to have vitality, reality and substance.

* See note by John Kirkpatrick, p.100.—Eds.

There can be nothing 'exclusive' about a substantial art. It comes directly out of the heart of experience of life and thinking about life and living life. My work in music helped my business and my work in business helped my music." *

* Henry Bellamann, "Charles Ives, The Man and His Music," *The Musical Quarterly*, January 1933.—Eds.

The Function of the Composer

[in teaching the general college student]

1951

Bulletin of the Society for Music in the Liberal Arts College, 3,1 (1952), Supplement 3

The subject which I have been asked to discuss with you, "the function of the composer in teaching the general college student," is one that runs at the outset on the horns of a dilemma. The place, as well as the point of view of the composer in our society, seem to be vastly different from the place and point of view of the teacher of the general student. A brief consideration of twentieth-century music reveals at once, I think, that today a composer's work is mainly prized, along with its artistic qualities, for its distinctness and uniqueness of personal character. The educated musical public and the composers themselves want new music to be a complete reworking of techniques in the interests of completely expressing a unique yet culturally responsible individual. The artist, today, seems to have been entrusted with the task of giving important meaning to the old figure of the individualist, to the "inner-directed man," whose actions are controlled by his own personal conscience, his own desires, his own ideas and beliefs. By contrast, most of

Address presented at the Annual Meeting of the Society for Music in the Liberal Arts College, held at Rochester, N. Y., December 29, 1951.

society seems to be drifting more and more into a conformist attitude. Most people tend to merge their tastes, feelings, and ideas with those of the majority, and these, in turn, are manipulated by those large-scale interests organized for the distribution of goods. The "outer-directed man" is more typical of the time. Apparently, it is both the artist's as well as the teacher's role to fight this collectivizing tendency in order to preserve that liveliness of the individual mind so important to our civilization. But teacher and artist carry on this attack from entirely different vantage points.

In his time-honored way, the professor, instead of testing every detail of his work in terms of his personal views, as a composer does, tests his ideas in the light of known facts. It is obvious that one who teaches the general student should be particularly apt at finding those grand, impartial, illuminating generalizations that fit and explain the facts of musical procedures and their historical development. Such great insights have always been the glory of the academic mind—rational, lucid statements that clarify where all once seemed confused. In the domain of music this illumination is particularly welcome, for as a fine art, music is a comparatively new arrival in the university. Because of its newness, there has not been that wealth of research and of insight that we find in the fields of literature or of the sciences.

As in other fields, the teacher of the general student in music aims for the all-embracing, the dispassionate view of his subject. By contrast, the composer is a person only occupied with those aspects of music most important to him as an individual. He is taking the next step along the path of musical history, willy-nilly, and, Janus-faced, he looks back at those aspects of older music which have a special meaning for him, and forward as he forms his own works. If he is adventurous and gifted, his works will help to continue and validate musical activity as it passes through the difficult period of adjustment to our society. But no matter what path he takes, his music will either contain significant things for the future or furnish a background for music that does.

The university teacher tries to find an harmonious and rationally explicable pattern in the past and present, and his efforts can be useful to the composer, especially now when a whole revision of musical theory is urgently needed. He is part of a grand, slow-moving enterprise in which many like-minded men are involved with similar points of view. The composer's life, on the other hand, is a private enterprise with no one to rely on but himself to produce his works.

Simply stated, the composer is a creator of works. He constantly comes to grips with what Hindemith calls "the stubbornness of the notes" and, to be sure, with performers not nearly as stubborn, fortunately. The teacher is up against the stubbornness of the facts, and these facts are mainly the works that composers have written out of their training, out of their experience, out of their instinct, often without being conscious of what choices they were making. And these facts are to be presented to students in a way that is consistent with the reasoned approach of the academic mind.

In the aggregate, composers are a very mixed lot, necessarily, while those who teach in university music departments are much more united in a common enterprise whose principles are more or less mutually agreed upon. Therefore to generalize about the composer's function outside of his composing is perhaps even more hazardous than to generalize about the university man's activities outside of his teaching. At first sight, it might seem that most composers had very little to offer the general student verbally. This contention is upheld by the fact that most eminent composers either do not teach in colleges, or, if they do, confine themselves to advanced students of composition.

In a recent article devoted to modern trends, Virgil Thomson said: "The neo-classic composers have all the good jobs in universities." Some years ago he suspected universities of supporting "academic modernism." Whether these statements are borne out by the facts or not, they are a typical reaction of artists of our time against the academy. It is often said that the official academic style of today is a sort of modern music, and a whole method has been devised in schools and colleges to teach young composers this official style. No wonder that composers who are more unorthodox in their view of contemporary music, who adhere to their own personal conceptions, are hesitant to become teachers. So this argument runs. There is, no doubt, some truth in this. One sometimes wishes that the academic situation were more flexible and could find various ways of using the talents of all different kinds of composers. The talents of some could be used for the benefit of the general student in other ways than in formal teaching, such as conducting, performing, or organizing concerts, if the university is to reflect the various aspects of our contemporary culture. The plan of having a resident composer, such as is found in some universities, is especially useful for promoting that kind of personal contact with the general student that in some ways can be the most useful of all.

But let us assume that there are some composers who can and will teach the general student. Their contribution to this important part of academic endeavor can be valuable in counteracting certain tendencies that very understandably crop up within the walls of the music department.

As everyone is aware, more than any other art today, music lives on its past, not only in universities, where this is important, but also among the public and among performers. Obviously music does present a wonderful reflection of former times, their glories, their sensitiveness, their charm, their depth of spirit. To most people at a concert this wonderful dream for a time seems like a possibility for the present. Such people are always asking, for instance, why contemporary composers do not write the way older ones did. But, as we are all aware, times have changed so much that most of us can no longer experience, except in imagination, the powerful forces of culture which unified past societies and formed the background for the musical masterpieces we love and respect. Concern with the past is indeed very inspiring if older works are approached as shining examples of what men have been capable of and what they may again accomplish, but as an escape from the conflicting and puzzling world of the present, this music is an unwelcome (though attractive) relaxation. Viewed in this way it does not invite the effort needed to create the new world of values which may once more unify society into those common and serious aims which will allow the arts to act once again as a vital force.

One function of the composer-teacher to which his creative effort naturally disposes him is to situate this past in the present, to make the past have a meaning for the general student in terms of his own life. This is something the general students want out of such a course of study and it is a question that is constantly being considered by the composer, more perhaps than by any other member of a music department. In fact with the other members there is always the danger that their more scholarly approach tends to emphasize the pastness of the past—an important affair for specialists who are seeking truths in the accumulation of history. But composers as well as general students are more engaged with the presentness of the past.

It is no secret that many people everywhere are deeply worried over our cultural problem in America today. Many of our best recent literary and sociological works have given an appalling picture of the cultural triviality of those very parts of society from which the majority of university students are recruited. For instance, in John W. Aldridge's recent book, *After the Lost Generation*, there is this remark: "The best literature in America will continue to be negative so long as the country's values are such that no writer of honesty or insight can possibly take them seriously."

This is, of course, one of many such statements that have been made about America with increasing insistence as the country has grown more mature, from the time of de Tocqueville through Sinclair Lewis's *Babbitt* down to the present. The incurable optimist sees in all this a long difficult transition from one set of values to another. Whether the new values will be as strong in survival power as the old ones, none of us here will probably ever know. But whether the new ones will favor the arts or not is in the balance. It is up to us in the artistic professions, who are convinced of the cultural value of art, to make sure that our students have such a strong sense of the validity of the arts, that as they go through life, the arts will always be a source of power and satisfaction to them. It is only in this way that we can be assured of the arts' continuance as an ever-present reality. Situating the Golden Age of art in the past and its decadence in the present, as is often done, is already a sign of defeat. Perhaps we are defeated. But there are some of us who do not think so.

In his book *The Aims of Education*, Alfred North Whitehead starts by saying: "Culture is activity of thought, and receptiveness to beauty and humane feeling. Scraps of information have nothing to do with it." Later on, he develops the idea that creative enjoyment of the arts by people busy in the commercial, productive, and scientific enterprises of our civilization, should be, as he put it, "analogous to sunshine in the physical world."

Under the present systems of education there is a perpetual danger that the teacher of the general student in the humanities or elementary elective courses, in despair, will settle for giving his students scraps of information, or "inert ideas," as Whitehead calls them. In despair, because of the limitations of time by comparison with the size of the subject, because of limitations of the student's musical training, and mainly because the larger issues of art are so controversial and difficult to present, and then, too, frequent enlightening contact with actual music is so difficult to make available. Scraps of information and inert ideas are useful for tests passed, which lead to courses completed, and this through the whole procession of academic credits, to be crowned with the laurel of a decently paying job. But it will be a job done, and a life led, by yet another poorly educated member of society.

Every honest member of the academic profession is aware that this pattern will never save us from cultural triviality. The composer, perhaps more than others, has a very real stake in imparting more than scraps of information, no matter how, and in constantly trying to find a more powerful method of making his students more culturally alive.

For at this point in history, we have got to help our students to realize that to enjoy the arts creatively and imaginatively will be far more rewarding to them as individuals in terms of stimulating vividness of thought and feeling, quickness of understanding, and ingeniousness in dealing with new problems—far more rewarding than the mere passive enjoyment which most mass-produced entertainment invites. Contemporary music can be made to play a part in this. In fact, it can be shown that the bewildering diversity of modern music presents a clear parallel with the best sides of modern life. Its qualities are very like the qualities of mind, a feeling necessary for an active, intelligent, and imaginative attack on the novel situations with which we are continually faced.

As has been frequently observed, most people in our society, through fatigue, bewilderment, and confusion, show an inability to face the constant violation of time-honored ways which offer little help in dealing with new situations. This often seems true of the musical world as a whole. Naturally people are very hesitant to change in those realms of feeling and fundamental belief most cherished by them. But what is fundamental and what is transitory and subject to change are undergoing a re-definition. It is activity of thought that is, as ever, one of the most important ways of dealing with the present.

It was this attitude that was taken by those who worked out the curriculum of study at St. John's College in Annapolis. This college, one of the first to revive the teaching of humanities, as you know, is the place where many of the important books of the past and present, literary as well as from the major fields of human thought, are read. The curriculum, required of every student, combines the reading and discussion of the books with extensive laboratory work and training in mathematics as well as in a classical language and a modern one. In this way Western culture is studied in its important manifestations, starting with the Greek contribution and coming up chronologically to those of the present in four arduous years, years that are full of intellectual stimulation and thoughtfulness, for the emphasis is on student discussion rather than on acquiring masses of facts.

Now, after this curriculum had been pursuing its course for some time, the faculty began to feel that the students were too exclusively occupied with technical questions in the books, with the philosophical, theological, moral, and scientific meanings. This was, of course, most bothersome in the discussion of the literary works. The students seemed to be missing almost entirely the artistic qualities of these works, which to anyone of awareness were written large on almost every page of every book. Besides this, the students had great difficulty in writing good, readable, literary English. Both of these deficiencies are, as everyone knows, common in many colleges and cause a great deal of concern especially in the English departments. The attempt to remedy this situation, made around 1940, suggests one of the basic reasons for teaching art to the general student.

For the faculty at St. John's decided to bring the matter of artistic quality and its accompanying problems into clear focus, so that every student would have to come to grips with it himself. They chose the study of music because it seemed to throw the matter into high relief with the fewest distracting elements. They called in a composer on the hunch that he would grasp the idea more than other members of the musical profession, and a plan was worked out from which it was hoped that students of widely different musicality could make contact with the art. As with all subjects, music was tied in with several aspects of the program. A number of physics laboratory experiments were devised to familiarize the students with the elements of music, the intervals, the tuning of scales, the construction of chords and of instruments. There was also a laboratory on the measurement of time and its relation to music. In all of these, emphasis was placed on how these factors contributed to music, melodies were played by each student on the sonometers and also simple harmonic progressions. There were several classes devoted to the elementary principles of musical notation. All these preliminaries led up to the thorough study of a very few works of music made available to the students not only on records but, where possible, in live performances in the concert series to which attendance was required. These few musical works appeared in their historical contexts, being studied at about the same time as books of the same period.

At the discussions of the music, which extended usually over two or three two-hour sessions devoted to one work, the students did most of the talking. Because of this, dealing with the particular work under consideration was difficult because the students were so beset with questions of a general nature—questions that perplex almost all general students and rarely receive attention in any elementary music course. In spite of the fact that the students who were not already familiar with music gained very little ability to grasp the detail of any particular piece, it was felt that the experiment did result in a considerable advancement in esthetic awareness on the part of students who did not already have it. Certainly the general interest in music was greatly stimulated, and many wanted to learn more about the whole literature.

While such an approach is out of the question in most humanities courses in colleges, it does indicate one way, as a composer sees it, that students might be helped to develop esthetic awareness. In fact, though a composer's point of view usually has its limitations, it often does have a consistency and a special kind of intensity which is not often found in other music teachers. For instance, his views on musical analysis can be of value to the student since it is his daily business to deal with the details and parts of a musical piece and to form them into a whole.

So the function of the composer, I think, can be summed up by saying that his emphasis will most likely be on the cultural wealth of music and its validity for the individual alive today. His coherent, practical ideas on the inner workings of any piece of music are valuable in showing what is routine and how it was transcended, what is imagination, what tradition. Through his constant dealings with the musical medium, he will be very aware of what artistic order and expression are, and of the host of things, details if you like, that help to give a work its liveliness, importance, and beauty.

But this reminds me that I have not included the one aspect of the composer's function which is directed toward all of society that will listen, including the general student, and that is his composition. It ought to be a self-evident fact that the composer's main function must always be, in respect to any part or all of society, to compose the best music he can, to give the best of himself to his composition.

This is easy to forget, for our society, which is fast becoming dominated by the figure of the non-skilled worker or business man, does not place a great value on skills that do not cater directly to the needs of the mass of people. In such fields, public interest is aroused more by reputation than actual product. Indeed once a composer's (or any other person's) reputation is even slightly established, no matter how, it seems as if society were ready to take its revenge on him. He is asked to serve on committees, to appear on quiz programs, to administer various projects, to write articles and the rest. All sorts of people and organizations try to get in on his prestige, appealing to his sense of public responsibility, to his desire to get works performed, and often to his need for economic support. These extraneous activities take a terrible toll of time and energy and thought away from his own work, the work which achieved his reputation.

Once these destructive forces are allowed too great an importance it can happen that the composer's activity becomes degraded to mere hack-work. He has to develop an ability to say no, for it is only then that we can get the best from him and it is only then that the musical profession can be refreshed and replenished with works of enduring validity, written in that kind of thoughtful concentration so difficult to provide in our time.

Thus it is important constantly to keep in mind that the best a composer has to give is in his compositions. If this is not so, he is not truly a composer. In his compositions he can teach, he can give life to and express all those things which, at best, he can but poorly indicate with words. And his function is most truly fulfilled toward the general student only while he is composing music—even if, at the time, the general student does not understand it. On the other hand, sometimes verbal teaching, that is, the articulation of the principles and ideas he strives to embody in his works, is a valuable part of his development as a composer; and in this case he can be a useful member of the academic world.

Wallingford Riegger

American Composers Alliance [ACA] Bulletin, 2,1 (Feb. 1952)

The present, belated recognition of Wallingford Riegger's music reveals, once again, that there are undercurrents, unsuspected depths to the American musical scene that are slow to come to the surface. But when they do, they give it greater importance and meaning. The fact that they finally emerge is refreshing at a time when so much musical activity happens in the full glare of publicity.

Riegger has followed the dictates of his own personality and musical instinct unobtrusively for years, without caring whether he was or was not in step with the fashions of the time, or, apparently, whether he would become known or his music would be performed. In a period when the prevailing styles of music were very different from his, he stuck stubbornly to his vision and wrote out of inner necessity. The general music public may have seen his name on his good teaching pieces and arrangements, but these works make no effort to reflect his highly individual style. Indeed, they seem to have been written by a different composer, and he does not include them in a list of his compositions. In this, as in all other matters, he has been quite indifferent to the familiar rules for building a composer's career. He never went in for catching the public's eye by some stroke of publicity, nor for gaining a position of power from which he could influence performers to perform his works. He has not written books, given public lectures, or written widely read articles.

While Riegger has been quietly writing music, a host of aggressive, younger composers has appeared, most of them more impatient than he to gain acclaim, or more cynical than he about the public's ability to recognize the good from the bad, or perhaps less sure than he that their music was of a quality that would eventually be noticed. So he was generally overlooked in favor of composers more determined and skillful about personal promotion. However, a number of still younger musicians, feeling the need for a change from points of view prevalent in the 1930s and '40s, have recently found him out and begun to take his music with the seriousness it deserves. So whatever success Riegger has had (and it is growing rapidly) has been purely on the basis of his music. This, after the satisfaction of actual creation, is what any composer most desires.

However, all the publicity which American music has attracted in the past twenty or thirty years has been very useful in educating the public to understand what is happening, and this increased understanding has helped the acceptance of Riegger's music. When Dimitri Mitropoulos conducts the New York Philharmonic in a performance of his *Third Symphony* later this season, the public will not consider the work difficult to understand. Yet, it is not too different in style from the *Study in Sonority*, performed by Stokowski about twenty years ago, which provoked a scandal at the time. His music still retains much the same kind of materials, but what was once so puzzling now seems fascinating and strongly expressive.

During the twenty years that elapsed between his first atonal works, such as the *Study in Sonority* written in 1927 and the *Third Symphony*, Riegger grew rapidly in stature and scope. He produced such exciting works as *Dichotomy* and his *First String Quartet* in relative isolation. As these and other of his works are played with increasing frequency, as they most surely will be, we will have added a new, important figure to the American scene and a new musical style to American tradition.

The Rhythmic Basis of American Music

The Score, 12 (June 1955)

It would be convenient if one could say—as so many have done—that the distinguishing mark of serious American music is its employment (or re-working) of the rhythms of our native folk or popular music, particularly jazz. Yet the attempt to reduce national characteristics to a few simple traits is a game that quickly wears thin in the artistic world, as in life itself. In earlier years when American music was just beginning to take shape, such an attempt may have been useful; but now that a substantial number of works has accumulated, neither critics nor composers feel it any longer necessary to emphasize national characteristics. On the contrary, instead of insisting that American music stands apart from that of Europe, it becomes interest-ing to consider the many foreign influences by which it has been nourished.

During the nineteen-twenties, jazz had a great influence on European music as well as on ours. Its impact in Europe was strong precisely because its techniques had already been anticipated by various composers. Bartók, Stravinsky, and even Schoenberg (in the first of his *Five Pieces for Orchestra*, written in 1909) had all been using irregular rhythmic patterns, and the appearance of jazz stimulated further interest in this rhythmic procedure. Indeed, European composers adopted only those aspects of jazz that had already been tried to some extent before its arrival. These very same aspects influenced the young American modernists of the time; but through greater familiarity with the source they had a different feeling for rhythm. As a result, jazz had far more effect abroad than in many quarters at home.

The American composer's relationship to jazz is in fact quite different from what one might expect. Heard constantly from every corner, this music has lost its original freshness; the techniques have become shopworn, the performances routined and dull. It is perhaps for these reasons that most composers have avoided using the jazz idiom in their concert music; and also because orchestral musicians often do not play jazz well, and cannot under the conditions of concert life be afforded the rehearsals needed for good jazz. Today in out-of-the-way places one can still find fresh lively jazz performances, and the improvisatory character of what is played is impossible to imitate with concert musicians. There are Marc Blitzstein, Leonard Bernstein, and Morton Gould, who, writing in the jazz idiom for popular consumption, have tried to place it (as Kurt Weill did) on a more meaningful and artistic level. But the majority of composers interested in this trend have drawn only on certain characteristics of popular music, combining them with other folk sources or neoclassic ones to produce works of larger scope, more interesting formal possibilities, and more variety.

There were four composers who helped to establish these techniques in the early stages of the contemporary movement in America. Roy Harris, Aaron Copland, and Roger Sessions followed the lead given them by contemporary European music and jazz and embodied a new feeling for rhythm in their music. The fourth, Charles Ives, living in seclusion, followed a different and more curious path, and his achievements are not yet well enough known to be properly judged.

Early in his career, Harris made a remark that has often been quoted: "Our rhythmic sense is less symmetrical than the European rhythmic sense. European musicians are trained to think of rhythm in its largest common denominator, while we are born with a feeling for its smallest units." Although this appeared after a number of outstanding works by Stravinsky, and Bartók had revealed the possibilities of irregular groupings of small units—which is what Harris is talking about—there is no doubt that he had a point in mind which becomes clear in the context of his own music and of jazz practice. For in spite of their irregular rhythmic patterns, written with constantly changing meters, Stravinsky and Bartók do often treat their irregular accents as displacements of regular ones by marking them with the same kind of vigor that was reserved in older music for syncopations. The quality of these accents is quite different from those used in jazz and in much new American music. In jazz, especially of the nineteen-twenties and thirties, the melodic line frequently has an independent rhythmic life; the metrical units are grouped into irregular (or regular) patterns, in melodic motives whose rhythm runs against the underlying 1, 2, 3, 4 of dance rhythm. Roy Harris carried this technique further by writing long, continuously developing melodies in which groups of two, three, four, or five units (such as eighth notes) are joined together to produce irregular stresses, but with the underlying regular beat of jazz omitted. Several such lines when sounded together produce interesting textures of "cross-accented counterpoint," which is not unlike such counterpoint found in the English madrigal school, although stressed more intensely and associated with very different types of melody. A characteristic example of this is to be found in the canonic last movement of his first *Piano Sonata* ([Op. 1] 1929).

Aaron Copland has been outspoken about his relationship with popular music both in his writings and in his composition. He drew from the jazz of the nineteen-twenties a principle of polyrhythm in which the melody is accented in regular groups of three quarter notes while the bass plays its conventional 4/4. In works closely concerned with the jazz idiom, like his *Piano Concerto* (1926), we find this polyrhythmic method extended to groupings such as 5/8, 7/8, and 5/4. In many sections of these works Copland followed jazz in sounding the regular beat but, as in Harris, there were places where the beat was not expressed. In works written a little later, such as the *Symphonic Ode* (1929) and the *Short Symphony* (1933), he dispensed with the regular beat altogether. Unlike Harris, Copland maintains a direct relationship with jazz or other kinds of American dance music, especially in his fast movements. For instance, in *El Salón México* (1936), he applied his rhythmic method to Mexican popular dances in which alternations of 6/8 (two groups of three eighth notes) and 3/4 (three groups of two eighth notes) are characteristic. Great portions of this work are made of the irregular rhythms that result from sounding these groups of two and three in such patterns as two, three, three, two, two, three. Similar patterns may be found in the faster parts of his *Piano Sonata, Clarinet Concerto*, and *Piano Quartet*. His style, far more incisive than that of Harris, has the variety of quality of accent characteristic of its American sources. But although he mentions the fact that jazz performers often play their improvisations with great rhythmic freedom, sounding their notes a bit before or after the beat, Copland has never incorporated this in his own music.

Roger Sessions carried the technique of irregular grouping to much greater extremes—particularly in contrapuntal textures—in the first movement of his *First Symphony* (1927), which is one of the most extensive essays in cross-accented counterpoint yet attempted. Although this work clearly derives from the European neoclassic school, its remarkable rhythmic shifts give it an American sound, and for this reason it exercised (together with Sessions's *First Piano Sonata*) a considerable influence on composers of the nineteen-thirties.

But this particular technique is only one of the many rhythmic devices to be found in jazz. It is well known, for instance, that in the actual interpretation of written notation a tradition of making slight distortions of note-values in the interests of rhythmic and expressive freedom has been handed down from one performer to another in the jazz world. It is a tradition surprisingly similar to that of the Baroque "notes inégales." In both, equal eighth notes are played in dotted fashion or as triplets of quarter note and eighth note. But jazz performers not only take liberties with notation, they also improvise so freely that their parts have an expressive rubato, slowing down and speeding up while the rhythm section keeps its steady beat. It is in this domain that Charles Ives worked, although much of his music was written before the technique became a common practice in jazz bands. It may already have been present, however, in the ragtime of Ives's day, as it is a tendency which is noticeable in any long-continued tradition of dance music, being occasionally found in the late periods of the waltz as well as in South and Central American popular music.

Ives went one step further than the composers mentioned above by exploring the realm of "artificial divisions"—triplets, quintuplets, and the like—to produce such complex polyrhythmic combinations that they seem to defy adequate performance or even audibility. His was usually a literary point of view in which fairly literal quotations of familiar patriotic, religious, or dance tunes are presented simultaneously with an expressive commentary in another remotely related or unrelated speed. For instance, in the second movement of *Three Places in New England*, a boy dreams of two groups of soldiers marching at different speeds, one disappearing as the other appears; in *The Unanswered Question*, the question is posed ever more insistently and rapidly by the winds while the strings play a quiet, meditative background, impassively unrelated in speed and harmony and requiring a separate conductor. This combination of different rhythmic planes involved Ives in complex problems of notation, especially in his later works, written between 1910 and 1920.

He uses three main procedures. The first consists in the superposition of different speeds that can be expressed in notation with a common unit, as in the following examples from the second movement of his *Fourth Symphony*, written in 1916 and revised and published in 1929.

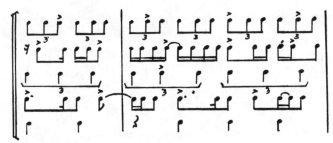

Ex. 1. Charles Ives: Symphony No. 4, second movement.
Copyright 1929 by Ch. E. Ives; © 1965 by Associated Music Publishers, Inc.

Later in the work [he shows a] greater freedom of rhythm. In Ex. 2 the second, third, and fourth lines are the rhythms of the brass and winds playing a dissonant harmonization of a national anthem, with the violas and cellos helping out in the line above the bottom. The sixth and bottom lines contain the rhythms of piano, bells, and basses playing a hymn tune in another system of dissonant harmony. The other lines are rhythms of various figurations, those of the quintuplets and septuplets belonging to the strings.

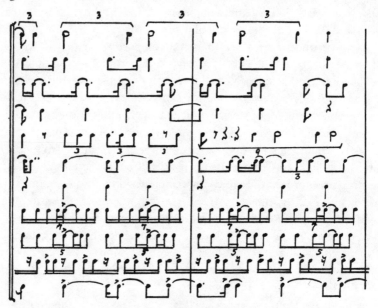

Ex. 2. Charles Ives: Symphony No. 4, second movement.
Copyright 1929 by Ch. E. Ives; © 1965 by Associated Music Publishers, Inc.

A second type of rhythmic device used by Ives consists in notated rubati on one level and strict time on another, as in *Calcium Light* (Ex. 3).

Ex. 3. Charles Ives: Calcium Light.

In a third type, two unrelated levels are heard simultaneously. In both *The Unanswered Question* and *Central Park in the Dark*, a quiet ostinato of strings directed by one conductor forms the background for faster, louder music directed by another conductor and played fragmentarily, allowing the soft background to be heard in the silences. Similar unrelated planes of music requiring the services of several conductors occur in the *Fourth Symphony* and other of Ives's later works.

These various procedures, so novel and occasionally of remarkable effectiveness, were described in Henry Cowell's book, *New Musical Resources* (New York, 1930), but have gained little currency because the great difficulties of performance that they involve have proved a real deterrent to a number of composers interested in continuing Ives's methods. A striking resolution of this problem has been made by Conlon Nancarrow, a composer who patiently measures and perforates his compositions on player-piano rolls. Not having to be concerned with performance, he has composed a number of interesting works, including three *Rhythm Studies* derived from the jazz idiom and employing unusual polyrhythms. In the most elaborate measures of his *Rhythm Study No. 1* four distinct planes of rhythm are combined, as will be seen in Ex. 4.

Ex. 4. Conlon Nancarrow: Rhythm Study No. 1.
Copyright 1952 by Theodore Presser Company.

Since the player-piano cannot accent individual notes, the third line of chords in this example marks the accents of the groups of seven of the notes on the first staff. The polyrhythmic combinations are: first and second staves—three against two, grouped in figures of seven and three, respectively; first and fifth staves—five against two; second and fourth—eight against three; second and fifth—five against three; fourth and fifth—five against eight. The whole produces a most novel sound.

The works of Ives and Nancarrow are scarcely known even in America,* but they attest to a continuing interest in rhythm which seems a part of the American scene. A few, such as Henry Brant and the author, have worked in this field. Brant has followed Ives in using a technique of unrelated or "uncoördinated" rhythm, as he calls it. The author's approach is discussed elsewhere in this issue.**

It must be said, however, that only a few American composers are seriously concerned with rhythmic problems. Owing to the influence of Copland, Harris, and Sessions, many seem to have an innate rhythmic sense that is different from that of European composers. But there has been little temptation to explore the field, since each of these three has lately become much more conservative in this respect, and performances of their rhythmically difficult works have been rare.

* This article was published in England.—Eds.
** William Glock: "A Note on Elliott Carter," *The Score*, no. 12 (June 1955): 47–52.—Eds.

Current Chronicle: New York, 1959

[Review of the *Violin Concerto* by Roger Sessions]

The Musical Quarterly, 45,3 (July 1959)

Roger Sessions's music has increasingly come to grips with the most serious and important issue that has faced contemporary music when considered in terms of its own internal development, that is, the important task of finding new forms for the new material. Many composers have been aware of the need to find a continuity that would allow them to translate into the most typical of musical dimensions, subjective time, the implications of the new 20th-century world of rhythms, linear and textural shapes, harmonic fields, and all manner of new qualities of physical sound. We can see Debussy facing this problem in his late sonatas and *Douze Études*, Schoenberg in occasional early and late works like the *Five Orchestra Pieces* and the *Trio*, Bartók in his *Piano Sonata* and *Third String Quartet*, Stravinsky in a number of works, particularly the *Symphony in Three Movements*. In this country, more than anywhere else, this matter seems to have engaged the attention not only of many younger composers, who have in their background a number of experimental works such as those of Varèse and Chávez, but also of the more traditionally oriented composers, of whom Sessions has been most devoted to this particular enterprise. It is a problem that has led the Darmstadt group to impatiently giving the whole musical vocabulary a thorough arithmetical shaking up, often without too much concern for producing audible and musically intelligible continuities of sound. For it is not an easy thing to develop a new and meaningful type of musical continuity. It must be undertaken by slow, rather intuitive steps, since the condition of "meaningfulness" presupposes a cooperative development in the composer and in some qualified listeners of a grasp of musical relationships not previously clearly recognized, coupled with an ability to test them against some standard of interest and meaningfulness.

Beginning with his music for *The Black Maskers* (1923) Sessions has gone through a musical evolution of unusual scope, since each of the three technical and esthetic areas of his time became in turn a center of interest for him and contributed to his way of musical thinking. The devices of blurring, of crowding sonorities by figurational activity in "close position," the meaningful use of instrumental and registeral tone-color, the shimmering backgrounds that in him have become contrapuntal—these are some of the marks of an Impressionism that was more prominent in his early works and that still can be glimpsed, although completely transformed, in such a recent work as his *Third Symphony*. Likewise, the sharply defined, vigorously incisive, rhythmic drive of primitivism and neo-Classicism as well as the intense, highly concentrated and characterized gestures of Expressionism furnished a springboard for the different techniques Sessions uses. To talk of his Impressionist beginnings of around 1923, his neo-Classic period from about 1926 to 1937, and his Expressionist period from then until now does great violence to the facts although it sheds some illumination. It is true that his "neo-Classic" works are much more tonally centered than his more recent works. They also contain certain turns of phrase, figurations, rhythms that link them to other composers' works in this style. The recent compositions, however, while approaching the "atonal," employ materials and methods very remotely related to any other composer's style. Even his use of twelve-tone patterns is freer and more personal than that of many others.

The significant continuity techniques, one of the explicable things that give his music its interest and importance, seem to have become much more focused and intentional in the *Violin Concerto** (1931–35) than in the previous *First Piano Sonata* (1930) and the *First Symphony* (1927), a fact, of course, that does not detract from these latter as works of art. These techniques can be best illustrated by a comparison of Exx. 1 and 2.

Ex. 1. First Movement (opening).

Ex. 2 Scherzo (second movement).

In Ex. 1, the very opening of the Concerto, the trombone plays directional motif "A," rising in five diatonic steps from tonic to dominant of B minor. This is immediately answered by the similar tone-color of the trumpet playing directional motif "B" in the same dynamic and note values, a figure whose overall pattern is a rapid rise and descent over a diminished eleventh. However, within this arch the figure changes direction every two notes except for the three that descend at the end of the measure. Its character, aided by a crescendo and diminuendo mark, is much more intense, both because of the expressive jumps of augmented fourth, major seventh, and diminished octave and the total distance it covers and because of its chromatic nature. Likewise there are a number of perfect fourths which are very much a feature of this motif, as can be seen in the harmonies of "B" in the first measure of Ex. 6. To these two brass figures, two flutes add, in homophonic style, the suggestion of an interrupted cadence in E minor, against a pedal of F♯. As any musician realizes at once, these brief, striking, yet rather bare measures are filled with implications—they are in fact a tiny summary of a great deal that is to follow, even prefiguring the final cadence, which holds F♯ and D after everything else has been stopped by a short, accented tonic note in the bass. The two directional motifs "A" and "B" are met with throughout the work. Whether this is a consciously contrived feature or whether it is the result of a very integrated conception of another sort would be hard to tell from the score, particularly because the connection between one idea and another is not always as clear as that which exists between Ex. 1 and the opening of the Scherzo (second movement) shown in Ex. 2.

In Ex. 3, a later episode in the Scherzo, motif "A" does not appear until an introductory motif of minor thirds is dwelt on—perhaps derived from the

Ex. 3. Scherzo (second movement).

first two eighths of Ex. 2. When it does appear, its intervals are different than in Ex. 1 or Ex. 2, its joint to motif "B" is like that of Ex. 2, and the pattern of reversal of direction at each two notes is more strictly adhered to than in Ex. 2. That these three thematic ideas are related would be grasped quite quickly by the listener.

However, in the opening of the short third movement, a Romanza (Ex. 4), one cannot be so sure whether the rise of five notes over irregular intervals should be related to "A" or not and even less sure whether the descent can be related to "B," although the last four notes suggest the possibility. Later in this movement the connection with "B" is made somewhat more definite. In the opening of the tarantella-like finale, a cadenza is played by the violin

Ex. 4. Romanza (third movement).

Ex. 5. Finale (opening).

alone (Ex. 5). Many would doubt whether the composer intended to recall the opening, although certainly the similarity cannot be fortuitous.

This brief survey of some of the themes of a work whose main feature is a wealth of long, beautifully shaped singing or rhythmic lines and figurations that move in very broad sweeps is not intended to state whether such an overall unification of the themes was striven for by the composer or not, but simply to examine the score, and to point out a tissue of connections which must strike the listener at once since it seems to operate not only on a large scale but also in the joining even of details, and of one small phrase with another. For instance, this is evidently at work in the connection between two relatively dissimilar contrapuntal lines, the beautiful cantilena with

Ex. 6. First Movement.

which the violin makes its first appearance and the slow motion of regular eighths played by the violas in octaves (Ex. 6). There are obviously many degrees of similarity possible between phrases controlled by the same directional motif, and when directionality is used with other kinds of remote relationships such as imitation of outline, ornamentation, and simplification, directional inversions, etc., the play of these could be likened to the use of metaphor and simile in poetry that results in the fascinating effects described in Empson's *Seven Types of Ambiguity*.

Ex. 6 also exhibits another important feature: the predominance of an overall process of continuity on which the harmonic, textural, dynamic, and expressive changes have only a slight deflective effect. Here the two separate registers, kept apart for many measures; the constant flow of eighths with approximately six in a group; the violin's gradual descent using a mixture of quarters, eighths, and long notes, with abrupt rises just before the beginning of each phrase; and the unity of dynamics represent a frame for uniform progress, just as Ex. 1 did. As in it, there are many sudden shifts of intervallic tension, both melodically and harmonically. This way of combining certain techniques used in a uniform, rather neutral way with others used in an intense or highly irregular way is like the use of harmony in some works of Brahms and Fauré in which an overall melodic and figurational pattern of considerable regularity and restricted range persists while sudden, very intense harmonic changes are taking place. Stravinsky's works abound in examples of such dissociations of techniques, Alban Berg's in the coordination of techniques.

During the progress of the overall continuity pattern Sessions uses, there is usually an increase and decrease in definition and individualization of motif, of rhythm, or of some other feature or group of features. Sometimes only the increasing or decreasing portions of this pattern are used. For instance, the first movement of the *Violin Concerto* comprises three clearly separated sections, each introduced by what sounds very much like (but never is) a transposed repetition of Ex. 1, each time more extended and differently orchestrated. The first of these sections, 56 measures, of which Ex. 6 gives the first ten preceded by the last measure of the introduction, emphasizes the particular expressive quality found in Ex. 1 that comes from its bareness of texture, its regularity of rhythm, and its abrupt changes of harmonic tension. Over the 56 measures this quality is made more intense in the middle and finally more attenuated with no more literalness of repetition than can be heard in Ex. 6. The second section, on the other hand, draws an entirely different consequent from Ex. 1, a graceful, light motion of sixteenths built of a mixture of staccato and legato, repeated notes, and the interval of a sixth, the repetition of which over a held chord forms the delicate climax of the movement. The falling away of this is accomplished by repeating the climactic moment each time more softly. Thus the second section brings into greater focus the graceful quality implied in Ex. 1. The third and last section recalls the other two, gradually reducing them to neutrality and quiet.

More and more the notion of extended, continuously flowing sections during which ideas come to the surface, gain clarity and definition, and then sink back into the general flow has characterized Sessions's unique style, and he seems to have striven for this first here.

When Sessions wrote this work, the 20th-century concerto had reached a rather fixed stage of development through the combined efforts of Stravinsky, Prokofiev, and Hindemith. Shunning the Classical opposition of solo and orchestra, it had turned, of course, to the Baroque form for assistance in finding a way to organize concertos in which the solo was the prime mover and in which the orchestra is used mainly to intensify and amplify the solo part. Sessions carries this method further than any of his predecessors. The violin dominates the orchestra in every sense, playing almost continuously a part of prime thematic or figurational importance; it is never dwarfed or overwhelmed in volume of sound, intensity of expression, or brilliance by the orchestra. Yet the orchestra has a typical life of its own. This remarkable feat not merely reveals high skill but must be the result of careful choosing of characters, themes, and all other devices with the final end in mind.

It was finished just before the *Violin Concerto* of Alban Berg, but under cultural conditions so vastly different that the achievement of such an outstanding work represents an even more remarkable artistic triumph—a triumph over the apathy, cultural confusion, and uncertainty that caused its subsequent neglect. For here there were then, and are even now, few incentives within or without the musical profession to recognize, encourage, cherish, or promote effectively such real excellence in our own music. If there were, this work would be as well known here (and elsewhere) as its outstanding European peers. Instead, like many important works it has been lent a specious importance by being tagged an "example" of some trend and thus given a ghostly existence in prose, when its special, powerful uniqueness that brings together so much into one imaginative whole is what gives it its importance. Even at the Thursday night performance, its première at the New York Philharmonic, played beautifully by Tossy Spivakovsky and conducted with care by Leonard Bernstein, the latter felt it necessary to introduce it by the brief description: "An example of complicated music written here during the thirties."

Current Chronicle: Italy
[Review of the ISCM Festival, Rome, 1959]

The Musical Quarterly, 45,4 (Oct. 1959)

The Italian Section of the International Society for Contemporary Music and the RAI-Radiotelevisione Italiana were hosts this June 10–16 in Rome to the ISCM delegates and to the unusually interesting festival for which their jury had chosen six programs. Two more concerts of prize-winning works in a contest sponsored by the Italian Section, the Radio, and a number of Italian publishers made up the generous number that formed the thirty-third festival held annually except during the war and the fifth given in Italy. Since the Society was founded in 1922 by a few far-sighted composers and musicologists, of whom the late Edward Dent was its active president for many years, the question of its continuation has come up repeatedly. For it has been beset by great political and artistic troubles, and the increasing public acceptance of new music, its more frequent and widespread performance, in the belief of many has robbed the Society of one of its main reasons for existence. Yet it persists and seems likely to go on, for unlike many similar organizations, this one has laid its main emphasis on live performance—performance of new, forward-looking works that were judged imaginative and talented and that would engage the attention of cultivated musicians—and not on the manufacturing of propaganda. Occasionally some of the works on the programs have been disappointing, yet at each festival enough were important or remarkable and enough more contained moments of special musical interest—sometimes combined with instructive miscalculations—to make the majority of delegates feel that the effort was worthwhile. Of course, besides offering this important professional experience to musicians, the Society has repeatedly brought to light new scores of merit that were later presented to a larger public. The opportunity for sympathetic performance before intelligent audiences and the possibility of arousing knowing enthusiasm and encouragement—familiar features of these festivals—have helped many a young composer over the trying period between his finding himself and his finding his public. It is hard to imagine how modern music could have become what it is without the Society's activity.

During each festival, delegates from the sections discuss, among other things, questions of policy that invariably arise from the stresses of the double commitment of the Society, "international" and "contemporary." When it was founded, there was no question about what kind of music it was committed to encourage. As its influence spread in the late twenties and early thirties, "advanced" young composers flocked to its performances— and stayed to run it in their middle age—now. Therefore, the problem of whether to continue as champion of the older, now accepted styles of many of its composer-members, indeed whether to perform older, established composers at all, or to keep up with the more advanced trends of the young has become a matter of controversy. Its present president, Dr. Heinrich Strobel, and one of its vice presidents, the young French critic Claude Rostand, are definitely in favor of rejuvenation, to a return, really, to the basic reason for existence of the Society. There are members of the German, Italian, English, Swedish, and Japanese sections of this opinion.

But to list these five sections is to imply the opposition or wish for compromise of others and at once the problem of the second commitment, international representation, arises. This problem has been much complicated by the large number of composers like Ernst Krenek or Roberto Gerhard who changed citizenship after establishing their reputations. For not falling clearly into a national group, they tend to be neglected, although in 1955 the English submitted a score of the former Spaniard, Gerhard, and the Swiss of the former Russian, [Wladimir] Vogel. Obviously the reason sections have joined this society is to present the new music written in their country before an international audience, to learn what is being done elsewhere, and to join in an exchange of music, experiences, musical judgments, and esthetics. To keep this exchange on a certain high level of quality and contemporaneity, the delegates screen quite carefully new applications for admission and watch over the progress of each section especially when there are drastic changes of personnel. Each section wants to be represented as often as possible on the festival programs, and considerable dissatisfaction is felt when its country's name is omitted for several years. Since the festivals have a maximum length in terms of both the interest of the audiences and financial outlay, various rules have been tried to assure fairness; the most recent, adopted shortly after the war, gave to each section in good standing the right to at least one performance every three years. The United States, under this plan, has figured as one of the favored nations, having had two or three works played each year, though this time but one.[1]

As a former international juror, this reviewer had it clearly brought home to him that the modern styles he was familiar with in America were prevalent in almost every country. To realize that each, whether a centrally located European country or one halfway around the world, had its representatives of the old-fashioned Romantic, the "motoric" neo-Classic, the folkloristic (whether polymodal or polytonal), and the Expressionistic schools and that the "advanced" of each country were adopting twelve-tone techniques and even, in some scattered places, the Darmstadt methods described in *die reihe*, gives one the impression that the ISCM has succeeded too well in exporting all the styles of Europe to the ends of the earth. But as a juror, one sees that what all jurors of this festival must have sought from the beginning was liveliness of imagination, avoiding the grey neutrality that infests these styles as they travel from country to country. One also realizes that the styles themselves have been enriched by ideas brought from elsewhere to these and similar concerts—ideas that, perhaps because of the incoherent cultural conditions in the places where they originated, were scarcely noticed, not developed, and seldom given the striking embodiment supported by cultural propaganda that they receive in the more unified and intellectually alert milieu of Europe. Cases of this are the contributions of such very diverse American musicians as Ives, Varèse, Babbitt, and Cage to the thinking of many younger Europeans, ideas that will become known in the world— even finally in the United States, through the works now being written abroad. Outside of Europe, few countries submit works of unusual character, it seems, with the possible exceptions of the U.S.A. and Japan. Often, as in the case of this festival, Japan has supplied a very striking work, such as the *Samai* [for orchestra (1957)] of Yoritsune Matsudaira—a compelling combination of total serialization and antique Japanese court dance music. The score provided a striking musical experience of the type that helps to make the festivals a success by offering relief from the rather routine quality of so many scores that have to be played because of the three-year rule. Also Milton Babbitt's *Two Sonnets*, although much milder in impact, owing to a restrained instrumentation, was a moment of highly organized music un-usual in approach. Both helped the programs on which they appeared and yet both certainly are not characteristic of the mainstream of their native music as many at home must see it. For choosing a series of interesting and varied programs out of the bundles of six scores submitted by the juries of each section leaves a great deal to chance. One year four violin concertos of similar style were submitted by four different countries, for instance. There-fore, it is not surprising that this year's jury included Stravinsky's *Agon*, Dallapiccola's *Tartiniana II* [for violin and piano (1956)], Boulez's *Improvi-sations sur Mallarmé*, Messiaen's *Oiseaux exotiques*, and Nono's *Incontri*, although not submitted by the sections, "in the general interest of the programs."

The review of his section's past year, usually given orally by each delegate, was dispensed with at Rome, and written reports were allowed to suffice. By far the most impressive was the 153-page *Neue Musik in* [*der Bundesrepu-blik*] *Deutschland 1958/59*, edited by the German Section, printed by Schott, and prepared, perhaps, to help persuade the delegates (who did not need it) to accept the German invitation of next spring's festival to Cologne. The booklet listed some 150 live concerts, 50 of them orchestral, entirely of contemporary music; also innumerable new works played on programs of old music and even more on radio programs during this past season. The quality was, on the whole, both high and challenging, and all schools were generously represented. Acknowledged masters like Stravinsky and Bartók led in number of performances. Schoenberg had about 36, which included several operas, numerous orchestral, and important chamber works. Ad-vanced young composers received sizable numbers. Luigi Nono, for in-stance, had 11, more than half of which were of large choral works. Of music recently composed, Stravinsky's *Threni* received 6, as did two works on the ISCM festival: Fortner's excellent twelve-tone *Impromptus* and Henze's highly romantic *Nachtstücke und Arien*. Pitifully few American works were played.

The Swedish report gave the programs of seven chamber music concerts, one of which was presented by John Cage and David Tudor along the lines familiar to their New York audiences. As a novel experiment the Swedish radio gave six live concerts of new music coordinated with the appearance of each of six issues of the new modern music magazine *Nutida Musik* in which was discussed the music about to be played at the concert.

The United States Section had no report to submit. Since the spring of 1955 it has given no concerts in New York, confining its activities to awarding commissions, paying its annual international dues and the costs of engaging soloists for the American works played at the festivals, electing a delegate to the central assembly, and choosing and sending its allotment of six scores annually to the festival jury.[2] Even in its most active years, the United States Section was never able to operate on the scale of those sections supported partly or wholly by state cultural funds or state radio taxes. Its fight for continuance during concert seasons was so demanding that it could never expand enough to be able to include foreign works in reciprocation for American works played abroad. All it could do was to give badly needed hearings to local composers and to works acknowledged elsewhere to be of prime importance and not known here, such as the all-Webern concert given in 1952 at New York.

The necessities involved in developing a contemporary musical culture seem to be fairly clear to the important European countries, necessities that are more difficult to satisfy in our widely spread-out country, perhaps, than in the close confines of a European one. Only frequent, widespread performance of the best, most interesting of American and other contemporary music before professionals and public can remedy this situation. At least, then, many would have a similar basis of experience and, one hopes, understanding. For no amount of panel discussions, congresses, reports, articles, and reviews will ever do much good unless they refer to the common musical experience of the speaker and reader. From what has been said above, it should be obvious that the Europeans have begun to accomplish this since the war and that Europe is fast becoming again the source of our musical culture. The fact that money can be found to print an English version of *die reihe* and none to print a contemporary music magazine of our own is a sign of our sad plight.

The difficulty the United States Section has of operating on a small scale becomes paralyzing whenever it has considered inviting the festival here. It is true that during the war the section gave two festivals, without, of course, the sanction of the central committee, which had ceased to exist. Now it is especially to be wished for, since we have been treated so generously at festivals and by the sections of many countries. Some of the directors of the United States Section thought it might be appropriate to give such a festival around the time of the opening of the Lincoln Center in New York City. But to find people familiar with the festival's problems who could also spend the vast amount of time and effort it would take to convince those who would have either to pay or play, and to do all this several years in advance of the fact (bids for festivals in '61 and '62 have already been made) was considered impossible. Indeed, in view of the far from brilliant record of performances in America of important new European scores, the delegates from other sections would need a lot of convincing that we would be able to meet the standards of performance common to most recent festivals. Because the international delegates must long ago have given up expecting either kind of reciprocation from the United States, one has a rather strange mixture of pride and embarrassment that so much American music has been played by the ISCM.

This reviewer does not feel that he can dismiss with a brief phrase the many fine, imaginative, and conscientiously composed scores heard in Rome—many of which need several hearings to be judged seriously. Quite a number certainly deserve the extended discussions frequently given in these pages to works that interest their critics, but because of the abundance at the festival, all must be penalized for lack of space.

Reflecting what seems to be an almost universal movement outside the Soviet Union and a few other countries not in contact with the mainstream of new music, almost all the scores, even of those composers who once wrote differently, could not have been written without the preparatory effort of the Viennese Three, either through their compositions or more often through the twelve-tone method by which these composers revealed the typical earlier 20th-century concern with musical design, or more indirectly through techniques derived from this method without concern for its original intentions, stressing instead "sound." As in Impressionism, here tone-color, register, attack, texture, perhaps dynamics, and "time"—the physical materials assume prime importance—are the subject matter of the composition, as "space," the physical materials of painting and their types of application, has become the subject matter of the Abstract Expressionist painter. In the music that depends on design, the colorist elements are used to emphasize or more completely characterize interval structure, motif, rhythm, and their combinations into musical "ideas," themes, chords. This kind of music assumes an experienced listener who can grasp and remember the initial groupings of these "ideas" and "follow" their uses and transformations. From this, musical meaning emerges. With the adoption of "sound" as the primary concept, the elements of design tend to be reduced to vagueness, to unobtrusive amorphousness, and so, in appealing to the ear's ability to distinguish contrasts of all kinds of physical sound-qualities, this procedure makes very little demand on the listener's memory and for this reason has frequently attracted with its striking sounds a musically inexperienced public that would be completely at sea in front of music that depended more on design.

In this festival more than ever before, this division was very pronounced. Almost all the works of the talented young European composers were written deeply under the influence of the "sound" concept, particularly as it has been developed in Darmstadt. One cannot fail to realize how much more fruitful in possibilities and more challenging to the imagination these new ideas are than were the neo-Classic ones the young subscribed to twenty years ago. Of course, just as then, there are a lot of unimportant taboos and formularized "musts" that the less individual composers faithfully repro- duce. Yet when one hears works of the young like *Prolation for Orchestra* by the Englishman Peter Maxwell Davies, or *Tre Studi* by the Italian Aldo Clementi, or the *Canticum Psalmi Resurrectionis* of the German Dieter Schönbach, the vast new domain of musical thought that is opening up offers an exciting prospect that gives their music much freshness.

The more completely realized works of the festival can be put fairly clearly into the two categories distinguished above. All three of the American works depended clearly on design. In Milton Babbitt's *Two Sonnets* and George Rochberg's *Cheltenham Concerto* (one of the prize winners) tone-color was soberly used; in Babbitt's work the expressive vocal line was allowed to be the main feature, in Ramiro Cortes's *String Quartet* (another prize winner) the lyrical quality came from linear design. Europeans were not so ascetic in the use of color to emphasize design. Wolfgang Fortner's *Impromptus* for orchestra have a bold, strong shape helped along by clear-colored orchestra- tion; relying much more on intervals and rhythmic motifs than on "themes," the work produces a striking impression. Don Banks's elegantly written and very changeable *Three Studies* for cello and piano made much of the instruments, while Michael Gielen's highly effective, clearly articulated setting of *Vier Gedichte von Stefan George* for mixed chorus, six assorted clarinets, and some other instruments was perhaps the most memorable of the works directly derived from the Viennese compositions, but nevertheless full of personal intensity. Of a somewhat freer type, depending on design, were Tadeusz Baird's unusual *Quatre Essais* for an orchestra that included two pianos, two harps, and harpsichord with the usual instruments, and Ingvar Lidholm's highly dramatic and declamatory *Skaldens Natt* for chorus and orchestra (a prize-winning work), filled with astonishing, abrupt changes of character. Even more free was Hans Werner Henze's *Nachtstücke und Arien*, three of the former alternating with two of the latter, for soprano and orchestra, which depended for their unity on intensity of poetic feeling and taste, since the variety of styles, textures, melodic shapes, and degrees of dissonance is so great that the listener might be reminded of certain not well integrated but extravagant moving picture scores if the music were not so imaginatively constructed and so unified in mood.

A few works fall between the two categories, like Goffredo Petrassi's *Serenata* and, perhaps, Messiaen's fantastic *Oiseaux exotiques*, a counterpoint of bird calls scored for piano and winds, in that they depend on design as well as sound for their effect. While those that feature the concern with "sound" were Yoritsune Matsudaira's *Samai*, [Luigi] Nono's *Incontri*, [Alois] Zimmermann's *Omnia tempus habent*, [Pierre] Boulez's *Improvisations sur Mallarmé*, and finally, the work that many thought was the best on the programs, *Ein irrender Sohn* by the youngest composer to be played, the Swedish Bo Nilsson.

This reviewer found great pleasure in Petrassi's fantastic little *Serenata* [1958] for harpsichord, flute, viola, contrabass, and percussion because of its great freedom of movement, which at times sounded like very advanced serial music while at the same time appealing to the listener's sense of audible order. It begins with a flute solo (Ex. 1) of the demanding nature that many

Ex. 1. Goffredo Petrassi: Serenata (1958).
Copyright 1958 by Edizioni Suvini Zerboni—Milan.

advanced Europeans now write encouraged by their champion, Severino Gazzelloni, the first flutist of the RAI orchestra, who delights in overcoming every difficulty (including double-stops) on his instrument.[3]

Especially interesting, because of its unusual use of sonorities, was the second of two *Improvisations sur Mallarmé* by Pierre Boulez, using the poem *Une Dentelle s'abolit* (Ex. 2). It treats piano, harp, vibraphone, bells, and celesta as ringing instruments, using percussion largely for producing upbeat crescendos leading to ictuses of the bell sounds. Against this a voice sings the text in elaborate Expressionistic vocalises. At first hearing, one is

Ex. 2. Pierre Boulez: Improvisations sur Mallarmé II.
Copyright 1959 by Universal Edition (London) Ltd.

struck by the constant use of unisons to prolong notes in ever-varying arpeggiation, and the slow introduction of one note after another into the ringing chords and their arpeggiation in the voice. The prolongation of chords and their slow shifting around common tones was, of course, characteristic of Impressionist composers (whom, perhaps because of the Mallarmé text, Boulez is evoking) and has been uncommon until recently. The groups of grace notes (as in Chopin) are to be played *ad libitum* before or within a beat, wherever they are placed visually.

This *ad libitum* playing, a feature given the approval of "new" at Darmstadt a few years ago (formerly used, of course, by composers to suggest to the performer a style of playing found in the improvisations of folk or popular performers, and for similar reasons in our time by Ives, who encouraged great latitude of interpretation in his prefaces and even in the notation of his scores), found an extreme demonstration in Bo Nilsson's 26-measure piece *Ein irrender Sohn* for alto voice, alto flute, and 18 other players,[4] all distributed, as in some works of Henry Brant, around the concert hall, according to a seating plan given in the score, with only the conductor on the stage. In Rome, the more conventional alternative of seating the performers on the stage was used with a good deal of reason, since some parts have many groups of grace notes and others are notated with even more rhythmic freedom—dots being placed in various parts of a measure without indicating time values—and if the instrumentalists were spread out, it might be difficult to achieve an ensemble. Especially if the exceptional places, indicated by vertical connecting lines, where notes are attacked together, are to be accurate. This work actually has a simple continuity established by a free-sounding improvisation of the alto flute for the first fourteen measures, continued at the fifteenth by the voice in the same style; later the two alternate until the end. Against this constant core of sound, all sorts of sudden high, low, loud, soft sounds are played in a highly irregular way, sometimes in groups, sometimes alone—all quite unpredictably. This surrounds the core with a hazy, uncertain, and agreeable dust of sound, which might perhaps be much the same, given the instruments and the above description, no matter what notes were played. Having heard several works of Nilsson, this reviewer finds them gifted and intriguing. One of the less complicated measures of the work will illustrate the notational method (Ex. 3; all notes sound as written).

A number of other Americans, besides the three composers, contributed to the success of this festival. Gloria Davy's marvelous performance of the two arias in the Henze work, Herbert Handt's expressive and accurate singing of the difficult vocal part of Klaus Huber's [cantata *Des Engels Anredung an die Seele*], and finally Francis Travis's conducting of the Bo Nilsson (which gives the conductor complete freedom as to tempos) showed that there are a number of Americans perfectly able to deal with the most

Ex. 3. Bo Nilsson: Ein irrender Sohn.
Copyright 1958 by Universal Edition (London) Ltd.

difficult problems of contemporary music. In the lavish program booklet designed and edited by the Society's general secretary, Robert W. Mann, the bobolink, the wood-thrush, the mockingbird, the Baltimore oriole, and many other American birds were credited with calls used in Messiaen's *Oiseaux exotiques*. For readers of these pages, perhaps the most interesting and concealed American contribution, in view particularly of his outspoken lack of artistic sympathy for it, is that of Everett Helm, who as U. S. Army Theatre and Music Officer in Wiesbaden, helped to establish the Darmstadt School after the war and at various times since has saved it from being overwhelmed by numerous situations that have threatened its existence.[5] By this he has earned the gratitude of a whole generation of young European musicians.

NOTES

1. Brazil, Czechoslovakia, Chile, Korea, Mexico, New Zealand, Norway, South Africa, Spain, and Switzerland were not played at the regular concerts in Rome. Germany and Sweden had three works apiece; Austria, France, Italy, and Poland two each; Argentina, Denmark, Finland, Great Britain, Holland, Japan, U.S.A., and Yugoslavia one each. To these the jury added five works not submitted by the sections (and not to be counted as national representations). The two prize-contest concerts added two more American and two more German works, and one each of England, Italy, Sweden, and Switzerland. Of the sections not performed, some were being penalized for not paying their dues, others did not submit scores, while the rest had not submitted works of sufficient interest to the international jury, and did not have to be played this year.

2. The few regional chapters that continue to give concerts have lost contact with the central section in New York, neither submitting scores for the U. S. jury to choose from for the festival, nor contributing funds to help pay the annual international dues, nor sending their programs to indicate whether the nature of their activities justifies their continued use of the ISCM name.

3. The Nilsson and Boulez examples are copyright 1958 and 1959, respectively, by Universal Edition (London) Ltd.; used by permission.

4. The instrumentation of Nilsson's work is interesting: alto voice, alto flute, viola and double bass (both played only pizzicato), piano, harp, electric mandolin, electric guitar, xylorimba, celesta, keyed glockenspiel, vibraphone, bells, timpani, very high and high maracas, medium and low Schellenbäume, high, medium, and low suspended cymbals, low and very low gongs, four Korean woodblocks from high to low, high and medium snare drums, low and very low tambourines, very high and medium bongos, low and very low congas, very high and high castanets, and very high, medium, and low triangles.

5. Described in Antoine Goléa, *Rencontres avec Pierre Boulez*, Paris, 1958, pp.72–75.

A Further Step / (1958)

The American Composer Speaks—1770–1965, ed.
Gilbert Chase (Baton Rouge: Louisiana State University
Press, 1966); originally published as "Un paso adelante,"
Buenos Aires Musical, 14, special number (Dec. 1959).

At present a new situation seems to be taking shape in the field of musical composition. Many young and a few older composers are being driven by what appears to be an imperious need to find a new principle of musical structure. Up to now, twentieth-century composers have explored new domains of harmony and their implications and have tried experiments with rhythm, timbre, and sonority; but for the most part they have employed these new materials in familiar contexts, and often produced expressive or formal effects similar to those found in older music. But today—as befits an art whose formative dimension is time—the techniques of continuity and contrast, of qualities and types of motion, of the formation and development of a musical idea or event, and in general the various kinds of cause and effect patterns that can be suggested in musical flow, occupy the attention of composers more than harmony or other matters all of which now become simply details in a larger kind of concern.

In this view, no item, no unifying principle or method of continuity is self-evident or considered a given part of musical process, but all are considered in the light of the whole and included or worked over so as to be able to fit the general scheme. Such a re-examination of musical discourse seems inevitable now, and a necessary culmination of all the different efforts of composers in our century. The intention is somewhat similar to the emancipation of musical discourse that took place during the time of Bach's sons and the Mannheim School, although today's is much more thoroughgoing. As in the products of that period, there have been many suggestions of change preceding the present transformation.

The first formulation of this recent direction was made by Debussy in his letters and articles, in which he made it plain that he was seeking a new and fresher musical psychology that did not use such classical devices as development and sequence. His ideas are, of course, wonderfully carried out in the later works, although within a limited frame. The influence of his point of view was widespread, leaving its effect on Stravinsky, particularly in the work dedicated to Debussy's memory, the *Symphonies of Wind Instruments*, and in the remarkable *Symphony in Three Movements*, a work that gives a first impression of being a loose construction of short condensed ideas but with familiarity reveals a tight organization of inner relationships that provides an entirely new solution for the problem of large-scale continuity.

In Vienna the influence of Debussy's ideas fell on fertile ground, as shown particularly in the works written there before the adoption of the twelve-tone method, such as Schoenberg's *Five Orchestral Pieces* and *Pierrot Lunaire*, Alban Berg's *Four Pieces for Clarinet and Piano* and *Three Orchestral Pieces*, and Webern's *Bagatelles*. These and other works of the time give a glimpse of a new universe of emancipated discourse, unfortunately quickly abandoned when Schoenberg returned to the classical musical shapes upon adopting the twelve-tone system.

Similar explorations can be found in some of the music of Sibelius and Janáček, in the early works of Chávez and [Arthur] Lourié, and to a lesser extent in Charles Ives and Roy Harris, as well as in a number of scarcely remembered Americans and in some Russians from before the time of Stalin. This trend remained secondary, emerging only from time to time, as in Schoenberg's *String Trio*, Opus 45 (1946), a work that is significant for its combination of the twelve-tone method with the emancipated discourse of his earlier period. Even today, this development is not clearly discerned by critics, who confound it with stylistic trends that have at times come to grips with the problem as "serial technique," "pointillism," or "expressionism." Clearly, none of these is necessarily associated with the other, nor are they mutually exclusive since each comes from a different category of description.

While it is not the point of this article to maintain the very dubious notion that artistic quality appears only in the musically advanced works, still it must be pointed out that new directions and ideas in art exercise in our day an increasing influence, even on conservatives. One of the present problems among musicians is that of keeping abreast of the time, since the musical world like any other professional world of today is in a state of very rapid change. The purpose here is simply to try to establish a general description of the direction which many different trends seem to be taking today, to consider a few of the many reasons for this, and to speculate on the problems of artistic quality and intelligibility that these new departures seem to raise. One of the most interesting and perplexing of these problems is that of the extent to which our judgment of "musicality," or of the possibility of important communication that a work contains, depends on the carrying over of pre-established patterns, both of attitude and of method, from familiar works that unquestionably have these qualities.

When listening to the recent works of Stravinsky, such as *Agon* or the *Canticum Sacrum*, or Copland's new *Piano Fantasy*, there can be no doubt in the mind of the listener accustomed to new music that these works make the kind of impression that more immediately accessible music never can. They may now be perplexing to many of the musical public because of their unusual sound and unfamiliar ideas and procedures; but to those listeners for whom modernity holds no terrors, they are on the same high level as many works of the older concert repertory. Hence they will, sooner or later, unquestionably become accessible to the larger public. At first hearing, we are struck by their artistic power and unity of vision, all the more remarkable as having been achieved by integrating very conflicting currents of feeling, thought, and technique, and by using this integration in a positive way to communicate a musical experience of commanding importance. Just as in the classics of the repertory, there are many levels of different pre-established techniques in these works. There is first of all the personal vision of the composer and his high standards of integration and of musical interest, which in turn are part of his sense of professional responsibility. There is the personal musical point of view that involves using a musical commentary on other styles as a feature of one's own expression. Then there are the many stylistic and formal features, small and large, that have become part of the composer's vocabulary over the years—a mixture of digested techniques drawn from other music, with predilections and inventions of his own. Lastly, in these particular works there is the use of twelve-tone technique (comparatively new in both composers), which Stravinsky and Copland have turned to their own uses. As in the case of the classics, a new work is made out of the materials of all these pre-established elements, each of them the result of slow, painstaking musical evolution.

A more trivial example may illustrate one kind of improvisation, at least, and its relation to pre-established techniques. Many of the older generation of French organists have developed an extraordinary ability to improvise on a given theme and occasionally give public demonstrations of their prowess, asking the public for the notes of a theme. At one of these sessions a particularly tortuous twelve-tone series was presented by a group of music students. With hardly a moment's hesitation the organist pulled out his stops and embarked on a half hour of variations, a passacaglia and fugue with many incidental canons; all quite audibly connected to the given theme, but all in the standard post-Franckian style with its Romantic altered chords, its modulating sequences—and winding up, of course, with an apotheosis of the theme against a background of rapid arpeggiation. The power of this highly developed, scholastic, pre-established world of musical devices was so great that it could meet any musical problem with a ready-made solution of great intricacy and refinement. There was, of course, no pretense that this was great music; it was intended simply as a demonstration of skill—much the same kind of skill (but with an added element of genius) that Bach must have revealed to Frederick the Great. But while in Bach's time, and especially in his later life, many more elements of general technique and of his own were "given" as part of his musical vocabulary, fifty years ago such was not the case, and it was unlikely that an improviser could do more than astonish his listeners with a display of remarkable musical ingenuity based on a whole group of academic or commercial routines. In fact, one might almost say that improvisation itself, if it is to be interesting to the listener, must have a whole set of pat, standardized, prearranged techniques, even though devised by the performer. Thus in improvisation as we know it today, especially in much popular music, the weight of pre-established routine is often great enough to carry the music forward like a well-oiled machine without reacting to any communication from the outside.

These two examples of different uses of pre-established compositional methods—the recent works of Stravinsky and Copland which reveal a living and meaningful sensitivity to the mutual interaction of details and whole and to differences of qualities and styles based on a thorough reworking of the inherited musical language; and the improvisation of the French organist that ticks away like a complicated clock, insensitive to the human meaning of its minutes and hours—should serve to clarify the new direction away from pre-established techniques which this article is attempting to describe. This new direction may be labeled "emancipated musical discourse" after the "emancipation of dissonance," which Schoenberg coined for the new trends in harmony.

One cannot escape the feeling that this new direction is a reaction to the extraordinary increase of interest in the past and the remote, bringing to what was once a product of Romantic nostalgia (and still is, perhaps) modern scientific precision and modern techniques. The bewildering wealth of all history and of all cultures has suddenly been made easily available through phonograph recordings and publications, and our temperaments do not permit us to dismiss older styles as most of the composers of earlier periods would have done. On the contrary, as everyone knows, the interest in older music even of rather obscure and not too interesting composers is on the whole greater than in that of contemporaries—a situation that would have profoundly shocked any of the older composers whose music is now being exhumed.

This vast array of information, of methods and ideas, increases the composer's range of possibilities so enormously that one of his greatest problems now is to make choices, to decide what to discard and what to keep for his own use. Even the most erudite composers of the past did not have so much to learn and so much to choose from. Therefore it becomes imperative for a composer to limit his range so that he can concentrate his efforts. This need for choice explains why young composers have relied on one dominating figure after another—following Stravinsky and others in neo-Classicism, or Schoenberg in Expressionism. In this matter the twelve-tone system has been particularly helpful, since it allows considerable latitude while limiting the composer's choices and giving these choices a kind of hierarchy of relationships. Once you have chosen the twelve-tone row, you have chosen a method of harmony and a collection of motives that are all interrelated. This is an enormous advantage, for it helps to put the composer in that situation of focused freedom that finds its counterpart in all species of musical training, from learning to play an instrument to writing an opera.

The resurrection of this vast world of forgotten music and the bringing into the living room of music from all parts of the world as it sounds is such a recent development that it is still intellectually and artistically undi-gested—quite unlike the situation in literature and the fine arts, where the opening up of the horizons of the past and of the remote took place some time ago, and several generations of critics and historians have had time to discover stimulating facts and to elaborate valuable ideas. Musicology has hardly passed the cataloguing stage, and so far has provided very little intellectual or esthetic stimulus. However, the activity of musicology which has, in America and elsewhere, raised music to a university discipline brings with it scientific attitudes —among them the analogy of the composer to a scientist in a laboratory who works for years on some piece of obscure research which will be brought to light only when popularized by a profes-sional popularizer, or when some imaginative scientist uses his data as part of a comprehensive theory of large application. Whether this attitude is healthy, when applied to the public art of music, remains to be proved. Likewise the amassing of vast amounts of information about all branches of this art tends also to draw it away from the general public, since there is so much to know that the public simply becomes discouraged.

For the composer, in spite of all, does write for a public. One might very well wonder *what* public, if it were not for the fact that the public is constantly changing, and one of the forces exerted upon it is that of the very works of music themselves. For now we can see that strong, commanding works of art, no matter how strange they seem on their first appearance, sooner or later reach the public. Their intrinsic quality acts as a centripetal force that first educates the musical profession and finally the public to understand. In the context of this article, the question to be asked at this point is whether the familiar, delayed public acceptance that has greeted so many contemporary works will not be delayed forever if works in the new advanced style eliminate too many of the pre-established techniques in their efforts to obtain complete consistency and very close coordination of all their elements. The effort of striking out along the new path, which was described at the beginning of this article, could result in complete hermeticism. How far along this road toward hermeticism one can go is perplexing to us today when we see the poems of Mallarmé and Valéry in our children's high school French book.

It is not an easy or a comfortable thing for a musician trained in the traditional techniques to break away from them—particularly from those discussed here which are so fundamental. One might suppose that a person without traditional training might be able to approach the problem more freshly. Yet in spite of the fact that musical training is still not at all adapted to deal even with the most familiar modern techniques, experience so far has shown that the results of practically all untrained musicians are either so chaotic or so pedestrian as to be without interest. Usually such people, like many listeners with little musical experience, are overwhelmed by the sheerly physical qualities of sound and can do little more than make a display of surprising sound effects like a display of fireworks, which pay slight attention to organization, since this seems meaningless to them. A knowledge and feeling for the high standards of coherence and meaning which the musical tradition has brought to great subtlety is probably much more important than many musicians of advanced tendencies have thought. What is needed is a restudying of existing music and the elaboration of a more significant kind of music theory that is more widely applicable. This inevitably goes with the point of view discussed here and is found reflected likewise in many places. The musicians of the United States have produced a number of important books, articles, and teachings in this field, which are revolutionizing the thinking of the present student generation of composers.

In Europe, the search for emancipated musical discourse has been much more closely associated with the twelve-tone system than in the United States. There it has taken its departure from Webern's pointillist works and has applied serial methods to other dimensions besides that of pitch. As a method of discovering new possibilities of momentary and unexpected sound effects, this exercise is useful. At its best it resembles the turning of a musical kaleidoscope that shuffles at random fragments of sound which may or may not fall into interesting patterns—the burden of reading meaning and of finding interest in these rests with the listener and not the composer. The real problem of such music-puzzles is illustrated simply by the verbal palindrome ("able was I ere I saw Elba"), which has to obey both a strict patterning of letters and has to make sense into the bargain. A palindrome of random letters is a bit pointless in itself. Although musical meaning is not quite so easy to establish, still up to the end of Webern's life this double standard of order and of meaning applied to all such types of musical ingenuity, with the exception perhaps of certain medieval and early Renaissance works. But the recent European school seems to have become occupied with pattern alone, hoping somehow that interest and meaning would emerge. Even on their own admission, this has not always been the case. This ordering according to the random application of number systems seems wasteful because it produces so many useless possibilities, like the monkeys at typewriters.

In the United States, the tendency has been to start with a co-ordinating principle having to do with techniques of listening or to begin with our experience of time and not some arbitrary numerological formula. Examples of emancipated discourse in America are beginning to be more numerous. Some of the abstract works of Copland and especially the recent works of Roger Sessions, such as his *Third Symphony*, and those of the writer of this article, strive for this principle using any system or musical procedure that seems suitable. Others, like Milton Babbitt, use the twelve-tone system emphasizing its co-ordinative possibilities rather than its disintegrative ones, as the Europeans do. Certainly, audible musical order that can be distinguished, remembered, and followed is a necessary condition for this new adventure.

The Composer's Choices

Commissioned by the Fromm Foundation
for Radio Broadcast (196–?)

[The following is a radio lecture with recorded musical examples. Even in the absence of the recordings, Carter's descriptions of what to listen for are, in our opinion, so clear and vivid that there is no doubt as to what he wishes to bring out. All of the music discussed has been published and recorded, with the exception of the *Holiday Overture*, for which no commercial recording is available at the time of this writing.]

The teacher to whom I owe the most, Mlle. Nadia Boulanger, frequently says to her students that a true artist can be recognized by the quality of his refusals, bringing sternly to our attention the critical activity that lies behind all good artistic work. To say that the higher the quality of ideas the artist rejects, the higher the quality of his final accomplishment, however, implies a commitment to an order of values that may be possible only in a unified culture such as that of France. For unless there is some general agreement about grades of quality, it is obviously impossible for different individuals to judge, according to the same standards as the artist, the quality of refusals, or even to agree on the quality of his final accomplishment.

Mlle. Boulanger's remark, partly because of its emphasis on rejection, suggests the typical, highly cultivated French artists of the turn of the century, such as Cézanne, Mallarmé, or Debussy, who not only rejected commonly held ideas about the subject matter of their arts that might have made them more immediately popular, but even within their own works were extremely fastidious about every detail regardless of all the obstacles that upholders of the conventions or ordinary life put in their way.

Something of the intensity of this devotion to art was made vivid to me while I was a student, on the day when the Stavisky affair resulted in bloody street rioting between rival political groups in Paris, closing all business offices and stopping public transportation. On this day our counterpoint class met. To reach it, some of us had to walk several miles across the frightening city. When we had assembled, Mlle. Boulanger criticized with melancholy exasperation the very few members of the class who had not appeared, saying that a riot might stop many ordinary affairs of life, but there was no reason why it should stop music.

I have thought of this day often when considering works created under difficult circumstances, and have wondered how many in our country would see any reason for a student to thread his way through a dangerous riot in which many were killed to learn the refinements of six-, seven-, and eight-part strict counterpoint—a discipline the nature of which few of them could understand, and the mastery of which still fewer would be able to recognize or value—and I have wondered whether this training or the precision of musical writing that results from it would seem to many Americans worth the risk which we took without question.

For few American composers can escape the impression that when serious music was brought over to this country, it was and still is but dimly realized by the public that the great compositions fundamental to the art were not things easily or cheaply produced, but were the results of human beliefs, of commonly shared moral and esthetic values, of orderly, logical thought, and of the practical musical experiences of generations. And the standards set up by the music profession that had directed the fascinating musical development we all love are a direct reflection of these qualities. For instance, the typical traditional training of a composer, even today, centers around the learning of techniques that imply an attentive listener, experienced in following musical thought, who is also a cultivated person in matters of taste, quick to understand, and impatient with the obvious. This training consists, at the very least, in developing a respect for such an intelligent listener's expectations and abilities, and, at the very most, in using these as a means for eloquent communication. However, as often happens here today, when a composer cannot always count on the listening ability of even a small part of his audience, or when this small part, if it exists, has no influence over the majority of listeners on whom most of the qualities and skills of even the accepted works of the standard repertory make little impression, what value can there be in learning to achieve the order and control which until now were thought to be so fundamental to the art?

It is against the background of this perplexing American situation that I would like to discuss some of the choices and refusals that I, as a composer, have made. Naturally I cannot judge their quality objectively, but in describing my musical development over the past twenty years, I hope to be able to dispel a little of the confusion and misunderstanding that surround the composer's work. If I dwell on the sound of the music—on what can be physically heard—it is because this can be talked about, while the musical content which must be grasped from direct attention to the sound cannot be put into words satisfactorily. It should be obvious that changes in musical vocabulary are the result of a human development in the course of which the musical content which I envisioned became more clearly defined and required a search for ever more adequate and precise means of expressing it; also as the character of the content changed and developed over the years, I was led to explore and invent other suitable new means.

My first large orchestral work, written in 1938—a ballet on the subject of Pocahontas—is full of suggestions of things that were to remain important to me, as well as of others, which were later rejected or completely transformed because they no longer seemed cogent.

Some of these features can be observed in the third movement of the ballet, a record of which you are about to hear. First, the overall style made up of irregular rhythms, dissonant harmony, and a combination of diatonic and chromatic elements has remained fairly constant, although in the years immediately following this work I made a brief excursion into a more diatonic style, and then, since 1946, became increasingly more chromatic and dissonant. The rhythmic structure found in this work was delved into, expanded, and finally completely transformed. The construction of phrases here already shows a tendency to change character quickly, a feature that became much more important in my later works.

On the other hand, the way of forming musical material and texture, and the type of flow and continuity were abandoned. Observe, for instance, how the main gist of this work is almost always presented in the form of themes or melodic lines, either based on reiterative motives—a method I soon found unsatisfactory—or on long spun-out phrases, usually leading to a climax—a pattern I rarely use today. The background is filled in with rhythmic chords, figurations, and simple contrapuntal lines. Today the texture of my music is seldom that of a thematic foreground with an accompanying background. Notice, too, the constant rhythmic drive running through the fast part—a technique I have modified a great deal in the interests of plasticity.

> [*Pocahontas—Ballet Suite*, third movement, pp.36–68 of
> printed score; begins ca. 9'28" from beginning of record-
> ing; playing time ca. 7'.]

This work, now so easy to listen to, was considered difficult to play and to hear at its first performance in New York in 1939, and was received very coldly indeed by the public and the critics. And those colleagues who were my friends and whose opinions I respected were hardly more encouraging. However, the *Suite* from the ballet was given the Juilliard Award for the Publication of American Music in 1941, and several hundred copies of the score and parts were printed only to gather dust on library and warehouse shelves, unused, until 1959, when the recording, part of which you have just heard, was made in Switzerland by the Zurich Radio Orchestra conducted by Jacques-Louis Monod.

After the experience of *Pocahontas*, I felt that I must write in a more controllable style, one that would be easier to perform and would appeal more directly to what I imagined to be the listening abilities of the average concert-goer, a point of view a number of American composers adopted at the time. Of the few works I wrote in what seemed a more acceptable style, from 1940 to 1944, the *Holiday Overture* was the last and already shows a turning to more elaborate textures. This work again won a prize of publication, and again remained unperformed in this country for a number of years, although it received many performances in the Germany of 1946 to 1947, none of which I heard. Recently it has been played by a number of orchestras here, among them the New York Philharmonic, directed by Dimitri Mitropoulos in 1958.

By the time I had completed the *Holiday Overture*, my interest was beginning to turn to other matters of a more specialized and personal nature. Since the music I had written with the aim of being accessible apparently interested few listeners and hence did not serve the purpose intended, I felt no compunctions about taking a direction that might be much more difficult to grasp.

By 1945, my preoccupation with modern dissonant harmony and what has since been called cross-accented counterpoint, of which the *Holiday Overture* is an elaborate example, was no longer central, and I became more concerned with the formation of musical ideas, of types and qualities of continuity, and with the fascinating possibilities of musical flow and change. The opening of my *Piano Sonata* of 1946 will illustrate what I mean. It is the first passage in my works that is not primarily thematic. Its central idea comes from the total sound of the piano writing. Notice particularly the variety and flexibility of rhythm, the frequent changes of character, the oppositions of register, of manners of playing, and of slow and fast. All of these were to become increasingly important.

[*Piano Sonata*, measures 1–82; playing time 2′30″.]

In the opening of my *Cello Sonata* of 1948, I was interested in the musical meaning resulting from two simultaneous, but differently characterized, planes of music—a type of texture used to great effect in many operas, but seldom in concert music. Here the clock-like regularity of the piano is contrasted with the singing, expressive line of the cello, which, although accurately written out, sounds as free from the underlying beat as the jazz improvisor from his rhythm section—the musical situation which suggested this passage:

[*Sonata for Violoncello and Piano*, measures 1–67;
playing time 2′30″.]

As time went on, all kinds of new textural and rhythmic ideas began to appear. For instance, one of my etudes from *Eight Etudes and a Fantasy* of 1950 is a musical mosaic made up of a two-note motive constantly repeated in different transpositions. Out of this neutral material an overall pattern with a more articulate shape of its own emerges:

[*Eight Etudes and a Fantasy* for woodwind quartet; Etude
IV, pp.7–11; playing time 1′38″.]

The last three examples briefly illustrate the numerous musical changes that occurred in my music from 1946 to the present. It is only in the realm of chamber music that such a change could have taken place and have been tried out in the America of these years, since it was, and still is, almost impossible to gain the necessary experience of actual live performances of works with any kind of unusual conception with the orchestras in this country. However, when the Louisville Orchestra commissioned a work from me, I decided to apply some of the ideas I had developed in my chamber music to the larger medium. I chose the form of a set series of variations, since the flow and change of musical character interested me a great deal at the time.

The work starts with activity on two different planes. On one there is a long singing line that flows calmly, resisting the change, and continuing through the introduction and the statement of the theme, gradually sinking below it. On the other plane, many brief dramatic ideas are presented during the introduction, followed by the statement of the lyrical theme which is the basis of the entire work, only part of which I shall point out now:

[*Variations for Orchestra*, measures 1–52; playing time
ca. 1′37″.]

Each variation has different features, and like different members of the same family, different relationships with the theme. For instance, in the fifth variation, all outlines are blurred and internal contrasts are reduced to accented attacks and held chords, which sound the notes of the theme together.

[*Variations for Orchestra*, Variation 5, p.62, measure 259
(beginning of cymbal roll) to end of p.70; playing time ca.
1'16".]

The work culminates in a rapid series of oppositions between many different characters, finally silenced by the trombones' loud statement of a new version of one half of the theme, while the strings play the other half softly.

[The broadcast ended with a performance of the
Variations in its entirety.—Eds.]

Sixty Staves to Read

This Was One of the Problems Faced by ISCM Jury in Cologne

The New York Times, Jan. 24, 1960. © 1960 by The New York Times Company. Reprinted by permission.

Cologne.—The festival jury of the International Society for Contemporary Music has just completed its choice of scores to be performed at the next, the thirty-fourth, annual ISCM festival, which will be given from June 10 to 19 in Cologne by the combined musical resources of the West, North, and Southwest German Radio Orchestras and the Cologne Opera.

The members of the jury, who were elected last spring by the assembly of national delegates in Rome, were Wolfgang Fortner (Germany), Karl-Birger

Blomdahl (Sweden), Guillaume Landré (The Netherlands), Marcel Mihalovici (France), and myself. We spent a week here looking through about 150 scores submitted by the national juries of the sections of twenty-one countries. Besides the six scores each section is entitled to submit, there were quite a number of works submitted by "independents," residents of countries of which they are not citizens, and still others were considered in the general interest of the programs.

SELECTION REQUIREMENTS

The problems of choice of these festival programs are manifold. Not only is it of utmost importance, obviously, for the music performed to be of very high quality and that the works can be juxtaposed to produce varied and lively programs, but it is also necessary, in order to keep the society together, to represent each national section on the festival programs, if possible, with at least one work every three years.

When this writer served on the same jury seven years ago, the jurists complained because there was too much music of conventional character. Now the scores using individual forms and strange titles are in the majority.

Along these same lines, a great many compositions were submitted describing the works of modern painters, especially those of Paul Klee, of Kandinsky, and of Hartung. The frequent preoccupation today with new qualities of sound, employing vibraphone, guitar, mandolin, celesta, crotales, bells, and many other percussion instruments, as well as with the re-seating of the orchestra to produce antiphonal effects, makes the jury's effort of imagining the sound of the music from the written page more difficult than ever.

The problem of unusual seating of the orchestra is perhaps most pronounced in the stereophonic distribution of six orchestras in Wlodzimierz Kotoński's *Musique en relief* (Poland). The jury had to be careful not to devise programs that involved so many changes of seating that more time was spent on this than on the music, as happened in a concert in Paris recently.

Too, quite a number of scores employed the orchestra with complete division of the string section, necessitating large numbers of staves. György Ligeti's *Apparitions pour Orchestre* (Hungarian, independent) employed mammoth scoring paper with sixty staves throughout.

The most troublesome difficulty for the jury was the number of scores that used various new notational techniques, ranging all the way from new ways of indicating changes of speed or dynamics to new ways of indicating rhythm or pitch, all of which required considerable study of prefaces and footnotes in order to find out what the composer meant.

Besides these technical matters, another question that we all took into consideration was presented to us by the society's president, Dr. Heinrich Strobel, before we looked at the scores. He pointed out that the ISCM, as well as the German Radio itself, had been the subject of much criticism in various quarters as being the promoters of twelve-tone music. We all agreed that it was as undesirable to promote this school as it was equally undesirable to promote the experimental school of Darmstadt—that we were interested in artistic quality no matter in what style it presented itself.

After looking through all the scores, however, although this matter was never again referred to, it was obvious to me that the preponderance of well-written, carefully planned works had some connection with the twelve-tone world. Most of the others were definitely of inferior character, a thing that was not true even seven years ago.

When the members of the jury had looked through all the scores, without consulting one another, we voted "plus," "Fragezeichen [question mark]," or "minus" on each and were surprised at how much we agreed. To me it was especially gratifying to find that, without any effort of salesmanship on my part, the United States scores were so generally liked.

It turned out that three American works, Arthur Berger's *String Quartet* [1958], Gunther Schuller's *Spectra 1958* [for orchestra], and Roger Sessions's *Fourth Symphony*, were chosen to be played. As a result, the United States had more of a representation than any other country except Germany, the country giving the festival.

Shop Talk by an American Composer

The Musical Quarterly, 46,2 (Apr. 1960)

[Carter wrote the following after a symposium at Princeton University, in an attempt to present a concentrated version of his ideas and the students' reactions and questions.]

When I agreed to discuss the rhythmic procedures I use in my music, I had forgotten, for the moment, the serious doubts I have about just such kinds of discussion when carried on by the composer himself. That a composer can write music that is thought to be of some interest is, of course, no guarantee that he can talk illuminatingly about it. It is especially hard for him to be articulate because inevitably his compositions are the result of innumerable choices—many unconscious, many conscious, some quickly made, others after long deliberation, all mostly forgotten when they have served their purpose. At some time or other, this sorting and combining of notes finally becomes a composition. By that time many of its conceptions and techniques have become almost a matter of habit for the composer and he is only dimly aware of the choices that first caused him to adopt them. Finally, in an effort to judge the work as an entity, as another might listen to it, he tries to forget his intentions and listen with fresh ears. What he is aiming at, after all, is a whole in which all the technical workings are interdependent and combine to produce the kind of artistic experience that gives a work its validity and in so doing makes all its procedures relevant. There is no short-cut to achieving this final artistic relevance. No technique is of much intrinsic value; its importance for the composer and his listeners lies only in the particular use made of it to further the artistic qualities and character of an actual work. If in discussing his works, therefore, he points out a procedure, he is bound to feel that he is drawing attention to something of secondary importance and by dwelling on it misleading others into thinking of it as primary. Schoenberg expressed such doubts in essays on his use of the twelve-tone method. And he was right, for certainly the twelve-tone aspect of his works accounts for only a part of their interest, perhaps not the most important part. For from Opus 25 to his last works the number of different kinds of compositions he wrote illustrates the very broad range of expression and conception and the wide variety of musical techniques that can incorporate the system and yet be distinguished from it.

In any discussion of specifically contemporary procedures, there are a few serious risks involved that must be constantly borne in mind. The first is the danger of rapid and wide dissemination of oversimplified formulas that shortens their life. It is obvious that one technical fad after another has swept over 20th-century music as the music of each of its leading composers has come to be intimately known. Each fad lasted a few years, only to be discarded by the succeeding generation of composers, then by the music profession, and finally by certain parts of the interested public, so that through over-use many of the striking features of the best works lost freshness. It was hard, therefore, for those close to music to listen to these works for a time, and many of the better works disappeared from the repertory without a trace. Such a formula as the Impressionists' parallel ninth chords, for instance, wore itself out in the tedious arrangements of popular music current until recently. Each of the trends of our recent past—primitivism, machinism, neo-Classicism, *Gebrauchsmusik*, the styles of Bartók and Berg and now those of Schoenberg and Webern—has left and will leave in its trail numbers of really gifted composers whose music, skillful and effective as it is, is suffocated, at least for a time, by its similarity to other music of the same type. Of course, ultimately this faddishness is trivial, but its mercurial changes today have made the life of many a composer a great trial, more even than in the time of Rossini, who is now generally thought to have been one of the first outstanding composers to have given up composing because he could not change with the times.

The tendency to fad has been greatly encouraged by the promulgation of systems, particularly harmonic systems. Many recent composers following Schoenberg, Hindemith, and Messiaen have gained renown by circulating descriptions of their systems even in places where their music was not known. This kind of intellectual publicity can lead to a dead end even more quickly than the older fads derived from the actual sound of music in styles the composer did not even bother to explain.

The popularity of modern harmonic systems is, unfortunately, easy to understand. Textbooks led music students to think of harmony as a well-ordered routine, and when they found it to be less and less so in the years from Wagner to the present, they were much troubled—and still are—by the gap between what they learn and what they hear in modern music. For mature composers, lack of system is usually not much of a problem since they write, as they probably always have, what sounds right to them. This "rightness" has come, I suppose, from a developed sensitivity and experience that take time to acquire. When modern systems of harmony that were orderly and easy to explain appeared they filled an important pedagogical need for the inexperienced.

The very ease with which any of these systems can be used has its obvious dangers, as I have said. With the help of these and other shortcuts a vast amount of music is being written today, far more than can ever be played, than can ever be judged or widely known. At the same time there seems to be little corresponding development of discrimination, or even of ability or desire to listen to new music, little expansion of opportunities for performance, at least in this country. The struggle to be performed and to be recognized makes it very hard for one not to become, even against one's will, some kind of system-monger, particularly if one uses certain procedures that are considered effective. For among students there is today a hunger for new formulas, and they constitute an interested public.

Obviously the only way to withstand the disturbing prospect of being swept away by a change in fad is to plunge into the even more disturbing situation of trying to be an individual and finding one's own way, as most of us have tried to do, not bothering too much about what is or will be sanctioned at any given moment by the profession and the public. We may then have to lead our lives producing works "too soon" for their time as Webern did, if they are not really "too late" since, if professional, they presuppose an attentive public which seems to be getting rarer. We are caught in a development dictated by convictions impossible to change with the fads.

All this is to say that I do not consider my rhythmic procedures a trick or a formula. I do not even feel that they are an integral part of my musical personality, especially in the way I used them in my *First String Quartet* (1951), which delves elaborately into polyrhythms. As I have suggested, all aspects of a composition are closely bound together, and for this reason I cannot give an orderly exposition of any without bringing in a large perspective of ideas. So I do not know where to begin, and I need your help in directing this discussion to regions that will be interesting and useful to you. Almost anything I might say, I suppose, preferably on musical subjects, might be considered relevant to the subject you have so kindly invited me to discuss here.

Question: In the program notes of your Variations for Orchestra *which you wrote for the Louisville performance, you described your method of variation as being a method of transformation, which you compared to the transformation from one life-stage to another of some marine animals. What did you mean by this?*

Answer: As musicians you are all familiar with the problems of program notes. Technical discussions baffle the greater part of the audience and the few who do understand are apt to feel that the composer is a calculating monster, particularly since musical terms are ponderous, not always very definite in meaning, and too often give the impression of complexity when describing something very obvious to the ear. If I had described the augmentations, diminutions, retrograde inversions as they occur, this would have been positively bewildering to the public and would not have helped it to listen—certainly not the first time. So I tried to find a comparison that would help the listener to grasp my general approach. Serious music must appeal in different ways. Its main appeal, however, emerges from the quality of the musical material or ideas and perhaps even more from their use in significant continuities, but does not always depend on grasping the logic of the latter on first hearing. There has to be something left for the second time, if there ever is a second time.

As in all my works, I conceived this one as a large, unified musical action or gesture. In it, definition and contrast of character decrease during the first variations, arriving at a point of neutrality in the central variation, then increase again to the finale, which comprises many different speeds and characters. This work was thought of as a series of character studies in various states of interaction with each other both within each variation and between one and the next. Activity, development, type of emphasis, clearness or vagueness of definition, I hoped would also contribute to characterization. Form, rhythmic and development processes, as well as texture and thematic material differ in each one for this reason.

The characteristic effort of the serious composer, as I see it, is not so much in the invention of musical ideas in themselves, as in the invention of interesting ideas that will also fill certain compositional requirements and allow for imaginative continuations. Serious music appeals to a longer span of attention and to a more highly developed auditory memory than do the more popular kinds of music. In making this appeal, it uses many contrasts, coherences, and contexts that give it a wide scope of expression, great emotional power and variety, direction, uniqueness, and a fascination of design with many shadings and qualities far beyond the range of popular or folk music. Every moment must count somehow, as must every detail. For a composer it is not always easy to find a passage that fits the particular situation and moment at which it appears in the composition, that carries to a further point some idea previously stated, that has the appropriate expressive quality motivated by what has been heard and yet is a passage that sounds fresh and alive.

As far as I am concerned, I am always interested in a composer's phrases and their shape and content, the way he joins them, the type of articulation he uses, as well as the general drift or continuity of a large section, and the construction of a whole work. The small details of harmony, rhythm, and texture fall naturally into place when one has interesting conceptions of these larger shapes.

Q: What do you mean by metric modulation?

A: If you listen to or look at any part of the first or last movement of my

First String Quartet, you will find that there is a constant change of pulse. This is caused by an overlapping of speeds. Say, one part in triplets will enter against another part in quintuplets and the quintuplets will fade into the background and the triplets will establish a new speed that will become the springboard for another such operation. The structure of such speeds is correlated throughout the work and gives the impression of varying rates of flux and change of material and character, qualities I seek in my recent works. The wish to accomplish this in the domain of heavily emphasized contrapuntal contrasts led me to work out the plan of metric modulation described by Richard Goldman.[1]

Q: *Why are the contrapuntal lines in your quartet so much alike, using equal note-values?*

A: You cannot have listened to the work very carefully or looked at the score. Of the nine notes in the first four measures, there are seven different lengths, the longest 18 times the shortest. There are, it is true, a few places near the beginning in which several contrapuntal parts, each of equal note-values, are combined, but in complete polyrhythmic contrast emphasized by intervallic, bowing, and expressive contrasts. In these I was particularly anxious to present to the listener the idea of polyrhythmic textures in its most definite form, for even this quality of texture develops during the work, leading, in the second movement, to a four-part fragmented canon in continuous sixteenths and, in later movements, to lines of much notational irregularity. But even if the values were more frequently equal than they are, as for instance in the polyrhythmic, posthumous *Études* of Chopin, I cannot see that this would be a real objection, as you imply. Many a fine work has dealt in continuous streams of equal note-values.

Q: *Does your music have any harmonic plan?*

A: A chord, a vertical group of pitches either simultaneously sounded or arpeggiated, like a motif, is a combination to be more or less clearly remembered and related to previous and future chords heard in the same work. Whether the composer is conscious of it or not, a field of operation with its principles of motion and of interaction is stated or suggested at the beginning of any work. The field may be tonal, employ traditional harmony, or it may be unrelated to traditional harmony, as my music seems to be nowadays, in which case I feel it imperative to establish clearly, near the beginning, the principles upon which the composition moves. Once this field of operation is established, its possibilities are explored, interesting new aspects of it are revealed, patterns of action of contrasting types emerge as the work goes along. A work whose world is not clearly defined loses a great deal of possible power and interest; one whose world is too narrow and restricted runs the risk of being thin, although if the world is unusual enough this narrowness can produce a kind of hallucinatory quality—one that I do not concern myself with in my own works. This extension of the traditional methods of coherence can rarely be attained nowadays solely by intuition, I think, because of the vast number of musical means, new and old, that we know. Some composers, it is true, insulate themselves from new musical experiences in an effort not to be distracted. Others, whose curiosity and interest prompt them to follow what is going on, feeling, perhaps, as Charles Ives did, that "eclecticism is part of his duty—sorting potatoes means a better crop next year," [2] have to make a number of conscious choices and establish the frame in which to work before they can compose at all.

In my *First String Quartet,** I did use a "key" four-note chord, one of the two four-note groups, that joins all the two-note intervals into pairs, thus allowing for the total range of interval qualities that still can be referred back to a basic chord-sound. This chord is not used at every moment in the work but occurs frequently enough, especially in important places, to function, I hope, as a formative factor. It is presented in various kinds of part-writing and interval combination, the number of notes is increased and diminished in it, in ways familiar to all of you. The chord, here in its closest position, showing its content of intervals of a diminished fifth and less, is also used both in many intervallic inversions and in total inversion (Ex. 1).

Ex. 1.

An example of its use in counterpoint (Ex. 2) occurs in measure 477 of the last movement, where the quality of the chord is strongly dwelt on—each vertical combination except the last being made up of it.

Ex. 2.

Q: Did you try to shape the free writing found in your quartet into formal patterns?

A: Since I consider form an integral part of serious music, I certainly did. Strange as it may seem, the intention of composing a work that depended so much on change of movement and polyrhythmic texture involved me not only in special questions of clarity and audibility that one does not usually have to face, but in special problems of form also. One of the solutions I tried, to keep this rather free-sounding technique from seeming haphazard and thus lose its connection with the progress of the work and the attentive listener's ear, was to establish thematic patterns made up of components of different ideas that could be separated. This feature emerges in the last movement, many of whose motifs are disintegrated to produce polyrhythms (Ex. 3). This is only one of the many ways I tried, hoping to give the impression of that combination of freedom and control that I greatly admire in many works of art.

Ex. 3.

Q: Do you use the twelve-tone system?

A: Some critics have said that I do, but since I have never analyzed my works from this point of view, I cannot say. I assume that if I am not conscious of it, I do not. Naturally out of interest and out of professional responsibility I have studied the important works of the type and admire many of them a great deal. I have found that it is apparently inapplicable to what I am trying to do, and is more of a hindrance than a help. Its nature is often misunderstood, it is a building material and not the building, and it allows, I think, for certain greater freedoms than were possible using traditional harmony with its very strict rules of part-writing, just as reinforced concrete allows for certain construction patterns impossible with stone. I must also say that having known many of these works all of my adult life, I hope the recent fad will not cause them to seem commonplace too soon. The results of total serialization are more recalcitrant to musical handling, I think.

Q: Do you mean to say that your rhythmic method is not a product of serialization?

A: It is not. But it is true that like all music, mine goes from one thing to another—the pattern on which serialization is based—but my choices of where to start and where to go are controlled by a general plan of action that directs both the continuity and the expression. Single details, chords, rhythmic patterns, motifs, textures, registers follow each other in a way that combines them into clearly perceivable larger patterns and then patterns of these patterns, and to me this cannot be easily accomplished with total serialization, at least the kind I study my way through in European articles these days. Perhaps another more useful and not so arbitrary kind of serialization could be devised. The present one resembles the turning of a kaleidoscope and usually produces not much more—or less—interesting results. Indeed it can be fascinating to listen to the total repertory of pitches, note-values, timbres, registers, and dynamics being touched upon in rapid succession and from a point of view we are unaccustomed to. But the cumulative effect of this is self-defeating since neither the attention nor the memory is appealed to. For who can decipher, by ear, the complexities of total serialization in most works of the sort? On the other hand, those in which this process can be followed are too obvious to be of any interest.

Q: What is your attitude about performance difficulty?

A: I realize with brutal clarity that orchestral music requiring a lot of rehearsal can, by the nature of American musical life, find very few, if any, performances. This is not true of difficult music for soloists or small stan-dardized instrumental groups, for obvious reasons. Our orchestral musi-cians are trained to play in the demanding scores of Strauss, Mahler, Debussy, Ravel, and early Stravinsky. One might imagine that one of the obligations of a present-day composer would be to use the skills of these excellently trained musicians to their full, lest their abilities deteriorate for want of use; that the challenge of good, effective yet technically advanced scores would be helpful in maintaining high performance standards in an orchestra, if not in raising them, as it did in the past. But this does not seem to be a consideration here, and, as you and I know, new works that make an immediate effect with a minimum of effort and time are favored. The real effort goes into the standard repertory, where it is more widely appreciated. Therefore, a composer who wishes to write orchestral music and get it played here has to tailor his work to these practical conditions, whether his ideas are suitable to such exploitation or not. Those who find that they can do nothing of interest under these conditions either give up writing orches-tral music or, if they cannot, hope for European performances of their works. For these reasons, the scores of our composers often show a lack of practical experience that reveals itself in conventionality and timidity. How can a man be adventurous, under the circumstances that obtain here? Any casual look at the European scores written since the war will show how far in advance of us even beginners are there in this respect. As in many other things, we may be willing to accept the final, accomplished results of European training and experimental efforts but we cannot afford and are impatient with the step-by-step experience needed to produce them.

Naturally, music that is both difficult and yet practical to play is not easy to write, and it may even be difficult to listen to. It does not make for a comfortable life to have this as one's mode of expression. There is an undoubted beauty in reducing things to their essentials or to their simplest form if something is gained thereby. When a composer cannot find an interesting and satisfying way of writing easy music, he is at least free, here, to use the level of difficulty he needs to set forth his ideas completely—even if this results in no performances. But I see no reason for being just difficult. Whenever difficult passages seem imperative in my works, I try to make them especially rewarding once they are played correctly.

For I regard my scores as scenarios, auditory scenarios, for performers to act out with their instruments, dramatizing the players as individuals and participants in the ensemble. To me the special teamwork of ensemble playing is very wonderful and moving, and this feeling is always an important expressive consideration in my chamber music.

Q: *Have you ever thought of composing electronic music?*

A: Naturally, I have often been intrigued with the idea of electronic music and have visited the Milan electronic studio several times to find out what is being done. I must say that almost all I have heard seems to me to be in a primary stage, and has not resolved some fundamental problems of matching and comparison of sounds that would raise it above the physical scariness that makes this music useful for television science fiction and horror programs. As far as composing it myself is concerned, you can imagine that since I am very enmeshed in the human aspect of musical performance, I would find it hard to think in terms of the impersonal sound patterns of electronic music. Certainly, impatience at not being able to hear my works in performance and impatience at the inaccuracies of some performances have occasionally made me wish that I could have a machine that would perform my music correctly and without all the trouble and possible disappointments associated with live performances.

Q: *What do you think of Charles Ives now?*

A: My opinions about Charles Ives as a composer have changed many times since I first came to know him during my high school years in

1924–25, but my admiration for him as a man never has. No one who knew him can ever forget his remarkable enthusiasm, his wit, his serious concern and love for music, and his many truly noble qualities, which one came to notice gradually because they appeared casually, without a trace of pompousness, pretension, or "showing off." Attracted to him by a youthful enthusiasm for contemporary music, I first admired, and still do, the few advanced scores privately available in those days, the *Concord Sonata*, the *Three Places in New England*, and some of the *114 Songs*. However, after I had completed strict musical studies here and abroad, I saw these works in a different light. Misgivings arose, which I expressed with considerable regret in several articles in *Modern Music* after the first performance of the *Concord Sonata* in New York in 1939. My doubts were of two kinds. First, there seemed to be very large amounts of undifferentiated confusion, especially in the orchestral works, during which many conflicting things happen at once without apparent concern either for the total effect or for the distinguishability of various levels. Yet in each score such as the *Robert Browning Overture*, the *Fourth of July*, and the second and fourth movements of the *Fourth Symphony*, where this confusion is most frequent, it is the more puzzling because side by side with it are a number of passages of great beauty and originality. Even more disturbing to me then was his frequent reliance on musical quotations for their literary effect. In spite of these doubts, I continued for many years to help bring Ives's music before the public since he would do nothing for himself, rescuing, among other things, *The Unanswered Question* and *Central Park in the Dark* from the photostat volumes of his work he had left with the American Music Center.* I arranged for first performances of these at a Ditson Fund Concert at Columbia University in, I think, 1949.**

What interests me now is his vigorous presentation in music and essays of the conflict between the composer with vision and original ideas, the musical profession, and the American public. It is the living out of this conflict, made poignant by his strong convictions, the anger it produced, the various actions and attitudes it led him to, the retreat into a subjective world, and, unfortunately, the terrible toll of energy and health it took, that makes of Ives an artist really characteristic of America, not unlike Melville. Without the dimension of this struggle and the quality it gave his scores, his *Emersons* and *Hallowe'ens* would be of superficial and transitory interest.

* See p. 100 fn.—Eds.
** 1946, according to "Documents of a Friendship," pp. 331–43 of this collection.—Eds.

His rage, which explodes between the waves of his transcendental visions in prose as it does in the scribbled comments in the margin of his musical manuscripts, reveals troubled concern over the problems of the American composer and his relations with the public. The music profession is castigated in one place as being more hide-bound, more materialistic, petty, bigotted, and unprincipled than the business world. The latter, his refuge from the bleak, meager life of the conventional American musician of his time, he respected and identified himself with enough to adopt an American businessman's view of the artistic profession, one that was especially characteristic of that time of wealthy art collectors. Making of the artist an anti-businessman, Ives saw him as a prophet living in the pure, transcendent world of the spirit, above the mundane matters of money, practicality, and artistic experience. The 19th-century American dream of art and high culture, which Henry James liked to project against the sordid European background from which it came, was the source, as Aaron Copland and Wilfrid Mellers have pointed out, of Ives's greatest misfortune. In gradually retiring into this dream, he cut himself off from music's reality. Too many of his scores, consequently, were never brought to the precision of presentation and scoring necessary to be completely communicative to the listener—or so it seems now. One could say that Ives was unable completely to digest his experience as an American and make it into a unified and meaningful musical expression. The effort of remodelling the musical vocabulary to meet his own personal vision, almost without encouragement or help, was too great, and too often he had to let hymn tunes and patriotic songs stand for his experience without comment.

As I have said, Ives's life vividly presents the special conflicts inherent in the American composer's situation. Today, even more than in his time, the division between the musician's professional code of ethics, his traditional standards of skill and imagination established at another time in another place, and the present standards of behavior respected, sanctioned, and rewarded by the society that surrounds us, is very pronounced. The familiar training of a composer giving him knowledge and skill in the accumulation of musical techniques, past and present, and the development of skill in notating them, presupposes trained copyists and performers who can grasp what he means and respect his notations. It also presupposes critics and, if not a large public, at least an influential élite that will be able to perceive the sense of the composer's efforts and skill, value them, and enable him to develop them further, by giving them careful consideration. When one or more of the links in this chain is not sufficiently developed or non-existent, as is often the case here today, the composer has a bitter fight just to keep his skill, let alone develop it.

This misfortune can be laid to the general lack of unanimity about and concern for the profession of composing on the part of the mass musical public that plays such an influential financial role in America. By training, the composer learns to write for a musically educated public that is also an influential élite, which does not exist and may never exist here. He cannot help but feel that he will be heard by a large majority of listeners and even performers that disagree with him, if they have any opinions at all, on the most fundamental issues of his art. Questions of style, system, consonance, dissonance, themes, non-themes, being original or an imitator, which imply some agreement on fundamentals, are not the stumbling blocks. A professional composer has today, as Ives certainly had, the training to be "communicative," "melodious," "expressive," qualities considered to have a wide appeal, just as he is now trained to use advanced techniques that will be appreciated by only a few professionals. How shall he decide? He is free, here, to do what he likes, of course, but it does not take him long to realize that whatever he chooses to do, radical or conservative, his music will further divide into small sub-groups the handful of people who will listen to contemporary music at all. Not one of these small sub-groups has the power or the interest to convince the large public by publicity or other means of the validity of its opinions, as happens in the other arts here. While diversity of opinion is much to be welcomed, where so little support exists such decimation of interest, one hesitates regretfully to conclude, can lead to cancelling of efforts and ultimately to their negation.

Even America's panacea, publicity, seems strangely useless in this field. Good reviews do not, often, lead to further performances, but they do help to sell more recordings. One might have thought that Ives, now so much discussed and publicly admired, would be often heard. That a number of his recordings have been discontinued, that only a few of his easiest pieces are heard while some of his more remarkable works are still unplayed or scarcely known, is surely an indication of how confused and desperate is the relation between the composer, the profession, publicity, and the musical public.

NOTES

1. Richard Goldman, "The Music of Elliott Carter," *The Musical Quarterly*, 43 (1957): 151.

2. Charles Ives, *Essays Before a Sonata* (New York, 1920), p.94 [p.79 in the Boatwright edition].

Current Chronicle: Germany, 1960

[Reviews of *Rasputin's End* by Nicolas
Nabokov and *Lady Macbeth of Mzensk*
by Dmitri Shostakovitch]

The Musical Quarterly, 46,3 (July 1960)

The almost simultaneous German premières of two operas about Russia, *Der Tod des Grigori Rasputin (Rasputin's End)* by Nicolas Nabokov at Cologne and *Lady Macbeth of Mzensk* by Dmitri Shostakovitch at the Düsseldorf opera, had an unexpected interest to the American observer unconnected with the German scene. It was the enthusiastic, lavish, interested productions given these works in two medium-sized Rhenish cities, on a par with Broadway at its most artistic and elaborate in direction, acting, and stage designing and with the Metropolitan Opera in musical performance. The ability to achieve such results suggests an unusual unanimity among supporters, managers, and directors as well as among all the collaborators about the importance of giving new works the most convincing and effective productions possible. The stage designers of both had created settings of high artistic originality that added very markedly to the effect of each and solved problems of change of scene, lighting, and action from different points of view, each fascinating in its own way—a way far removed from the stiff world of painted flats and old-fashioned lighting common in most American opera productions. The remarkable, moody sets by Teo Otto for *Lady Macbeth* were outdone by the elaborateness and mobility of those by Caspar Neher for *Rasputin*. The stage direction of Bohumil Herlischka for the Shostakovitch and of Oscar Fritz Schuh for the Nabokov were on a level with the best of Harold Clurman or Tyrone Guthrie. These efforts, combined with imaginative and well-trained musical performances, avoided any of the sense of fatigue or tedium arising from lack of conviction that makes performances of older operas intolerable but that, in new works, is complacently overlooked because it is so common that they are expected to be tiresome. If contemporary opera is to be done, it is clear that it must be done with a conviction that kindles the enthusiasm and imagination of everyone concerned, including the supporters, who must feel that the enterprise is so important that enough money is allotted to allow for the proper fruition of commanding conceptions. Certain opera houses in Germany seem willing enough to do this occasionally, even with works, such as these, by non-Germans.

Shostakovitch's *Lady Macbeth* in its first and only version so far, the version performed in Cleveland and New York in 1936, was withdrawn from circulation after the composer was reprimanded officially before the war. Still taboo in Russia, its present production, although forbidden in vain by the composer, was possible because a score nobody thought existed was discovered. Since the composer is said to be rewriting the work, he will certainly try to prevent further performances.

As an indication of the cultural condition of Russia of the '20s and '30s by a child of the time, the score presents a terrifying example of musical genius, vitality, and skill put to purely opportunistic uses with total disregard for musical unity, taste, and coherence. In its lack of concern for any consistent point of view, moral, political, or even artistic, it resembles a "comic" book, particularly since it is the expression of a temperament that only gives evidence of a craving for grim physical excitement, but does not always succeed in expressing even this, because of an inability to clarify intentions and consequently to be self-critical. Styles of Alban Berg, Hindemith, Mahler, Tchaikovsky, Mussorgsky, and Offenbach confront each other without transition. Genuinely inventive passages follow others of extreme mechanical dullness. The timing is haphazard. A long scene of wrong-note operetta music pokes fun endlessly at the ineffectuality of the local police, while one of the culminating scenes—that in which the heroine mixes rat poison, feeds it to her father-in-law (who has just horsewhipped her lover), and watches his death agonies impassively—is dismissed briefly and weakly. The relation of the music to the action is unaccountable, ranging from opposition, as in the scene in which the heroine and her lover strangle her husband on a large stage-sized four-poster bed to a lively dance tune, to the more familiar underlining of action and mood. Today, the makeshift and callous quality of all this recalls poignantly the description of those years in Russia in Boris Pasternak's novel *Dr. Zhivago*, when values that had always given human meaning to the individual's life were ridiculed and rejected. The gusto and very real musical talent with which the composer expresses his sense of physical excitement, of rowdy comedy, and of disgust make the opera worth hearing, no matter how disturbing it is as an example of an artist looking coldly on a society of passionate people living violently and brutally, and giving no sign of sympathy or of understanding in his music. The very possibility of human understanding itself seems banished along with any ideological point of view that at least might have helped to give the work some serious justification.

Nicolas Nabokov's *Rasputin's End*, with a libretto by Stephen Spender, in almost complete antithesis to this, is a sympathetic and convincing portrayal of human characters and situations with a comparatively unified musical vocabulary which is affecting not because of its surprises, brutality, and brashness but because of its aptness and explicitness and warm, human lyricism. A revision of the composer's earlier *The Holy Devil*, commissioned, performed, and recorded by the Kentucky Opera Company as part of the Louisville commissioning project, the new version is definitely grand opera in that it requires elaborate staging, good voices, a big orchestra, and many rehearsals. The action is a series of flashbacks occurring like a nightmare during the moments after Rasputin has been given the poison by the conspirators in the first scene and before he awakes in the last scene to the realization of the plot against his life, attempts to escape, and is shot. All this takes place behind a scrim curtain, scenes fading in and out noiselessly with the flexibility of a moving picture and without pauses or musical interludes, except for the intermissions. Thus the music is always directly connected with the persons on the stage, the lurid and violent aspects of the action are played down, and the human traits and feelings of the characters emphasized. The composer never overwhelms his listeners with an orchestral comment of any length, but like a very sensitive dramatist brings into vivid focus the moods and feelings of his characters, their conflicts, and their relation to the general character of the scene. Yet, theatrically effective as this score is, it also is, as that of any good opera must be, interesting in its own right. The skill with which arias, ensembles, and other "numbers" are made to take shape and conclude is unusual since one is hardly aware of these musical events apart from their function within the stage action itself.

The scene of Rasputin's "cure" of the young Czarevitch's haemophilia is most memorable because in it are kept distinct many different strands of human attitudes and each is given convincing musical expression—the Countess Marina's disapproval of Rasputin, the Czarina's fanatic faith, and Rasputin's intense, personal, spellbinding quality as he tells the boy a childlike bedtime story and finally induces him to get out of bed and walk. This many-faceted scene is convincingly presented as one complicated ensemble piece, and each situation is played off against another with a very strong sense of theater, and yet all is worked out in a beautiful musical form that makes sense in itself. The same is true of the scene in which the Countess Marina, as a nurse sitting in a little cubicle in the middle of the provisional military hospital that has been made out of her ballroom, writes to her husband at the front, recalling their past happiness, and describing her anxiety for the future, against a background of bedridden, wounded soldiers calling for water, crying out in nightmares, or singing love songs. Against this same background, the conspirators come in, discuss the reasons and plans for the assassination of Rasputin, arguing with the Countess, who is against taking this step. Another such complex ensemble scene is that of Rasputin's dream during his visit to the gypsy's house, in the course of which each of the principal women in the opera appears singing important themes of the opera while a chorus of monks accuses Rasputin and he tries to placate them. Such scenes, especially when produced as effectively as they were in Cologne, make the opera memorable both as theater and as music.

To integrate many "characteristic" styles such as those of Russian folksongs, soldiers' songs, religious chanting, gypsy music, and a French chanson in the popular style of the period (played on a scratchy phonograph record) into a score featuring the elaborate and cultivated vocal, ensemble, and orchestral techniques that are an accepted part of this medium, is difficult without destroying the immediacy and directness of reference of the "characteristic" music. This muting of character is very noticeable in *Wozzeck*, for instance, where, because of Berg's obliqueness of reference, the meaning of the whole opera loses its sense of particular locale, becomes more generalized and fantastic and probably more inaccessible to the larger musical audience that must now be appealed to, it seems, in order to justify the great expense of effort and money opera requires. The Nabokov work, unlike that of Shostakovitch, reveals an awareness of this problem, a new one, since certainly many older operas encompass a great variety of musical styles that nobody is bothered by. But today the importance of stylistic unity as an indication of the composer's integration of outlook, personality, and artistic approach is thought by many to be so fundamental that any stylistic mixture is unacceptable, no matter how skillfully the composer manages transitions or has tried to establish an all-encompassing musical frame that makes all stylistic divergences related, as Nabokov has. This type of criticism of the score overlooks its effect in the theater, where it makes a stirring impression. Indeed the recall of various styles of music helps to set the stage by evoking the special "feel" of the place and time, as must happen in such a realistic story. In other places, when the composer speaks with his own voice, the work is most convincing, and worth all the effort and imagination spent on it at Cologne.

The Milieu of the American Composer

Perspectives of New Music, 1,1 (Fall 1962)

The constant desire of American composers is to find a music that will have a real connection with the life we lead today, both as members of our society and of our profession. To an American musician, the post-war European trends seem to have been directed toward the disintegration of the routines and formulae that characterized the highly accomplished techniques of all previous, great European composers. To us this appears to have been undertaken in a spirit that is very thoroughgoing, even to the point of denying the fundamental reasons, traditionally put forth, for writing music. A definite break with the past on every level seemed urgent to the younger European composers. This attitude led to the applications of various arithmetical plans or methods of random which take no account of the special order related to the human ear and, through it, the human abilities to discriminate, organize, and remember patterns of sound. Their position, to us, represents an unwillingness to admit the possibility of highly purposeful communication. Such a view is nearly impossible to hold seriously in America, where the musical tradition and its accompanying danger of academicism do not count for so much. Indeed, in our country, almost all new techniques, including the serial and electronic, have been thought of as ways to broaden the communicative possibilities of music through the human perceptions.

Even the most anarchic tendencies in our music cannot be considered purely destructive because audiences here are too concerned with the novelty of hearing music in a concert, too interested in trying to understand what kind of experience this is, to be willing to accept a nihilistic attitude as the motivation for some of the strange theatrical events that such concerts occasionally turn out to be. In defense of these events, such explorations of the relations of the composer, the performers, the public, to the environment of a concert hall may be somewhat fruitful, in the sense of making the matter of musical communication more vivid to those who have not given it much thought and who find that music of a more highly specialized nature, which requires experienced listeners, eludes them.

But such experiments in the musico-theatrical situation do not represent the general attitude of the most advanced, and naturally not that of the more conservative. Here there is a fundamental belief in the development of music that reaches the human feelings and brain through the ear. Unlike many Europeans, apparently, the American believes that such communication is possible. This carries on a similar belief implicit in the older tradition of art music.

Having to face the continual uncertainty that surrounds his small, financially unprofitable, and but slightly respected artistic efforts, the American composer is almost forced into a position of affirmation if he is to compose at all. Professionally destructive efforts are scarcely meaningful in this situation, although exasperation with the poor quality of our mass entertainment is widespread and sometimes leads to great pessimism and rebellion. Indeed the tendency to adopt positions counter to those accepted in the society in which they live is characteristic of many contemporary artists and intellectuals, especially when faced with the low grade of mass culture. And this position leads the artist to reaffirm the traditions of Europe as a gesture of reaction against his society. A person with this point of view has, therefore, no inclination to turn to the almost nihilistic defiance, so understandable among advanced thinkers and artists in Europe today. Nor does the American composer need to deny the value of experiment by holding to an equally nihilistic cultivation of naïveté. It is by carrying on the European tradition and by following the methods of some of its experiments in the different context of his own experience that our composer affirms his identity and the identity of American music.

Thus in America a composer of art music comes face to face with many of the most urgent problems of modern civilization. Living in a situation where routine, custom, and habit no longer insure the continuity of culture but where such culture needs to be continually retested and reaffirmed before a mass public apathetic to these interests, he fights a special kind of adventurous battle. The fact, for instance, that compositional skills are laborious to master well enough to promote the imaginative conceptions of the composer, and that these skills are still being learned at a time when they seem unimportant to a profession which has, under public pressure, been forced to devote its abilities to the performance of works of the past, makes the composer's struggle seem quixotic. Yet this struggle is entered into by more and more young people every year, and this small fraction of a small minority group—the music profession—whose importance is not generally accepted by a large enough part of our citizenry to provide adequate support, forces the profession to meet the very difficult challenge of constantly proving its worth. The fact that this struggle is increasingly carried out under the protection of the universities implies the danger, on the other hand, that music may be assimilated to other university disciplines that deal in historical, semantic, acoustical, or psychological research, and thus be destroyed as a public artistic communication. Once compositions are treated as illustrations or examples of general principles rather than for what they are in themselves they lose a large measure of their significance. On the other hand, so many people are becoming involved with this field that certainly some will constitute part of the future musical public who can influence the less trained members. In any case, the random development of music here, without the imposition of authoritarian and customary attitudes and tastes, will be the prime factor in molding our own music into something of its own, with a freshness, we hope, drawn from these very circumstances; and a quality, not necessarily more simplified or naïve, perhaps the very reverse of this, that exhibits a vivid sense of what it is to communicate through the sound medium itself.

Art music in America has been like a plant, transplanted in a new place that provides a very different environment from the one in which it originally developed. In this new situation, hitherto unrealized qualities inherent in its nature begin to appear, and the special challenge of trying to live and develop under new circumstances may produce a considerable mutation. The plant is sturdy, the environment strange to it, the desire for adaptation great, and the process of adaptation filled with difficulties which at times seem insurmountable and threatening to the life of the plant, yet its wish to live and develop is very strong.

Letter from Europe

Perspectives of New Music, 1,2 (Spring 1963)

The proliferation of European festivals and conferences focusing on contemporary music is becoming so great that if any of the group of musicians regularly invited were to accept all his invitations, he would be kept busy almost all year simply in traveling from one country to another. For there is a small nucleus that meets over and over again, once even in Tokyo (as happened last year [1961]) but most often at the annual festivals, such as the "Biennale" in Venice in April, the Zagreb Festival in May, the ISCM Festival at the beginning of June—last year [1961] in London, this year in Amsterdam—and, during the summer, in the courses at Darmstadt, Dartington Hall, Cheltenham, etc.; then again in September in Warsaw, in early October either at Palermo or Berlin, and at Donaueschingen in late October. Although each of these festivals has its local supporters, performers, composers, and a special public that has grown rapidly in recent years, there is an increasingly large itinerant group of young enthusiasts that goes from one place to the other. To everyone's amazement (but to the delight of only some), modern music festivals are becoming increasingly successful. This year the size of the audiences for the third annual Palermo festival (about 2,500 for each event) has stimulated other less thriving Italian music festivals of other types to rethink their plans for next year in an attempt to attract some of this modernistic public, even though modern music festivals are notoriously expensive to give, requiring sometimes extravagant numbers of rehearsals and sometimes the assistance of one of the special group of conductors and performers accustomed to the problems of new music.

The main artistic orientation of these festivals has become more and more that of the Darmstadt school, not so much because its members have made a concerted effort to control the programs, but because increasing amounts of music of an interesting nature have their source there. By now it is clear that the members of this school have become the arbiters of what it is to be "modern" in Europe, for the novelty of their music and their ideas have been intensively and quite intelligently promoted by many different agencies. Sometimes it seems that the very fact of such musical activity within a limited sphere, brilliant and fascinating as it sometimes is, will lead quickly to surfeit, but right now this is the lively school and its influences are felt everywhere in Europe where young composers try to strike out for themselves against the older generation and find recognition among their younger colleagues.

Although apparently all of a piece, sometimes subsumed under the general critical heading of "post-Webernism," there is really quite a large number of different concepts and methods distinguishable at Darmstadt. Many of the important composers of the school alternate between "total serial" and "aleatoric" compositions, between compositions using, as sound-sources, ordinary musical instruments, percussion instruments, or electronic instruments, as well as myriad combinations of all of these. Yet, for all their seeming variety, all these various methods and sound materials coincide in revealing an acceptance of the same few aspects of some works of the Viennese school, of Debussy, and of Varèse as almost the sole models of procedure from the past, and only the ideas of theorists like Cowell, Hába, Hauer, Schillinger, and others who participated in the avant-garde movements of the 1910s and 1920s. In continuing the trends initiated in that lively time, atonalism, bruitism, dadaism, microtones, polyrhythms, and the imposition of rather arbitrary arithmetical patterns such as are found in Schillinger, they have been faced with all the problems and contradictions which were some of the causes that led to the decline of that earlier period. Like the old avant-garde, the neo-avant-garde has a very great preoccupation with the physical materials of music—sounds, their instrumental and mechanical sources, their projection in halls, and finally their method of notation. The presentation of these in time concentrates at present on producing varied or kaleidoscopic alternations such as are inevitably achieved by either total serialization or the use of aleatoric devices. There seems to be very little concern with the perception of these sounds, their possibilities of intellectual interrelation by the listener, and, therefore, their possibilities of communication on a high level. Most of the time the possibility of communication is denied, or, if admitted, kept on the primitive level of any music that has only a sensuous effect. The most talented works, by very definition, communicate, apparently almost unintentionally, while a greater part of the others consist in an auditorily random display of unpredictable groupings of sound, rather violently opposed in pitch, speed, intensity, and color. The fundamental frustrations resulting from this apparent refusal to deal with the matter of communication, and even the denial of its possibility, explains a great deal about the various directions this school has taken. Yet many of these have considerable interest, and since they are approached from such an untraditional point of view have an important effect on esthetic and philosophical ideas about music; perhaps they could even become useful if given direction by equally "advanced" concepts arising from an awareness of the listener's psychology. But without these, even in the most stimulating sound combinations, there is usually a stultifying intellectual poverty that no amount of arithmetic patterning will overcome; for either such a pattern can be heard by the listener, in which case it is usually far too simple to be of any interest, or it cannot, in which case an impression of pointless confusion results. For the most part, the Darmstadt music seems to waver between these two extremes—that is, when it is heard in large amounts—for there is no denying that on first impression some of the works are quite striking.

It is interesting to try to classify the various methods, in order to formulate a position about them, and to sift out what seems significant from all the welter of publicity, propaganda, and articles. First of all, as noted, this is a neo-avant-garde school and as such its direction has, up to now, been away from the "traditional" and the "conventional" toward the "future." The judgment of how "advanced" a work can be, since this is still considered a virtue, is a very relative matter; to those familiar with musical history of the twenties very little that happens today seems really "advanced," although the present movement occasionally has more sophistication and interest than the often foolish experiments of previous times. Thus it is misleading to establish categories and trends based on "advancement," but perhaps one can find degrees of difference from the Viennese school from which this movement claims to have taken its start.

The furthest away (from this school) is, of course, the neo-dadaist school, of which there are a number of small "anti-music" groups in various places that operate on a more primitive level than John Cage and Dieter Schnebel (whose "Visible Music" amused many at Palermo this year). The best that can be said of them is that they test the audience-performer-composer relationship and violate the faith that underlies the conventional acceptance of the pattern. Certainly the poverty of communication and often its complete dissolution in the tedious routine of many concerts of familiar format become more infuriating to musicians each year, since their art is based on the quality of commanding experience that can be communicated to the audience through the important works. The familiar efforts to arouse listeners from their apathy today rely on publicity. The kind usually used stresses all the superficial aspects of musical life, personalities, buildings, etc., and is really not so far from the dadaist assault, which also results in publicity. Both assault the naïve faith in the possibility of important communication and draw attention to the peripheral at the expense of the central. Both interest the news reporter in an effort to attract audiences not primarily interested in or able to grasp serious music. It could be that the neo-dadaist is more honest in his attack on the concert ritual; certainly he is more interesting and amusing, if not actually to witness, at least to think and talk about.

The usual complaint, that the musical iconoclasts are heaping opprobrium and ridicule on the musical profession, and if allowed to go too far in the use of musical facilities will finally destroy themselves and the profession too, was made a number of times at the UNESCO conference on Music and Its Public, which took place in Rome (September 27–October 3, 1962). Although the counterpart of this idea, that the traditional methods of musical dissemination were becoming less and less effective and were all leading in the same direction, was never stated, the conference gave the impression that all its participants—educators, critics, directors of radio stations, concert managers, and a few performers and composers—felt that the growth of serious music was not keeping pace with almost any other field of public artistic and intellectual endeavor today. All seemed to share a sense that music was declining rapidly in widespread cultural importance. However, as often happens at such conferences, no clear idea of why this was or what could be done to remedy the situation could be agreed upon. In this predicament, the ambivalent comic anger, the mystifications and absurdities of the neo-dadaist are sympathetic, if scarcely helpful, and perhaps less destructive than the big-time publicity efforts which have still less relevance to the problem.

To take all this seriously is no doubt foolish, and maybe the interest in the neo-dadaist can be laid to the deplorable decline in circus and vaudeville, where the musical clown once was a staple feature. Harpo Marx, Grock, and, in motion pictures, the concert given by Buster Keaton and Charlie Chaplin in *Limelight*, or Laurel and Hardy in an upper berth with a cello, accomplished such feats as we see today, using the physical material of music to ridicule pretentiousness and giving a glimpse of the musician's battle to communicate amid the recalcitrant apathy of instruments and public. Anyone who witnessed such remarkable performances as that of the clown who tore the piano to pieces playing a pseudo-Saint-Saëns concerto and was swept away with the debris (and did this six times a day) can never find these new musical "happenings" really entertaining.

On the other hand, the Darmstadt group which deals directly with the organization of music is a little nearer to the familiar situation, although when pushed to extremes, its results are indistinguishable from those of the neo-dadaist. One type of this, less characteristic now than before, is "total serialization" and another is "aleatoric." By turns, each of these concepts has captured the imaginations of many composers, first in Darmstadt and then elsewhere, just as for a moment similar ideas captured the fancy of many earlier composers (Mozart, *Musikalisches Würfelspiel*). For instance, a number of less advanced Polish composers like Witold Lutoslawski in his *Jeux vénitiens* and Tadeusz Baird in his *Etiuda* have written aleatoric scores. The degree to which chance is controlled or directed, how much is left up to the performer, allows for a very great variety of types. At one extreme are the blank pieces of paper with the direction to the performer at the foot: "Play anything you like but be sure to put the title and my name as composer on the program," at the other is the figured-bass, or the "ossia," which gives alternatives that are easier, or harder, than the version in the text. As one progresses in degree of control from the latter to the former, the question of authorship becomes more acute (one could imagine, on the analogy of Bach-Busoni, such attributions as Tudor-Cage, or Fortuna-Bussotti), and a host of dadaist problems arise, not the least of which are the matters of predictability of result and the effects of repeated hearings. The decision to play such and such a work, by a program committee or a jury for a festival, the announcing of a work to the public—and the relationship of these predictions of what is going to happen to what actually does happen—involves a complex, many-sided responsibility, and finally again brings into play the peripheral concern with what can be expected from the performer and the composers and not with what the actual work will be. In a way such works receive many first performances and have to be conceived in a very different way from other music: since to be worthwhile they must be immediately intelligible and effective, the methods must be very simple and definite although in a different but equally effective way at each performance. As the amount of carry-over from one repeated hearing to another is sometimes slight, the listener cannot get to know the work better and grasp the relevance of more of its facets. From the example of this that I have heard played in many different ways by the same pianist, Stockhausen's *Klavierstück XI*, the aleatoric principle has come to seem grafted onto the work from without, since there are really only a few effective orders of performance.

This aleatoric method has its direct counterpart in our educational training today, which encourages us to classify artistic works by trends, similar procedures, concepts, etc. (as I am doing here), rather than to look at specific works and recognize their special qualities in all their uniqueness. Aleatoric pieces with any degree of free choice are simply demonstrations of certain general styles or methods of composition without ever becoming concrete individual works in which every detail, and aspect of order, contributes in some way or other to the total effect. In considering this kind of music, one cannot help thinking that for some composers it might very well have become a matter of indifference just what shape the small details of a work would take, so long as a certain general effect is produced, and they came to think that it might be reasonable to let the performer choose how he wanted to make this effect—especially since so many listeners could not tell the difference anyway.

The other prevalent way of organizing music, "total serialization," is actually quite similar to the aleatoric methods except here the elements of random choice come in at the compositional rather than the performance level. For, while the music is written out, giving fairly precise directions to performers, the methods of relating a pattern of pitches to durations, intensities, and tone colors, etc., is highly arbitrary because intervallic relationships (such as the motion from E to F) have an entirely different perceptual meaning than intervallic relationships in durations or intensities (such as following a duration of eight sixteenth-notes with one of nine sixteenths, or of getting slightly louder—from mezzo forte to forte). Each of the "parameters" has a different way of being perceived and hence cannot be organized according to the same system of serialization and have any similar effect. Yet, as in all periods of art where "conceits" of this sort were practiced, it is possible to derive an artistic result from such an apparently arbitrary patterning, but it takes a musician with a strong sense of artistic value not to fall into the trap of producing something of no quality at all.

The more fundamental matters of textural organization, of musical flow, and the combination of a large repertory of sounds to produce these has been a less expressed, but more important concern in the Darmstadt school than the above, and have been the real controlling factors determining many of the "total serialist" and aleatoric choices made. As is often pointed out, one of the main tendencies of this school has been the persistent avoidance of the usual notion of theme or melody as the basic factor in musical organization and also of the shaping effects of regular rhythmic patterns and pulses. This avoidance has led to a focusing of musical invention on many other aspects not previously of so much concern. One of the concepts of textural organization, supplanting previous "pointillist" methods was, perhaps, first developed in compositions such as *Pithoprakta*, by the Greek composer Iannis Xenakis, and carried further by Penderecki, Gorecki, Ligeti, and a host of others. This technique uses many striking contrasts of thin and thick textures of many different qualities and draws continuities from their evolving and changing progress, making previous "one-note-at-a-time" textures seem a little faded and thin. For the isolation of single notes by pitch, dynamics, timbre, and their brief or prolonged overlapping, once used so delicately and effectively by Webern and further developed with more dramatic intensity by Luigi Nono, as in his *Canto sospeso* (1956), is a device that no longer seems to stimulate the writing of interesting music, while the thick, packed, dissonant textures and vivid juxtapositions of whole clusters or constellations of notes seem to lead, these days, to livelier results. Xenakis, using terms borrowed from probability theory in the impenetrable explanations of his works in program notes, calls his music "stochastic." Actually his point of view has evidently led him to think about the behavior of large groups of notes, rather than single ones, and this to the development of complex and strangely organized textures, usually without reference to counterpoint.

With this new textural development naturally goes an exploration of new possibilities of sound, an increasing interest in percussion and in novel ways of playing the more familiar instruments. Penderecki's most impressive score, *To the Victims of Hiroshima, Threnody*, for 52 strings, calls for a host of new methods of playing these instruments aside from using all the effects found in the Viennese scores. It asks for "highest sound without pitch, play between the bridge and the tailpiece, arpeggio on 4 strings behind the bridge, play on the tailpiece," as well as quarter-tones and vibrati of several different speeds and widths. This exploitation of some of the cruder and more uncharacteristic sounds of the instruments borders on the dadaist, in some cases; in others, as here, the extremely violent, almost "anti-artistic" expression of the music justifies the means.

Such searching into the physical aspects of musical production also leads to considerable interest in new, more graphic ways of notation, which sometimes result in a clearer depiction of the composer's intention than conventional notation affords, but often puts up an enigmatic barrier between his imagination and the possibility of physical sonic realization. The highly skilled and costly efforts of some publishers, particularly those in Poland, to follow composers in this direction is amazing in view of the very limited number of such scores that can be sold.

It is important to realize that this entire school of music, with its great preoccupation with physical sound, can have a wide appeal on a simple sensuous level, and often attracts those not trained to expect and grasp the higher types of order found in older music. In this it parallels, on another level, the return to the more fundamental and primitive level, elements of music characteristic of "folkloric" tendencies; interestingly, the *Rite of Spring* seems to point in both directions at once. The fact that this new music can have a strong appeal was particularly evident in the Warsaw Festival this year [1962], where it was repeatedly hailed with great enthusiasm by large audiences.

This, the most elaborate of annual festivals, celebrated its sixth anniversary between September 15 and 23, 1962. Extensive as it is, it forms only part of the still larger Warsaw Autumn, held to commemorate the gradual resurrection of the city since its almost total destruction during the war. Each year some new section is rebuilt, and each year's festival features a new step in Poland's artistic post-war renaissance. In a few years, the grand old opera house, reconstructed with one façade in its old neo-Classic style, will reopen with entirely new equipment; plans for a huge commissioning project of new operas and new productions of leading contemporary operas are already at an advanced stage. In general, the festival seems to act as a safety valve for all the somewhat submerged advanced tendencies in iron-curtain countries. Since the Polish government provides lavish financial support and allows artists and composers themselves to decide freely what they want to present, the programs and exhibits attract the more progressive from East Germany, Hungary, Czechoslovakia, Rumania, Bulgaria, and the Soviet Union to a reunion where they can mutually discuss their ideas and where their works can be presented before a sympathetic public.

Last September there were eight symphonic concerts, one ballet evening, one electronic and nine chamber orchestra or chamber music programs, each containing from two to two and a half hours of music, all contemporary. Besides this intensive listening, there was much social activity, for "observers" had been invited from everywhere, and those countries where there is state support for musicians' traveling expenses (the Polish government paid expenses within Poland) were well represented. There were, it seemed, twenty observers from the Soviet Union as well as several busloads of Moscow Conservatory students, who reacted vivaciously to the advanced scores, both pro and con. Also quite a number came from Bulgaria and other iron-curtain countries, a few from Western Europe, and from our hemisphere, a lady from Cuba and myself. There were no orientals or Africans present. Each morning a polylingual (Polish, Russian, French, German) discussion took place, called a "press conference," but in reality it was a good-natured social meeting in which the composers and performers, or conductors of the previous day's concerts, were questioned and their works discussed. All were very attentive, particularly the Russians, who took elaborate notes on what was said. In private talks with them, it was impossible to fathom what motivated their special interest, since like everyone else, they seemed well versed in the Viennese school and in the schools of music presented, and were eager, as we all were, to hear the new works. To my amusement one of the Russian musicologists criticized my *Eight Etudes and a Fantasy*, brilliantly played at the festival by the Dorian Wind Quintet, as not being advanced enough. The Russians I met, in fact, seemed unexpectedly knowledgeable and aware, were familiar with some American scores, and were especially enthusiastic about those of Sessions. Wishing to know more, they, like many Western Europeans, regretted that it was so difficult to learn about our music without being overwhelmed with scores and information about works that did not interest them. I pointed out that we had to suffer under the same kind of unselective representation from the Soviet Union. The same problem bothered the festival directors, who were much interested in American music but had a hard time finding the kind of scores that would fit into the rather advanced yet highly developed context of their festival. Varèse's *Arcanes* was played, and I arranged to send a number of scores of some older Americans like Ives, Ruggles, Riegger, and Cowell that did not seem to be known. The interest in the United States was very genuine, and the two concerts played by Americans, that of the La Salle Quartet and the Dorian Quintet, were packed with standees.

This year, more than ever, the festival favored the advanced school of Polish composers, Penderecki, Gorecki, Kotoński, Serocki, Schäffer, and that of the conductor Jan Krenz. Of these the first three seemed to be the most effective. The young Polish student of Nadia Boulanger, Wojciech Kilar, provided one of the "wows" of the festival, *Riff*, "*62*" for orchestra, which combined the tone-cluster technique of Penderecki with remote suggestions of very rowdy jazz. The packed hall gave the work such an ovation that it had to be repeated. Other interesting scores were *Aprèsludes* by the Italian Niccolò Castiglioni, *Lyrische Gesänge* by the German Dieter Schönbach, two interesting violin-piano sonatas by the Soviet composers Halina Oustvolska and Boris Klouzner, and works by the Rumanian Aurel Stroe, and the Bulgarian Lazar Nicolov. Unusual works by Bartók, Stravinsky,

Schoenberg, and Webern were played, but only two works of the older neo-Classic tendency, one by a Pole and the other, Shostakovitch's *Eighth Symphony*.

It is clear that in Poland, as in most countries where there is considerable state support of serious music, subsidy came as a continuation of the types of support possible under aristocratic patronage, which comprehended all the important aspects of professional activity, and with it plans for educating more professionals and audiences to keep the whole enterprise alive. It was, therefore, only natural that when the state took over its almost total subsidy, contemporary composers, performers, orchestras, as well as educational institutions, the public, and those invited from the outside to observe and comment, should be included. There is even a far-sighted policy in the importation of foreign performing talent and foreign compositions, for it is by such contact with the international musical world that the local activity can maintain an important standard and avoid the provincialism that isolation invariably produces. The Polish Composers Union is allotted a fairly large sum annually to distribute as commissions to its members by the government. Composers, themselves, make applications for a commission to an annually elected board of composer-directors, presenting a project for the size and kind of work they intend to write. The board decides how much to allot, taking into account not only the dimensions of the projected work but the composer's importance and reputation and the total sum to be distributed. The composer usually receives enough to live on reasonably during the writing of the work. This plan applies to composers of all schools. The completed works are usually printed by the state Polskie Wydawnictwo Muzyczne or by other publishers, performances are found for them, they are put on tapes distributed to radio stations abroad, and they are often recorded by the state recording company, Polskie Nagrania.

Obviously the amount of effort, thought, planning, and expenditure incurred by such a festival is tremendous, but the results were indeed remarkable. Every important orchestra in Poland—the two in Warsaw, the Cracow Philharmonic, the Silesian Philharmonic, the Pomeranian Philharmonic of Bydgoszcz—presented a program or two, and at each of these concerts at least one or two of the advanced works were played with remarkable seriousness and care for the total effect. One reason that could be perceived for spreading the work over many orchestras is that the players and their local audiences are thereby kept in touch with present-day tendencies.

Besides providing the observers with much to discuss, the festival revealed to us how many similar attitudes and experiences we shared about new music. Strangely, most of what was expressed, especially by those not specifically involved in the Darmstadt movement, was discussed in the preface to the printed program taken from an article written in 1926 by Szymanowski, Poland's most revered recent composer:

> The intellectual atmosphere of the most cultivated strata of contemporary life, the stage on which is acted out the fierce struggle for a new form, for a new expression of reality, becomes more and more complicated, bringing into play ever more specialized and subtle concepts. This process, by the nature of things, has brought the artist into the very heart of ideological conflicts, opposing his intuitive and instinctive method of work to the effect of the concept of art as an objective esthetic problem. Already with Wagner, theoretical considerations on the nature of the musical drama preceded in large measure the artistic concretion of the idea essential to many of his most remarkable works. This excellent example is an irrefutable argument against the (conservative) type of critical thought which (apparently) wishes to see the checkmate of contemporary art in its excess of intellectualism, in its abstraction, which results, so it is said, from theories made *a priori*. In reality, there is in this a clearly elementary misunderstanding which consists in confusing (more or less consciously) the notions of form and content in art, and in ignoring their organic interrelationship. . . .

One cannot describe the spirit of the contemporary European musical world today without mentioning Hans Rosbaud, whose death was a great loss to the entire contemporary music movement. The level of this man's cultivation, even aside from musical gifts, was extraordinary: he spoke English, French, Italian, and, of course, German perfectly, and up to the end of his life, took daily lessons in Russian, Greek, and advanced mathematics. He had a phenomenal power of concentration, was able, after the first reading of a complicated orchestral score, to grasp all its details—as I was able to observe at the ISCM Festival in London—and to deal with orchestral matters with a sure sense of the totality, as well as explain patiently to the performers how this was to be achieved—even at a time when obviously he had very little physical energy left. His quiet humor, his extraordinarily cultivated knowledge of literature and art, as well as his adventurousness in tackling any score, no matter how problematic, in which he found something valuable, made him one of the truly remarkable human beings of our time. It is to the credit of the Southwest German Radio, the Zürich Tonhalle, and the Chicago Symphony, among others, that he was so frequently engaged to present, in his inimitable way, the masterpieces of the twentieth century and other works he believed in so deeply. These scores he conducted with enormous care and precision, bringing out their innermost musical qualities and beauties, unbelievably and almost effortlessly, it seemed, without show, without extravagant gestures, but as a truly cultivated and civilized man would, by persuasion and not by force.

Expressionism and American Music

Perspectives on American Composers, ed. Benjamin Boretz and Edward T. Cone (New York: W. W. Norton, 1972); revised version of article originally published in *Perspectives of New Music*, 4,1 (Fall–Winter 1965).

The tendency for each generation in America to wipe away the memory of the previous one, and the general neglect of our own recent past, which we treat as a curiosity useful for young scholars in exercising their research techniques—so characteristic of American treatment of the work of its important artists—is partly responsible for the general neglect of the rather sizable number of composers who in their day were called "ultramodern," and who wrote in this country during the early decades of our century. And it is also part of this unfortunate pattern that interest in these composers is being awakened now because their music fits into a new frame of reference imported from Europe since the war, thus confirming the disturbing fact that the world of serious music here is still thought of as an outpost of that European world which Americans have so often found more attractive than the reality of what they have at home. In fact, it often seems as if we have no genuine interest in looking at our own situation realistically—at least in music—and developing ourselves for what we really are, but are always trying to gain admission into the European musical world (which, at present, is rapidly losing its inner impetus and is fading into a lifeless shadow of what it was).

When interest in Schoenberg and his circle began to be imported into America some years after the war and various of our agencies sent Americans abroad to learn what Europeans were doing and invited Europeans over here to reveal their secrets to us, those who had been close to this music all along began to be treated with a little more respect, while previously their efforts (including those of Schoenberg and his followers living in this country) had been dismissed as meaningless. Thus with the introduction of the post-Webern music and esthetic here, it was only natural that we should begin to take more interest in our early ultramoderns, whose techniques and outlook had much in common with the Viennese school of about the same time.

The long neglect of these American composers has resulted in a lack of information about them, and unfamiliarity with their ideas and music, and often a falsification of facts, so that it now is important to reconsider our attitude about them in the light of actual information in order to understand our own musical situation more clearly. The purpose of the series of articles which *Perspectives of New Music* is devoting to various composers of that time is not a nationalistic one in the European sense at all. It is undertaken in the attempt to clarify the special attitudes these creators developed in relation to the unusual musical situation of America, which gave an entirely different direction to this group than that of its counterparts in Europe. For they came at a time when ideas that were to change the face of each of the arts were widespread, and the same sort of thinking which formed the background of the Central European Expressionist movement also informed the thinking of artists both in Russia (which does not concern us here) and in the United States.

Because of many similarities of outlook, the great amount of analytical and philosophical thought which has recently been lavished on German Expressionism by European and even American scholars can perhaps be helpful in filling the large empty gap of serious criticism which surrounds the works under consideration, and can be helpful in understanding what went on in this country almost independently. The works produced at that time here, some of clearly great interest, others simply curiosities, have the special traits of the artistic milieu out of which they came, which has not changed much in the intervening years. Very little serious thought and criticism is devoted to our music even today except by composers themselves, and this can be laid partially to the conflict between the American reality and the American dream of Europe which patrons of music try to perpetuate in our musical institutions.

During the period with which we are concerned, a great deal of contemporary music was performed in New York, Chicago, Boston, and San Francisco. The Metropolitan Opera House kept *Petrouchka*, *Le Rossignol*, de Falla's *Vida Breve*, Gruenberg's *Emperor Jones*, and Carpenter's *Sky-*

scrapers in its repertory. The International Composers' Guild and the League of Composers organized many important performances, including *Wozzeck*, Schoenberg's *Glückliche Hand*, and Ives's Prelude and second movement from his *Fourth Symphony*. There was an interest in microtonal music,[1] and besides the concert of Hans Barth and Ives discussed by Howard Boatwright,[2] the League of Composers presented a *Sonata casi Fantasia* in quarter, eighth, and sixteenth tones by the Mexican composer Julián Carrillo for guitar, octavina, arpa-citera, and a French horn made in New York that could play sixteenth tones, in 1926, on the same program as the first U. S. performance of Schoenberg's *Wind Quintet*. In the next year Carrillo appeared with a larger ensemble of microtonal instruments and recorded his *Preludio a Cristóbal Colón* for Columbia Records. But the two important rivals in presenting modern music to the large musical public were Leopold Stokowski—an irrepressible experimenter, in those days, who played Schoenberg, Varèse, and Ruggles, and was a supporter of the more extreme "ultramodernists"—and Serge Koussevitzky, also dedicated to the new, but really most interested in the Franco-Russian schools and in launching the (then) younger generation of American composers, giving them the kind of enthusiastic support he had previously given to young Russians in Europe. At that time these institutions felt it their obligation to keep their audience abreast of new developments—especially those coming from abroad, and in the case of Koussevitzky of the American composers he sponsored, just as art museums still do today. Few good scores (given, of course, the particular tastes of the conductors) had to wait for any length of time to be heard. Each new work of Stravinsky, for instance, was heard within a year after it was composed, performed with serious devotion by one of the outstanding orchestras, quite contrary to the situation today. In the end Koussevitzky's energy and persistence won a larger audience for the new American neo-Classical, folkloric, and populist school and adherents of other esthetics were more and more bypassed and forgotten.[3]

It was in the early, more advanced stages of this period that the American ultramodern school was especially active, but when the Boston Symphony composers began to dominate the scene in the mid-thirties most of this activity came to a standstill. If there had not been such a drastic change, it is possible that Ives, Varèse, Ruggles, Rudhyar, Cowell, Riegger, Ornstein, [John J.] Becker, [George] Tremblay, and those a bit younger, like [Ruth] Crawford, [Gerald] Strang, and [Adolph] Weiss, among many others who are beginning to be heard again, would have had an entirely different development. In any case, Cowell's *New Music Edition* carried on valiantly from 1927 to the present, keeping the scores of this group in circulation and thus enlivening the sometimes very pessimistic outlook for the "ultras."

It is at first surprising that the American group seems to have been but dimly aware of its counterparts in Vienna and Russia, but on closer familiarity with the period, it becomes clear that the general opinion here of the Viennese school, particularly as regards Schoenberg and Webern, was of a kind that would lead few to become deeply involved in their music. Paul Rosenfeld, for instance, whose enthusiastic and sympathetic criticism was influential even among musicians in the twenties, found that Schoenberg's works "baffle with their apparently willful ugliness, and bewilder with their geometric cruelty and coldness. . . . It is only in regarding him as primarily an experimenter that the later Schoenberg loses his incomprehensibility."[4] When one realizes that Rosenfeld knew the early tonal works and Opp. 11, 16, and 19 when he wrote this, it is easy to see how the appearance of twelve-tone works must have strengthened this opinion which is still widely held in America, despite the evident fact, revealed by a number of recordings, that quite the opposite is true. This attitude persisted to the very end of Schoenberg's life in this country and succeeded in restricting his influence to a much smaller circle than he deserved, and kept most of the composers discussed from coming to grips with his music. Cowell, however, did publish the second of Webern's *Drei Volkstexte*, Op. 17, in 1930 (in a slightly different version from the one now published by Universal Edition) and Schoenberg's Op. 33b in 1932 in *New Music Edition*, yet in his book, *New Musical Resources*,[5] he mentions a new system of tonal organization used by Schoenberg but shows no understanding of it, perhaps because the book had been written, so the author explains in a preface, in 1919. Until around 1930, and even after, it is hard to escape the impression that the Viennese music left very little impact on most of the ultramoderns. Riegger, it is true, did start to use a very simplified version of the twelve-tone system then and wrote his *Dichotomy* (published 1932) incorporating this method but in a way utterly different from the Viennese.

The reverse influence is interesting to speculate about. We do know that Webern directed works of Cowell, Ruggles, and Ives in Vienna in 1932, that Slonimsky conducted works of this school in various places in Europe, and that Schoenberg left among his posthumous papers an oft-quoted statement about Ives. Certainly an American is tempted to be reminded of the tone-cluster writing of Ives and Cowell when it appears so baldly on the piano in Berg's *Lulu* (mm. 16, 79, and in a number of other places, particularly during the recitative by Rodrigo, the athlete, mm. 722–768—perhaps to characterize and develop the idea of "Das wahre Tier," which is introduced by the tone-cluster in the Prologue. There may even be a reminiscence of Henry Cowell's *Tiger* here).

To clarify certain esthetic, artistic, and technical matters central to this group, it is useful to compare them with those central to the composers associated with German Expressionism. A number of papers presented at the Convegno Internazionale di Studi sull'Espressionismo of the Maggio Fiorentino of 1964 are particularly relevant.[6] The problem of trying to define and delineate the special features of this movement is troublesome, naturally, and there has been a tendency by German musical scholars and Luigi Rognoni to insist that it be limited only to the works of the Viennese—and to all of their works, although the paper of Dr. Stuckenschmidt was inclined to include some Russian and a few of the American composers to be discussed in this series. In any case, the basic manifesto of the movement, *Der blaue Reiter*,[7] was the first attempt to clarify its aims. In this pamphlet, music holds a central position since by its very nature music is not a representational art but an expressive art[8] (a point of view derived from the type of thinking that put music at the top of the hierarchy of the arts, as in Walter Pater, in Busoni, and in Ives). *Der blaue Reiter* contained four important articles on music: Schoenberg's "Das Verhältnis zum Text"; [Leonid] Sabanieff's "'Prometheus' von Skrjabin"; [Thomas] von Hartmann's "Über die Anarchie in der Musik"; and [N.] Kulbin's "Die Freie Musik." Other statements about expressionism and music are to be found in Kandinsky's *Über das Geistige in der Kunst*,[9] in Schoenberg's *Aphorismen*[10] and his *Harmonielehre*,[11] and more peripherally in Busoni's *Entwurf einer Neuen Aesthetik der Tonkunst*. Comparison with the general tenor of statements in these works and those made in Ives's *Essays Before a Sonata*,[12] as well as the critical writings of James Huneker and Paul Rosenfeld reveals many similarities.

The main difference, as always, is that the state of American musical life was so inchoate that a revolutionary movement in this art would necessarily be less well thought out, less focused, and more of an affair of individuals only agreeing in a general way, hence less corrosive of the fundamental aspects of what seemed to all a moribund musical tradition, since the situation was not seen with any clarity—and for that reason tended to dissipate itself in superficialities and absurdities, as so often happens even today.

The basic point of agreement is Hegel's statement (quoted partially by Ives)[13] that "The universal need for expression in art lies, therefore, in man's rational impulse to exalt the inner and outer world into a spiritual consciousness for himself, as an object in which he recognizes his own self." This statement as quoted by Ives omits the words "and outer" and the last phrase "as an object . . . ". Both of these omissions are very significant, for they reveal how close Ives's thinking was to that of the Expressionists, for whom the inner world was of prime importance, and for whom art was not an object but a means of embodying his own spiritual vision, for himself, and, in view of other statements, for others to share through what was later called an "intersubjective relationship." [14]

Rufer's excellent paper attempts to give a general definition: [15]

> There too (in painting and music) is an eruption into chaos, a state of total unrelatedness (which, however, manifests itself in formlessness!), intoxication, ecstasy, the undermining of the very foundations of representative art. "There are no 'objects' or 'colors' in art; only expression." (Franz Marc, 1911). . . . Music of intensely romantic—one might as well say expressionistic—character, with an increasingly pronounced tendency toward breaking the bounds of tonality, toward apparent destruction of musical coherence and traditional formal schemata. Everything was called into question and always seemed to lead into chaos. Today, in retrospect, it seems self-evident that so many fine talents were destroyed in this atmosphere. Only a chosen few, through the force of their genius and the strengthening effect of constant trials, found themselves again. And here I can do no better than quote Gottfried Benn: "The expressionists in particular experienced the profound, objective necessities demanded by craftsmanship in art: the ethos of professionalism, the morality of form."

The actual texts of the period stress truthfulness of expression and the inner necessity of the artist to express his transcendent experiences, as Kandinsky writes: [16]

> [This] inner beauty arises from the pressure of subjective necessity and the renunication of the conventional forms of the beautiful. To those unaccustomed to it, it appears as ugliness. Humanity, in general, is drawn to external things, today more than ever, and does not willingly recognize subjective necessity. The refusal to employ the habitual forms of the beautiful leads one to hold as sacred all the procedures which permit the artist to manifest his personality. The Viennese composer Arnold Schoenberg follows this direction alone, scarcely recognized by a few rare and enthusiastic admirers.

Schoenberg himself writes: [17]

> Beauty begins to appear at that moment when the noncreative become aware of its absence. It does not exist earlier because the artist has no need

of it. For him, truth suffices. It is enough for him to have expressed himself, to say what had to be said according to the laws of his nature. The laws of the nature of men of genius, however, are the laws of future humanity. . . . Nevertheless, beauty gives itself to the artist even though he did not seek it, having striven only toward truthfulness.

Ives, in an elaborate discussion of form versus content and manner versus substance—a discussion which identifies form and manner with the generally accepted traditional forms and styles of music language, and content and substance with the artist's feelings and vision seeking expression:[18]

> Beauty in its common conception has nothing to do with it [substance]. . . . substance can be expressed in music, and that is the only valuable thing in it; and, moreover, that in two separate pieces of music in which the notes are almost identical, one can be of substance with little manner and the other can be of manner with little substance. . . . The substance of a tune comes from somewhere near the soul, and the manner comes from—God knows where.

Curiously enough, although the Expressionists were very aware in their writings that an inner vision was the driving force behind their search for new artistic means, Ives and Cowell, who were the only ones who wrote extensively about this music, did not state this idea directly in words. It must also be pointed out that the influence of mysticism—in Kandinsky[19] the theosophy of Blavatsky (which is also partially evident in certain ideas of the Viennese composers), and in Ives the transcendentalism of Emerson[20] —formed the basis for this sense of the importance of the inner vision and the disdain for the "material" world. Ruggles, to judge by the titles of his works, and Rudhyar also were deeply influenced by mystical thought. The power of the inner experience to force these composers to find a new means of expression led in two apparently opposite directions, called by Benn, "chaos and geometry" (recalling, oddly, Pascal's *l'esprit de sagesse et l'esprit de géometrie*). The former was the direction toward the basic, elemental aspects of human experience (and the elemental materials of art): Whitman's "barbaric yawp"—the baby's first cry at birth—what was sometimes called the *Urschrei* or the *Urlaut* (Busoni also discusses, in another sense, *Urmusik*)[21] —the primeval, immediate expression of basic human emotion. Mittner's paper is valuable on this point:[22]

> The two main artistic procedures of expressionism are the primordial utterance (*Urschrei*, or in the terminology of Edschmid, *geballter Schrei*, almost "compressed cry") and the imposition of an abstract structure, often specifically geometric, on reality. These two procedures seem, and

often are, diametrically opposed, since the 'cry' arises in the soul of the seer who envisions or witnesses the destruction of his world, while 'abstraction' is, primarily, the work of an ideal architect who strives to reconstruct the world or construct a completely new one. The relationship, however, is reversible, since geometry can deform and even disintegrate, while the 'cry' can turn into an ecstatic shout of jubilation which invokes or creates a new world, an ideal world. . . . The *Urschrei* of German expressionism almost never realizes the "We," and thus reveals the tragic position of uncertainty of the bewildered bourgeoisie. It is rarely the vaunted shout of rebellion and liberation, but primarily a cry of anguish and horror. The parallel with atonal music is significant. The *Urschrei* is most tellingly evoked in the monodrama *Erwartung*, which records with the precision of a psychograph the various moments of spasmodic expectation indicated by the title, followed by a series of cries of horror and desperation.

Mittner also points out the relation of the *Urschrei* to silence:[23]

> In contrast to this concern for the lacerating, primordial 'cry,' a new power is found in *silence* which, paradoxically, is considered its metamorphosis, since a tragic occurrence is presaged or experienced in a silence analogous to an internal 'cry' of the soul.

Among the American ultramoderns, the urge for such intensification of expression is particularly in evidence in Ruggles, in Rudhyar, and to a certain extent in Ives. Certainly his song *Walt Whitman*, which has something of a caricature about it, perhaps, strikes a character of expressionistic intensity in its first measures, that is similar to the opening pages of the "Emerson" movement of the *Concord Sonata* and to the first movement of Ruggles's *Men and Mountains*.

The opposing expressionist tendency, as Mittner points out, is that of constructivism, familiar to Americans as an attitude through the esthetic comments of Poe. In the American period under consideration many kinds of "geometrical" schemata were applied to music, as they were also in Europe and Russia. The rhythmic experiments of Ives partly come out of this thinking, as do those of Varèse, while Ruggles, Ives, and Varèse seem to have experimented with pitch organization in comparative isolation. Ruth Crawford, in particular, developed all kinds of patterns of this sort. Her *Piano Study in Mixed Accents* (1930) uses variable meters and a retrograde pitch plan that reminds one of similar methods of Boris Blacher, while her *String Quartet* (1931), especially the last movement, juggles with quite a number of different "geometric" systems, one governing pitch, another dynamics, and still another the number of consecutive notes before a rest in any given passage. Besides, the whole movement is divided into two parts, the second a retrograde of the first a semitone higher. Cowell's book, *New Musical Resources*,[24] has a chapter dealing with the association of pitch-interval ratios with speed ratios after the manner "discovered" later by certain Europeans. During the late twenties and thirties, Joseph Schillinger, who had come to America from Russia, bringing with him the fruits of similar thinking there, taught here; and after his death, his *The Schillinger System of Musical Composition* was published (1946) with an introduction by Cowell, which although attempting to be an all-embracing method of explaining the technique of music of all types is, ultimately, simply another example of this aspect of expressionist "geometry" in that it applies "extrinsic" patterns derived from other fields of systematization and theoretical description to music, often without sufficiently taking into account the "intrinsic" patterns of musical discourse. As Mittner points out in this connection, "geometry" can be a way of building an entirely new world or a way of deforming or dissolving the old. It is possible that an illogical, disorganized geometry or a totally irrelevant one can be just as much of a deforming or even constructive pattern as one more obviously relevant and logical (although the chances are obviously higher that the latter will be more fruitful) in the hands of an imaginative composer. The history of the canon in all its phases is a clear demonstration of this.

To get down to actual musical practice, the most obvious similarity is that of the "emancipation of dissonance." Just when this began has not yet been explored and hence it is difficult to say, as is often said, that Ives worked independently and before Schoenberg at this, since there may have been a prior obscure source, as there is to microtonal music. Certainly René Lenormand's *Étude sur l'Harmonie Moderne*[25] gives examples from [Ernest] Fanelli's *Tableaux Symphoniques* of 1883 containing whole-tone progressions, Erik Satie's chords constructed on fourths in 1891, and a twelve-tone chord used by Jean Huré in 1910. It is true that Ives seems to have tried a tremendous variety of harmonic methods from about 1900 on. With his point of view, he experimented not only with passages of consistent harmonic structure (such as is common in Scriabin) in works such as the songs *Evening*, *Two Little Flowers*, *Harpalus*, *Walking*, and *Soliloquy*, and with very great diversity of harmonic structure, as in *Majority* and *Lincoln*, as well as with polyphonic textures derived from these opposing attitudes toward harmony. Ruggles, Ornstein, and Rudhyar maintained a very much more consistent harmonic approach. Ruggles, in particular, shows a great sensitivity to the handling of major sevenths and minor ninths and their interrelationships with other intervals. The fourth *Evocation* is a particularly fine example of this. Tone-clusters, which might be considered a reduction of harmony to its most primitive and undifferentiated state, may have been first used by Ives in his *First Piano Sonata* of 1902 and then by Cowell in 1917. By 1912, Ives was writing large tone-clusters for divided strings in his orchestra music, especially in the *Fourth of July*, in which several streams of tone-clusters rush up and down scales in contrary motion simultaneously. Berg uses clusters in the men's chorus in the first tavern scene in *Wozzeck*. Indeed both tavern scenes in this opera have a strikingly similar character to those works of Ives that suggest crowd scenes, like the one mentioned above, and the second movement of the *Fourth Symphony*. The strings divided into tone-clusters, which seems to have been one of Ives's discoveries, did not come into wide usage until very recently in the works of Xenakis, Ligeti, Penderecki, and Cerha. Ives's attitude toward dissonance is summed up:[26]

> Many sounds we are used to do not bother us, and for that reason we are inclined to call them beautiful. . . . Possibly the fondness for individual utterance may throw out a skin-deep arrangement which is readily accepted as beautiful—formulae that weaken rather than toughen up the musical muscles.

Although Cowell wrote a number of piano works exploring polyrhythms (and using a notation devised by him for the purpose) and Ornstein used irregular bar lengths—and Rudhyar and Ruggles used irrational note divisions in order to give the impression of rubato and rhythmic freedom—it was again Ives who explored the field of rhythm most extensively, using precompositional patterns of note-values, all types of polyrhythms, of approximately coordinated instrumental groups, of passages more or less improvised rhythmically, carrying such exploration much further than any composer of his time. In a desire to make the performance situation vivid, Ives sometimes wrote remarks in the score directed to the performer to encourage him to give free rein to his fantasy. His remark "Perhaps music is the art of speaking extravagantly" [27] gives some clue to his general approach and links him once again to the expressionists.

One of Ives's most puzzling aspects is his extreme heterogeneity, a characteristic of some of Cowell's and Ornstein's music, too, but not shared by the other Americans who resemble much more closely the more acceptable attitude Schoenberg stated in his early essay, indicating the kind of thinking which would eventually lead him to adopt the twelve-tone method: [28]

> Inspired by the first words of the text, I had composed many of my songs straight through to the end. It turned out that I had never done greater

justice to the poet than when, guided by my first direct contact with the sound of the beginning, I divined everything that obviously had to follow the first sound with inevitability.

Thence it became clear to me that the work of art is like every other complete organism. It is so homogeneous in its composition that in every detail it reveals its truest, inmost essence.

Such a sense of inner cohesion is closely allied with the general tendency among Expressionists toward "reduction" in technique, to finding the basic material of any given work. This method became acutely important to musicians as the form-building function of tonality was eliminated, obviously, and also as various familiar methods of beginning, stating, developing, and ending began to seem outworn because they weakened the intensity and vibrant immediacy of individual musical moments. As in literature, much concern and invention was lavished on new methods of fragmentary presentation, such as starting *in medias res* or ending with an uncompleted phrase. Closely allied with this was the tendency toward very short, concentrated totalities after the analogy of a Chinese character or a hieroglyph. The works of Schoenberg and Webern of this type are well known. It is interesting that among the Americans only Ives attempted this in works such as the songs *Anne Street, Maple Leaves, 1,2,3,* and *Soliloquy.*

But not only this type of fragmentation was common among Expressionists but also the fragmentation of the materials of the work. In this respect the music of Varèse is particularly significant in that its material is made up of small fragments for the most part and these fragments are generally reduced to very basic, elemental shapes—melodic material made of repeated notes, repeated chordal sounds depending for their telling effect on their instrumentation, vertical spacing, and timing. Varèse's music corresponds very closely to Mittner's delineation of several stages in the development of the expressionistic vision as seen in poetry and painting: [29]

> The visionary power of expressionism did not result in a sudden turning away from the observation of reality, but reached this goal through a series of steps. The first was a reduction of sense data. [Ernst] Barlach, in his sculptures, took a most important step in this direction in 1901 . . . he began to reduce methodically the lines of his figures to those which seemed to him the most important, and so achieved a new, vigorous, and very plastic presentation of the essence of his subjects. The second step consisted of the extraction and separate use of each aspect of the total sense perception as a thing in itself, detaching it from the object to which it belongs, with the consequent deformation of reality as an entity. Such a procedure evolved also in poetry through means specifically derived from painting, where it had caused a revolution in the field of color. . . . Color was no

longer added to figure, but figure to color. From such an unnaturalistic coupling of color and figure it is but a short step to the unnaturalistic coupling of any of the other elements of reality.

The dissociation of the various elements of reality and their reassembling in new ways, isolating, as Kandinsky did, color from shape, etc., is paralleled by the dissociation, first, of the various so-called "elements" of music— melody, harmony, rhythm. The next step was the more subtle one of dissociating certain qualities from others, such as tone-color from the above three, and finally the dissociation of all the presently called "parameters" from each other. All of these tendencies along with the "reductive" method are evident in Varèse.

In passing it is interesting to point out that the development of the resources of instrumental techniques, which was not so common in Europe until recently, had during this period an important exponent in America. Carlos Salzedo's *Modern Study of the Harp* (New York, 1921) presents a whole new repertory of effects for that instrument that are still not incorporated into our composers' vocabulary, as are the latest tapping and scraping of the violin from France and Poland.

Perhaps the other striking feature of resemblance between these two groups is the avoidance of repetition and the sense of continuous variation. Ives's statements about this are very indicative:

> Unity is too generally conceived of, or too easily accepted, as analogous to form, and form as analogous to custom, and custom to habit.[30]
>
> Coherence, to a certain extent, must bear some relation to the listener's subconscious perspective. But is this its only function? Has it not another of bringing outer or new things into wider coherence?[31]
>
> There may be an analogy—and on first sight there seems to be—between the state and power of artistic perceptions and the law of perpetual change, that ever-flowing stream, partly biological, partly cosmic, ever going on in ourselves, in nature, in all life . . . perhaps this is why conformity in art (a conformity which we seem naturally to look for) appears so unrealizable, if not impossible.[32]

NOTES

1. F. Busoni, *Entwurf einer neuen Aesthetik der Tonkunst*, Leipzig, 1907. References are to the English translation by Theodore Baker, *The New Aesthetic of Music* (New York, 1911). On pp.31–33 Busoni makes out a case for the division of the whole tone into sixths and refers to an American acoustician, Thaddeus Cahill,

whose Dynamophone could produce any division of pitch required of it. Also see D. Rudhyar, "The Relativity of our Musical Conceptions," *Musical Quarterly* (Jan., 1922), for a discussion of microtones.

2. *Perspectives of New Music*, Spring–Summer, 1965, pp.22–31.

3. Ives was a subscriber to a box at the Saturday afternoon concerts of the Boston Symphony at Carnegie Hall, and the author of this article remembers being invited to join him and Mrs. Ives at concerts where Scriabin's *Poème de l'Extase*, *Prométhée*, Stravinsky's *Sacre*, and Ravel's *Daphnis* were performed.

4. P. Rosenfeld, *Musical Portraits* (New York, 1920), pp.233ff., but compare his praise a few years later: *Musical Chronicle* (New York, 1923), pp.300–314.

5. H. Cowell, *New Musical Resources* (New York, 1930).

6. L. Rognoni, "Il Significato dell'Espressionismo come Fenomenologia del Linguaggio Musicale." J. Rufer, "Das Erbe des Expressionismus in der Zwölftonmusik." H. H. Stuckenschmidt, "Expressionismus in der Musik." L. Mittner, "L'Espressionismo fra l'Impressionismo e la Neue Sachlichkeit: Fratture e Continuità."

7. *Der Blaue Reiter*, a German collection of articles, reproductions of art works, music, etc., of the avant-garde of the early 1900s, ed. Wassily Kandinsky and Franz Marc (Munich, 1912); reprinted with extensive commentary in 1965 by R. Piper & Co. Verlag, Munich. It includes Schoenberg's "Das Verhältnis zum Text," an English version of which—"The Relationship to the Text"—appears in Schoenberg's *Style and Idea* (New York: Philosophical Library, 1950).

8. Walter Sokel, in *The Writer in Extremis (Expressionism in German Literature)* (Stanford: Stanford University Press, 1959; McGraw-Hill Paperback, 1964), devotes a whole chapter, "Music and Existence," to this subject.

9. W. Kandinsky, *Über das Geistige in der Kunst* (Munich, 1911); English trans., *Concerning the Spiritual in Art* (New York, 1947).

10. A. Schoenberg, "Aphorismen," *Die Musik* (Berlin 1909–1910); Italian trans. in L. Rognoni: *Espressionismo e Dodecafonia* (Milan, 1954).

11. A. Schoenberg, *Harmonielehre*, third ed. (Vienna, 1922).

12. Charles Ives, *Essays Before a Sonata, and other Writings*, ed. Howard Boatwright (New York: W. W. Norton, 1962).

13. Ibid, p.96 (p.81 and editor's note p.141 in Boatwright edition).

14. L. Rognoni, *Il Significato* . . . , p.9. "Just as expression is only possible in spoken language if an 'intersubjective relationship' is established, so it is in an even more direct and immediate way in musical language."

15. Rufer, pp.3–4.

16. Kandinsky, pp.31–32 (my translation from the German).

17. Schoenberg, *Harmonielehre*, p.393.

18. Ives, pp.89, 90, 91 (pp.76, 77 in Boatwright edition).

19. Kandinsky, op. cit.

20. Ives, p.36.

21. Busoni, p.8.

22. Mittner, pp.43ff. On this point Mittner has a footnote referring to another interpretation of the dichotomy by Sokel (op. cit.), who traces, as he calls it, "Pure Form and Pure Formlessness" back through German literary history in an attempt to show that it is a special product of the German cultural situation.

23. Mittner, p.36.
24. Cowell, op. cit.
25. R. Lenormand, *Étude sur l'Harmonie Moderne* (Paris, 1912).
26. Ives, pp.118, 119 (pp.97, 98 in Boatwright edition).
27. Ibid., p.57 (p.52 in Boatwright edition).
28. Schoenberg, *Style and Idea*, p.4.
29. Mittner, pp.32ff.
30. Ives, p.119 (p.98 in Boatwright edition).
31. Ibid., p.119 (p.98 in Boatwright edition).
32. Ibid., pp.82, 83 (p.71 in Boatwright edition).

The Time Dimension in Music

Music Journal, 23,8 (Nov. 1965)

[This article is based on a lecture given at the University of Texas at Austin.]

It should be obvious that music must participate in the time dimension and all that this implies. A work that does not take into account the listener's ability to distinguish sounds, to grasp, remember, and compare in some way their combinations, both sequential and simultaneous, in small durations, intermediate lengths, as well as over the whole composition, is very unlikely to hold a permanent interest for the listener.

It is toward this time dimension that my own interest has been directed since about 1940, and whatever musical techniques I have used are contributory to the main concern of dealing with our experience of time, trying to communicate my own experience of it and my awareness of this experience in others. This, as I listen to most other contemporary music, is dealt with in a very routine way, in spite of the fact that sometimes most unusual and fascinating combinations of sound are being presented.

Before discussing my main topic—the time dimension and its various ramifications in contemporary composition—I would like to say a few words about the situation of many composers such as myself who grew up in the generation after the great musical revolutions brought about by Schoenberg and Stravinsky. It seemed to us at that time that the music of these important composers had completely re-examined the traditional postulates about music and the hearing of music. The "basic dimensions" of music—pitch, duration, volume, and timbre—had been "separated out" and examined anew. For example, we have Schoenberg and Hauer's isolation of the pitch component—a process which eventually led to the twelve-tone system. We have works such as the third movement from the *Five Orchestral Pieces* of Schoenberg and various "Klangfarben-Melodie" works of Webern, in which the element of timbre is more or less isolated and dealt with in a systematic fashion. Works such as the *Rite of Spring* and others of Stravinsky showed an analogous re-examination of various rhythmic and durational procedures. We were all aware almost intuitively at that time that these procedures were going on, but it was only later that the exact systematic significance of these developments became clear to us. It was this music, along with that of Americans such as Charles Ives, which was most interesting to me in my youth and which opened up enough possibilities in music to cause me to dedicate my life to it.

But this music was also part of a general cultural pattern. Many of these works which were so impressive to us as works of art contained in their hyperexpressivity a reflection of the retreat from reason and emphasis on "emotion," which was then current in all the arts and, for that matter, in the very fabric of our social life. The appeal to the baser elements in man's nature through mass propaganda, the rise of Hitler to power, the inability of many of the world's leaders to face the issues necessary for their survival—all these elements seemed to be a disastrous result of one aspect of a general point of view, another of whose aspects had furnished the artistic vision of the composers whose music we loved. For this reason, many of these earlier works lost their urgency—although, naturally, not their musical interest. However, it was through contact with the works of Schoenberg written during the war, and especially with performances of his works I helped to arrange during the war and shortly thereafter, that this music began to have a more important meaning for some of us who were led to study it more carefully than we had. Contact with this and with the music of Ives and Ruggles led a few of us at that time to rethink our musical development and to strike out on a path still frowned on by the musical public and much of the profession in the United States, perhaps because of the poor, unenthusiastic performances that have given rise to much misunderstanding here.

To show one example—not directly related to rhythmic procedures—of how this idea of rethinking the basic materials of music had significance for me, let me quote the Fourth Etude from my *Eight Etudes and a Fantasy for Woodwind Quartet*. Here the "simplest" possible interval—the ascending minor second—is made the sole basis for an entire movement. The second is, of course, transposed and moved to different metrical positions. But it is always a minor second up and it is always stated in contiguous eighth notes. This seemed to me to create a very interesting structure which I had never heard used before in music—a structure very similar to that of the parquet floor on which we are standing. You see, it is made of small blocks of wood—all of the same dimension.

In pieces such as my *Piano Sonata* and my *Sonata for Cello and Piano* . . . I began to work with the rhythmic procedures which have proved to be so interesting for me in my later music. In the *Cello Sonata*, for example, the piano begins with a steady rhythm and plays that pattern for most of the first movement while the cello enters with a more free metrical pattern. This "stratification" of musical elements by metrical and other means became very important for me in such works as my *First String Quartet*. Here the first movement is a contrapuntal fantasy which is built on four main and several subsidiary themes each in a different speed and each having a different character. These themes of course have influence on each other and modify each other in the course of the piece. Yet a great deal of the interest in the first quartet comes from passages in which four themes are stated simultaneously—interacting somewhat, yet also stratified by means of their being in different tempos. The fact of each theme being associated with a different tempo builds into the work the possibility and the necessity for metric modulation—a procedure in which the tempo or "beat" speeds up in an ordered manner between measures. Often, after many of these metrical modulations—which are in a sense analogous to the changes of key in a piece of tonal music—the piece will return to the original tempo. In my first quartet, for example, the material played by the cello at the beginning of the first movement is marked quarter-note equals 72. When this material returns in the first violin near the end of the entire piece, it returns at the speed of quarter-note equals 72—though in this case the pitches are transposed up an octave and a fifth.

In this piece I was also very interested in examining the effects of the speeding up or slowing down of themes. The last movement, a set of Variations, is made up of a number of ideas which become slightly faster with each repetition until they reach the "vanishing point"—until they can no longer be perceived as the same idea. The "minor-third idea" heard originally in the cello reappears frequently throughout the movement, gradually gaining speed until it is turned into a tremolo near the end of the movement. Another aspect of this idea (the same is true of the other ideas of the Variations, but is more obvious in this case) is that it is obviously not new to the movement marked Variations, but has been going on for some time in the previous movement. This brings us to the question of the plan of movements in the piece—a plan which is very much related to the general idea of metrical modulation.

Note that while there are really four movements in this piece, only three are marked in the score as separate movements, and these three do not correspond to the four "real" movements. The four "real" movements are Fantasia, Allegro Scorrevole, Adagio, and Variations. But the movements are all played *attacca*, with the pauses coming in the middle of the Allegro Scorrevole and near the beginning of the Variations. Thus there are only two pauses, dividing the piece into three sections. The reason for this unusual division of movements is that the tempo and character change, which occurs between what are usually called movements, is the goal, the climax of the techniques of metrical modulation which have been used. It would destroy the effect to break off the logical plan of movement just at its high point. Thus pauses can come only between sections using the same basic material. This is most obvious in the case of the pause before the movement marked Variations. In reality, at that point the Variations have already been going on for some time.

My interest in the speeding up and slowing down of themes is also reflected in various procedures in the *Variations for Orchestra* and the *Double Concerto for Piano and Harpsichord with Two Chamber Orchestras*. For instance in the *Variations*, of two secondary themes usually associated with the main theme throughout the work, one becomes successively slower and the other successively faster at each appearance. This kind of technique is demonstrated more obviously and on a smaller scale in variations four and six. Variation four has a measured ritard over a four-measure phrase from an original tempo to one half of that tempo (which is then doubled), and variation six has a measured accelerando over a six-measure phrase to three times the original tempo (which is then divided by three). The balance of each of these movements repeats the respective metric pattern of speeding up or slowing down. The combination of these two procedures is found in my *Double Concerto for Piano and Harpsichord*. Beginning in measure 453 the harpsichord and all other instruments except the piano begin a measured ritard over a span of four measures to one half the original tempo. This same ritard pattern is repeated three times after the original and then slows, in one large measure, to ¼ the original speed. Meanwhile the piano has begun (in measure 453) a pattern of acceleration which continues throughout the ritards of all the other instruments. These means of metric stratification can be used in various ways to express different effects in the course of a work. In all these works I have tried to be as precise as possible about the effects desired and their manner of execution. Thus I do not write simply Accelerando and Ritardando at appropriate places, but I usually give specific metronome indications of the change desired. In a "measured accelerando" from MM 70 to MM 140 over a four-measure span, for example, one needs the MM indications 70, 83, 99, 118, and 140—adding 13, 16, 19, and 22, respectively.

As a final example, I would like to say a few words about my *Second String Quartet*. Here the four instruments are stratified according to their repertoire of intervals, their repertoire of rhythms, and their repertoire of musical gestures. The first violin, for example, specializes in the intervals of the minor third, perfect fifth, major ninth, and major tenth. Its fantastic and ornate character is borne out by its rhythmic repertoire, which is extremely contrasted. The second violin, on the other hand, shows very regular motion and moves steadily at its own metronome markings of 140, 70, and sometimes 280. The viola specializes in rhythmic relationships which are usually in the ratio 2:3 or 3:5, and the cello does not move at a steady tempo, but rather has accelerandos and ritards built in. This stratification of the instruments can be heard very clearly at the beginning of the piece. As the piece progresses, the diverse "characters" of the beginning come to influence each other and the repertoires of each "actor" begin to be shared. The work progresses through a climax involving each instrument's sharing the repertoires of each of the other instruments to an ending which serves a double function. There is a return to the intervallic stratification of the beginning, but there is also a sharing of functions—a fact made especially clear by the phrasing of the second violin, whose notes (usually individual pizzicato double-stops), serve to end motives that had been played up to then by other instruments.

Current Chronicle: New York

[Edward Steuermann]

The Musical Quarterly, 52,1 (Jan. 1966)

The striking text of Kafka, *Auf der Galerie*, used by Edward Steuermann for one of his last works, a *Cantata* for mixed chorus and orchestra (1964), furnishes such a significant comment on the type of performance to which he devoted an important part of his life, and his choice of this particular text such an insight into what must have been one of his attitudes about performance, that this discussion must begin by quoting it:

> If some frail, consumptive equestrienne in the circus were to be urged round and round on an undulating horse for months on end without respite by a ruthless, whip-flourishing ringmaster, before an insatiable public, whizzing along on her horse, throwing kisses, swaying from the waist, and if this performance were likely to continue in the infinite perspective of a drab future to the unceasing roar of the orchestra and hum of the ventilators, accompanied by ebbing and renewed swelling bursts of applause which are really steam hammers—then, perhaps, a young visitor to the gallery might race down the long stairs through all the circles, rush into the ring, and yell: Stop! against the fanfares of the orchestra still playing the appropriate music.
>
> But since that is not so; a lovely lady, pink and white, floats in between the curtains, which proud lackeys open before her; the ringmaster, deferentially catching her eye, comes towards her breathing animal devotion; tenderly lifts her up on the dapple-gray, as if she were his own most precious granddaughter about to start on a dangerous journey; cannot make up his mind to give the signal with his whip, finally masters himself enough to crack the whip loudly; runs along beside the horse, openmouthed; follows with a sharp eye the leaps taken by its rider; finds her artistic skill almost beyond belief; calls to her with English shouts of warning; angrily exhorts the grooms who hold the hoops to be most closely attentive, before the great somersault lifts up his arms and implores the orchestra to be silent; finally lifts the little one down from her trembling horse, kisses her on both cheeks and finds that all the ovation she gets from the audience is barely sufficient; while she herself, supported by him, right up on the tips of her toes, in a cloud of dust, with outstretched arms and small head thrown back, invites the whole circus to share her triumph—

since that is so, the visitor to the gallery lays his face on the rail before him and, sinking into the closing march as into a heavy dream, weeps without knowing it.[1]

In spite of a typical Kafkaesque ambiguity, on one level at least, this can be read as a double view of the performing situation, contrasting the "behind the scenes," tired, routined "professional" aspect with its communicative, evocative intention. The deep ambiguity about which aspect is "real" and which "imagined" for the various participants, and also the comment one aspect makes on the other, is not lost on the "young visitor." Steuermann's setting casts a mask of highly sensitive, beautifully connected phrases over the whole text, avoiding any direct reference to the circus world but for an occasional drum roll and any other mimicry. In one continuously developed movement that minimizes the contrast between the two paragraphs and dramatic moments such as the young visitor's "Stop" or the rider's "great somersault," it passes these over quickly to emphasize a fleeting, alternately shadowy and excited nervous character. The score is one of delicate shadings, smooth transitions, with a mosaic of contrasting bits of material of much greater variety, character, and expressive scope than those of the late Webern cantatas, which it remotely resembles, although actually closer in character to the pre-twelve-tone Viennese works. In emphasizing musical over dramatic development, it bears out Steuermann's statement to Gunther Schuller: "His [Schreker's] approach was a little *theatralisch*, which was against the spirit of the Schoenberg school."[2]

This *Cantata* was given its posthumous first performance at the Juilliard School at a memorial concert devoted to Steuermann's works, one year after his death, and like the three other original works on the program: *Drei Chöre*, for mixed voices with instrumental accompaniment (1956), the *Suite for Piano* (1954), and the *Suite for Chamber Orchestra* in four movements (1964)—to which was added a charming arrangement for three pianos of Schubert's *Wohin*—represents his personal development of the general style of the Schoenberg school, in an apparently original way. I say "apparently" because Steuermann's music and indeed a great deal written by those associated with or influenced by this school (other than Berg, Webern, and perhaps Krenek, Eisler, Pisk, and Weiss), like that of many who came to maturity before the Second World War, is hardly known in spite of the interesting but far too sketchy account of their work in Leibowitz's *Introduction à la musique de douze sons* (Paris, 1949) and a few articles by Adorno. This lack of recognition, performance, and publication prevents us from knowing the many interesting developments of this style and the mutual influences as well as the individual originalities. That there was such a development can be clearly seen in works of Wellesz, Gerhardt, Kahn, Apostel, Gielen (to name but a few at random), and Steuermann himself. The works of the last-named heard at this concert represent what must have been a long development in a special direction. The style differs from the known one by a much greater freedom in pitch recurrences within each statement of the row, octave encounters, octave transpositions, and even tonal references. Partly because of similarities in technical features and in general character, this reviewer was reminded of some of the music of the very youngest generation of Polish composers—Krauze, Madey, and Meyer—heard at the Warsaw Autumn this year. This may represent a reaction against the "post-Webern" style, so different from the music of Steuermann, which emphasizes sensitivity, fanciful variety, and "heard" inner organization.

The special quality that informed his thinking, aside from the musico-grammatical traits mentioned above, is evident in all four compositions played, particularly the two composed in 1964. These reveal a wealth of imagination about musical syntax, as regards construction of motifs and textures into phrases, phrases into sentences, paragraphs, total composi-tions, and the inner articulation of all of these. There is even a complexity of articulation that resembles the interplay of verbal syntactical structures and versification structures, which fall into lines and stanzas not necessarily coordinated with the former. Much imagination is expended on such things as the preparation for the beginning of a phrase, its type of actual "begin-ning" with varied degrees of new or referential assertiveness or with direct linking with previous ones, its "middle" comprising perhaps an expressive or accented point of emphasis, and its "end"—strong or weak, abrupt or prolonged. Similarly there is a great concern for interrelation of phrases, of cross-cutting one with another, of sharply delineated or ambiguous and concealed articulations. The *Suite for Chamber Orchestra* (1964) in particu-lar maintains an interesting flow of constantly evolving dialectical state-ments made of short strands (often three-note motifs) of contrasting inter-vallic, rhythmic, timbral, and dynamic content that in combination produce flexible phrases in a logical and expressive continuity (see the example).

Note the transition from 14 to 15 with the pivotal A passed from guitar doubled by viola to the cello, and the descending melodic interval A–C♯ in eighth-notes, *piano*, suddenly expanded to A–C by the cello, in sixteenths, *forte*, also the linking fourth G♯–C♯ starting in 16 in the viola pizzicato, then picked up the violin tremolo, sul ponticello, each softly, then suddenly attacked by the marimba tremolo *sforzando-piano*, which is held as a new phrase enters in 18, started by the viola, which refers, near its end, on the last quarter of the measure, to the pitches in question. This example, besides showing a frequently employed method of pivotal tones, also shows a linking by similar sonorities (the diminished triad in 14 is heard transposed in 15), and the interweaving of short motifs of different character and intervallic content.

It is impossible to point out many such devices within the cumbersome limits of a printed discussion. But in thinking about them, the remarkable performance of Chopin's Preludes given by Steuermann a few years ago at the Juilliard School is brought to mind. For many this was one of the more memorable musical experiences of recent years. Discussing this performance after the concert, he explained, humorously referring to the fact that he was a Pole, too, that he had tried to find in each of these pieces that which interested him most as a composer and to bring them to the attention of the listener, without, of course, violating Chopin's intentions. In performance, each prelude became a work of special character, different from the others not merely in general expression and sonority but even in thought process. Certain moments left a lasting impression—the way, for instance, the much-discussed E♭ came in at the end of the F major Prelude as a structural event prepared throughout the piece, not as the commonplace effect of sonority it is usually thought of. And this moment was made to seem part of a whole series of similar events in other preludes, as part of the logic of the entire set. His performance made the listener sit up and listen so as not to miss the wealth of freshness seen in a work that is only too familiar.

Theodor W. Adorno, who studied piano with him in 1921, says:

> It is however true that the discipline and control that this kind of performance exacts from the performing musician is more than unusual and approaches the unbearable. Steuermann increased the ability to analyze concretely to a point of magnificent defeatism of Kafka proportions. When he despaired of all his pupils and wondered if they would ever learn to play the piano properly, he was animated by the fact that he asked the same question of himself—a question he expressed frequently and very seriously. . . . With talmudic strength, by interlinear vision, so to speak, he made the signs and markings of the score speak to him. But equally strong was his expressionist impulse: as a pianist, Steuermann freed musical expression in agitated eruptions from its taboos.[3]

Steuermann was born in Poland in 1892, went to Vienna to study with Busoni shortly before 1914, and joined the Schoenberg circle, to which he devoted his remarkable musical abilities not only as a pianist who cham-

ELLIOTT CARTER

Edward Steuermann: Suite for Chamber Orchestra (1964).
Reprinted by permission of Clara Steuermann.

pioned Schoenberg's and other modern works from then until the end of his life, abroad and here, but as an arranger of them for piano, as their analyst, and as a coach imparting information about their performance that he had received from Schoenberg. His contact with this music gave a special, urgent quality to his playing of the classics. As Adorno says:

> Steuermann not only had an open, receptive mind for the modern radicals, but he was part and parcel of their very existence, and embodies the refutation of the fatal habit of separating actual composing from music making. The interpreter is doomed when he feels closer to music of a different age and relating to circumstances now remote, than to music that rises from his own historic moment.[4]

In his years in this country from 1936, he was at first in the difficult position of a refugee, and then during the '40s and '50s of the typical advanced musician living in a society that did not favor his particular talents; like many others of the time—Roberto Gerhardt and Egon Wellesz in England, Wladimir Vogel in Switzerland, Stefan Wolpe, Erich Itor Kahn, Ernst Toch here, and a host of others composing in a style unappreciated at the time—he suffered tragic neglect. By the time Schoenberg came to this country in 1933 the earlier period of interest and even enthusiasm for the musical avant-garde both of America and Europe had passed. Enthusiastic support to these, as was given by Huneker and Rosenfeld in their criticisms of the early '20s and by Stokowski at Philadelphia Orchestra concerts, had given way to the views of a new generation, which looked back on this music as "old-fashioned modernism." Conductors were following the lead of Koussevitzky in hailing neo-Classicism and populism as the vital new trend. Nevertheless, the previous modernist groups never ceased entirely to be active and fought to give performances. One of the most energetic in this was Steuermann himself, who, with Mark Brunswick and Roger Sessions, gave a series of Contemporary Concerts in 1939 and 1940 in which those interested heard, perhaps for the first time in America, excellent performances of the Viennese composers and others that had figured in the Viennese concerts whose programs these followed. The very smallness of this effort, which continued, always aided by Steuermann as adviser, as organizer, and as performer, during the active years of the ISCM and then of its combination with the League of Composers well into the '50s, had a very selective effect on the choice of music. Works of a composer such as Steuermann were by the very nature of things neglected, even by himself, in the effort to present performances of the as yet unfamiliar works of the well-known Viennese, those of the older American avant-garde, and those of the few young Americans who were developing along these lines and could find no place else to hear their works. The patient and self-denying attitude of many in Steuermann's position at that time helped to lay the groundwork for the rediscovery of this avant-garde, which took place after the war, and helped to keep alive a way of thinking about music, of composing, that for a time seemed about to disappear. American musicians owe an immense debt of gratitude to this group and to Steuermann for, first, having kept alive our faith in this music and, second, having made it as meaningful in performance as it had seemed in score.

His own attitude is best summed up in an article he wrote on the occasion of Schoenberg's seventy-fifth anniversary for the Australian journal *The Canon*:

> All this is Schoenberg's life: fight, incessantly from the very beginning; fight for the future, fight for the past—the past he overcame to show the future, the future he showed to preserve the past. These battles are history by now. . . . There is hardly a musician of our time not influenced by him, hardly any music conceivable which by-passes his work and thought.
>
> As the memory of the struggle becomes more distant it seems as though the fight had raged mostly around misunderstandings: matters of style, method, theory. These have been accepted, voluntarily or subconsciously, in faith or in protest, possibly laying the ground for new misunderstandings.[5]

Now that the music he fought for is being recognized, it is important for us to know the music of those, who like Steuermann, continued to carry its implications in unfamiliar directions.

NOTES

1. Translated by Willa and Edwin Muir.

2. Gunther Schuller: "A Conversation with Edward Steuermann," *Perspectives of New Music*, Fall–Winter 1964, p.23

3. T. W. Adorno: "Nachruf auf einen Pianisten: Zum Tode von Eduard Steuermann," *Süddeutsche Zeitung*, Nov. 28/29, 1964.

4. Ibid.

5. E. Steuermann: "A Great Mind and A Great Heart," *The Canon—The Australian Journal of Music*, Sept. 1949, p.111.

Introduction to a Poetry
Reading Session by W. H. Auden

Hunter College Playhouse, January 1969

As a composer of music, I would like to use this opportunity to thank Mr. Auden publicly for his wonderful writing for and about my art. What musician can resist the line "Music is the brandy of the damned." Or what composer, the lines about him:

> Only your notes are pure contraption,
> Only your song is an absolute gift.

Or about his work:

> You alone, alone, imaginary song,
> Are unable to say an existence is wrong.
> And pour out your forgiveness like wine.

From this and other things he has said, we can see he's an ideal listener, having a great fondness for the art, which led him to wide experience of its literature, and this in turn has resulted in wise thoughts and judgments, essays, libretti, and, finally, poems.

Because of his direct experience of music's immediacy, he never falls into that only too common kind of cultural alienation which substitutes abstractions about music for the imaginative involvement with what [Karl] Marx called "the living flower." This cultural alienation results in the non-listening to works of music and joins large parts of the establishment to whole sections of the avant-garde. Mr. Auden's breadth of comprehension and interpretation, based as it is on listening, keeps him above such trivialities and makes him someone to pay attention to even if you don't agree with him.

Much of his musical writings are occupied with the fundamental question—the attempt to define the identity of Western art music, describe its characteristics, and relate them to those of the other arts and, finally, to life. Thorny questions all of them.

He often says things forgotten by musicians themselves, such as: "A verbal art like poetry is reflective; it stops to think. Music is immediate, it goes on to become."

In extolling the particular quality of Western art music he points out that it is unlike all other kinds because it, as he says, "deals with our experience of Time in its twofold, natural or organic repetition and historical novelty created by choice. And the full development of music as an art depends on a recognition that these two aspects are different and that choice, being an experience confined to man, is more significant than repetition."

To a composer his most fascinating encounter with music is the way in which he and Chester Kallman tackled the matter of opera libretti and produced three excellent ones: *The Rakes' Progress* for Stravinsky's master-piece, as well as *Elegy for Young Lovers* and *The Bassarids* for Hans Werner Henze. In seeing and hearing these works, a composer, especially, ap-preciates the fact that Mr. Auden never forgets that the music is the main thing in an opera and that the libretto should give ample opportunity for it.

Messrs. Auden and Kallman realize, as few librettists have, that the basic problem is to justify art music as the central element in the stage production. This justification has to be intrinsic to the plot or to the subject matter itself, has to inform every dramatic situation and verbal text to make the enterprise convincing—as it so seldom is nowadays, so seldom, indeed, that many have wondered whether opera could ever become a living art form again. Mr. Auden has made a significant effort to revalidate it.

Of opera he remarks: "A credible situation in an opera means a situation in which it is credible that someone should sing. A good libretto plot is a melodrama in both the strict and the conventional sense of the word; it offers as many opportunities as possible for the characters to be swept off their feet by placing them in situations which are too tragic or fantastic for 'words.'"

Finally in this connection, let me read something I have always enjoyed very much although I don't agree with it since, being a musician, I don't have a very clear idea of what the word *sensible* means. He writes: "The theory of 'music drama' presupposes a libretto in which there is not one sensible moment or one sensible remark: this is not only difficult to manage, though Wagner managed it, but also extremely exhausting on both singers and the audience, neither of whom may relax for an instant."

And so now let's hear something sensible from Mr. Auden.

Charles Ives Remembered

Charles Ives Remembered: An Oral History, by Vivian Perlis
(New Haven: Yale University Press, 1974).

[This article was written by Carter *after* his interview with Vivian Perlis, i.e., as a result of the interview; it is not a transcript of the interview itself, as the term *oral history* might suggest.]

In 1924, when I was a student at Horace Mann School in New York City, my music teacher, Clifton Furness, who knew Ives, showed me some of his music. Furness was interested in contemporary arts of all kinds—it wasn't merely Ives's music, but also various performers of new music like Katherine Ruth Heyman, artists like the Russian refugees David Burliuk and Nicholas Roerich. Also, through Eugene O'Neill, Jr., a fellow high school student, we followed the lively productions of the Provincetown Playhouse on Mac-Dougal Street [New York]. It was an exciting time for contemporary arts: *The Dial*** was in full swing: *Ulysses*, which we all read, was banned; and O'Neill wrote one remarkable play after another, stirring up a great deal of controversy.

Miss Heyman, a very progressive pianist for those days, had been a friend of Ezra Pound in London before the First World War, had befriended the much neglected Charles Griffes here, and was regarded by her circle as a spokesman for the avant-garde "great" from the immediately previous period, both as a musician and a conversationalist. It was at her weekend afternoons, in a loft apartment on 15th Street and Third Avenue, in a little triangular building (now razed) that I first heard parts of the *Concord Sonata* around '24 or '25. She played much other new music for her friends then, particularly Griffes, Emerson Whithorne, Dane Rudhyar, Ravel, Debussy, Schoenberg's opus 11, no. 2, and especially Scriabin. The group that came to these dimly lit gatherings admired the latter very much. I myself, enthusiastic, soon acquired all the late works at considerable effort and practiced the polyrhythms in works like *Vers la flamme* and the *Eighth*

---

* A monthly published in Chicago, 1880–1929.—Eds.

Etude of Opus 42. Ives used to appear occasionally at these private recitals, but whether I met him there for the first time or where, I really couldn't say.

Both Furness and Miss Heyman, along with a few habitués who came to these séances, were involved with what might be called extra-musical ideas. She was committed to mysticism, having been a member of the Annie Besant theosophical circle in her London days, while Furness was drawn to Rudolf Steiner's anthroposophy. I myself read quite a number of Steiner's works with great interest in those days. Therefore, the mystical, transcendental aspect of Ives's music had a particular appeal to the group. There was, however, a strong feeling among this group against Schoenberg's music, which was considered a kind of dangerous black art (the "Satanic" side of Liszt and Scriabin, on the other hand seemed perfectly OK). From this point of view, Ives was considered a kind of white god and much reverenced. The mystical bias in all of this appealed to an adolescent, though it was not long before I began to feel these judgments unreliable when it came to artistic matters. In retrospect I would have thought that Ives would not have liked this kind of thing.

My impression, then, however, was that Ives had a rather restricted world of musical contacts, limited to the few that really admired his music, and it was understandable that he would be drawn to interested musicians, no matter what their other views, in a desire for human talk about contemporary music.

Ives was certainly involved and interested in music of his time and didn't remain aloof from it: as much as he could be, he was part of it. He was very generous to *New Music Edition*, which published modern scores quarterly for years, of which Henry Cowell was editor. Later, when I succeeded Cowell, for a while we continued to receive an annual contribution from Ives of a thousand dollars, which, in those days, went far to printing modern scores. Besides this help to other composers, Ives subsidized the printing of many of his own music scores and his *Essays Before a Sonata* and sent these around to libraries all over the country, including, to my surprise, the library of the American Academy in Rome, where I found copies a few years ago. He was not a recluse in the sense that he didn't want his music to be known to the music profession, which he looked on with some suspicion; on the contrary, I think he was making a distinct effort to take his place among the composers of his time.

When Ives expressed opinions about the music profession as it existed in his time in America, there was much anger at its timidity and its secondhand cultural attitudes. He expressed himself in the *Essays*, verbally, but also in the many marginal comments in his music manuscripts. Some of the music itself is a direct reflection of his scorn and anger—poking fun at the music profession and sometimes, I think, punishing it by intentionally peculiar cacophony or vulgarity. Every American composer cannot help but understand this attitude. During Ives's lifetime, Dvořák was brought over here to explain and demonstrate what American music should be, and now we subsidize Stockhausen and others as if they could show us the way.

Like many composers of his time, he was sensitive about the criticism that the modern composer really didn't know how to write "music." Once in talking about this he told me that in order to prove that he could write in a conventional style, he had written his *Third Violin Sonata*. He then played this with comments for me on a privately made recording by a violinist who had played all four sonatas the previous year, I think, at Aeolian Hall. It was at this same meeting, I believe, that he showed me the score of his *First Symphony*, written as a student of Horatio Parker, and pointed out details Parker had objected to, particularly modulations that did not follow the then accepted sonata-form formulas. How scornful he was of the latter— saying, as has often been said more recently (and also at that time by Debussy), that the great sonata writers had never followed the rules.

One of the most vivid memories I have of Ives is of an afternoon when he lived on East 22nd Street, near Gramercy Park. It may have been our first meeting, where we were invited after a concert on a Sunday afternoon, which I described in an article in *Modern Music*[1] when my memory was fresher. It was perhaps in the years '24–'25, when I was occasionally invited to sit in the Ives box (which he subscribed to for the Saturday afternoon Boston Symphony series at Carnegie Hall), and I remember returning with him to excited discussions of the new music at his house. I was then very surprised about his attitudes and so remember quite distinctly what he thought. He invariably felt that each of the new pieces like, I think, Ravel's *Daphnis et Chloé* or Stravinsky's *Rite of Spring*, although I am not sure it was the latter, revealed extremely simple-minded ways of dealing with new harmonies and rhythms. I remember vividly his "take-off" at the piano of the Ravel chord and of the repetitiousness of Stravinsky. Ives was very literate and sharp about this—he seemed to remember quite clearly bits of what he had heard and could parody them surprisingly well. His point was that most all contemporary composers of the time had chosen the easy way out. Perhaps out of deference for our interests at that time, I don't remember his taking off on Scriabin, although both *Le Poème de l'extase* and *Prométhée* were heard occasionally then. Scriabin's music might well have been criticized for the same reasons as the others—excessive repetition, mechanical formalism, and the isolation of some small formula in an unwillingness to deal with a large body of musical material. Ives's *Essays*, too, which contain rather pointed asides about Stravinsky and especially Debussy, express some disagreement with his musical contemporaries. But, in spite of what he said, I think Ives had a genuine interest in new music. I remember seeing, to my surprise, the score of Prokofiev's *Love of Three Oranges* lying on a desk in his house in Redding [Connecticut]. I couldn't believe he could be interested in Prokofiev at that time, although it was right after the opera, commissioned by the Chicago Opera, had been performed. One of the myths that has grown up about Ives is that he never knew about and never heard contemporary music. This may have been true in his early years, but by the time I met him it was not. By then surely he had heard some of the piano pieces of Schoenberg[2] and Scriabin, and works of Stravinsky and others, and had read about all of these and others in the pages of the *Pro Musica Quarterly*,* copies of which he must have received as one of its sponsors, and also the scores of *New Music Edition*, which printed many new works besides his own.

I seem to remember—it's hard for me to believe now—that it used to be said among us that after a few social evenings early in their married life, at which Ives's excited, enthusiastic outbursts had overpowered the gathering, Mrs. Ives had considered it more prudent not to accept such invitations any more, as her husband could not be counted on to take a social situation into account. He was, as is well known, secretive with his business associates about his music. He would tell how he had gone up in the elevator to his office with someone who said, "Ives, you know, yesterday I heard *Parsifal* at the opera. It's a fine thing. You should go to the opera sometimes." He seemed ruefully proud that he kept all of this from the people in the office, but the other side of the story, apparently, was that they all knew of his music but played the game.

He was a complicated, quick, intelligent man with, obviously, an enormous love and wide knowledge of music, and with a determination to follow his own direction, believing in it deeply. Yet he seemed to have been almost unwilling to witness the imperfections of the performances he had and reluctant to face and solve them. It may have been too disturbing for his excitable nature to discover his works did not come out as he wanted, either

* Periodical of the Pro Musica (formerly Franco-American) Society, published from 1920 to 1932.—Eds.

because they were not carefully or practically enough marked with dynamic indications—the score of the second movement of the *Fourth Symphony*, printed after the 1927 performance, shows an elaboration of dynamic markings seldom found in others—or else because musicians had not rehearsed sufficiently. So he seems to have avoided concerts where his own music was played, although attending the rehearsals, as he did with the performance of the *Fourth Symphony* movement. The suspense and excitement of public performance and the ensuing reaction were said to be too much for him to bear. I remember a dismaying demonstration of this overexcitability which occurred when he was playing parts of *Emerson* for me at Redding. A vein on the side of his neck began to bulge as if it were going to burst with the tremendous energy and excitement he was putting into the performance. Apparently accustomed to this, he stopped playing, pinched the vein as if to stop the flow of blood, and went to lie down on a sofa to recover, his wife bringing him a glass of milk. Perhaps he had been warned by a doctor that he must avoid excitement, and it's possible that for this reason he did not go to concerts.

In any case it seems in retrospect he had already begun to withdraw from active life by the time I met him, although this tendency, perhaps, had always existed. But it seemed clear even at that time that there had been a great disillusionment with America as it emerged from the First World War, a crass, materialistic society that no longer lived up to the ideals he so worshiped. I suppose his reputed refusal to read the New York newspapers, subscribing instead to the London *Times*, was a symptom of this. For in talk about contemporary politics, he seemed profoundly disturbed by the bungling and compromising that had gone on with the peace settlement and the postwar negotiations which had destroyed the illusion that the war had been fought for a noble cause.

Yet being the idealistic man he was, such things were not in the foreground of his thought. It was part of his attractiveness that he was so lively, so full of enthusiasm, and, except in the instances mentioned above, not given (at least at any time I saw him) to bitterness and pessimism. In fact, he was so uncritically enthusiastic about the things he cared for that there seemed to be little counterbalancing cool judgment or cynicism, which might have helped him to be more realistic about the notation of his more intricate scores.

A matter which puzzles me still is the question of Ives's revisions of his own scores. I can remember vividly a visit on a late afternoon to his house on East 74th Street, when I was directed to a little top-floor room where Ives sat at a little upright piano with score pages strewn around on the floor and on tables—this must have been around 1929. He was working on, I think, *Three Places in New England*, getting the score ready for performance. A new score was being derived from the older one to which he was adding and changing, turning octaves into sevenths and ninths, and adding dissonant notes.[3] Since then, I have often wondered at exactly what date a lot of the music written early in his life received its last shot of dissonance and polyrhythm. In this case he showed me quite simply how he was improving the score. I got the impression that he might have frequently jacked up the level of dissonance of many works as his tastes changed. While the question no longer seems important, one could wonder whether he was as early a precursor of "modern" music as is sometimes made out. A study of the manuscripts would probably make this clear. It's obvious to me both from his music and his prose that Ives was really familiar with Debussy, for there are many piano figurations and conceptions of music that seem derived from the French composer, although, of course, he transformed them in a most original and personal way. Ives, although he was not aware of it, probably belonged to the 1890–1920 period with a strong retrospective view of the transcendental–Civil War period. This was brought home to me very intensely at our last meeting.

When my father and mother were living in Westport, Connecticut, I remember driving their car over to Redding with some music, showing it to Ives, and spending a whole day with him talking and walking around in the woods behind his house. My family was so upset about my becoming a musician that I thought I ought to get the advice of respected people before I really broke away and became the rebel I had to be. This was in '28 or '29, during my college years. Ives was certainly not enthusiastic about the neo-Classic music I was then writing. My memory is that he had seen other music of mine before I went to college which he thought more promising and had on the basis of that encouraged me to go on. (Just before Henry Cowell died, he returned one of my boyish compositions submitted to *New Music Edition* in the '20s that had gotten lost in his files. It wasn't much good, I must say. It's a wonder Ives or anyone else could have seen anything in it.) That day was the last I saw Ives, except for occasional times when I used to take the morning train from Westport to New York during the summer, which stopped at South Norwalk and picked up passengers from the Danbury spur, among whom occasionally was Ives on his way to his office. When I saw him get on, I usually would wait until the last stop before New York before going to talk to him.

Ives's influence on my music has varied greatly from '24 to now. It was very important before I actually decided to become a musician. But when I began to study music formally at college in '26, its value diminished a great deal, because I was anxious to learn how to write music step by step, not only by traditional methods but from the new music that was within my grasp to imagine auditively and to formulate clear ideas about. From that time there was a mounting sense of frustration when I returned to Ives's music, which I have done frequently, because much of it then seemed so disordered and even disorganized that, given the point of view I held then, it was nearly impossible to understand how or why much of it was put together as it was. This experience, coupled with a growing anti-Romantic outlook characteristic of most young composers of the '30s and '40s, led me to try to cultivate clarity and sharp definition of musical material, qualities antithetical to Ives's work.

Out of this attitude, a distressing dilemma arose, for when John Kirkpatrick finally gave the first performance of the complete *Concord Sonata* at Town Hall in 1939, I was disappointed in the piece that had previously meant so much to me. Unfortunately, being the critic for the magazine *Modern Music* and being quite knowledgeable about the sonata and about Ives, I felt I had to write a long review of the work expressing my views.[4] The critic's obligation to speak his thoughts frankly, painful as it was to me as one who wanted to admire Ives, made me very sad. After what I wrote then, I never had the heart to see Ives again.

Later in the mid-40s, I began to think I had been wrong about the *Concord Sonata*, that I should go back and reconsider all of Ives's works more closely.[5] I plowed patiently through the eleven-volume photostat collection of his unpublished works that Ives had deposited at the America Music Center.* As I did, frequently surprised and delighted, I began to list pages out of order, hardly legible, or apparently missing. It became clear to me that a great deal of work needed to be done to get some of the manuscripts in shape for performance, and it would help if Ives could be consulted, even in his sickness, before he died. I got in touch with Mrs. Ives to propose such a project, asking if Ives would cooperate. They agreed, so I began to work on one piece after another, raising questions, planning for copying. Unfortunately I found very quickly I was temperamentally unsuited to unscramble the confusion of many of the manuscript sketches. Not only would they take inordinate amounts of time (with no certainty that an

* See also the footnote by John Kirkpatrick on p.100 of the present collection—Eds.

actual piece would emerge), but I could not make the rough decisions necessary, for only too frequently there was a palimpsest of three or four alternatives. The mounting sense of confusion with which his music has at times overwhelmed me was at this juncture too much for me to take, and I stopped, but not before finding others, in particular Lou Harrison and Henry Cowell, who were devoted to the project and more able to face its problems. At about the same time, I planned a book on Ives with [critic] Paul Rosenfeld, but the latter's death put an end to this.

As I scanned the Ives manuscripts, the *Fourth Symphony* looked the largest and the most important. However, unlike the other three movements, the last was scribbled in pencil with many perplexing alternatives sketched in the margins. I remember a few measures for six trombones, a number never called for again. I began to wonder whether this movement could ever be gotten into playable shape. The second movement was printed after a concert performance in 1927 (Ives had invited the New York Philharmonic percussionists to his house and beaten out the complicated rhythms on the dining room table until they learned them). Its markings, as I have said, are much more elaborate and carefully done than in any other Ives scores—which usually content themselves with very vague indications that force the performer, often, to invent his own. Perhaps if Ives had had more and better performances during his life, the other scores would have been similarly marked.

The first and third movements of the *Fourth Symphony* have been printed very much as they appeared in the photostated volumes. The third, which is about seventy-five percent the same as the first movement of the *First String Quartet*, has a few irregular bar lengths, polyrhythms, and dissonances added especially at the expanded climax near the end. Comparison between these two shows, in small, how Ives revised his works to suit the changes brought about by his musical development, as do, in a much more problematic way, the incorporation of parts of the *Hawthorne* movement of the *Concord Sonata* into the piano part of the second movement of the *Fourth Symphony*.

It is most mysterious that it took musicians and public so long to catch on to the fact of Ives's music, once the contemporary movement began to take hold in the United States during the '20s. Quite late, perhaps during the Second World War, I think, I can remember talking Ives over with Goddard Lieberson,[6] who in turn arranged a lunch with Stokowski to try to convince him that there were a lot of remarkable pieces that ought to be played. The latter was very cautious, saying that the works were complicated, hard to rehearse, and would take much more time to prepare than could be arranged for.

With this and similar scenes in mind, I attended the ISCM festival in Baden-Baden in 1955, the year after Ives died, being one of the members of the Central Committee and having my *Cello Sonata* played there. I was immediately impressed by what was, to me, extraordinary, for I witnessed what was said to be the fiftieth (or so) rehearsal of Boulez's *Marteau sans maître*, at which the conductor, Hans Rosbaud, was still picking apart little details, patiently getting an instrument to play the part exactly as written with the right dynamics, and so on. I immediately talked to the director of the Südwestfunk [SWF], Dr. Heinrich Strobel, saying, "You know, there's a very wonderful work of Ives, the *Fourth Symphony*, that the SWF Orchestra should play. It is probably the only orchestra that could afford the rehearsals of such a complicated piece, and with its conductor who is so interested in new music and so painstaking with it, you would be helping the cause of new music by presenting this important work in a fine, well-rehearsed performance." Strobel got in touch with the various people in the United States who had custody of the score, as I suggested. This led to those in the United States being disturbed by the possibility that the German radio might get the first performance of the work, and so they busied themselves with getting the score, especially the last movement, in shape, copying the parts, and finally convincing Stokowski to do it. It took a request by the German radio to get the ball rolling, which ended in the typically American "big-time publicity" given to Ives's music.[7]

Many another remarkable work, like the *Browning Overture*, had to wait until the publicity had sifted down and done its work, while prior to this, efforts to get the orchestral works played in America by the major orchestras met with the kind of rebuff I described (except during the '30s when Nicolas Slonimsky conducted a few, as did Bernard Herrmann).

In spite of the efforts of some of us to get Ives's scores in shape, the declining health of Ives and his consequent inability to check on the orchestra parts of some of his available works meant that some of these were very badly, at times unprofessionally, copied. I know this, because when I was on another jury in Italy, I happened to have with me the old printed score of *The Fourth of July*, which I'd owned for a long time. When I presented this score to the music director of the Italian radio (who had never seen it), he burst with enthusiasm and said, "We've got to play this—it's one of the most interesting pieces I've ever seen." (Quite different from the reactions one used to get from musicians in important positions in the United States.) So the radio sent for the parts, which turned out to be so mixed up and confusing that the radio librarian had to have them copied all over again. The director of the radio station was quite angry and almost canceled the performance because of the mess in the original parts, which, I believe, Ives had had extracted for *New Music*. Now the work is published by another publisher, and there are probably better parts.

Each work has its difficulties because of Ives's inability in his later years to cope with musical situations. I remember that after I had looked through the volumes of photostated manuscripts, two of the works which intrigued me a great deal were *The Unanswered Question* and *Central Park in the Dark*. As I was then teaching at Columbia University and there was an annual Ditson Festival, I persuaded the festival committee to include premieres of these two works on the program [May 11, 1946]. I wrote to Mrs. Ives to ask if these were in fact first performances and for other program information. She wrote back a very charming letter quoting her ill husband, that they would not want to say those works were having their premieres—Mr. Ives wanted to be fair to those "old fellers" who had played them in between the acts of a theatrical performance around 1907 or 1908.

I don't think Ives had much influence on other composers until the *Fourth Symphony* publicity after his death; for Ives's music is, for the most part, very programmatic, and during the period of his life most composers of concert music were interested in writing "abstract" music, that is, music that depends on its design for its expression. Movie scores are different, and certainly those of Bernard Herrmann, who performed a lot of Ives's music with the CBS Symphony in the late '30s and '40s, were much influenced, particularly the one for *The Red Badge of Courage*, which sounds very much like Ives, I think.

As for myself, I have always been fascinated by the polyrhythmic aspect of Ives's music, as well as its multiple layering, but perplexed at times by the disturbing lack of musical and stylistic continuity, caused largely by the constant use of musical quotations in many works. To me a composer develops his own personal language, suitable to express his field of experience and thought. When he borrows music from another style and thought than his own, he is admitting that he did not really experience what he is presenting but has to borrow from someone else who did. In the case of early music, like masses on *L'homme armé*, or cantatas on Lutheran chorales, the original melody has a deep religious meaning so that, understandably, a very devout composer feels he needs to borrow it as a basis, since its expression transcends his own religious experience. These old tunes both united the composer to his listener and were very close in style to the music for which they formed a basis. At the other extreme of borrowing are the endless variations on popular or famous tunes in the nineteenth century, a very few of which produced great music, not really because of the tunes. Then there were the entertaining potpourris or medleys of patriotic airs, sometimes arranged humorously for band concerts; these have no artistic pretensions and reveal little fundamental musical imagination. Some of Ives's works belong close to this latter category, except for his daring "take-off" technique that often makes these pieces resemble "realistic" sound pictures of festive scenes. It is, to me, disappointing that Ives too frequently was unable or unwilling to invent musical material that expressed his own vision authentically, instead of relying on the material of others. But what is striking and remarkable in his work, like much of the *First* and *Second Piano Sonatas*, is an extraordinary musical achievement.

NOTES

[BY VIVIAN PERLIS]

1. Elliott Carter, "The Case of Mr. Ives," *Modern Music* 16, no. 3 (March–April 1939): 172–76 [pp.48–51 in the present collection—Eds.].
2. Mr. Carter later supplied the following footnote: "After having made this statement, I read in *Charles E. Ives Memos*, edited by John Kirkpatrick, that Ives wrote E. Robert Schmitz in 1931 that he had never heard a note of Schoenberg's music, and I realized that he must have been absent on each of the infrequent occasions when Miss Heyman played the Schoenberg piece (Op. 11, no. 2)."
3. *Three Places* was being prepared by Ives and Nicolas Slonimsky for the première performance of the work (1931) by Slonimsky's Boston Chamber Orchestra. (Since the work had originally been scored for full orchestra, it became necessary for Ives to rescore it to accommodate Slonimsky's small orchestra.)
4. Carter, "The Case of Mr. Ives."
5. Carter wrote a second article in 1944 discussing various works by Ives. Elliott Carter, "Ives Today: His Vision and Challenge," *Modern Music* 21, no. 4 (May–June 1944): 199–202 [pp.98–102 in the present collection—Eds.]
6. See Goddard Lieberson, pp.206–209 [in *Charles Ives Remembered: An Oral History*].
7. During the preparation of the score and parts of the *Fourth Symphony* for its first complete performance by the American Symphony Orchestra under Leopold Stokowski (April 26, 1965), it was discovered that a few pages from the fourth movement were missing from the American Music Center's collection of photostats of Ives's music. A search was made and these pages were found. It was claimed that

the fourth movement had been lost and was recovered as a result of the first performance preparations. Actually, all of the manuscript pages were complete and safe in West Redding, and it was only a few pages of negative photostats which had been temporarily mislaid.

Sonata for Cello and Piano (1948)
Sonata for Flute, Oboe, Cello, and Harpsichord (1952)

Program notes for Nonesuch recording H-71234 (stereo), 1969

> . . . *out of what one sees and hears and out*
> *Of what one feels, who could have thought to make*
> *So many selves, so many sensuous worlds,*
> *As if the air, the midday air, was swarming*
> *With the metaphysical changes that occur*
> *Merely in living as and where we live.*

In prefacing a chapter about my music with this quotation from Wallace Stevens,* Wilfrid Mellers, author of *Music in a New Found Land,* draws attention to some of the main aims of my work. It is quite true that I have been concerned with contrasts of many kinds of musical characters—"many selves"; with forming these into poetically evocative combinations—"many sensuous worlds"; with filling musical time and space by a web of continually varying cross references—"the air . . . swarming with . . . changes." And to me, at least, my music grows "out of what one sees and hears and out/Of what one feels," out of what occurs "Merely in living as and where we live."

The two pieces on this record are examples of this, since they treat of "metaphysical changes." For they were written during a time (1945–55)

---

*From *Esthétique du mal* (New York, 1950).—Eds.

when I was preoccupied with the time-memory patterns of music, with rethinking the rhythmic means of what had begun to seem a very limited routine used in most contemporary and older Western music. I had taken up again an interest in Indian *talas*, the Arabic *durub*, the "tempi" of Balinese *gamelans* (especially the accelerating *Gangsar* and *Rangkep*), and studied the newer recordings of African music, that of the Watusi in particular. At the same time, the music of the early *quattrocentro*, of Scriabin, Ives, and the techniques described in Cowell's *New Musical Resources* also furnished me with many ideas. The result was a way of evolving rhythms and rhythmic continuities, sometimes called "metric modulation," worked out during the composition of the *Cello Sonata* (1948) and further developed in the other sonata on this record.

To sketch briefly another part of the background of these works (although they are to be considered primarily for themselves and not in relation to their time or their composer), I became interested in music as a boy through the exciting early works of Stravinsky, Bartók, Varèse, and others. Later, while a music student in the late '20s and early '30s, the contemporary fashion changed and the latest thing—like, perhaps, live electronic music today—was the neo-classic revolt against the expressive and primitivist of the previous period. Music was to be anti-individualistic, to sound almost machine-made, and to use bits of "everyday music," pop, Baroque—anything that could be denatured into the cool, depersonalized character so much sought after. I found both directions increasingly unsatisfactory, and a return to older, "common-practice" music out of the question, so I took the steps described above.

Naturally any serious concern with rhythm, time, and memory must include the shaping of music, and I began to question the familiar methods of presentation and continuation, of so-called "musical logic," based on the statement of themes and their development. Certain older works, particularly those of Debussy, suggested a different direction. In considering change, process, evolution as music's prime factor, I found myself in direct opposition to the static repetitiveness of most early 20th-century music, against the squared-off articulation of the neo-classics and, indeed, against much of what is written today in which "first you do this for a while, then you do that." I wanted to mix up "this" and "that," make them interact in other ways than by linear succession. Too, I questioned the inner shape of "this" and "that"—of musical ideas—as well as their degrees of linking or non-linking. Musical discourse needed as thorough a rethinking as harmony had at the beginning of the century.

These two pieces are, then, steps along the way from a prevalent neo-classicism toward a freer, more vital and sensitive musical language. Both relate to their time and also look forward. The *Cello Sonata* uses bits of pop, but manipulates these in a way that produces the special rhythmic handling characteristic of most of my subsequent music. The *Sonata for Flute, Oboe, Cello, and Harpsichord* (1952) ends with another kind of "everyday music"—a Venetian gondolier's dance, the *forlana*—but draws out of the characteristic rhythmic cell of that dance all sorts of rhythmic changes, a continuity which only later was to become widely used. Both works are also prophetic in that, encouraged, perhaps, by the example of Debussy's last sonatas, they avoid classical development, use sonority as an item of musical thought, and aim for a fluid, changeable continuity. The later sonata starts its slow movement with a one-note theme, continuing the idea of my one-note piece in the *Eight Etudes and a Fantasy* of 1949, a conceit that has become the stock in trade of the avant-garde during the past few years (the *Etudes* were played at the 1958 Warsaw Festival).

Finally, because these works are virtuoso pieces for all the performers, they were considered impossibly difficult to perform when they were written; but now, after frequent performances, these scores seem to have taught musicians to play them with comparative ease and fluency, so that the attention is not on the technique but on the music, as this record demonstrates.

When I was asked in 1947 to write a work for the American cellist Bernard Greenhouse, I immediately began to consider the relation of the cello and piano, and came to the conclusion that since there were such great differences in expression and sound between them, there was no point in concealing these as had usually been done in works of the sort. Rather it could be meaningful to make these very differences one of the points of the piece. So the opening *Moderato* presents the cello in its warm expressive character, playing a long melody in rather free style, while the piano percussively marks a regular clock-like ticking. This is interrupted in various ways, probably (I think) to situate it in a musical context that indicates that the extreme disassociation between the two is neither a matter of random nor of indifference, but one to be heard as having an intense, almost fateful character.

The *Vivace*, a breezy treatment of a type of pop music, verges on a parody of some Americanizing colleagues of the time. Actually it makes explicit the undercurrent of jazz technique suggested in the previous movement by the freely performed melody against a strict rhythm. The following *Adagio* is a long, expanding, recitative-like melody for the cello, all its phrases interrelated by metric modulations. The finale, *Allegro*, like the second movement based on pop rhythms, is a free rondo with numerous changes of speed that ends up by returning to the beginning of the first movement with the roles of the cello and piano reversed.

As I have said, the idea of metrical modulation came to me while writing this piece, and its use becomes more elaborated from the second movement on. The first movement, written last, after the concept had been quite thoroughly explored, presents one of the piece's basic ideas: the contrast between psychological time (in the cello) and chronometric time (in the piano), their combination producing musical or "virtual" time. The whole is one large motion in which all the parts are interrelated in speed and often in idea; even the breaks between movements are slurred over. That is: at the end of the second movement, the piano predicts the notes and speed of the cello's opening of the third, while the cello's conclusion of the third predicts in a similar way the piano's opening of the fourth, and this movement concludes with a return to the beginning in a circular way like Joyce's *Finnegans Wake*.

The *Sonata for Flute, Oboe, Cello, and Harpsichord* was commissioned by the Harpsichord Quartet of New York and uses the instruments of which that ensemble was composed. My idea was to stress as much as possible the vast and wonderful array of tone-colors available on the modern harpsichord (the large Pleyel, for which this was first written, produces 36 different colors, many of which can be played in pairs, one for each hand; the Dowd that Paul Jacobs uses for this recording even has "half-hitches," which permit the different colors to be played at half as well as full force). The three other instruments are treated for the most part as a frame for the harpsichord. This aim of using the wide variety of the harpsichord involved many tone-colors which can only be produced very softly and therefore conditioned very drastically the type and range of musical expression, all the details of shape, phrasing, rhythm, texture, as well as the large form. At that time (in 1952, before the harpsichord had made its way into pop) it seemed very important to have the harpsichord speak in a new voice, expressing characters unfamiliar to its extensive Baroque repertory.

The music starts, *Risoluto*, with a splashing dramatic gesture whose subsiding ripples form the rest of the movement. The *Lento* is an expressive dialogue between the harpsichord and the others, with an undercurrent of fast music that bursts out briefly near the end. The *Allegro*, with its gondolier's dance fading into other dance movements, is cross-cut like a movie—at times it superimposes one dance on another.

The performances on this record* are remarkable, especially in view of some I have had to suffer through in the past. The outstanding technical and interpretative skill of each performer, each with his own individual way of playing and of joining the ensemble, comes through strikingly. The sonatas are reincarnated in a new, yet faithful way. Playing by such excellent performers brings to light new, unexpected aspects of these precisely notated pieces and is as lively, novel, and fresh as if the players were improvising.

*Cello Sonata: Joel Krosnick, cello; Paul Jacobs, piano. Sonata for Flute, Oboe, Cello, and Harpsichord: Harvey Sollberger, flute; Charles Kuskin, oboe; Fred Sherry, cello; Paul Jacobs, harpsichord.—Eds.

String Quartet No. 2 (1959)

Program note for the performance by the Composers Quartet (Anahid Ajemian and Matthew Raimondi, violins; Jean Dupouy, viola; Michael Rudiakov, cello) at Alice Tully Hall, Lincoln Center, New York, April 15, 1970.

My *Second String Quartet* was begun in August 1958, and finished in May 1959. In it the four instruments are individualized, each being given its own character, embodied in a special set of melodic and harmonic intervals and of rhythms that result in four different patterns of slow and fast tempos with associated types of expression. Thus four different strands of musical material of contrasting character are developed simultaneously throughout the work. It is out of the interactions, combinations, and oppositions of these that the details of musical discourse as well as the large sections are built. Up to the end of the second movement (*Presto scherzando*) the various facets of each instrument's character are presented quite distinctly. In the third and fourth movements (*Andante espressivo* and *Allegro*), there is a growing tendency to cooperate and exchange ideas, while in the cadenzas, opposition between the solo and accompanying instruments grows. The *Conclusion* returns to the state of individualization of the first part of the work.

The first violin reveals itself in its cadenza and elsewhere as fantastic, ornate, and mercurial, in rapid figurations and variously expressive phrases. It dominates the first movement, partially imposing its ideas on the others. The second violin, dominating the second movement and the *Conclusion*, plays a part which consistently projects regular rhythms. It has a laconic, orderly character which is sometimes humorous. The viola adds its repertory of expressive motives to the group, coming to the fore in the third movement, expanding ideas first heard in its cadenza. The somewhat impetuous cello part frequently breaks out of the rhythmic scheme, a feature which reaches its greatest freedom in the cadenza and finally draws the other three into an agitated *accelerando* at the end of the fourth movement. The form of the work does not follow traditional patterns but is developed directly from the relationship and interactions of the four instruments, which result in varying activities, tempos, moods, and feelings.

[The *Second String Quartet* won the 1960 Pulitzer Prize, the 1960 New York Critics Award, and the 1960 UNESCO First Prize.]

String Quartets
No. 1 (1951) and No. 2 (1959)

Program notes for the Nonesuch recording by The Composers Quartet, H-71249 stereo (1970).

Hearing these two quartets now, I get the impression of their living in different time worlds, the first in an expanded one, the second in a condensed and concentrated one—although this was hardly a conscious opposition at the times of their composition. Each presents as different a version of humanly experienced time as the two imagined by Thomas Mann in "By the

Ocean of Time," a chapter in *The Magic Mountain*, where he writes: "It would not be hard to imagine the existence of creatures, perhaps upon smaller planets than ours, practising a miniature time-economy. . . . And, contrariwise, one can conceive of a world so spacious that its time system too has a majestic stride. . . ."

Although both quartets are concerned with motion, change, progression in which literal or mechanical repetition finds little place, yet the development of musical expression and thought during the eight years that separate them seems to me far-reaching. The difference, aside from that of their time-scales, might be compared to the types of continuities found in Mann's own writings, where in the earlier ones, characters maintain their characterized identities with some revelatory changes throughout a work, while in the Joseph novels, each character is an exemplification of an archetype whose various other incarnations are constantly referred to (as Joyce does in another way in *Finnegans Wake*). Recurrence of idea in the *First Quartet* is, then, more nearly literal than in the *Second*, where recall brings back only certain traits of expression—"behavior patterns," speeds, and interval-sounds—that form the basis of an ever-changing series of incarnations but link these together as a group. The musical language of the *Second Quartet* emerged almost unconsciously through working during the '50s with ideas the *First* gave rise to.

The *First Quartet* was "written largely for my own satisfaction and grew out of an effort to understand myself," as the late Joseph Wood Krutch (a neighbor during the 1950–51 year of this quartet) wrote of his book *The Modern Temper*. For there were so many emotional and expressive experiences that I kept having, and so many notions of processes and continuities, especially musical ones—fragments I could find no ways to use in my compositions—that I decided to leave my usual New York activities to seek the undisturbed quiet to work these out. The decision to stay in a place in the Lower Sonoran Desert near Tucson, Arizona, brought me by chance into contact with that superb naturalist Joe Krutch, who was then writing *The Desert Year*. Our almost daily meetings led to fascinating talks about the ecology of the region—how birds, animals, insects, and plants had adapted to the heat and the limited water supply, which consists of infrequent, spectacular but brief cloudbursts that for an hour seem about to wash everything away, and then very long droughts. There were trips to remote places such as Carr Canyon, the wild-bird paradise, but mainly it was right around the house that exotica (for an Easterner) could be seen—comic road runners, giant suguaros, flowering ocatillos, all sharing this special, dry world. It was indeed a kind of "magic mountain," and its specialness (for me) certainly encouraged the specialness (for me at that time) of the quartet as I worked on it during the fall and winter of '50 and the spring of '51.

Among the lessons this piece taught me was one about my relationship with performers and audiences. For as I wrote, an increasing number of musical difficulties arose for prospective performers and listeners, which the musical conception seemed to demand. I often wondered whether the quartet would ever have any performers or listeners. Yet within a few years of its composition it won an important prize and was played (always with a great deal of rehearsal) more than any work I had written up to that time. It even received praise from admired colleagues. Up to this time, I had quite consciously been trying to write for a certain audience—not that which frequented concerts of traditional music, nor that which had supported the avant-garde of the '20s (which in the '40s had come to seem elitist) but a new, more progressive and more popular audience. I had felt that it was my professional and social responsibility to write interesting, direct, easily understood music.

With this quartet, however, I decided to focus on what had always been one of my own musical interests, that of "advanced" music, and to follow out, with a minimal concern for their reception, my own musical thoughts along these lines. Now, in 1970, I think there is every reason to assume that if a composer has been well taught and has had experience (as was true of me in 1950), then his private judgment of comprehensibility and quality is what he must rely on if he is to communicate importantly.

Like the desert horizons I saw daily while it was being written, the *First Quartet* presents a continuous unfolding and changing of expressive characters—one woven into the other or emerging from it—on a large scale. The general plan was suggested by Jean Cocteau's film *Le Sang d'un poète*, in which the entire dream-like action is framed by an interrupted slow-motion shot of a tall brick chimney in an empty lot being dynamited. Just as the chimney begins to fall apart, the shot is broken off and the entire movie follows, after which the shot of the chimney is resumed at the point it left off, showing its disintegration in mid-air, and closing the film with its collapse on the ground. A similar interrupted continuity is employed in this quartet's starting with a cadenza for cello alone that is continued by the first violin alone at the very end. On one level, I interpret Cocteau's idea (and my own) as establishing the difference between external time (measured by the falling chimney, or the cadenza) and internal dream time (the main body of the work)—the dream time lasting but a moment of external time but from the dreamer's point of view, a long stretch. In the *First Quartet*, the opening cadenza also acts as an introduction to the rest, and when it reappears at the end, it forms the last variation in a set of variations. Not only is this plan like that of many "circular" works of modern literature, but the interlocked presentation of ideas parallels many characteristic devices found in Joyce and others—the controlled "stream of consciousness," the "epiphany," the many uses of punctuation, of grammatical ambiguities, including the use of quotation. This quartet, for instance, quotes the opening theme of Ives's *First Violin Sonata*, first played by the cello in its lowest register after each of the other instruments has come in near the beginning. A rhythmic idea from Conlon Nancarrow's *First Rhythmic Study* is quoted at the beginning of the *Variations*. These two composers, through both their music and their conversation, had been a great help to me in imagining this work and were quoted in homage.

Since both these quartets are made up of many-layered contrasts of character—hence of theme or motive, rhythm, and styles of playing—they are hard to describe without adding to their apparent complication. Briefly, the *First* is in four large sections: *Fantasia, Allegro scorrevole, Adagio,* and *Variations*. This scheme is broken by two pauses, one in the middle of the *Allegro scorrevole* and the other just after the *Variations* have been started by the cello, while the other instruments were concluding the *Adagio*. The first section, *Fantasia*, contrasts many themes of different character frequently counterpointed against each other. It concludes with the four main ideas being heard together, fading in and out of prominence. This leads directly to a rapid *Allegro scorrevole*, a sound-mosaic of brief fragments, interrupted once by a dramatic outburst, then resumed, again interrupted by a pause, again resumed, and finally interrupted by another outburst that forms the beginning of the *Adagio*.

During this extended slow movement, the two muted violins play soft, contemplative music answered by an impassioned, rough recitative of the viola and cello. This *Adagio* forms the extreme point of divergence between simultaneous ideas in the quartet and has been led up to and is led away from by many lesser degrees of differentiation. The last section, *Variations*, consists of a series of different themes repeated faster at each successive recurrence, some reaching their speed vanishing point sooner than others. One that persists almost throughout is the slow motive heard in separated notes played by the cello just before and after the pause that precedes the *Variations*. This motive passes through many stages of acceleration until it reaches a rapid tremolo near the end.

Written in 1959, the *Second Quartet* represents quite a contrast to the *First*. In it, as mentioned previously, there is little dependence on thematic recurrence, which is replaced by an ever-changing series of motives and figures having certain internal relationships with each other. To a certain extent, the instruments are type-cast, for each fairly consistently invents its material out of its own special expressive attitude and its own repertory of musical speeds and intervals. In a certain sense each instrument is like a character in an opera made up primarily of "quartets." The separation of the instrumental characters is kept quite distinct throughout the first half of the work but becomes increasingly homogenized up to the *Conclusion*, at which point the separation reemerges. The musical contrasts of behavior and material associated with each instrument can be brought to the listener's attention by a special stereophonic placement which helps to sort them out—as accomplished in this recording—although this is not absolutely necessary, since the total effect at any given moment is the primary consideration, the contribution of each instrument secondary.

The form of the quartet itself helps to make the elements of this four-way conversation clear. The individuals of this group are related to each other in what might be metaphorically termed three forms of responsiveness: discipleship, companionship, and confrontation. The *Introduction* and *Conclusion* present in aphoristic form and in "companionate" manner the repertory of each instrument. The *Allegro fantastico* is led by the first violin, whose whimsical, ornate part is "imitated" by the other three, each according to his own individuality; the same occurs in the *Presto scherzando* led by the second violin and the *Andante espressivo* led by the viola. The final *Allegro*, although partially led by the cello—which eventually draws the others into one of its characteristic accelerations—tends to stress the "companionship" rather than the "discipleship" pattern.

In between these movements are cadenzas of instrumental "confrontation" or opposition: after the *Allegro fantastico*, the viola plays its expressive, almost lamenting cadenza to be confronted with explosions of what may be anger or ridicule by the other three; after the *Presto scherzando*, the cello, playing in its romantically free way, is confronted by the others' insistence on strict time; finally, after the *Andante espressivo*, the first violin carries on like a virtuoso, to be confronted by the silence of the others, who, before this cadenza is over, commence the final *Allegro*. Throughout the entire quartet, the second violin acts as a moderating influence, using its *pizzicato* and *arco* notes to mark regular time, its half, or double—always at the same speed.

On this record, Anahid Ajemian plays the second violin part with fascinating wit and humor where needed and with refined expressivity or robust vigor elsewhere. Indeed, all the members of The Composers Quartet—Matthew Raimondi, Jean Dupouy, and Michael Rudiakov as well as Miss Ajemian, accomplishing the difficult and unprecedented feat of maintaining both quartets in their repertory simultaneously—play their parts as if they meant what they were doing, as if it were very important, in order to reveal what both pieces are about, to play them accurately and musically. What more could a composer want of performers?

"The Composer Is a University Commodity"

Answer to a questionnaire: The Composer in Academia—Reflections on a Theme of Stravinsky
College Music Symposium 10 (Fall 1970)

[The Symposium (a questionnaire) to which Carter contributed this article posed as its theme a quotation from *Conversations with Igor Stravinsky*, by Stravinsky and Robert Craft (Garden City, N.Y., 1959, pp.153–54). In it, Stravinsky maintains that "a composer is or isn't; he cannot learn the gift that makes him one." He also "warns young composers . . . against university teaching" because "teaching is academic," it conforms to conventional rules, and it may therefore "not be the right contrast for a composer's noncomposing time."]

The effect of teaching in universities by young composers, on them and their works and on the public and music profession, will have to go through many stages and be reconsidered many times before it can be evaluated, if it ever can. Certainly between 1959, when Stravinsky wrote his advice, and 1969, when I write this, so much has happened in American society and its relation to education and so much within the field of music that one hesitates to give any general answer at all—music is not what it was in 1959—and neither are universities.

One can, now, as then, list the goods and bads only and not predict. But there is one fundamental question—the one of education itself as a pattern which indicates that it could be an unhealthy situation for composers to be too much involved with education, especially in a university. For the age level of students, and their preparation is always the same in each new class, from year to year, while the composer changes and develops and naturally grows older—and more experienced in the ways of his own generation (often thought nowadays to be irrelevant to the next generation). This constant rebeginning for the sake of the young is not always the best atmosphere for a composer to develop in.

Also the fact that the university is a passing stage, a preparation (?), a training (?) for life outside of the university for students, means that the academic society itself should have this as its goal and not become too much involved with itself—which it very often tends to do, and therefore a composer living in this atmosphere could lose the sense of writing for the outer society which he should be helping to develop. One could imagine students today being very critical of many of the more recondite activities of American graduate schools, including music schools.

To come down to more precise matters:

BAD: The American composer, like his colleagues on university faculties, tends to be treated as a commodity with these tangible assets: *reputation* (the kind formed by American publicity, or taken up by American publicity from foreign cultural propaganda), which the university does little to help him to increase once engaged, and hence which often deteriorates during the teaching years; *verbal articulateness* (not characteristic of composers *qua* composers, although sometimes found even in good ones); *new ideas* about music techniques, analysis, theory, and teaching techniques (preferably those that will evoke publicity—now computer methods, etc.); *closeness to the "new" trends*, as defined, of course, by the news media.

While one can have no objection to having all of these taught in a university (except on the basis of the quick obsolescence of most of the "new" in art), the emphasis on these is hardly conducive to the composer's own development. For the composer's own work becomes of small importance to his department (which explains the American Society of University Composers) unless it can get important write-ups in the news, or unless the composer is willing to tear his own pieces apart, explain them in detail, and show his students how to do it in a few easy lessons. Thus his work is of little importance, so it often seems, unless it can be transformed into the tangible assets of "reputation" or "articulateness."

BAD: Since composers seem to be regarded as immediate (and often dispensable) commodities both by university management, by most of his students, and even by his departmental colleagues (for the most part), he becomes part of a competitive market and he cannot help but be aware that there is a constant look-out for others with greater assets, especially reputation. Since universities usually tend to downgrade composers' reputations, once employed by them, there is a look-out for those previously not associated with U.S. universities—composers whose reputations are made and sustained by effective cultural propaganda from the country of their origin, not available to American composers. Many of these from other countries continue to profit by the cultural propaganda of their country even while employed here, thus putting their American colleagues in the shade.

Naturally, one would not want to eliminate the important thought and contribution of non-Americans to our culture; it is simply that in terms of the particular asset of "reputation" they have a much better opportunity than any American composer—and have often been inflated far beyond their intrinsic value.

BAD: The effort to develop in his own way is met, for a composer, with constant frustration by the very demands of the situation. What appears to be an utter lack of responsibility toward the needs of its compositional faculty seems to be characteristic of most university music departments today. To make matters worse, departments are often willing to pay high prices for those who have profited by the culturally more responsible situations that exist outside the U.S. This is profoundly disturbing to all involved in it and should be to all American graduate students. For the latter cannot fail to realize that, if things keep up this way, they will be put out of jobs by young professionals trained elsewhere under more culturally responsible situations, when they graduate. We don't even approve of the results of our own education, so it seems (perhaps because education itself is not a commodity, only the act of educating). In fact, in music one cannot help but feel that in composition, education is a training in obsolescence and is likely to be a hindrance in future teaching—for only thus can certain members of university faculties be explained today.

BAD: In 1969 (as not in 1959) the question of what can be useful to the next generation and how it can be presented has reached crisis proportions. If this continues to be the (what seems to me, healthy) situation of universities, teaching should be done by those who can constantly be concerned with the young and their attitudes, and not by composers who can only hope to interest the next generation by their honest work.

GOOD: In 1959 it used to be said that the university in America was the home of the arts—a place where they could be taught, studied, discussed, enjoyed, and developed outside of the mercantile pressures that link our society together. It is possible and much to be hoped that this continues and will continue to be true until the time when our society can find the kind of cultural consensus which will allow a large enough community of citizens to encourage musical composition outside of the university.

The Orchestral Composer's Point of View

From *The Composer's Point of View: Essays on Twentieth-Century Music by Those Who Wrote It*, edited by Robert Stephan Hines. Copyright 1970 by the University of Oklahoma Press.

Merely to consider the possibility of writing orchestral music of any quality as a field of endeavor for a composer in the United States calls up a barrage of contradictory problems, each of which would seem to militate against any kind of new, vital, or original music being produced. It would even seem impossible to work out an intelligent program that would provide a situation in which this could be accomplished by anyone but a confirmed masochist seeking a heavy burden of self-punishment. The fact that such music has been written here, though not often, amid miserable circumstances, at great human cost to its creators, and in almost utter neglect—that Edgard Varèse, Charles Ives, Carl Ruggles, Stefan Wolpe, and others fought this desperate battle—means that these composers had such a strong inner vision that they were able to overlook the preposterous circumstances that surrounded them in our musical society, particularly in the orchestral field. Younger composers who write in an original way are often filled with illusions about the present situation (which, it is to be hoped, is changing), encouraged as they are by commissions, fellowships, and contests bent on stimulating what must seem like an appalling overproduction of an unwanted commodity. Such commissions, for instance, are very often given by those entirely concerned with publicity, a kind that feeds on the composer's reputation but is not interested in his actual work. This is clear from the fact that commissions are too often given by groups who have shown no previous interest in a composer's work by performing it or arranging for performances of it. Very often, a little research will reveal that the commissioners do not even know what kind of music the composer has written and hence is likely to write—with the curious result that the finished score comes as a disagreeable surprise to conductor and performers, who then churn through it desultorily or with hostility misrepresenting the score to the public and ruining the possibility of future performances for a long time. The commissioning sums, themselves, are seldom attractive, and are usually far less than a professional copyist would be paid to copy the score. The rewards, if one cares about them—artistic results, kudos, and money—are each so small that commissions rarely seem worth the trouble.

Composers with fewer illusions about the present orchestral situation in our country suffer through these nonsensical performances in the hope that they will get ones supported by educational funds, such as the Rockefeller Foundation-supported modern-music symphony concerts played in universities, or performances with some of our better conservatory orchestras (Oberlin, Iowa, Michigan, or the New England Conservatory), where student performers are eager to play new music and have plenty of time to rehearse and be taught the score by a conductor who really knows it thoroughly. A somewhat similar result can sometimes be obtained by performances with European radio orchestras, which do not play as well as American orchestras but can devote much more rehearsal time to new music. In fact, a number of American composers living abroad have been able to develop styles of orchestration by constant contact with orchestral performances that they could not have evolved in this country.

Because it is difficult to get multiple performances with American symphony orchestras, since they are interested mainly in *premières*, composers do not write for this medium unless they are commissioned or have the stimulus of a prize contest. There is little satisfaction in a poorly rehearsed *première*. And, under the present rehearsal and performance situations, there are such absurdly small performance and royalty fees that the copying of the parts is seldom repaid except by potboilers. (No performance or royalty fees would be given if a number of us had not fought a bitter battle twenty-five years ago to try and establish what one would have thought was an obvious principle.) Prize contests do not solve the problem any better since the authority of juries is infrequently respected by musicians. Even when an honorific prize like the Pulitzer Prize has been given in music, sometimes resulting in a number of performances (as with my *Second String Quartet*), this can cause a great deal of dissatisfaction on the part of those who question the jury's choice.

Here is an example of what can happen at a prize contest: My *Holiday Overture* won a prize of $500, publication, and performance by one of the major symphonies, whose conductor was one of the jurors. The score and parts were taken from me, remained in the orchestra's library four years without ever being performed, and were then returned. I had no copy of the parts, and I could not get other performances during this time, for when I tried to withdraw the parts, the possibility of a performance that might take place very soon and which I might lose if the parts were not in the library was held before me. Finally, I sneaked the parts out without the librarian's knowing it, had them photostated, and returned. From these parts the work got its first performance in Frankfurt, Germany, and later in Berlin with Serge Celibidache conducting. The American orchestra never knew of this. Why it held up the *Holiday Overture* I never learned, but the experience did not add to my desire to deal with American conductors and orchestras.

Such mishaps are a constant part of the composer's routine. Conditions do not improve much even when such relationships are handled through a publisher, as has been my frequent experience since 1936, when my first orchestral work was written. The reasons for these vexations and others have been a constant source of concern for composers, yet no one has been able to find a way to solve them. Perhaps all these problems can be traced to the habit of applying traditional economic standards by a large segment of our population to all its efforts and products, which inevitably causes confusions and misapprehensions between composers and many performers, critics, publishers, and publics. Looked at in this way, a piece of music is assimilated to a typical item of consumption in the traditional frame of a consumers' market. However, such a piece cannot be physically owned as can a painting or sculpture, cannot generally be figuratively owned by being retained in the memory as the contents of a book, movie, or play. This very fact means that its consumption value lies only in the immediate present during which it is heard and during which it must be experienced, if it is. Hence, it must cater to the listener's immediate abilities, interests, and experiences, in much the same way a performer does on a far more accessible level. Although recordings have somewhat lessened the composition's mere present existence for the public, still it is the very evanescence, which is part of its attractiveness, that makes it an anomaly as an item of consumption and alters drastically the bases on which music can be compared to any of the other arts, both in terms of historical development and economic remuneration. This accounts for the underdeveloped nature of its economic aspect; particularly in America it was (and probably still is) assumed that musical repertory is a European importation and that Europe can take care of composers' payments and exploitation while we do not have to consider these seriously. From this follows that the investment of money in publicity and salesmanship in compositions in the United States need be very little since so little return can be expected.

However, with the explosion of the publicity industry, more and more emphasis has been put on the public image of the composer as the real item of consumption. His musical composition is only one of the contributing elements, others being his ability to perform, to talk, to write, to teach, and to be photographed—all of these being more salable, and hence more highly paid, than his music. The public, often, must wonder why composers persist in writing music that so few can understand. They must think—and perhaps rightly—that the musical work is intended to help his public image through reviews and reports in widely circulated periodicals, and thus lead the composer to more important positions in domains peripheral to composition, but more remunerative.

Except for American opera, symphony orchestra, and community-concert subscribers where the group must be very small, there usually exists a sizable minority of musical public that understands what an important role new music could play. This special public realizes that the development of musical composition is affected by many more important factors than that of immediate popular consumption. This group has little power, even though its point of view—that contact with the new brings new attitudes toward the old, new insights into the art itself, and interesting, even important new experiences—is generally accepted in the other arts and in most of American life. Contemporary music, music that is to be listened to for itself rather than for its performance, is in another class from older music, and this distinction keeps it out of competition with the "performance industry," where the stakes are high, and whose efforts assume the solid foundation of accepted "masterworks."

A solid foundation? Commercial exploitation is destroying this as it did forests in the nineteenth century. So far, in America at least, no concerted effort of musical reforestation of the rapidly dying repertory of increasingly tired and worn-out classics is planned. (The mortality of the Francks, Regers, and Saint-Saëns is very high these years.) This improvident depletion of the repertory has gone on for years, while the twentieth-century composers were producing work after work that have been treated as seasonal novelties and dropped instead of being drawn in to replenish the failing repertory. The American public of symphony subscribers has not yet caught up with the Viennese music written fifty years ago, nor that of Varèse which is thirty or forty years old. However, there is evidently another public for such music, as was proven by the success in New York of the all-modern music repertories of the BBC Orchestra and the Hamburg Opera in 1967. But the average subscriber has no part of this literature. For him the gap between contemporary music and his understanding has grown wider through the years, and it is ever harder for him to catch up. Unless this situation can be remedied it will have a severe effect on the future of orchestral music. Often in recent years, composers have felt that the future of the symphony orchestra was doubtful. Needless to say, the artist who puts his faith in future recognition thinks a long time before he wastes a lot of time and effort on a medium which many think is dying. The contrast between this situation and that of chamber music, where contemporary music is welcomed, serves to emphasize that this plight is strictly a matter of the orchestral situation and not that of the composers, as described in Henry Pleasant's book *The Agony of Modern Music*. The orchestral brontosaur staggers with inertia and ossification; its very complexity resists change.

Now let us look at that institution, the conductor (seldom an American) of an American symphony orchestra. He is involved in a complex of economic and social problems in his community and orchestra that threaten to draw his attention away from musical ones: in tea-party strategies to keep and augment his audiences, in making himself a public personality, in helping to raise money, in getting better pay for his performers through recording contracts, in maintaining and raising the performance standards without causing ill-feelings. Keeping the orchestra alive and functioning must often seem to be the primary issue, while the actual giving of concerts and learning new repertoire becomes almost a secondary responsibility. Yet these latter duties—the backbone of his role as conductor—form a very taxing schedule. The extended seasons of the major orchestras devour an enormous number of standard works, few of which can be repeated more than once every two years, none of which can be performed without rehearsal and, on the conductor's part, without restudy and rethinking of interpretation. Understandably, the conductor has little time left to study the few new scores he may have scheduled, none to look through the piles of new music sent to him every year, and, certainly, very little time to keep up with the progress of contemporary music by following new trends through scores and recordings. His impossibly demanding tasks naturally force him to find time-saving solutions and not do anything which will augment his problems. To satisfy the pressure of the progressive minority of his audience, he must inevitably find works that do not require much rehearsal, will not cause much dismay, or be too long or too unusual. He can hardly be blamed for not choosing more important scores under the circumstances. In fact, it is remarkable that as much important new music is played as there is.

The situation of the orchestral musician is not much better with regard to new music. The high cost of living in the United States naturally forces him to need high pay for his very skilled efforts. He must participate in as many higher-paid services as possible (concerts, broadcasts, and recordings) and as few lesser-paid ones (rehearsals). This state of affairs limits the repertory of concerts drastically and, when combined with the extended seasons of many orchestras, results in overwork, fatigue, and tedium. When such musicians are faced with a new work which has been allowed a small amount of rehearsal time insufficient to produce a good performance, many players, otherwise sympathetic to new music, become disgusted while the unsympathetic performers are annoyed at being required to do many difficult and unfamiliar things that seem to lead to a pointless result. At a recent rehearsal of my *Piano Concerto*, an orchestral musician said to me: "Your music does not make sense unless the dynamic markings are fol- lowed." At most rehearsals and the majority of performances of new orchestral music, the players are so occupied with playing the right notes that they often forget to follow the instructions to play them softly or loudly.

Music requiring careful observation of these distinctions needs extra rehearsals, therefore, in order to "make sense." A work like my *Holiday Overture*, in which the variety of dynamics is produced almost automatically by the addition or subtraction of instruments, can make sense without such care being taken although it makes better sense when it is. One can easily imagine the frustration of an orchestral musician who works hard to master his part only to discover that he is being entirely covered by a neighbor who, instead of playing softly as his part indicates, is giving all he has.

Often the blame for the growing gap between audiences and new music is laid at the door of the orchestra's board of directors or of the audience itself. Most of the time with both of these groups, there has been and still may be an interest in new music, in small amounts. However, if this curiosity is satisfied by poor contemporary music and not by the finest, a receptive attitude can readily turn to animosity, as has happened only too often. Many times when looking over the modern music played by orchestras for a certain period or season, one gets the impression of visiting an art museum where no examples of Picasso, Braque, Kandinsky, Klee, et al., but only the works of the latest recipients of Guggenheim Fellowships had ever been shown. Everybody concerned with music—composers and musicians, as well as the public—has constantly to develop a background of understanding based on the best works of the recent past if they are to come to terms with new compositions. Recordings and scores can and have helped the public and composers, but the conductor and performer must have had direct performing contact with these works in order to be able to make quick sense out of the welter of new musical methods developed over the past sixty years. Most practitioners do not have the time or the encouragement from a good majority of those connected with music who are shortsightedly still milking the "masterpieces" dry.

As if all these practical problems were not enough to keep a composer from writing orchestral music, and they are not, the very instrumental make-up of the orchestra itself presents many serious difficulties in these years. Developed to play romantic music based on a common practice of standardized harmony, rhythm, and counterpoint, of singing themes, of widening sonority by octave doubling, the orchestra seems to require this kind of music to justify its existence. Since most contemporary composers do not wish to compose this way, the orchestra has to be forced to do things which seem to violate its fundamental nature. For example, the dry incisiveness and powerful rhythmic articulation of Igor Stravinsky's music since

1920 does not fit the sonority expected from the orchestra. Also the whole growth of the orchestra, intensifying its romantic character with Bruckner, Mahler, Strauss, and early Schoenberg, made the works of these composers and others unplayable outside large cities, especially in the United States, where they are a drain on the budgets of orchestras. Many European composers still feel the need, today, to write for large orchestras and can get their works played because of state subsidies—the Stalinist symphonies of Dmitri Shostakovitch and quite a few recent Polish and German works. American composers ruled out this possibility long ago. Aaron Copland recently revised his *Symphonic Ode*, written originally for a large Boston Symphony Orchestra, for a smaller group of instrumentalists.

Aside from the enlargement and increasing technical demands made by composers in the late nineteenth and early twentieth centuries, which limited their works to special situations that became rarer with each passing year, there came forth a realization which was expressed by many composers that the orchestra is no longer useful. Schoenberg complained in 1928 to Erwin Stein, in an interview translated in the booklet accompanying the Columbia Records of the works of Schoenberg, Volume II:

> If it were not for America, we in Europe would be composing only for reduced orchestras, chamber orchestras. But in countries with younger cultures, less refined nerves require the monumental: when the sense of hearing is incapable of compelling the imagination, one must add the sense of sight. . . . But disarmament is as slow here as it is in other areas; so long as there continue to be nations which, in art, have not yet won their place in the sun, so long will America demand large orchestras and Europe maintain them; Europeans will remain incapable of acquiring that finesse of ear that artists long to see generally acquired as long as they continue to maintain large orchestras.[1]

It is significant that quite a number of the twentieth century's best composers—Schoenberg, Bartók, Webern—seldom wrote for the orchestra.

The orchestra's very instrumental make-up severely limits its possibilities of sound. All of the instruments of the usual orchestra playing a *tutti* can only be written for in a very few ways that will produce a balance of sound in which each element contributes significantly to the whole and is not partially or totally blotted out by more powerful instruments. A flute, for example, as sometimes happens in the Ives scores, playing a theme in its medium-low register against a full, loud orchestra playing above and below it, is unlikely to be heard at all, and scarcely contributes anything to the total effect. The fewer the instruments that play, the more possibilities of combinations there are. Recent Stravinsky works, like *Agon* and the *Variations*, treat the orchestra as a storehouse for many changing chamber music combinations, avoiding its full sound almost throughout. This requires sensitive playing by the musicians and careful listening by the audience, which neither are prepared for, especially when many orchestral concerts take place in halls where acoustics prevent great delicacy of sound from being heard distinctly.

If there is still any point in composing for orchestra, it is to treat the medium with as much novelty of concept as one does harmony, rhythm, or any of the older musical methods, so rethought in our time. It is the compositions that are written for orchestra that will make it live. If these are dull and routined in the use of the medium itself, not consistent with the composer's thought, then the orchestra has to be left to the ever-diminishing repertory of the past.

To compose for the orchestra, as far as I am concerned, is to deal practically with the instruments, writing idiomatic passages for them, and, particularly, to compose music whose very structure and character are related to the instruments that play it. The entrance, register, sound of an oboe or a solo viola must be a matter of formal and expressive signification for the whole piece. The combinations of instruments are as much a compositional consideration as the material they play, even to determining the material, and all must reflect the overall intention. The handling of the orchestra must have the same distinctiveness and character as the other components of the work. This concept of orchestral writing takes considerable imaginative effort, increased, as has been said, by the many built-in routines which the orchestra was developed to accomplish. The uses of any one of these would be as much out of character in my music as a passage of conventional four-part harmony.

It took me many years of experience and thought to arrive at this technique of orchestral practice. My first works, the *Tarantella* (1936) for men's chorus and orchestra and the ballet *Pocahontas* (1939), were orchestrations and amplifications of prior piano four-hand scores, while the *Symphony No. 1* (1941) and the *Holiday Overture* (1944) each began to move away from this procedure, the symphony dealing with orchestrally thought textures and the overture with orchestrally thought counterpoint. In fact the *Holiday Overture* began to use consciously the notion of simultaneous contrasting levels of musical activity, which characterizes most of my more recent work. *The Minotaur* (1947), a ballet, is another step toward direct orchestral thinking, which culminated in my *Variations* (1954), conceived as it is entirely in terms of the orchestra for which it is written. After this, each of my two concertos used a different approach to orchestral sound. The *Double Concerto for Harpsichord and Piano with Two Chamber Orchestras* (1961) makes the percussion the main body of the orchestra, the pitched blown and bowed instruments secondary, with the two soloists mediating between them. The *Piano Concerto* (1965) uses the orchestra mainly as an elaborate ambiance, a society of sounds or a sounded stage setting for the piano.

In every case, these works have taken into account the practical situation of the American orchestras that might be their performers at the times they were written. The complete change of aim and direction, amounting to a private revolution in musical thought, which went on through all these years in my chamber music, hardly found its way into my orchestral work until the two concertos. There was good reason for this decision since I was—and am still—made painfully aware with each orchestral rehearsal that the type of writing found in almost every measure of my chamber music could never come out under American orchestral conditions that I know or imagine. Orchestral passages of a far simpler structure have often proved serious stumbling blocks to musicians who always seem to face my scores with the belief that they will never make sense—although occasionally some performers find that they were mistaken. For these reasons, I have sought different goals in orchestral scores than in chamber music.

Up to now, although finding these were useless precautions, I have tried to fit the situations for which my music was written, carefully. The ballets used the size of the orchestra that would fit into the pit of Broadway theaters; the Martin Beck in the case of *Pocahontas*, and the former Ziegfeld with *The Minotaur*. The *Variations*, commissioned by the Louisville Orchestra, used the exact number of instruments that comprised that orchestra—a very small number of strings (nine players of first violins, etc.) and the normal-sized brass section, which could cause serious problems of balance. My score allowed for possible enlargements of the string section in other performances. The *Piano Concerto*, partly to save rehearsal time, relegates much of the difficult playing to a concertino of soloists. Each of these self-imposed restrictions affected the form and plan of the work drastically, of course, and seem in no way to have helped the performance prospects of the work, as they have gone unnoticed. In the case of my *Variations*, when played by the Philadelphia Orchestra, the entire wind section was doubled through most of the work, as is sometimes done in Beethoven symphonies, without my knowing, until I arrived at the last rehearsal when the work was completely rehearsed. This resulted in a rather intense and coarse sound in fast passages, which I did not want. I realized, however, that this amplification of the orchestra was probably necessary because of the bad acoustics of the then recently opened Philharmonic Hall at Lincoln Center. When the work was performed there, one of the critics wrote that this work was seldom performed because it required such a large orchestra!

I made unusual orchestral demands in the score of my *Double Concerto* because the generous commissioner of the work, Paul Fromm and the Fromm Foundation, assured me of excellent musicians and sufficient rehearsals. Unlike my other compositions, this one presents many kinds of special performance problems, the main one being the harpsichord itself. The instrument is of always unpredictable volume, which varies from hall to hall as well as from instrument to instrument—a fact that I was so aware of that during the work, all the other instruments usually stop altogether or play their softest in their dullest registers when the harpsichord is playing. These precautions do not prevent it from being lost and requiring amplification under many performing conditions but, as it is the soft member of a dialogue "pian e forte," it cannot be amplified very much. The balance and accuracy of the percussion, its damping, its sticking, have to be worked out with great care, otherwise the work will sink into a miasma of confusion, as it has on a number of occasions, especially when the hall is too resonant.

The work is built on a large plan, somewhat like that of Lucretius's *De Rerum Natura*, in which its cosmos is brought into existence by collisions of falling atoms, in the music by ten superimposed slowly beaten out regular speeds—five for the harpsichord and its orchestra on one side of the stage, and five for the piano and its orchestra on the other side of the stage. A musical interval is associated with the attacks of each of these and used in the introduction as if it were a percussive sound. The distribution of the speeds and intervals is given in Ex. 1a. As can be seen, the smallest ratio of speeds is 49:50, which is the one first presented. This fans out to the largest, 1:2, in intermediate steps, reading from right to left, during the introduction. 49:50 is presented by alternating rolls of the snare drum on the piano side of the stage at metronomic speed 25, and of the cymbal on the harpsichord side at speed 24.5, starting in an ornamented way in measures 7 and 8 and resolving to the pure lengths combined with the associated intervals in 10–12. Then harpsichord speed 28, perfect fourth, and piano speed 21⅞, major seventh, appear in measures 13 and 14—piano speed 21, major sixth, and harpsichord speed 29⅙, augmented fourth, in measure 17—harpsichord speed 19⁴⁄₉, minor third, measure 20; piano speed 31.5, perfect fifth, measures 23 and 24—finally harpsichord speed 17.5, minor seventh in

RATIO	BETWEEN				SPEEDS		METRONOMIC SPEEDS	PIANO	HARPSICHORD
2					1/5	10	35	♪	
	81					9	31½	♪	
		25			1/6		29⅙		♪
			32			8	28		♪
				50	1/7		25	♪	
				49		7	24½		♪
		25			1/8		21⅞	♪	
	18					6	21	♪	
	50				1/9		19 4/9		♪
1					1/10	5	17½		♪

Ex. 1a. Double Concerto.
Examples 1a–c copyright 1964 by Associated Music Publishers,
Inc.

measure 31, and piano speed 35, major third, measure 36. During these
measures some of the layers of speed that have been introduced drop out,
but they all begin to be sounded as the two climaxes, made by rhythmic
unisons, approach. Four of the speeds that fill in the ratio of 35:17.5 are in a

ratio of reciprocals, as the chart shows, and these reach a rhythmic unison in measure 45, while the other four speeds fill in 35:17.5 in a ratio of whole numbers and come to a rhythmic unison in measure 46. The two systems engender a pattern of regular beats in the case of the reciprocals and a pattern of acceleration and retardation in the case of the whole numbers as shown in the diagram, Ex. 1b.

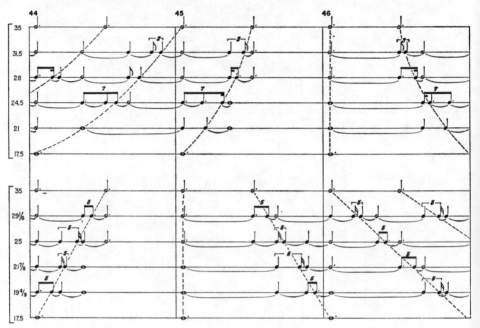

Ex. 1b.

After the introduction, the various speeds and their intervals are joined together to produce polyrhythmic patterns of a lesser degree of density but a higher one of mobility and articulation, different combinations producing different sections. How this is done can be seen in the harpsichord and piano cadenzas in which almost the entire repertory of both parts is presented in aphoristic form. The slow movement which emerges from the previous fast one at measure 312 and continues to measure 475, overlapping the beginning of the next section, uses alternations of accelerating and slowing up in a pattern that runs around the outside of the orchestra counterclockwise (percussion 4,3,2,1, harpsichord, contrabass, cello, piano) when accelerating and clockwise when slowing up. The central part of the orchestra, the

TWO ALL–INTERVAL TETRACHORDS, WITH CHARACTERISTIC INTERVALS
USED IN DOUBLE CONCERTO

COMBINATION
OF
TETRACHORDS

Ex. 1c.

winds, play a slow piece not related rhythmically to these motions, but maintaining their interval identity in each orchestra. Until the coda, the two orchestras adhere to a system of interval interrelationships that is different for each, as indicated in Ex. 1c. In general the piano and its group specialize in rhythmic ratios of 3:5 while the harpsichord group uses that of 4:7. The coda extends these ratios over many measures, producing long, slow waves of oscillating sounds, an orchestration, so to speak, of the sound of a tam-tam heard in 619, dying away over many measures. The piano group at this point has important attacks every seventh measure with subsidiary ones every thirty-fifth quarter, while the harpsichord group emphasizes every fifth measure and secondarily every thirty-fifth dotted eighth—all with many subsidiary patterns and accents. The coda is the dissolution of this musical cosmos—Lucretius's "Destruction of Athens" or, perhaps, the triumph of Chaos at the end of Pope's *Dunciad.* *

As in all my music such intervallic schemes provide a somewhat ordered substructure (like the triadic harmony of the common practice period, but more freely used because it is not adhered to so strictly) as a source of ideas of many degrees of interrelationship on several different levels at once.

With the many performances this work has had, I had a great deal of opportunity before the score was printed to try and get all its indications as foolproof as possible. There is a constant stream of unfamiliar ideas that can hardly be expected to come out "all by themselves" if musicians have never participated in a work that presented these particular problems before. It is a great advantage not to conduct the music myself, so that I can find out just how explicit the score is to the conductor and players. When it is not, then I can make it clearer so it will come out well when I am not present. In it there are many problems of notation—the awkward dotted notations, used for quintuplets and septuplets in compound time, that have bothered performers in Warsaw and elsewhere. In defense of them, I do not think many passages which use dotted and undotted notes simultaneously could have been notated as clearly.

If I had not had the experience of my *Variations* behind me, I do not think I would have ventured to write orchestral works of the unusualness of the *Double Concerto* or the more recent *Piano Concerto*. It is strange to have a work like the *Variations* over the fourteen years of its existence not only become easier and easier for performers to play and for listeners to grasp but also gradually sound more and more the way I intended it to sound with each new performance. At its *première* in Louisville in 1954, the music sounded so confused, particularly in the very resonant gymnasium in which it was played, that I wondered if I had not gone off the deep end and written a score that would never sound as I imagined it. Although by far the hardest work the Louisville Orchestra had commissioned to that date, so I was repeatedly told, it was far simpler in performance demands than the chamber music I was writing at the time. The conductor, Robert Whitney, and the orchestra worked hard and well and made the fine Louisville recording of the *Variations*. After that, the work received, I think, no performances in the United States until 1964, although it was performed in the interim at Donaueschingen, Rome, Stockholm, Paris, and Liverpool. During its first years of existence, I was particularly eager to learn from live

---

* See p.348 of this collection.—Eds.

performances with different musicians in different halls, so that I could witness for myself just what was difficult, what was easy and why, what always came out well, and what was troublesome. I would have needed to hear lots of such performances by competent orchestras while the score was still fresh in my mind, in order to profit from its lessons in my next works. This did not happen, and by the time the score began to be played fairly frequently in places where I could be present, I had written my *Double Concerto*, which approached the orchestra in an entirely different way.

Under present conditions in America, it seems to be very nearly impossible to develop a personal orchestral style that also takes into account the practicalities of the performing situation. Either a composer must use the standardized, "tried and true" orchestral routines, or he must suffer for years through misrepresentative, tentative performances, which teach him very little. In situations where new music is taken more seriously, as in Germany, Italy, Sweden, Poland, and elsewhere, the composers' contacts with orchestral performances have often allowed them to develop highly distinctive, yet practical techniques. In the United States, the prospect of troublesome situations is very discouraging—situations in which the performers assume that the composer does not know what he is doing, in which the score cannot come out as intended for lack of rehearsal time or because the conductor is unable to imagine how the score might sound if played correctly. These painful prospects, which a composer must face every time he plans an orchestral work, make it hard for him to follow his own ideas and to take the whole operation of composing orchestral music with the seriousness that he might devote to chamber music, where the musicians are eager to discover precisely the composer's intentions and to play the work to his satisfaction.

My most recent work for orchestra, the *Piano Concerto* (1965), presents a number of quite different concepts in orchestral use that involve difficulties of balance and, to a lesser extent, playing. For conductors unfamiliar with the late scores of Charles Ives and others, the orchestral score presents a forbidding appearance with its pages that sometimes divide the strings into many single parts. These pages are hard for performers to grasp and interpret, too, since they comprise as many as seventy-two different parts that need to be balanced and coordinated—especially in the fast passages near the end, in which the orchestra plays in 3/2 while the concertino plays in 12/8. The work consists in a different dimension of dialogue from the *Double Concerto*, the solo piano is in dialogue with the orchestral crowd, with seven mediators—a concertino of flute, English horn, bass clarinet, solo violin, viola, cello, and bass. These share with the piano its material and various characters. Like the *Double Concerto* it employs no pre-established form but is a series of short, usually overlapping episodes, mosaics of fragments that derive from parts of the basic material combined in different ways. This basic material is formed of the twelve different groups of three notes, triads, six assigned to the soloists and six to the orchestra. Each of the twelve triads is related to one or more speeds and characters, as the chart shows in Ex. 2.

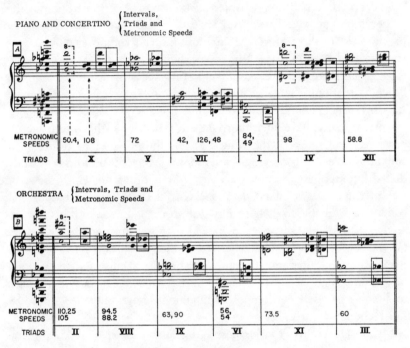

Ex. 2. Concerto for Piano and Orchestra.
Copyright 1967 by Associated Music Publishers, Inc.

The triads, written in whole notes, show how each participates, and in what register, in the two twelve-note chords: *A* for the soloists, *B* for the orchestra, which dominate the first movement and conclude it. The main triad for the soloists is VII, for the orchestra, VIII, both sharing the augmented fourth. This relationship is stressed in measures 19–22. After these, triads I and IX are frequently used. The black-headed notes in the example show the other spacings of the triads used, while the two-note intervals in boxes indicate the interval of the triad which is most frequently stressed.

Each triad has its associated character or characters, and hence its own kind of continuity. Triad III, for instance, is constantly superimposed on itself in a way which leads to the large tone clusters in the strings, which become thicker and more frequent as the work proceeds. The first movement stresses the similarities between the triads of both groups. After the opening of the second movement—its first thirty measures, 349–378, being a transition from the first to the second large section—the music stresses the difference between the two groups. The orchestra has a constantly changing series of slow, soft chords that gradually become denser over many measures. At the same time, it keeps up a web of accented beats in many different speeds between 105 and $10\,5/13$ in as many as eight different layers going on at once. The piano and occasionally the concertino play a series of rhapsodic, cadenza-like sections based on the chords and intervals used in the first movement with the addition of the perfect fifth and the major seventh. Sometimes these soloists play accelerandi and ritardandi against the regular beating of the orchestra. The many-voiced chords of the orchestra become thicker and the eight polyrhythmic, regularly beaten-out accents of the orchestra gradually approach a rhythmic unison as the piano dies away repeating a single note. At this point the slow accents of the orchestra become very emphatic, the piano and concertino take up their parts, and the whole leads into a kind of battle between the soloists and the orchestra, with the orchestral strings playing fast passages of twelve-tone chords. The music subsides with a short piano solo in which all of its chords and characteristics are stated in a brief summary of its entire part, recalling each idea with quiet insistence.

Before the first rehearsal of the *Piano Concerto*, I was presented with the alternative of signing away my right of refusal to allow the work to appear on a recording (allowing the conductor alone to make this decision) or not having the recording made at all. Reluctant as I was to give this right up, since I could not be sure whether on hearing the piece for the first time "live" I would be satisfied with every part of it—or, even if I were, whether the performance would present the piece adequately—I decided to take the chance and was fortunate to have had two unusually good first performances from which to make the tape. Naturally, this surprising request was connected with the record's financing and other aspects of commercial recording ventures. Nevertheless, such a curious lack of consideration for the composer's artistic rights only adds to the general reluctance to write for orchestra that he gradually develops.

For all these reasons and others which come to mind every time I plan an orchestral work, I hesitate a long time. My first conclusion usually is that given the large amount of imaginative effort, skill, and experience such a work as I am interested in writing demands, it will not be worth the effort (particularly in view of the disagreeable, absurd, and hypocritical situations that it will give rise to) since I always write music that cannot be expected to be a "hit" or a "scandal" with the audiences we know. The two or three thousand dollars (the Louisville was one thousand) I am paid for commissions recompenses my work at the rate of about twenty-five cents an hour. Artistically, there is not much to be said, either, for making the effort, given the inadequacies of most American performances, the apathy of most conductors and orchestral performers, and the consequent disaffection of audiences. As the satisfaction of a personal artistic need to write for masses of instruments, there is perhaps more point. Although if the composer feels this need without the concommitant one of writing for the public situation, there is no reason why he should use the usual orchestral setup, considering it stereotyped, but invent his own combinations, which in the United States would, no doubt, rule out all possibility of performance. All in all, it is hard to understand why composers commit the folly of writing for orchestra in our country in recent years. They do. Is it quixotic? Certainly the answer cannot be expected to come from our orchestras, who are too busy with their own organizational and financial problems to bother seriously about the work of composers foolish enough to see something in the orchestral medium.

NOTE

1. Courtesy of Columbia Records.

Igor Stravinsky, 1882–1971

Perspectives of New Music, 9,2 (1971)

In this period of sorrow, immediately following Stravinsky's death, it is hard to find words to express the many thoughts and impressions that must occupy the minds of many composers and musicians. For me the periods of overwhelming illumination and of profound gratitude for them, of irrepressible wonder crowd into my mind, as I recall the first time I heard the *Sacre* (which I already knew in a four-hand piano arrangement) played live at Carnegie Hall, conducted by Pierre Monteux in the mid-twenties and decided there and then to become a composer, or the subsequent fascination with which I was on the lookout for each new work, many of which, like the *Symphony of Psalms*, *Perséphone*, *Jeu de cartes*, *Orpheus*, *Symphony in Three Movements*, the *Mass*, the *Cantata*, *Agon*, *Threni*, *Abraham and Isaac*, and *Requiem Canticles*, I had the good fortune to hear in their first performances. This experience, which I actually sought out, out of enthusiasm for the composer's work, was, of course, in this case, filled with amazement and surprise since his growth was a series of unexpected renewals of approach from *Fireworks* to *The Owl and the Pussycat*. Of course, it was easier during the late twenties and early thirties to keep up because the Boston Symphony played each new Stravinsky work almost as soon as it was finished (unlike orchestras today) and kept some, like *Apollo* and *Capriccio*, in the repertory for years. It was because of this opportunity to know Stravinsky's works that the *Symphony of Psalms* was so much appreciated by the audiences of the Boston Symphony—the orchestra that commissioned it in 1930. The same cannot be said of the *Symphony in Three Movements*, commissioned by the New York Philharmonic, whose audiences are still "protected" from the new. (It is to be hoped that Boulez will change this.)

Later, when Stravinsky's remarkable piano playing, filled with electricity, began to be heard here, as well as his conducting, many of us were grateful that this great composer had decided to come and live among us. I myself have a very vivid memory of him playing over the score of *Perséphone* (the humanistic rite of spring) with René Maison singing the part of Eumolpe, at the apartment of Nadia Boulanger in Paris a few days before its première. What impressed me most, aside from the music itself, was the very telling quality of attack he gave to piano notes, embodying often in just one sound the very quality so characteristic of his music—incisive but not brutal, rhythmically highly controlled yet filled with intensity so that each note was made to seem weighty and important. Every time I heard him play, in the Salle Pleyel, in Town Hall, or wherever, the strong impression of highly individualized, usually detached notes filled with extraordinary dynamism caught my attention immediately—and this was true in soft passages as well as loud.

Then, to my own surprise, I was privileged to meet and to come to know him and witness this remarkable man with his penetrating, brilliant, and original mind and dedicated spirit in action. A highly concentrated inner force, although then considerably reduced in expression, seemed to govern him even during my last visit in December 1970, when we listened to recordings and followed scores together of *The Song of the Nightingale* and the last act of *Magic Flute*, which he particularly enjoyed, shaking his head and pointing out special beauties on the page.

Through these recent years, when I saw him now and then, certain things that I wanted to make clearer, at least to myself, have nagged at me, but I was never able to formulate them into questions that would bring the answer I wanted. The possibility of such questions came to me first during a time when Robert Craft was conducting my *Double Concerto* in Los Angeles, and Mr. and Mrs. Stravinsky invited me to their house on North Wetherly Drive. A little discouraged and shy in the midst of such august figures as Spender, Isherwood, and Huxley, who were also there, I went off into a corner, soon to be joined by Stravinsky himself, and we began musicians' talk until I got up the courage to ask him how he composed. At which he took me to his work room, and showed me a large book of blank pages onto which short fragments of musical sketches, roughly torn out of larger sketch-pages, had been pasted. Since the original sketch-pages had been papers of different qualities and colors and the musical fragments (sometimes only two or three notes) had been written on staves that were hand-drawn, often in quite fanciful curves, the scrapbook itself gave a very arresting visual impression. This was the work book for *The Flood*, which I don't think had yet been performed. He proceeded to explain how he chose fragments from his sketches, tore them out, shuffled them in different orders until he found one that satisfied him, and then pasted them down. I was genuinely surprised to learn of such an unexpected way of composing, which, if I had not known whose music it was, I might have had doubts as to the results; indeed I was so surprised that I did not think of the questions which would continue to nag me from then on. Naturally, he explained that all the fragments were derived from one chosen piece of material (as was evident), but what was not evident to me was how these fragments could be made to fit together. Of course, the printed score of this "Musical Play," which I saw much later, contains passages of short bits of music interspersed between lines of speaking, and these do look very much like what I remember seeing, even in print.

Some time later, I began to realize that what I saw corresponded to glimpses I had had of this technique in his music elsewhere. The description and quotation of Stravinsky telling how he cut up the final "fugue" of *Orpheus* and inserted fragments of harp figurations characteristic of the work, given in Nicholas Nabokov's *Old Friends and New Music*, as well as in a brilliant lecture by Edward Cone on the *Symphonies for Wind Instruments*, recalled to me how pervasive cross-cutting was in the music. I had not expected to see it so graphically demonstrated.

In Cone's lecture, he shows how the *Symphonies* are made up of a series of different musical movements, each cross-cut into the other. Sometimes the edges of the cuts are joined together by transitions or marked by cadences, but usually they are abrupt, coming at a point where the statement of a unified concept or impression is incomplete. In this, these cuts are unlike the articulations of literary works into chapters, stanzas, or of musical works into movements, or even of serialized movies or TV shows, all of which conclude with a completed action, although raising the question of "what happens next?" In Stravinsky, these are more often like random cuts, aimed, probably, as similar devices in the movies, particularly those of Eisenstein, to give a sense of sampling different kinds of things from which the observer can form his concept of the whole.

Such abrupt articulation seems to have become a conscious device with Stravinsky from about 1916 (*Renard*) on. Naturally one of the questions this brings up as far as music is concerned (since visual things have a very different quality of concreteness) is how these abrupt fragments can be joined into continuities that give the listener a unified musical idea or impression.

In connection with this, one of the things I had always wanted to discuss, especially after I had publicly read the text of the soldier's part of *The Story of a Soldier* (with Aaron Copland as narrator and John Cage as devil) for a performance given by Lukas Foss, was the lack of the usual continuity in the plot. For I was struck by the fact that there are at least three almost unconnected stories presented one after the other as if they were continuous. The second story starts back where the first one did with the soldier trudging down the road, as if it were the first time. I had also noticed that there was a similar plot structure in *Renard*, and a similar isolation of events so that previous actions seem not to affect succeeding ones—although the final result, the victory of the devil over the soldier or that of the barnyard animals over the fox (each finale presented almost as a separate story), fulfills expectations. In these two stories, the characters on stage and the audience are dealt with as if they had no memory, as if living always in the present and not learning from previous events—a dramatic situation that suggests the puppet world, like that of Punch and Judy, as the authors certainly intended, and also in a larger sense inescapable fate and universality of action such as that in the Everyman plays or that of the shades in the Hades of Gide's libretto for *Perséphone*, who ceaselessly repeat the gesture of living.

Whatever the intention, this kind of almost disjointed repetition immeasurably increases the pathos of both works. In fact, I came to believe, as I studied the soldier's part, that it was just because of this curious plot repetition, especially as it is coupled with music, that, although almost continually different in tiny details, is always drawing attention to its repetitive form, particularly harmonically and motivically. And it is through this that these two works gain their very urgent, compelling quality. For the soldier's violin seldom departs, from beginning to end of the work, from its basic musical material, drawn as it is out of the very fundamentals of violin playing, and from this is derived the tango, waltz, fox-trot, devil's dance, as well as the striking end. Because of this underlying continuity of material, all the brief, almost discrete fragments, however roughly they connect with each other, end up by producing a work that holds together in a very new and telling way. Disjunction of motive exists in much of Stravinsky's music before this time—such as in the fisherman's song in the *Nightingale*, in which (especially as it is presented at the end of the opera) each measure, although motivically related to its neighbor, is not connected to it by phrasing, harmonic leading, or rhythm.

Already in *Petrouchka*, of course, there is both a harmonic separation of crowd music from puppet music with a cross-cutting of a rather conventional kind from one to the other. In the *Sacre*, too, there is a use of different chord structures to characterize and unify each dance and to isolate it from its neighbors, a device that had already been used by Bartòk in his piano *Bagatelles*, by Schoenberg in *Erwartung*, and in works by Scriabin and also by Ives. One question I did ask was whether all the chords in the *Sacre* were related to one source chord (which may be partially or completely stated in the introduction). It was in January 1962, when I was teaching a course that dealt with the *Sacre* and thought I had discovered such a chord. I showed him my conjecture and he politely turned away from it, saying that he had forgotten whether or not or how he had organized this work. (In connection with this I had meant to ask about the three or four different editions of the *Danse Sacrale*, with different orchestrations and with the shift of the corona from the first to the third beat in the first measure, which, along with the change in harmony in the first and second chords and other similar places, not to speak of changes in bar lines in the 1943 version, reveal either a change in the idea of the phrasing of the movement—or a clarification of what was originally intended, all of which invalidates some French attempts at analysis.)

But to continue about the matter of "unified fragmentation," which really seems to have been carefully studied during the writing of works after the *Sacre*, like *Pribaoutki* (1914). The idiosyncrasies of Russian folk song and liturgy, of jazz and military band playing, of the parlor parodies of Satie, seemed to have played a role in this, which, once it was developed, furnished a pathway out of Russian folklore into an ever broadening musical world of technique and expression—always marked by what came to be recognized everywhere as the highly original and compelling voice of Stravinsky.

As a postscript, I quote my tribute written for the June 16, 1962 issue of the Hamburg newspaper *Die Zeit*, which, unlike American papers, contained a page of tributes to him written by composers from everywhere for his 80th birthday:

> Stravinsky's music is filled with a remarkable sense of the power, strength, and movement of human life. As no one before him, he captured the immediate moment in all its freshness and vividness and welded it into sequences of music that enhanced its life. Formulae, schemata, and other routines which can fill out musical time and space have no place here. Everything is shaped by the musical concept, which he presents in the most telling and direct way. His entire work—a very personal, almost autobiographical mirror of the development of a composer in our time—when considered as a whole forms a typical composition by Stravinsky. It lives in and grows out of the present through which it passes, finding unexpected but highly evocative and convincing ways of progressing. It denies itself the tried patterns by which similar problems were solved in the past. It is founded on a new approach to musical statement and expression often called 'objective' but no less human for that.

The career of Stravinsky serves as an example of a highly civilized creator aware of the disasters and glories of our period, from which he has drawn very important musical conclusions. His art represents a profession of faith in the value and importance of music to which his work lends new glory.

Igor Stravinsky, 1882–1971

[Eulogy delivered December 10, 1971]

Proceedings of the American Academy of Arts and Letters and the *National Institute of Arts and Letters*, second series no.22 (1972)

If anyone can be said to have *lived* the artistic history of his time and embodied it in outstanding works, it was Igor Stravinsky. In mourning his death, musicians of succeeding generations suffer this loss as a loss of part of their world. The horizon has suddenly become narrower. For while each generation has tended to live out its particular version of the twentieth century, Stravinsky encompassed them all. The general public, however, for whom he was, as he was for musicians, one of the leaders of his time, mourns the Stravinsky of the early part of this century, when it was still possible for a composer to become world famous. It was a great privilege to have lived in his time, to have awaited year upon year the appearance of new works, each an unexpected departure, a new challenge, and yet always totally engrossing and convincing. He never gave up his status as an advanced composer, as he once said jokingly of himself.

Understandably, many have, and the temptation to continue in the same direction must have been very great for one who between 1910 and 1913, from his twenty-eighth to thirty-first years, caused an international furor with the three ballets, written in quick succession, that have remained in the repertory ever since. They revealed a composer who understood the style of ornamental, romanticizing Russian folklore inherited from Rimsky-Korsakov, and could present it more convincingly than anyone else. Yet the line of a development which led him so quickly from the *Firebird* to *Pe-*

trouchka and then to *Le Sacre du printemps* indicates that he was already on the way to a complete change of style. He had the courage to follow this direction, which found support from the new artistic trends in France at the time he finally settled there at the end of the First World War.

Here [in the U.S.] he soon became the leading figure of the post-war generation, the so-called neo-Classicists, in sharp revolt against the former Romanticism, Impressionism, and Fauvism. From then until the end of the Second World War, he explored many facets of this esthetic with matchless power to convince, ranging more widely than other composers. So widely, in fact, that by 1945 there were indications that still another stylistic change was in progress. And, during the '50s, he became the leader of this second post-war generation—sometimes called "serialists" because they followed the twelve-tone methods of Stravinsky's contemporary Arnold Schoenberg. From around 1954 to 1967, from his seventy-second to eighty-fifth years, he embraced the methods of this Viennese composer who had long been considered his opponent, outstripping in originality and power all the younger followers with some of his finest works. Naturally each of these about-faces violated public and critical expectations, dismaying and often angering admirers and discouraging many of his disciples.

Yet in no way could this development be considered an effort to be up to the minute, since the works at every stage carried such conviction and imposed themselves by so many remarkable qualities. All are decisively marked by the composer's highly individual way of thinking and expression, by a passion for his particular kind of order and symmetry, and by his quick and intense temperament. The approach to these conflicting styles was that of a poet or novelist toward different subject matters, the invariable being the artistic vision, expression, and handling. In Stravinsky the style was truly the man himself, his own voice, not the "styles" he used.

In fact, the voice became more itself through the adoption of these different esthetics. In the nine large religious works, spread throughout his life, the sharpening of focus on personal religious experience, the gradual elimination of the extraneous with a consequent increase in seriousness fuses the great variety of methods into one coherent development. The non-religious works as well mark this progression toward the discovery of the essence of their respective genres.

Yet for all Stravinsky's deep artistic commitment, there is much lightness and wit. Impatient with romantic gestures, his was a quick, ironic yet compassionate nature, expressing itself in the brilliant flashes so evident in his secular works, his television appearances, on the recent Columbia record of rehearsals, in the transcripts of his conversations, and in his actions. He could truthfully answer at eighty-five, with his broad smile, when I asked him what he was composing: "What can you write after a *Requiem* but a setting of the *Owl and the Pussy-Cat*?"

Variations for Orchestra (1955)

Program note originally written in 1955 and revised for the performance by the New York Philharmonic, April 1972, Lorin Maazel, conductor.

My *Variations for Orchestra* was written for the Louisville Orchestra during 1955 from sketches made in 1953 and 1954. The project of writing such a work had interested me for some time, as I was eager to put into concrete musical terms a number of ideas I had about this old form. Traditionally, of course, this type of composition is based on one pattern of material, a theme or a succession of harmonies out of which are built many short contrasting pieces or sections of music. The theme and each little section form musical vignettes usually presenting one single, unchanging mood or character and often only one musical idea or technique. Viewed as a series of separate pieces of sharply defined character, a set of musical variations resembles certain old literary works such as the collection of brief, trenchant delineations of *Ethical Characters* by Theophrastus, held together by one common idea or purpose. Such a set implicitly gives expression to the classical attitude toward the problem of "unity in diversity."

In this work I was interested in adopting a more dynamic and changeable approach. The general characteristics of the form are maintained—one pattern of material out of which a diversity of characters come, but the principle of variation is often applied even within the scope of each short piece. In some, great changes of character and theme occur; in others, contrasting themes and characters answer each other back and forth or are heard simultaneously. By these and other devices, I have tried to give musical expression to experiences anyone living today must have when confronted by so many remarkable examples of unexpected types of changes and relationships of character, uncovered in the human sphere by psychologists and novelists, in the life cycle of insects and certain marine animals by biologists, indeed in every domain of science and art. Thus the old notion of "unity in diversity" presents itself to us in an entirely different guise than it did to people living even a short while ago.

Musically, the work is based on three ideas. The first two, ritornelli, are repeated literally here and there throughout the work in various transpositions of pitch and speed, while the third is a theme that undergoes many transformations. Of the ritornelli, the first, rising rapidly shortly after the opening, becomes progressively slower at each restatement (Variations I, III, VIII, and the Finale). The material of the main theme is used in many different ways, and its characteristic motive is frequently referred to.

The large plan consists in a presentation of degrees of contrast of character and their gradual neutralization during the first four variations. In the Fifth Variation, contrast is reduced to a minimum, and from there on there is increasing definition and conflict of character until, in the Finale, the restatement of the notes of the theme by the trombones reestablishes unity.

Each variation has its own shape, since shape, too, as a mode of musical behavior, helps to define character. For instance, the First Variation and the Finale are both rapid dialogues of many contrasting motives in contrasting rhythms. The Second Variation presents contrast of character by quoting the theme almost literally and confronting it with its own variants derived alternately by intervallic expansion and intervallic diminution. The Third contrasts textures of dense harmony and expressive lines with transparent fragmentary motives. The Fourth Variation is a continual *ritard*, and the Sixth an accelerating series of imitations. The Fifth obliterates contrast in a succession of chords using the notes of the theme. The Seventh is an antiphonal variation presenting three different ideas played in succession by the strings, brass, and woodwinds, and representing three different rhythmic planes. The line the woodwinds play in Variation VII is continued and developed in Variation VIII, while ideas of a much lighter musical nature are presented against it. The same idea is carried over into Variation IX, where it is rejoined by the other two ideas from Variation VII, now played simultaneously. The Finale is a rapid interplay of different characters, finally called to order by the trombones, who restate the notes of the first half of the theme while the strings play those of the second half softly.

The orchestration in detail, and the orchestral style of the whole was conceived taking into account the exact size of the Louisville Orchestra with its limited string group, though of course the work can be played by a symphony orchestra of the customary size. The following are called for: two each of flutes (second doubling piccolo), oboes, clarinets, and bassoons; four horns, two trumpets, three trombones, tuba, percussion (two players), harp (two harps ad lib), nine first violins, six second violins, six violas, four cellos, and four basses.

Music Criticism

Read over the BBC as part of a series on "Composers and Criticism," edited by Elaine Padmore (Aug. 1972).

The interplay between words about musical compositions and compositions themselves is very interesting to speculate about. Yet what impresses a composer about any attempt to verbalize about musical composition is the inadequacy of words to grasp something which is far more real to him in many important respects than words can be. Musical sounds are notoriously resistant to description, and so, to a composer, any attempt to discuss them always tends to be a matter of "flawed words and stubborn sounds"—the line from Wallace Stevens I used as the title of a recent book of conversations between Mr. Allen Edwards and myself.*

Beethoven's answer to someone who asked questions about some music he had just played was to play it over again. This is, of course, the composer's true response about his own work.

Yet writing about music, music criticism does play an important part in musical life, and in one way or another affects the musical public, performers, and even composers. In cases where society gives fairly clear directives as to what music shall be—as in most periods of the past before the Romantic, or in socially conscious societies like that of the United States in the '30s or that of the Soviet Union for most of its existence—the influence of dominant ideas and procedures as expressed in musical criticism is very

---

* Allen Edwards, *Flawed Words and Stubborn Sounds—A Conversation with Elliott Carter* (New York: W. W. Norton, 1971).—Eds.

powerful and pervasive. In our present Western society, such social directives are not clearly defined, so that a wide range of different methods and esthetics, originated by composers and their critics, admits different attitudes, none of them binding. Works of great quality elicit very different criticism from one cultural milieu and period to another, and seem to change their meaning and character, and therefore their influence, for one place and time to another. Even so perceptive a critic as the American Paul Rosenfeld changed his mind about Schoenberg's music between 1920 and 1923. At first he describes the Viennese composer as

> the great troubling presence of modern music. His vast, sallow skull lowers over it like a sort of North Cape. For with him, with the famous cruel five orchestral and nine piano pieces, we seem to be entering the arctic zone of musical art.[1]

Later, in 1923, after hearing *Pierrot Lunaire*, Rosenfeld wrote:

> The human torso of this time is in the music of Schoenberg. He is the thing without arms, without legs, without organs of communication, without a phallus. He is the helpless, quivering pulp; blindly stirring, groping, stretching. . . . Anguish speaks out of the sweetest dreams. "Eine blasse Wäscherin" is like a cool hand upon a pain-rent head; like the cool linens that release the body after states of exhaustion. It is out of some starvation-pit that Pierrot yearns for Columbine. She is the drink of water to a black and leathern mouth.[2]

This description seems preposterous if considered out of the context of its time, and when compared to what Pierre Boulez says of the work in 1961:

> The esthetic of *Pierrot Lunaire* is not so distant—disregarding questions of temperament and of musical characterization—from certain works of Debussy, like the *Sonata for Cello and Piano*. . . . As far as the instrumental writing goes, Schoenberg is at the height of his invention and originality: using a free language, he organizes it into sonorous shapes with more or less thematic tendencies, occasionally using the strictest forms of counterpoint. Oddly enough, it is the use of these forms which struck the earliest listeners, or at least the earliest chronicle writers and reviewers . . . even though these are far from being predominant.[3]

Schoenberg himself described the work in a letter of 1940, written about a performance he was to give and record in New York:

> at least for this time I intend to catch perfectly the light, ironical, satirical tone in which the piece was actually conceived. Then, too, times and ideas have changed a lot, so that what might have sounded Wagnerian or at worst Tchaikovskian to us then would remind us of Puccini or Léhar or worse, today.[4]

It is obvious that each of these writings about the same piece has some relevance to the music, yet is even more revealing about its time and milieu. Schoenberg, himself, points out how tastes and even perceptions change from period to period. In rereading the criticisms of Paul Rosenfeld today, it is hard for me to remember why it was that they stimulated such a great interest in the work he described and led me to it. Now, of course, the descriptions seem almost totally irrelevant, as the music itself has become a primary consideration.

For the importance of critiques and descriptions of music in drawing a listener's attention to certain qualities and procedures and leading him to grasp things that would have otherwise escaped his attention, is certainly very great. When listeners not accustomed to hearing Western music first encounter polyphony, they hardly notice what is happening unless their attention is drawn to it, just as those unfamiliar with East Indian music have difficulty hearing the characteristic inflections of pitch and attack. It is entirely possible that many developments in the arts would never have taken place if there had not been critics to explain to listeners what they were hearing and to develop their judgment by drawing attention to qualities, subtleties—and faults. The very elementary descriptions of the differences between consonances and dissonances by the early Western theorists were a way of making listeners conscious of what they were hearing as well as a way to teach musicians to produce these effects. How serious music would have developed without its accompaniment of verbiage is hard to imagine, and it seems that in most cases it was the composer who led the way with new ideas and approaches, such as those of Haydn, Beethoven, or Wagner, and these in turn have given rise to the vast cloud of words that occasionally confounds us.

Yet it is not only words that serve to define and clarify the new in music, it is also previous works themselves. Just as any new composition can be considered as a criticism of the past, throwing into question some of the assumptions it was based on, and making us hear it in a different perspective, so a knowledge of older works makes us hear new ones differently. The effect of Stravinsky's neo-Classic music, with its motoric vigor, was to force us to hear the rhythm of Baroque music in a new way, just as much music of the '50s and '60s makes us understand much more vividly the hocketing of thirteenth- and fourteenth-century music. Constant expansion of our horizon through familiarity with the sound of many kinds of old and new Western and non-Western music on gramophone recordings has changed the orientation of listeners and indeed all interested musicians in a way that is still hard to describe.

In the midst of changes and historical developments, composers themselves, naturally, are always considering and reconsidering their musical experiences, and these are expressed in their music and sometimes verbally. Usually, in his writings, the composer-critic is trying to clarify or change his attitudes and feeling about certain elements of his own style by discussing other related things. Wagner, for instance, whose early music was much influenced by Meyerbeer, gradually rid himself of this dependence by attacking Meyerbeer's music on extra-musical grounds. The same pattern can be seen on a less dramatic scale in Charles Ives, who in his *Essays Before a Sonata* reveals an extensive knowledge of his immediate European predecessors and contemporaries. He tells of his admiration for Brahms, Elgar, Franck, D'Indy, of his contempt for Wagner and Strauss, and his uncertainty about Reger and Mahler. His criticism, like that of many Romantic composers, is usually on moral or esthetic grounds, as this, for instance:

> We might offer the suggestion that Debussy's content would have been worthier of his manner if he had hoed corn. . . . Or we might say that his substance would have been worthier if his adoration or contemplation of Nature—which is often part of it, and which rises to great heights, as is felt, for example, in *La Mer*—had been more [of] the quality of Thoreau's. Debussy's attitude toward Nature seems to have a kind of sensual sensuousness underlying it, while Thoreau's is a kind of spiritual sensuousness.[5]

The criticism of Debussy is made even more direct in Ives's setting of Rupert Brooks's *Grantchester* in which Brooks's line "Clever modern men have seen a Faun peeping through the green" is accompanied by a quotation from Debussy's *L'Après-midi d'un faune*. In all of this, Ives, like every composer, is seeking his place and his own style in relationship to other music as he hears and experiences it, and this is as true of his discussions of old music as it is of his criticism of Stravinsky's *Firebird*, which he heard in 1919 or 1920 when he wrote, "I thought it was morbid and monotonous; the idea of a phrase, usually a small one, was good enough, and interesting in itself, but he kept it going over and over and it got tiresome."[6] Underneath these criticisms, however, there is a clear note of respect for what Ives calls the "manner," and an evident awareness of much that was going on. He was far from being the recluse that some have pictured.

Similar things can be found in almost any composer, in Mozart, for instance, whose letters contain many fascinating remarks, criticisms, and descriptions of other music. These, too, show him revolving and reorienting his thoughts. Perhaps the most crucial reorientation is described in the letters of March and April 1782, when he was twenty-six, at the time when he married Constanze Weber, and at the time when he first had extensive contact with the music of Handel and J. S. Bach. He first gives an indication of his new interest in a letter to his father, when he says he is collecting the fugues of J. S. Bach as well as those of his sons. Further evidences of this are the arrangements for string trio and quartet he made of many fugues from the *Well-Tempered Clavier*. In a letter to his sister[7] just after his marriage to Constanze he says:

> The reason this fugue has come into the world is really my dear Constanze. Baron von Swieten, whom I visit every Sunday, has sent me works of Handel and Bach, which I play for him. When Constanze heard the fugues she fell in love with them—she only wants to hear fugues and especially those of Handel and Bach. As she has often heard me improvise fugues, she asked me if I had written any of them out; and when I said, No, she scolded me for not writing the most ingenious and beautiful kind of music there is. So I busily wrote the *Andante Maestoso*.

Mozart is referring to his fugue in C major, seemingly patterned on that in C minor from the first book of the *Well-Tempered Clavier*. Contact with Bach developed Mozart's taste for counterpoint a great deal, for in the same letter he dismisses the work of a contemporary as not worthy to stand by Handel and Bach. This contact was, as everybody knows, to have far-reaching effects on Mozart's use of counterpoint, which up to that time had been derived from the academic precepts of Padre Martini. Alfred Einstein, in his book *Mozart*, discussing the impact of Bach, says

> Mozart was too great and fine a musician not to feel deeply and painfully the conflict produced when his habit of thinking in terms of "galant" and "learned" music was shaken by the encounter with a living polyphonic style. . . . Mozart was never completely finished with this experience but it enriched his imagination and resulted in more and more perfect works.[8]

Cases of the critical impact of one composer on another, with the latter assimilating the former into his own world of self-criticism, could be multiplied. Debussy's attitude about thematic development as derived from Beethoven and taught at the Conservatoire is well known. Whether Debussy's ideas were derived from those of Satie on the same subject is not clear, but such ideas did exert great influence on Stravinsky, who adhered to them from the time of the *Sacre* on. It is also because of such avoidance of thematic development that the Schoenberg school looked so askance at Debussy and

Stravinsky. This division of opinion is at the basis of Theodor Adorno's attack on Stravinsky and his praise of the Second Viennese school in his *Philosophie der neuen Musik.**

The role of critics like Adorno, in directing the course of history, seems to be a relatively new one, and perhaps inevitable. For although critics do tend to try to be fair to new music, and try to separate the good from the bad, still they, like composers themselves, cannot fail to have their own preferences and their own picture of what the future has in store for us. Unlike the composer, though, the critic cannot *make* the future, although he can try to prepare a way, even if it is not the way that the future finally takes. Yet in the twentieth century with its very wide variety of esthetics and supporting arguments, each exemplified in results of vastly different qualities, it often happens that critics, or art historians, have a better grasp of the complex ferment of points of view in the recent past and present than most working artists can have and so seem to be in a better position than they to indicate where the next step lies. Everybody knows the fable of the art critic who knew so much more about art movements in our time than any artist, and who was able, therefore, to go from city to city in his country and invent a special new movement with an esthetic and supporting ideology for each city and thereby convince local artists in each place to follow his suggestion, pointing out, too, how they would not be repeating their colleagues in the next city. Being also influential as a critic and curator of exhibitions, he later made a harvest of works for a big annual exhibition, and could point out the unusual variety of the works and their excellences, and award prizes.

In America such a role often seems to be played by art and music departments in universities, bent on extrapolating what the next step in their fields will be. After all, one could extrapolate a program for what some consider avant-garde music very easily. Since repetition of a short stretch of music about ten times produced a scandal in the early twenties, but no longer does, the number must be increased. We have reached well above a hundred now. Likewise, the hushed and almost noteless silences found at the end of the last Mahler works were a great surprise in their day but now are accepted, so we must have softer music, fewer notes, and more silence. The progress from the delicate click of the typewriter in the scoring of Satie's *Parade*, to airplane propellers has recently reached the highly amplified scraping of metal on glass. Or, consider the composer: can he be replaced by a machine or by improvisation? Is the player-piano or the electronic

*Tübingen, 1949.—Eds.

playback a substitute for the performer? How about giving the listener sounds and theatrical situations he cannot pay attention to in the usual way! However, just as we have seen Schoenberg noticing the change in listening habits from one period to another, it is now clear that the joke of one period can become the serious effort of the next. And vice-versa—even without the assistance of the critics and educators.

Journalist critics are naturally very concerned with such matters as news-producing scandals, oddities that give them scope to write entertainingly, as well as predictions and efforts to force the hand of history even when it involves distorting facts. How else could one explain the following, which is the opening of an article intended to show that there is to be as drastic a change in contemporary music as there was between the Baroque and Classical periods:

> Can we even imagine what their music might have been like if Schoenberg had grown up not knowing the works of Wagner and if Stravinsky had known nothing of Rimsky-Korsakov? Except possibly for Ives, it is hard to find such innocence and insularity in our century. And yet that is what happened to Mozart, he knew the music of Bach's sons intimately, but not that of the father, who stood for everything Mozart's own idols found repellent in the Baroque. . . .

This appeared in July 1972, in the *New York Times*, the only New York paper in these years which reviews the musical scene. Like others that used to but failed, the *Times* may be fighting for its life, so that inaccuracy and sensationalism must inevitably permeate even its music reviews. This, on the part of a paper which is read throughout the United States, is profoundly distressing for an American musician, and appears to be in very great contrast to the literate kind of music writing found in English newspapers and periodicals. Our American weekly and monthly magazines devoted to music, too, are nowhere near the caliber of English ones. We do not understand why this is so, for certainly there are as many literate music-listeners in America as in England. A number of periodicals have been launched in the past twenty years in America—only to fail. On the other hand, academic periodicals supported by private individuals or university music departments, which deal with music in a theoretical way for specialists, seem to have a longer life. Thus there is almost no corrective for the musical journalism which, by necessity, has to be more responsible toward selling the papers than toward music. It is hard to gauge how much good a composer derives from reviews in these papers, how much they help in getting his works considered by the lay public.

Within the confines of his own development the composer really has only two critics, in our situation: his own works and his alter ego—his self-critical activity. His works, as they mount up, each tend to suggest new paths of development, or, having fulfilled their particular vein, bring it to a halt. It is quite a common pattern for composers to write successive works exploring opposing areas of experience or technique—the comparison of Beethoven's *Eighth* and *Ninth Symphonies* shows this, as do the like-numbered ones of Mahler, as indeed do the three symphonies Mozart wrote in 1788. The carrying out of a general tendency from work to work, such as, for instance, the reduction to essential brief elements found in the series of works Webern wrote up to Op. 11, or a similar pattern of reducing rhythm, tempi, and texture to their simplest expression in his last series of works represents, of course, the opposite tendency.

The development of the self-critical power which leads a composer to try and write the work he would most like to hear—or perhaps what he would like others to hear—involves his commitment to society, to art, as well as to the materials of music. That Ives in the setting of Rupert Brooks's *Grantchester*, mentioned above, chose to illustrate some words about "clever modern men" with a quotation from Debussy, a method quite characteristic of him, indicates that he could not, so to speak, assume the role of a clever modern man and present it out of his own experience. The lapse in style shows that Ives's inner self-criticism did not extend to include the very basic lesson learnable from all art works of any importance, which takes as a fundamental that every part should be marked with the artist's vision, with the corollary that what falls out of the frame falls out because it has not been assimilated.

Thus the inner criticism, or self-criticism, of a composer becomes a demonstration of his relationship with his society, embodying as it does his courtesy to his listeners and performers, by first inducing him to find visions or messages which seem important to communicate, and then communicating them in a way that can eventually lead to understanding. This self-criticism cannot come from without, although acceptance or rejection of a work may reinforce the composer's inner conviction or change its direction.

NOTES

1. Rosenfeld, *Musical Portraits* (New York, 1920), pp.233–43.
2. P. Rosenfeld, *Musical Chronicle* (New York, 1923), pp.300–14.

3. P. Boulez, *Relevés d'apprenti* (Paris, 1966), pp.355–56.

4. Letter to Fritz Stiedry, August 31, 1940, in Josef Rufer, *The Works of Arnold Schoenberg—A Catalogue of his Compositions, Writings, and Paintings* (London, 1962).

5. Ives, *Essays Before a Sonata*, p.97 (p.82 in the Boatwright edition).

6. John Kirkpatrick, ed., *Charles E. Ives Memos* (New York: W. W. Norton, 1972), p.138.

7. April 20, 1782.

8. A. Einstein, *Mozart* (New York: Oxford University Press, 1945), p.153.

In Memoriam:
Stefan Wolpe, 1902–1972

Perspectives of New Music, 11,1 (Fall–Winter 1972)

Comet-like radiance, conviction, fervent intensity, penetrating thought on many levels of seriousness and humor, combined with breathtaking adventurousness and originality marked the inner and outer life of Stefan Wolpe, as they do his compositions. Inspiring to those who knew him, these inspiring qualities reach many more through his music. A man, a musician for whom everyone who came close could not help but feel admiration and affection. Contact with him was such an important experience that he was understandably surrounded by many devoted, convinced friends and students who helped with his problems of publication, performances, helped in finding him teaching positions, helped to save his manuscripts during the fire of a few years ago, helped him to move about when his physical condition was deteriorating. The force of his artistic personality, motivated as it was by deep conviction and by an innately original way of doing things, occasionally seemed to be utterly unconcerned with prudence and caution, yet frequently what he did turned out to be the only right way of acting.

I remember a very vivid day in England, when I was teaching at the music school at Dartington Hall, where Stefan had come to visit. I asked him to teach my class of young English student composers—feeling really, that he, at least, would give the students one worthwhile class. He started talking about his *Passacaglia,* a piano work built of sections each based on a musical interval—minor second, major second, and so on. At once, sitting at the piano, he was caught up in a meditation on how wonderful these primary materials, intervals, were; playing each over and over again on the piano, singing, roaring, humming them, loudly, softly, quickly, slowly, short and detached or drawn out and expressive. All of us forgot time passing, when the class was to finish. As he led us from the smallest one, a minor second, to the largest, a major seventh—which took all afternoon—music was reborn, new light dawned, we all knew we would never again listen to music as we had. Stefan had made each of us experience very directly the living power of these primary elements. From then on indifference was impossible. Such a lesson most of us never had before or since, I imagine.

Stefan's work first came to my attention in the 1920s when he wrote workers' songs, somewhat of the type of Weill and Eisler, during the Weimar Republic. When he left his hometown, Berlin, as the Nazi menace grew, he went to Russia, Rumania, Austria, and the then Palestine. During this period little of his was heard here until he came to America to live in 1939. It was about that year that I reviewed his *March and Variations* for two pianos, written in 1931, as "the only work on the program with signs of real originality." But it was with his *Songs from the Hebrew,* sung here at McMillan Theater, that Stefan became one of the moderns I was and still am most enthusiastic about. Then we heard the piano *Passacaglia,* the amazing *Battle Piece,* the many wonderful chamber works, and finally the *Symphony* written in 1955–56, comissioned by Rodgers and Hammerstein in collaboration with the League of Composers–ISCM. It turned out to be one of the most remarkable but also one of the most difficult-to-perform pieces of our era.

When it was finally accepted for performance by the New York Philharmonic, six years after its completion, Stefan, already ill, had the parts copied hastily so that later, at the last moment, the Philharmonic librarian had to do many of them over, for which many of his friends contributed. The music itself proved beyond the level of difficulty that the Philharmonic could cope with, given its lack of experience with new music and its limited rehearsal schedule, despite the good will and valiant efforts of many of the performers and of Stefan Bauer-Mengelberg, who had been called in to conduct. As all his friends remember bitterly, only two of the three movements were performed and these not well.

Tragically, shortly before this performance-ordeal, while Stefan was at the American Academy in Rome, he began to show signs of the illness,

Parkinson's disease, which from then on fell like a heavy shadow on the physical body of this extraordinarily animated man. For from about 1961 until his death in the spring of 1972, physically weakened often to the point of not being able to push a pencil across a piece of paper, he still continued, undiminished in spirit, to teach, think, and compose, producing more of his remarkable works. In this phase of his life, the courage, determination, and will to live and act through his art were inspiring. Few have been put to the terrible test that he endured and few that have, have been able to carry on as he under the circumstances.

Now, his physical life over, what emerges more clearly than ever is that the surpassing moral fortitude Stefan exhibited in these last years is the very quality which gives the radiant power and originality to his work. His music, to me, unequivocally expresses his deeply felt conviction about the values of art and life—makes them immediately graspable—a most inspiring thing in these unencouraging times.

String Quartet No. 3 (1971)

Program note for the Columbia recording by the Juilliard String Quartet (Robert Mann and Earl Carlyss, violins; Raphael Hillyer, viola; Claus Adam, cello)—M32738 (1974).

[Introductory note by Robert Hurwitz, followed by Carter's remarks.]

The *Third Quartet*, like the *Second*, deals with the relationship of instruments, but, instead of constantly shifting attention to one of the instruments vs. the other three, as he did in the *Second*, Carter divides the players into two pairs: Duo I for violin and cello; Duo II for violin and viola.

Duo I is set in a quasi rubato, "expressively intense, impulsive style," and plays four movements: *Furioso; Leggerissimo; Andante espressivo;* and *Giocoso.* Duo II plays its six movements in strict time: *Maestoso; Grazioso; Pizzicato giusto, meccanico; Scorrevole; Largo tranquillo;* and *Appassionato.* Carter has supplied the following comments on the workings of the *Third Quartet*:

The movements of both duos are broken into substantial fragments, played in other orders than the four listed for Duo I and the six for Duo II (see plan below) so there is a constant interlacing of moods and materials; for the change within either duo from one movement to another always occurs while the other duo is carrying on the same movement.

The work begins with Duo I playing *Furioso* (associated with the major seventh) against Duo II's *Maestoso* (perfect fifth). Later, I's *Furioso* reappears during II's *Pizzicato giusto, meccanico* (augmented fourth) and continues when II changes to *Grazioso* (minor seventh). Later I's *Furioso* is expanded for a longer stretch, coming in while II plays its *Largo tranquillo* (major third) and continuing through II's pause and part of II's *Scorrevole* (minor second). The *Maestoso* of Duo II can be traced in a similar way: at the beginning it is combined with I's *Furioso*, and continued through I's short pauses, stopping after I has taken up *Leggerissimo* (perfect fourth). Later II's *Maestoso* returns during I's *Pizzicato giocoso* (minor third), continuing during part of I's *Andante espressivo* (minor sixth). A similar plan can be traced for all the movements, as can, perhaps, be seen from this plan:

Duo I (played continuously)   Duo II (played continuously)

Furioso .... Maestoso ⌐
(pause) .... Maestoso |
⌐Leggerissimo .... Maestoso ⌐
|Leggerissimo .... (pause)
⌐Leggerissimo .... Grazioso ⌐
⌐Andante espressivo .... Grazioso ⌐
⌐Andante espressivo .... Pizzicato giusto, meccanico ⌐
(pause) .... Pizzicato giusto, meccanico |
⌐Pizzicato giocoso .... Pizzicato giusto, meccanico ⌐
|Pizzicato giocoso .... (pause)
⌐Pizzicato giocoso .... Scorrevole ⌐
(pause) .... Scorrevole |
⌐Leggerissimo .... Scorrevole ⌐
⌐Leggerissimo .... Pizzicato giusto, meccanico ⌐
⌐Furioso .... Pizzicato giusto, meccanico ⌐
⌐Furioso .... Grazioso ⌐
(pause) .... Grazioso |
⌐Pizzicato giocoso .... Grazioso ⌐
⌐Pizzicato giocoso .... Maestoso ⌐
⌐Andante espressivo .... Maestoso ⌐

```
⌈ Andante espressivo  . . . . . . . . . . . . . . . . . . . . . . . . . . . . . . . . (pause)
⌊ Andante espressivo  . . . . . . . . . . . . . . . . . . . . . . . Largo tranquillo ⌐
  (pause)  . . . . . . . . . . . . . . . . . . . . . . . . . . . . . . . Largo tranquillo │
⌐ Leggerissimo  . . . . . . . . . . . . . . . . . . . . . . . . . . . Largo tranquillo ⌟
⌊ Leggerissimo  . . . . . . . . . . . . . . . . . . . . . . . . . . . . Appassionato ⌐
⌐ Pizzicato giocoso  . . . . . . . . . . . . . . . . . . . . . . . . . Appassionato ⌟
⌊ Pizzicato giocoso  . . . . . . . . . . . . . . . . . . . . . . Largo tranquillo ⌐
⌐ Furioso  . . . . . . . . . . . . . . . . . . . . . . . . . . . . . . . . Largo tranquillo ⌟
│ Furioso  . . . . . . . . . . . . . . . . . . . . . . . . . . . . . . . . . . . . . . (pause)
⌊ Furioso  . . . . . . . . . . . . . . . . . . . . . . . . . . . . . . . . . . Scorrevole ⌐
⌐ Andante espressivo  . . . . . . . . . . . . . . . . . . . . . . . . Scorrevole ⌟
⌊ Andante espressivo  . . . . . . . . . . . . . . . . . . . . . . Appassionato ⌐
  (short pause)  . . . . . . . . . . . . . . . . . . . . . . . . . . . . Appassionato │
  Furioso  . . . . . . . . . . . . . . . . . . . . . . . . . . . . . . . . . Appassionato │
  Coda:Furioso; Andante;                        ⌐
     Leggerissimo; Pizzicato giocoso⌟. . . . . . . . . . . . . . Appassionato ⌟
```

The above sections are not, of course, of the same length nor their components of the same salience, since each whole movement, although fragmented, has its own overall shape, with some sections more emphatic than others.

Dramatically and technically one of the principal interests of this formal play was the possibility of contrasts between the 'unmotivated,' abrupt changes from one movement fragment to another with the 'motivated' continuities within the movements in which one thing clearly grows out of another.

Brass Quintet

Introductory talk for the BBC première, October 20, 1974

I am particularly happy that the world première of my *Brass Quintet* should be given as part of the BBC's celebration of Charles Ives's hundredth birthday, because it helps to repay the great debt I owe him personally and musically. In 1924 and 25, when I was making youthful blunders in composition, Ives, whom I used to see at that time, encouraged me, and even over a number of years took an interest in my aspirations to become a composer. His remarkable personality has always been a great inspiration to me, but perhaps even more than that, the copies of the privately printed *Concord Sonata, 114 Songs,* and the photostat of the *First Violin Sonata* which he gave me formed a sometimes perplexing, but always exciting visionary bible during my formative years.

I can remember, vividly, the last time I saw him, when, as a college student I had started to write the kind of Hindemith-like neo-Classic music, characteristic of the then young composer's revolt against the dissonances and confused romantic textures of the earlier time. He looked at a little piano sonata and, I guess, rather disappointed, took me out for a walk in the summer woods overlooking the Connecticut valleys of Redding, where he spent his summers. Nature was at its most lush, and I remember clearly the mottled sunlight on the paths and rocks and his turning suddenly to me and saying something like: "How can anyone deny that there is a great being behind all this?" expressing typically pantheistic views, already well known to me then. In retrospect, this could have been taken as a kind of rebuke for the rather artificial music I was trying to write, but at the time, overcome by the beauty of the day and a profound respect for the man, I did not think so, although I did realize dimly that our directions were beginning to be different.

Yet now I see that many of our aims are similar, particularly in the primary concern for musical expressivity. For me this quality can be heightened, focused, and when necessary dramatized both in detail and in larger relationships, in a way that did not always interest Ives. Like him, I enjoy writing music of constant variety and change, but within a more highly focused and coherent sound-character and musical style than interested Ives. Coming at a later period, I have been much more concerned with flexibility and variety of texture and sound, while Ives, like many early modernists, relied at times on rather routine procedures to make dissonances, like the pedantic canon in *From the Steeples and the Mountains,* or the rigidly systematic use of harmonies built on other intervals than thirds found in *The Fourth of July* and the song *Soliloquy.* Unlike him, I have been concerned with finding idioms that would help express the special vision behind any particular work, that would give it its own identity and differentiate it from others. For this reason I have avoided conscious quotation of other music except for the one case in my *First String Quartet* of 1951, in which I quoted the opening theme of Ives's *First Violin Sonata* as a tribute to the composer whose works had suggested some of the general ideas of my music. Indeed Ives's music is one source of the notion of multilayered texture which has preoccupied me since 1948, the other sources being, of course, the operas of Mozart, Verdi, and Mussorgsky.

The *Brass Quintet*, which you will hear shortly, was written this past summer for its present players, the American Brass Quintet. It is representative of many things I have mentioned. Being almost constantly multilayered, like my *Second String Quartet*, it separates the players by individualizing their parts, but not as completely as did the string quartet, because each instrument shares parts of its repertory with one of the others. The first trumpet, for instance, near the beginning plays in a trio with the second trumpet and the tenor trombone, featuring the minor sixth in light, irregular chords, of which the character and interval become part of the repertory of the three participating instruments. A bit later the first trumpet plays another trio with the horn and the bass trombone, which features fanfares and quiet majestic music based on the perfect fifth, which then become part of the repertory of these three instruments. The horn, however, which has the largest repertory of all, also frequently uses the augmented fourth, which it does not share with any of the others.

All of these contrasting characters and their related musical intervals form a multilayered piece planned along the following pattern: Every third (that is the first, fourth, seventh, etc.) of its overlapping nineteen short sections is a brief five-part quodlibet in which the instruments oppose each other with contrasting parts of their individual repertories. Between these is a duo preceded or followed by a trio in which the two or three instruments join in music of similar character. Each duo and trio has a different instrumentation.

Just to make the general plan clear let me describe the shape of a few of the initial sections: The opening quodlibet starts as if it were a slow movement but is suddenly interrupted by the horn. This causes an outburst from all the five, each contributing a characteristic fragment. Immediately the first trio starts, with the two trumpets and the tenor trombone playing short, light chords in irregular rhythm, while the horn and the bass trombone continue the slow music of the beginning. These latter two stop for a bit and then start a somewhat rough, fast duo in which the bass trombone takes the lead. The trio still continues above this, pauses, and then starts up the slow music which leads to the second quodlibet. This general pattern is followed throughout much of the piece, with variations of emphasis, timing, and, of course, contrasts of expression and character. At one point, for instance, the two trumpets and the horn play soft, rapid, smoothly flowing music that soon is combined with a duet for the two trombones playing glissandi.

The general plan is interrupted, midway through the work, by a relatively extended unaccompanied horn solo, which is cut off by angry octaves from the others. The slow music which began the piece and forms the background of the first three quodlibets is abandoned after the last of these, only to return in extended form near the end. The entire work, in fact, can be heard as one long slow movement with interruptions.

Indeed another way of hearing the piece is to consider it as a meeting of five brass players who have come together to play slow, solemn music. As they start to do so, entering one after the other, the weak member of the group, the horn, interjects irrelevant, disruptive ideas that momentarily upset the plan. Given the atmosphere of discord that arises between the players, each begins to assert himself, joining partners in small groups while the excluded ones try to bring back the slow music. The light, comic, flowing, excitable or lyric duos or trios heard between passages during which all five altercate, gradually stray from the project of playing slow music. Midway through, the horn deplores its alienation in a long unaccompanied solo, which arouses the others to a menacing duo for trumpets and an angry trio for trombones and horn. All this leads to a violent altercation that finally is settled by an agreement to continue the slow music of the beginning. After quite a period of unanimity the players again begin to disagree: the tenor trombone, never having had a proper solo like the others have had, stops them for his, which is accompanied by a muted trumpet. There is an abrupt and aggressive ending.

This quintet, rather than employ all the resources of color possible with modern mutes for the brass, relies primarily on linear material, textures, and the instrumental virtuosity for which the American Brass Quintet is notable.

Double Concerto
for Harpsichord and Piano
with Two Chamber Orchestras
(1961)
Duo for Violin and Piano (1974)

Program note for the Nonesuch recording H–71314 stereo (1975). *Double Concerto*: Paul Jacobs, harpsichord; Gilbert Kalish, piano; The Contemporary Chamber Ensemble, Arthur Weisberg, conductor. *Duo:* Paul Zukofsky, violin; Gilbert Kalish, piano.

Both pieces on this record, although written thirteen years apart, derive their music directly from the performing situation. It was considered a matter of great importance that the expression and thought arise from the unique sound and performance techniques of the harpsichord, of the piano, and the violin. There was a desire to get down to the physical origins of musical sound and to take off from there. The *Double Concerto*, in fact, actually has a shape that parallels this attitude, starting as it does by presenting gradually changing percussion sounds that first "give birth" to a few musical pitches that in turn bring on the sound of the piano and then the harpsichord, which in their turn become more and more articulated and differentiated, only to sink back eventually to a more chaotic, undifferentiated state near the end.

Both of these works were written in response to specific requests; both had to wait until ideas arose whose expression seemed to require those pairs of instruments for which I had been asked to write. This was particularly true of the *Duo*, where the right idea presented itself only after about ten busy years of writing other things. In the case of the *Double Concerto*, the response to a request from Ralph Kirkpatrick for a piece for harpsichord and piano ended up in music that surrounds each of the soloists with a small orchestra and two percussion players, serving sometimes to intensify the special qualities of the solo instruments and at other times to blur their differences.

Each of the works heard here has two sound sources treated as opposing members of a pair, with differences of sound quality and types of expression reinforced by giving each member of the pair individualized musical materials, harmonies, and rhythms. In the *Duo*, the contrast between the violin and the piano, both stringed instruments, is fundamentally a gestural one—between stroking and striking. Using a great variety of bow strokes, the violin can be made to produce many different types of attack: it can also prolong its sounds and give them a variety of tone colors and inflections, such as swelling and fading or becoming more, or less, intense. On the other hand, the finger of the pianist strikes a key that catapults a felt-covered hammer up to the string more or less suddenly and forcefully, depending on how the key is struck. Once the hammer has started the string vibrating, the player has no further control over the sound—which immediately begins to die away—except that he can cut short this decay by raising the finger from the key, activating a damper.

The piano's loss of control over its sound is shared with the harpsichord, which, moreover, has only a remote control of dynamics—these are scarcely affected by the pressure of the finger on the key, being produced mainly by stops (operated, in this case, by pedals) that add or subtract the number of strings set into vibration by the plectra when the key is struck. These stops, however, give the two keyboards of the harpsichord a vast array of tone colors, since they control jacks that vary in their plucking materials—quills or leather—and pluck the strings at different places along their length.

The piano has eighty-eight notes (usually) and can play very loudly and very softly; the violin covers only about the upper fifty-three notes of the piano's range and can be overwhelmed by the piano even when playing its loudest. The harpsichord called for in the *Double Concerto* lacks the piano's uppermost seven notes, but has four rather soft notes below the lowest piano note (these are heard in the harpsichord's last chord, just before the end); even at its loudest, it is very much softer than the piano playing moderately (in the fast duet in the middle of the *Concerto*, the piano has to play very softly for the harpsichord to be heard). This contrast between the two solo instruments dictated the antiphonal character of the *Double Concerto*, so that the harpsichord would not be overwhelmed by the piano. The changes of stops that give great variety to the harpsichord's sound were worked out as carefully as possible (harpsichords are not standardized), with certain harpsichord timbres being associated with particular effects in the orchestra, as at the end of the introduction, when the harpsichord's mute (lute) stop is answered by wood percussion and pizzicato strings. The harpsichord's solo cadenza has a great number of sudden changes of registration, which reveal almost the full color range of the instrument.

Given the point of view from which these pieces were written, there is little question of one instrument's imitating another in sound (as often happens in the Classical style), and for this reason there is almost no imitation of musical material between the members of each pair. The harpsichord and piano in the *Concerto*, and the violin and piano in the *Duo*, are each given music idiomatic to their instruments, meant to appeal to the imaginations of their performers and cast them into clearly identifiable, independent roles. The intention is to stimulate performers into giving vital, personal performances and through these to transmit the message of a new, important, and special experience to the listener. Since the instruments and the highly developed ways of playing them already possess a quality of special experience in and of themselves, frequent exploitation of unusual sound effects or of chance playing was avoided, for in these works it would have reduced that special quality to the ordinariness and obviousness of chaotic confusion.

The music gives the impression of being continuous, of evolving constantly from beginning to end. Although the *Double Concerto* falls more clearly into sections than does the *Duo*, it is constantly prefiguring what will happen and recalling what has happened, bridging the pauses and changes of character by numerous internal connections. The [seven] sections of the *Concerto* are symmetrically arranged. The brilliant *Allegro scherzando* and the *Presto* [sections 1 and 6] each feature one of the two solo instruments, the piano in the former, the harpsichord in the latter; in each movement, the featured instrument and its orchestra are frequently interrupted by the other instrument and its orchestra playing at a dynamic level opposite to that of the main group. In the central *Adagio*, the "choreography" changes: the entire wind section, in center stage (although still divided into groups), plays slow music, while in the background the two soloists, strings, and four percussionists surround the winds with accelerating and decelerating patterns that alternately move clockwise and counter-clockwise.

The Introduction and Coda also form a fundamentally symmetrical pair. The Introduction "breaks the silence" and gradually piles up two-by-two, polyrhythmically, the ten speeds and associated tone colors and musical intervals used in the entire work. The Coda begins with a crash and then, like a large gong, dies away over many measures in wave-like patterns, with many diverse tone colors fading out and returning—each time slightly different, and each time with less energy—until the work subsides to a quiet close.

Thought about this work suggested *a literary analog to the concerto's expected form—Lucretius's *De rerum natura*, which describes the formation of the physical universe by the random swervings of atoms, its flourishing, and its destruction. Bit by bit, however, a humorous parody of Lucretius in Alexander Pope's *Dunciad* took over in my thoughts, in lines like:

> All sudden, Gorgons hiss, and Dragons glare,
> And ten-horn'd Fiends and Giants rush to war;
> Hell rises, Heav'n descends, and dance on earth;
> Gods, imps, and monsters, music, rage, and mirth,
> A fire, a jig, a battle, and a ball,
> Till one wide conflagration swallows all.

The beautiful end of Pope's poem seemed to articulate in words the end of the work I had already composed:

> —the all composing hour
> Resistless falls; the Muse obeys the power.
> She comes! She comes! the sable throne behold
> Of Night primeval, and of Chaos old!
> Before her Fancy's gilded clouds decay,
> And all its varying rainbows die away.
> Wit shoots in vain its momentary fires,
> The meteor drops and in a flash expires.
>
> Nor public flame, nor private, dares to shine;
> Nor human spark is left, nor glimpse divine!
> Lo! thy dread empire, Chaos! is restor'd;
> Light dies before thy uncreating word:
> Thy hand, great Anarch! lets the curtain fall;
> And universal Darkness buries all.

The *Duo*, as has been said, derives its character and expression from the contrast between its two very dissimilar instruments—the bow-stroked violin and the key-struck piano. The mercurial violin music, at times intense and dramatic, at others light and fanciful, constantly changes its pace and tone of expression; the piano plays long stretches of music of consistent character and is much more regular both in rhythm and in style. The piano

---

* The text from here to the end of the poetry has been inserted from an earlier program note.—Eds.

makes extensive use of the pedal to mask one sonority with another and then gradually to uncover the second—as in the very first measures. In fact, the long opening section for the piano forms a quiet, almost icy background to the varied and dramatic violin, which seems to fight passionately against the piano. After this beginning, the music is joined seamlessly until the end.

In the course of the work, the violin focuses on one aspect of its part after another—and often on two or more aspects at a time—playing in a *rubato*, rhythmically irregular style, while the piano constantly plays regular beats, sometimes fast, sometimes slow. Toward the end, while the violin is involved in a very fast and impassioned music, the piano becomes more and more detached, playing a series of regular rhythmic patterns, each successively slower than the previous one. As the piano reaches a point of extreme slowness, the violin is heard increasingly alone, isolating for a few measures at a time the various elements of its part, with the quiet and more lyrical aspects given more prominence than previously.

The general form of both works on this record is quite different from that of the music I wrote up to 1950. While this earlier music was based on themes and their development, here the musical ideas are not themes or melodies but rather groupings of sound materials out of which textures, linear patterns, and figurations are invented. Each type of music has its own identifying sound and expression, usually combining instrumental color with some "behavioral" pattern that relies on speed, rhythm, and musical intervals. There is no repetition, but a constant invention of new things— some closely related to each other, others, remotely. In both the *Double Concerto* and the *Duo* there is a stratification of sound, so that much of the time the listener can hear two different kinds of music, not always of equal prominence, occurring simultaneously. This kind of form and texture could be said to reflect the experience we often have of seeing something in different frames of reference at the same time.

The *Double Concerto* was commissioned by the Fromm Music Foundation and is dedicated to Paul Fromm. It was written during 1959–1961 and given its première in New York,* September 6, 1961, at a concert for the Eighth Congress of the International Musicological Society. The *Duo for Violin and Piano* was written in 1973–74 to fulfill a commission by the McKim Fund in the Library of Congress and is dedicated to my wife, Helen. It was first performed by Paul Zukofsky and Gilbert Kalish at a New York Philharmonic Prospective Encounter, March 5, 1975.

* Ralph Kirkpatrick, harpsichord; Charles Rosen, piano; Gustav Meier, conductor.—Eds.

Documents of a
Friendship with Ives

Tempo, 117 (June 1976); originally published in *Parnassus*, Summer 1975.
© 1975 The National Institute of Arts and Letters.

These letters and sketches of letters which the curator of the Ives Collection at Yale University, Mr. John Kirkpatrick, has been kind enough to allow us to copy give the history of a warm and inspiring friendship with Charles Ives. It started around 1924, when Mr. Clifton J. Furness, a music teacher at the Horace Mann High School in New York City, where I was a student, introduced me to him. From what I can remember, we went to Ives's house by Gramercy Park on a dark, rainy Sunday afternoon, and stepped into a cheery, old-fashioned interior, discussing excitedly modern music all afternoon. After this, I met Ives occasionally, sometimes when he invited me to join Mrs. Ives and him in their box at the Saturday afternoon Boston Symphony concerts at Carnegie Hall, or at Katherine Ruth Heyman's loft in a building that no longer exists, on Third Avenue and 10th Street huddling under the El, or later at his house on East 74th Street opposite the Mannes School.

To assist my entrance into Harvard in 1926, Ives graciously allowed me to use his name as a reference in my application for admission as a Freshman. The typescript copy, which has scrawled across the top in his handwriting, "letter to Harvard Dean in re Elliot [sic] Carter," has this to say:

> Carter strikes me as rather an exceptional boy. He has an instinctive interest in literature and especially music that is somewhat unusual. He writes well—an essay in his school paper—"Symbolism in Art"—shows an interesting mind. I don't know him intimately, but his teacher in Horace Mann School, Mr. Clifton J. Furness, and a friend of mine, always speaks well of him—that he's a boy of good character and does well in his studies. I am sure his reliability, industry, and sense of honour are what they should be—also his sense of humour which you do not ask me about.

After going to live in Cambridge, I was to return fairly often to New York either by hitchhiking or by train, especially for concerts of contemporary music, and kept in touch with Ives, as the next two letters show. The first was written just after the first performance of the second movement of Ives's

Fourth Symphony, given in New York at a Pro-Musica concert under the direction of Eugene Goossens. This Pro-Musica Society, which listed Ives as a sponsor on all its programs and periodicals, gave many seasons of concerts of contemporary music in New York, as did its chapters around the country, and published an important magazine, *Pro-Musica Quarterly.* It also sponsored the first tours of Bartók and Prokofiev around the U.S. At the time of this letter, the organization was sponsoring a tour of Darius Milhaud.

C–22 George Smith Hall
Cambridge, Mass.
Feb. 19, 1927.

Dear Mr. Ives,

　　I am sorry that I was unable to come to see you that Sunday afternoon nor later to hear your symphony. As I am interested very much in your music I would like to *hear* it once instead of having to *work* over it to make it sound at all.

　　I wonder if it would be possible to have a few more records of your violin sonata. Or is the stamp lost? Recently I have been greatly interested in recordings. I have eight records of 'Pelleas and Melisande', 'Pacific 231', Stravinsky's 'Petrouchka', 'Firebird', 'Ragtime', as well as Scriabine's 'Poem of Ecstasy'—only to mention moderns. I find the victrola a great help in studying Beethoven and Brahms. Unfortunately very little good Bach has been done.

　　I am sending you a very interesting magazine dealing with recordings entirely. In it, this month, has appeared an account of private recordings. I wonder if Pro-Musica could not have a department for recording its more popular modern works. 'Pierrot Lunaire' and other things are waiting to be done as well as some Scriabine.

　　The subscription record idea seems a very good one (at least to me) and would help in the understanding of modern music. I wish it were possible to start a modern music group here in Boston—it has never been done though we hear a great deal from Koussewitsky.

　　I am coming to Miss Heyman's concert Sunday evening Feb. 27. I hope I shall see you there.

Sincerely yours,
(Signed) Elliott C. Carter, Jr.*

The violin sonata referred to in this letter was the *Third,* privately recorded by Jerome Goldstein, I think. Miss Katherine Ruth Heyman, another friend of Ives, was an American pianist who had lived during the Bloomsbury days in London (Ezra Pound dedicated "Scriptor Ignotus" in *A*

---

*A facsimile reproduction of this letter appears in Vivian Perlis, *Charles Ives Remembered: An Oral History* (New Haven: Yale University Press, 1974), p.132.—Eds.

Lume Spento to her) but at this time was New York's principal exponent of Scriabin's music, as well as that of other moderns—Ravel, Schoenberg, and Americans like Emerson Whithorne, Charles Griffes, and Ives. Her book, *The Relation of Ultra-Modern to Archaic Music*, along with Claude Bragdon's *Dynamic Symmetry* and Ouspensky's *Tertium Organum*, was almost required reading for this somewhat Blavatskian circle.

The above letter reveals a concern for the presentation of contemporary music to the public, an activity which was to absorb almost all of my time in the late Thirties, Forties, and Fifties, what with writing reviews and organizing concert seasons of modern music for the League of Composers and the International Society for Contemporary Music.

The next letter to Ives from Cambridge, with date and address left off, revealing no doubt the progress of my education, can be dated by the mention of Rudhyar's *Paeans*, published in January 1928. All the music of mine it refers to has been lost except a setting of Joyce in 5/8 time submitted to *New Music Edition* around the period of this letter and neither published nor returned until a few years ago when Henry Cowell turned it up among his old papers. *New Music Quarterly* (later called *Edition*) was devoted to the publication of "modern" scores no other publisher would print. It was run single-handed by Cowell from October 1927 (its inaugural issue was the score of Ruggles's *Men and Mountains* discussed in this letter) to around 1942, when Cowell tried to retire and encouraged a number of us, including myself, to run it. We shortly turned the entire catalogue of music over to a commercial publisher. The *Quarterly*, I presume, was partially subsidized by Ives from its inception. When I was its president we received a contribution of $1,000 from him annually. It was said among us that he had subsidized the publication of his own large orchestral scores and perhaps those of Ruggles and Cowell.

New Music fulfilled much the same role in music that the old *Dial* or *transition* did in literature. It made known the work of North Americans primarily, some Central and South Americans, some Soviet radical composers, and assorted others, including the first publications anywhere of Schoenberg's *Klavierstück*, Op. 33b, and Webern's *Geistlicher Volkstext*, Op. 17 no. 2

Among its steadies were, of course, Ives, Ruggles, Ruth Crawford, Carlos Chávez, and Dane Rudhyar (misspelled by me in the letter reproduced below). Enthusiasm for the music of the last-named, discussed below (who, besides being a composer, is an astrologer—his real name is Daniel Chennevière), has grown since I have come to know more of his music.

The following letter seems to be a thank-you note for scores Ives sent me. The *New Music* scores (Ruggles's *Men and Mountains* and Rudhyar's *Paeans*), being among the *Quarterly*'s first publications, were probably sent as an inducement to subscribe. The Ives *Violin Sonata* (the *First*, of which I still have the photostat copy) apparently was also included, as, perhaps, were the *Three Transcriptions from Emerson* in photostat (which I later heard Ives play at Redding) drawn from the Emerson movement of the *Concord Sonata*. Several years before this, Ives had given me a printed version of the latter with quite a number of notational changes in his hand, which I have treasured for years.

> Dear Mr. Ives,
>   These examinations are something of a waste of time and they have taken me away from my music. Before they began I wrote two more songs and planned partly another movement of that string quartet.
>   I am getting together some fellows up here to play it and also that violin sonata of yours. I have not had time to look it over but it looks very good so far. I have not tried to fit the Emerson movement together yet. But the violin sonata seems to me to have the quiet emotionality which is the real inspiration of music. Music should be admitted to have an affect on people and more that has a good effect should be played.
>   Your violin sonata seems to make ideals and serenity sprout out of one as Brahms and Bach do. Mr. Furness has played Emerson for me and I think it is wonderful too. I have always wanted to hear you play these and possibly learn some one of them (as much as my poor technique would allow).
>   And then too those . . . *New Music*. That is really a great thing. Henry Cowell deserves much praise. I can hear some of 'Men and Mountains' but Rhudyar's 'Paeans' are good but they seem a little too majestic, too much of his own greatness taken for granted.
>   Anyhow, thank you very much for all these, they will last long and mean much. More, now, than I can say and certainly more than I have as yet discovered.
>
>   (Signed) Elliott C. Carter, Jr.

My meetings with Ives stopped when, like many others who must have felt as I did, I left the conservative teaching I had been receiving in America for that of a more progressive Europe. In the United States, at that time, contemporary music was generally brushed aside by most musicians as the work of lunatics. I had complained to Ives that most of my teachers, except for Walter Piston, seemed to hold this opinion. I was particularly disgusted by and scornful of those who raged against Ives's work after having thumbed through the privately printed scores he had sent to many college libraries and been appalled. Understanding my attitude, Walter Piston advised me to study with someone who took contemporary music seriously: Mlle. Nadia Boulanger, and this took me to Paris. While there, I witnessed the massacres connected with the Stavisky affair and the terrifying rise of Hitler. I returned to the U.S. of the Depression in 1935, but remained out of touch with Ives until our paths crossed in what was for me, at least, a disastrously traumatic way.

For, as a sometime-critic (for the magazine *Modern Music*) I was put into the personally very dismaying situation—routine, probably, for profession-als (else how to explain their callousness)—of having to give an unfavorable review of a work which I had once loved and whose composer, Ives, I counted as one of my great friends. For I had to review the world première of his *Concord Sonata* given by John Kirkpatrick at Town Hall, New York, on 20 January, 1939. Indeed, this was the first of two performances, because hardly any critics except for Lawrence Gilman and myself, indeed hardly anyone, showed up. At Gilman's suggestion it was decided to repeat the concert about a month later after a concentrated publicity campaign had been undertaken—which did succeed in bringing in public and critics—proving what should have been obvious: that most music critics do not review, nor does the public applaud, the music *per se*, but rather the publicity that surrounds it—the present explosion of interest in Ives unfor-tunately is no exception.

By the time this première took place my taste in contemporary music had changed considerably from my college days. With the extravagant, bawling, impassioned demagoguery we witnessed on newsreels and heard on the radio emanating from Italy and Germany, it was hard to be taken in by or even be sympathetic to Romantic flamboyant gestures of any kind as we once were (sometimes in a joking way) and were to be again. At that particular time Ives's *Concord Sonata*, for all its qualities, seemed, at least to me, to have a strong element of extravagant Romantic gestures, however sincere, and it was impossible for me not to express my genuine antipathy to them, even though by doing so I was violating something I treasured a great deal. I don't know how much Ives was hurt by what I wrote. I know that I was deeply, so much so that I never had the heart to see him again.

From that time the distress caused by my own review, coupled with a growing sense of how remarkable the man and his music were, as I recap-tured my early point of view, led me to take practical actions to further Ives's cause. My new thoughts were expressed in several articles, "Charles Ives, His Vision and His Challenge" in *Modern Music*, May 1944, and "An American Destiny (Charles Ives)" in *Listen*, November 1946. Replying to me about the 1944 article Ives, as was his habit during these years, wrote out a rough first sketch and then a second, more finished one, in pencil in his irregular, nervous handwriting. Oddly, these were written from the point of view of Mrs. Ives, who then would transcribe and sign the letter. Here is the final version sent to me by Mrs. Ives—12 June, 1944.

Dear Mr. Carter—

I am writing for Mr. Ives who, as you know is not well and it is difficult for him to do so.

He appreciates very much your interest in his music and your kindness in writing the article in Modern Music Review. You have put things in a most interesting way. He feels there are some things not quite accurately referred to—though it is hardly your fault.

For instance, the 2nd Symphony was for the most part completed before Mr. Ives' father died fifty years ago (tho' it was fully scored a few years later) & Mr. Ives had not then heard or seen any of Dvorak's music which you assumed influenced this symphony. He says the themes in this were a kind of reflection of—or at least a hope to express in some way—the spirit of Stephen Foster, even if occasionally some of the old barn dance tunes were strewn over it—also themes from the old Camp Meeting hymn tunes, and in the last movement the stirring excitement the boys felt when the Danbury Cornet band of the '80s was marching down Main St. playing "The Red, White & Blue."

The 3rd Symphony, particularly the 1st & 3rd Movements he played as organ pieces and so not as fully as in the score in church services over 40 years ago and before he had heard or known any of Caesar Franck's music which it is inferred influenced it.

The last movement of the Holiday Symphony "Forefather's Day" Mr. Ives feels strongly is not dithyrambic—at least he hopes it reflects in no way the sallies of a crowd of revellers of Bacchus—no more than does that great solemn old hymn which a chorus sings towards the end of the Movement "O God, beneath Thy guiding hand Our exiled Fathers crossed the Sea."

In his chamber music there may be, he says, a poor joke or two but no parody of modern music was intended.

We hope that the inference in the last paragraph that no real considera- tion has ever been given to his music will not be misunderstood, that is, taken too literally nor seem unfair to those who have played, sung, con- ducted some of his music, written about it & "stood up for it" even when, as he says, some of them felt that in so doing they would probably get in wrong with some of "the powers that be"—& be not for that matter.

However, most of the above matters are secondary and rather unimpor- tant. He feels that your thoughts as to the fundamentals of music are "thoughtfully and beautifully expressed" and that they seem to suggest something that may be seen in a "scenic landscape of an Art-Philosophy"—

He is deeply grateful for what you have done on behalf of his music & sends you his sincere thanks.

We were so glad to see that your Symphonies are being played & hope they were well performed & fully appreciated.

Mr. Ives hopes when he is better to have the pleasure of seeing you again.

With kindest remembrances from both of us I am

Sincerely yours

Harmony Ives

I cannot resist, however, making a few comments on the changes that occurred between the three versions of this letter. Ives's first sketch is far more friendly than either the second sketch* or Mrs. Ives's copy. The first version remarked in the first pargraph "a very well-written article," which recurred in the second but was crossed out. The short paragraph about the chamber music did not appear until the second sketch, nor did the sentence about being unfair to those who have performed the music. Evidently Ives read my article several times and became more and more severe about it. This caused him to eliminate the touching reference to their cat, occurring only in the first sketch, with which it concludes:

> . . . and sends you his sincere thanks. He hopes to have the pleasure of seeing you again—and we won't let that old cat crawl on your shoulder again and try to take your coat off—You remember that happy day—She is now nearly 20 years old and now so polite and sedate. With kindest remembrance, Yours_____.

This last is a reference to what was an embarrassing moment for me as a youth at the Iveses' house, when their kitten crawled into the sleeve of my jacket and wandered around inside it behind my back, while I was trying to appear calm and collected. We had often laughed over this. It is entirely possible that if I had received the first version of this at the time, instead of seeing it for the first time now, I would have immediately gone to see him. Then, I received the version above addressed "Dear Mr. Carter," while all other letters were addressed "Dear Eliott."

Continuing my active efforts for Ives's music, I decided to start an Ives Society with the primary aim of getting some of his more muddled manuscripts into playable shape, with clear copies of score and practical parts, while he was still around to help with advice. This project was to be a special one connected with the American Music Center. The following letter is self-explanatory:

---

* A facsimile reproduction of its first page appears in Perlis, p.140.—Eds.

Chairman of the Board: Otto Luening — Executive Secretary:
Harrison Kerr — Assistant Secretary: Shirley Brandt —
Treasurer: Marion Bauer — Assistant Treasurers:
Aaron Copland, Douglas Moore, Quincy Porter

AMERICAN MUSIC CENTER, Inc.,
250 West 57th Street, New York 19, N.Y.
For the Distribution of Published and Recorded American Music

Board of Directors: Marion Bauer — Aaron Copland —
Howard Hanson — Philip James — Harrison Kerr — Otto Luening —
Douglas Moore — Quincy Porter — Oscar Wagner

October 20th, 1944

Mr. Charles E. Ives
West Redding, Connecticut
Dear Mr. Ives:

In recognition of your outstanding achievement as a composer, and in
acknowledgment of the many contributions you have made to the cause of
American music, the Charles Ives Society wishes to send you greetings on
your 70th birthday.
Representing a group of creative people to be known as the Charles Ives
Society, I wish to tell you that it is our intention to assist in familiarizing the
people with your works, feeling that they are entitled to the widest possible
understanding.

Sincerely yours,

(Signed) Elliott Carter

EC:rw

This provoked the following reply, which exists in the Yale archives only
in Ives's first and second pencil sketches, which differ primarily in that the
first is warmer in tone while the second is more coherent—I give the second
here: The words in parentheses are inserts, sometimes substituting for and
sometimes adding to, the text:

> Mr. Ives was deeply affected by your kind letter and says he cannot find
> words to express his great appreciation of all you, Henry, and other kind
> friends are doing on his behalf but he feels that he doesn't deserve it
> all—and to form a society named after him is not fair to many other
> American composers and also that it will bring you all too much trouble
> and take too much (of your) time.
>
> Just now he is so overcome and so embarrassed that he doesn't know
> what he ought to do about it all. When Henry wrote that an informal
> committee has been formed he felt somewhat embarrassed about that—
> but a Charles Ives Society of new composers* that's too much he says unless
> not only his name but the names of all American composers your commit-
> tee approves of, can be nailed all over it.

He is not at all well as you may know, and can't do many things he would like to, or take an active part in any work (he couldn't go to meetings) and so he feels he should not let his generous friends put themselves so much out for his sake, he says. There are other composers (he says) who need your help too—among them Carl Ruggles, and in the next generation Henry Cowell and a younger friend of his, Elliott Carter, whom you probably know (may have met) and also others whose music should be widely known and often played.

But he does thank you all from the bottom of his heart.

He doesn't feel quite right about having a society named after him (he says it makes him feel like "sort of like a Hog") some of his friends (on the high way) may infer as has happened before that there is an old friend he doesn't stand up for enough—that one "is his music."

However, later on when he is better able to attend to things—and hears whatever you, Henry, and other friends think ought to be done, he will try to do.

But he does thank you from the bottom of his heart all for your generous friendship and interest.

*The previous three words have been crossed out in the original; "new" is a conjecture—only the "n" is legible.

The Ives Society project continued for a number of years and involved the devoted activities of Henry Cowell and Lou Harrison, who prepared the scores of the *Robert Browning Overture*, the *Second* and *Third Symphonies*, and the *First Piano Sonata*, among other things, for performance and publication. I remember working on the *Trio* for violin, cello, and piano. This effort, which was mainly concerned with scores of which Ives had never had the occasion to make a fair copy, consisted not only in deciding which of the many palimpsest versions of the MSS were usable but sometimes in composing little connecting passages, submitted, of course, for Ives's approval. In all of this, I found myself becoming more and more aloof, for the confusion found in many of the manuscripts began to keep me awake nights trying to decide how to make Ives's highly personal music emerge from his incomplete and often jumbled sketches.

During these years (1944–47), I met quite regularly with Paul Rosenfeld, the most intelligent and hospitable critic American music has had the good fortune to have, to plan a book on Ives—he, taking care of the biography and I, the music. This was cut short by his death in 1946.

In the spring of 1946, Columbia University, which had inaugurated an annual series of festivals of contemporary American music, was persuaded to present some of Ives's works. At first, it was uncertain whether *The Unanswered Question* and *Central Park in the Dark*, which I was particularly anxious to have performed since no one had heard them and few even knew of their existence, would be part of a concert of Ives's works or not, and so a series of communications about other possible works took place to gather information, as the following answers by Mrs. Ives to my various requests show:

164 East 74th Street
March 14, 1946

Dear Elliott—

Mr. Ives thinks the enclosed may do as programme notes to the 3rd Symphony. He had some notes years ago but they are not around any more now. We think Herrmann's article nicely expressed.*

If it is too long the sentences marked may be omitted.

Hoping this will answer—Mr. Ives greatly appreciates all you are doing and hopes someday he may do something for you—

Mr. Ives will be glad to have Mr. Pagano make a copy of the Symphony and says it must be done only at his expense—As he remembers there were 2 or 3 measures in the 1st violin and flute parts in which a note or two were not as they were in the old sketch. The last time he played it over several years ago the first way seemed better. However he says they were unimportant, and this page could be made over easily later after the score is copied. Also at the very end a kind of ad lib. chords for bells off stage were to represent distant church bells—but they can be left out until the sketch copy can be found—

Of course Mr. Pagano will understand that the clarinet and horn parts are in the actual notes and not transposed as they should be in the score and also the viola part is not always in the viola clef—As I said to you over the phone the other day, the key signatures sometimes left out are throughout in the 1st movement B♭ and in the 2nd E♭ and in the 3rd B♭.

Mr. Ives says he hates to give you all this trouble—he feels it is an imposition and is very sorry!

With our best wishes

Sincerely yours
Harmony T. Ives

Mr. Carl Pagano, who for many years has been a great help to contemporary American composers through his patient and careful efforts as a copyist of their scores, had become quite an expert in dealing with Ives's scores. Part of the activity of the Ives Society of that time was meeting with Mrs. Ives to ask her to find out which scores Mr. Ives wanted to have worked on, then "editing" them when necessary, giving them to Mr. Pagano to copy

---

* Bernard Herrmann, "Four Symphonies by Charles Ives," *Modern Music*, 22,4 (May–June, 1945):215–22.—Eds.

and extract parts, and then proofreading these. Henry Cowell also became active at this time in interesting publishers in accepting these works for publication. There had been a parallel effort by Bernard Herrmann, the conductor of the Columbia Broadcasting Orchestra, to get some works into performable shape, and he gave a number for the first time over the air and had written an enthusiastic article about Ives's work, which was included in the above letter. The next letter followed immediately:

164 East 64th Street
New York City
Sat. Ma. 16 1946

Dear Elliott

Mr. Ives has decided he wants one sentence in the Herrmann notes left out—The last sentence in the first paragraph.

'Ives in the role of preacher speaks words of comfort, tenderness & hope'.

He feels that it is appropriate in a magazine article but not in a programme note,

With best wishes

Sincerely
Harmony T. Ives

P.S. It would be well, Mr. Ives thinks that the title of the score 'Central Park in the Dark' be changed to 'Central Park in the Dark Some Forty Years Ago'.

We are giving you lots of trouble.

[top of next page] *Unanswered Question*

Enclosed is a page from the 'Boletin Latino-Americano de Musica' which is marked to show that the passage in the square should be in the upper part of the score staves and not where it is written in the lower ones.

Mr. Ives doesn't know if Mr. Schenkman is using this score—he has no photostat score here but doesn't think it is put down this way in the latter.

Mr. Ives doesn't know if it will help to have the notes on the 2nd Str. Quartet used—and says to do whatever you think best.

As the Columbia University concert approached, plans for it began to change. For one thing Lou Harrison conducted a New York performance of the *Third Symphony* (which was to win Charles Ives the Pulitzer Prize for that year), and it was decided to include some works of Ruggles on the concert. So a further telephone call elicited this letter:

164 East 74th Street
New York City 21
April 9th 1946

Dear Elliott,

Miss Dower telephoned me today asking me for programme notes & dates to be sent to you for the Columbia concert on May 21st.

On the last page of both scores 'The Unanswered Question (or Cosmic Landscape)' & the 'Central Park in the Dark Some 40 years ago' are typewritten photostat copies giving some description of the music from which programme notes could easily be made. These scores we think are at the Music Center. If not we will have photostat copies made & sent to you tho' if you are in a hurry for these it might save time if you call the Quality Photostat Studio—VA6–0358—& order them—the bill to be sent to Mr. Ives of course. Ask for Index nos. 229–230.

As to the 2nd Violin Sonata Mr. Ives says the titles to the 3 movements would almost do as programme notes. l. Autumn. 2. Barn Dance. 3. A Revival.

The dates you ask for are 'The Unanswered Question'—sometime before June 1908 'Central Park in the Dark—' 1906 2nd Violin Sonata—1903–1910.

Mr. Ives hopes you do realize how very appreciative he is of all you have done & are doing for his music—You will of course send bills for any expense incurred to him. We are going to West Redding on the 15th of this month I think you have our telephone number if there is anything further you want to ask about.

I enjoyed the concert so much & was so glad Lou Harrison got such good criticism.

With our warmest best wishes

Sincerely yours

Harmony T. Ives

In the Yale Library there is, in Ives's hand, a "sketch for postscript to 9 apr. 46 (not sent)":

Though it is not an important matter, it would be well,—unless the programs for your May concert are already printed—not to put as a first public performance the 'Central Park—some 40 years ago'.

As it was cut down some in instrumentation for Theater orchestra (Mr. Ives doesn't remember the details) and (it) played between the acts in a downtown Theater in NY.

—He doesn't remember the exact date or the name of the Theater. There was no programme, but he thinks it was in 1906 or '07.

The players had a hard time with it—the piano player got mad, stopped in the middle and kicked in the Bass Drum. However don't put the above in the program—just not 'First Performance'—as he feels if not, it would be hardly fair to those old 'fellers' who stood up for a 'dangerous job.'

After the concert, since I was in touch with Mrs. Ives by phone, I called her up to have her tell Mr. Ives about the strong impression his works had made on many of us. We had done *The Unanswered Question* and *Central Park* at McMillan Theater with the "off-stage" string orchestra behind a curtain and the other orchestra in front of it, which gave a particularly magical effect.

After this, I was frequently away from New York and there seems to have been no correspondence, until I learned of Ives's death while I was a Fellow at the American Academy in Rome in 1954. My letter of condolence to Mrs. Ives, not yet found, was answered:

West Redding
Connecticut
October 3, 1954

Dear Elliott,

From the length of time it has taken me to acknowledge your most kind and truly valued letter written me at the time my husband died you might think I was not as moved by it as I was—I loved the things you said about him. I remember your visit here and Mr. Ives telling me, 'He says people think I'm crazy, *really crazy*'—and he used to recall that remark rather with wonderment.

I am by no means adjusted to a life without him. He has for so many years been my care and my joy that my life seems emptied of its contents and I do not know how I shall fill it.

Henry Cowell tells me you are still abroad—I know Rome and love it—better than Florence and hope you are gaining inspiration and laying up a store of rich memories and experiences.

Thank you so warmly
with kindest wishes
Harmony T. Ives

John Kirkpatrick and Henry Cowell have been a great help to me in going over and rearranging Mr. Ives' MSS which are in a state of confusion.

Music and the Time Screen

Current Thought in Musicology, ed. John W. Grubbs (Austin: University of Texas Press, 1976)

The sense of the above title was suggested to me by Professor Edward Lowinsky, the well-known musicologist, once when I was lecturing at the

University of Chicago. He said something to the effect that "time is the canvas on which you consider music to be presented, just as the spatial canvas of a painting furnishes the surface on which a painting is presented." Such a provocative comparison reaches in so many directions that it is difficult to discuss it in some clear and intelligible way. Analogies between the structure and character of time and those of space tend to be superficial, if not pointless, because we experience these dimensions in such different although interconnected ways. Yet, if the "time screen" on which music in this statement is said to be projected is considered to be a stretch of the measurable time of practical life, while the music itself may be incorporating another kind of time but needs measurable time for its presentation, then it can, no doubt, be compared to the space screen of a flat, rectangular canvas on which the imaginings of the artist about space are projected, and there is some point to the comparison.

However, it becomes much more tenuous if we try to compare the connections a composer can make in a composition between "sooner and later," which, although existing in "clock time," can also gain many special meaningful relationships because they involve patterns related to the experience of time of both composer and listener, and the "up and down" or "right and left" of a picture, elements that, although also physically in the picture, also participate in the artist's and observer's common experience of weight, shape, color, and visual texture, which can only be applied to time metaphorically.

It is not my intention here to indulge in such comparisons but to describe how, out of a consideration for the special temporality of music, I have attempted to derive a way of composing that deals with its very nature. To start with, I must briefly deal with the formidable subject of time, a most confusing one because no common vocabulary exists to help us—the "real time" of the Bergson school is very far from that of electronic composers, and the various conceptions of "ontological time" do not relate to each other, while the relationship of "public time" (of Martin Heidegger) to "clock time" (for some, synonymous with "mathematical time") and the latter to such a notion as Pierre Suvchinsky's "chronometric time" is hard to establish. In an effort to isolate the particular field under discussion, I would like to start by quoting Charles Koechlin, who proposed four aspects of time:

> 1. Pure duration, a fundamental of our deepest consciousness, and apparently independent of the external world: life flows by. . . .
> 2. Psychological time. This is the impression we have of (the above)

duration according to the events of our existence: minutes that seem centuries, hours that go by too quickly. . . . That is, duration relative to the circumstances of life.

3. Time measured by mathematical means; all of which depend on visual methods—sand clocks, clocks, chronometers. . . .

4. Finally, I would like to talk of "musical time." To us musicians this fact does not present itself as it does to scientists. Auditory time is without a doubt the kind that comes closest to pure duration. However, it appears to have some connection with space in that it seems to us measurable (by ear) and divisible. The divisions embodied in musical note-values (whole-notes, half-notes, etc.) lead to a spatialization of time very different from that (based on vision) which Bergson talks about. Besides, as concerns the measure of this (musical) duration, the role of musical memory possesses an importance that seems to escape many.[1]

To expand these aspects further: the first, "pure duration," is evidently the same as Bergson's "real" or "subjective time," *la durée réelle*, which can be known only by intuition, or, as Suzanne Langer, whose *Feeling and Form* has been illuminating on these matters, comments: " . . . every conceptual form which is supposed to portray time over-simplifies it to the point of leaving out the most interesting aspects of it, namely the characteristic appearances of passage."[2]

Koechlin's second aspect, "psychological time," would be more or less clear from his definition if Heidegger had not expounded a whole philosophy in *On Time and Being*, which, as I understand it, combines the first and second of the above aspects in an impressive demonstration that every human (*Dasein*)[3] is experiencing duration according to his own life pattern, tinged as it inevitably is with expectation, dread, and with the certainty of an end in death, as well as with the sense that the experience of living in time is a common human condition.

Of Koechlin's third aspect, "mathematically measured time," Langer says it is "a special abstraction from temporal experience, namely *time as pure sequence*, symbolized by a class of ideal events, indifferent in themselves, but arranged in an infinite 'dense' series by the sole relation of succession. Conceived under this scheme, time is a one-dimensional continuum."[4] Finally, of "musical time" with its relation to "pure duration," Langer remarks: "The direct experience of passage, as it occurs in each individual life is, of course, something actual, just as actual as the progress of the clock or speedometer; and like all actuality it is only in part perceived, and its fragmentary data are supplemented by practical knowledge and ideas from other realms of thought altogether. Yet it is the model for the virtual time created in music."[5]

The ambiguity of the term *time screen* becomes evident with the isolation of such aspects, for while it can be said to be a mathematically measured stretch of time (painfully evident at broadcasting or recording sessions), still, the fact that music is intended for listeners creates the impression that "musical" or "virtual" time is being projected on a time screen of the listener's "pure (or 'subjective') duration," with all its added capabilities of interpretation, memory, and shifts of focus of attention. The relationship between two of these aspects is made clear in Langer's discussion of the experience of time, which is based on contrasting it with "clock time,"

> whose underlying principle is *change*, which is measured by contrasting two states of an instrument, whether that instrument be the sun in various positions, or the hand on a dial at successive locations, or a parade of monotonous, similar events like ticks or flashes, "counted," i.e., differentiated, by being correlated with a series of distinct numbers . . . "change" is not itself something represented; it is implicitly given through the contrast of different "states," themselves unchanging.
>
> The time concept which emerges from such mensuration is something far removed from time as we know it in direct experience, which is essentially *passage*, or the sense of transience. . . . But the experience of time is anything but simple. It involves more properties than "length," or interval between selected moments; for its passages have also what I can only call, metaphorically, *volume*. Subjectively, a unit of time may be great or small as well as long or short. . . . It is this voluminousness of the direct experience of passage that makes it . . . indivisible. But even its volume is not simple; for it is filled with its own characteristic forms, as space is filled with material forms, otherwise it could not be observed and appreciated. . . . The primary illusion of music is the sonorous image of passage, abstracted from actuality to become free and plastic and entirely perceptible.[6]

Such ideas as these did not become important to me until around 1944; up to that year I had been concerned with other matters and thought of "time" much as many others did. I was familiar (but somewhat suspicious of) the various proposals made to organize time according to mechanical, constructivist patterns frequently discussed in the twenties and thirties. Like many other approaches to music of the period, this was primarily concerned with purely physical possibilities and their juggling. Some applied numerical patterns to note-values derived from the tuning of the musical scales (as Henry Cowell proposed in *New Musical Resources*[7]); others followed the schematic methods presented in *The Schillinger System of Musical Composition*[8]—two points of view taken up later and subjected to serial permutation by Olivier Messiaen, Pierre Boulez, Karlheinz Stockhausen, and others. As the first phase of modernism began to die away with the rise of Populist ideas during the late thirties and forties, composers, for the most part, returned to the more or less familiar ways of musical thought, and this matter, which began to interest me then, found little corroboration among most of my colleagues.

As one whose interest in music was aroused by hearing the "advanced" music played in the twenties in the United States and whose musical education took place during the years of change to the Populist style, and who then, out of political sympathy, wrote for a while in this style, I still view with considerable perplexity the renewal of many of the so-called experiments of the earlier avant-garde style, few of which led to interesting results then and seem, even today, to be rather unproductive. In any case, around 1945, as the Populist period was nearing its end (as we now see in retrospect), I felt I had exhausted my interest in that style and started a thoroughgoing reassessment of musical materials in the hope of finding a way of expressing what seemed to be more important matters—or at least more personal ones.

In retrospect, I can see that it took several years to clarify intentions. During this time I wrote my 1945 *Piano Sonata*, my 1947 *Emblems*, and my 1948 *Wind Quintet* and *Cello Sonata*, all of which foreshadow future preoccupations. By 1948 and 1949 I had become very concerned with the nature of musical ideas and started writing music that sought to find out what the minimal needs were for the kind of musical communication I felt worthwhile. There were the *Eight Etudes and a Fantasy for Woodwind Quartet* and six of the *Eight Pieces for Timpani*. The seventh of the wind etudes, based on the note G (which can be played on all four instruments), draws out of the four possible tone colors and their eleven combinations and many variants due to dynamic and attack differences, a musical discourse entirely dependent on contrasting various types of "entrances": sharp, incisive attacks as opposed to soft entrances. In the third etude, the three notes of a soft D-major chord are given different emphases by changes of tone color and doublings. In the fourth etude, a unit of two eighth notes, rising a rapid semitone and resting, serves as the generator of an entire piece constructed after the fashion of measures sixteen to thirty-five (Ex. 1), a mosaiclike technique I have used in many different ways.

At the same time, a whole complex of notions about rhythm, meter, and timing became a central preoccupation. In a sense, this was explored according to the principles of "clock," or in this case "metronomic," time, but its relationship to the jazz of the thirties and forties that combined free improvisation with strict time, and with early and non-Western music, as well as that of Alexander Scriabin, Ives, and Conlon Nancarrow, made

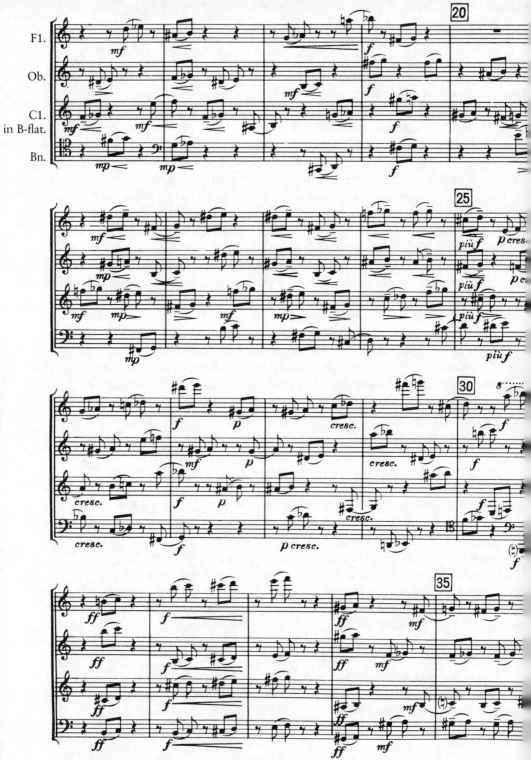

Ex. 1. Eight Etudes and a Fantasy for Woodwind Quartet
(1950), No. 4, mm.16–35.
Copyright 1959 by Associated Music Publishers, Inc.

me always look toward ways that could incorporate into "musical time" the methods that interested me. The desire to remain within the realm of the performable and auditorily distinguishable divisions of time kept me from exploring the field of polyrhythms, for instance—as someone else might have done who was primarily concerned with mathematically measured time.

A few years previous to 1948, I had come across the ideas of Pierre Suvchinsky in his article in the May–June 1939 issue of *La Revue musicale*[9] and in Igor Stravinsky's long discussion of them in *La Poétique musicale*.[10] Here again, it was a question of the experience of time with an opposition between what Suvchinsky calls "Khronos," which appears to be a version of "pure duration" ("real" time), and the many different "psychological" times—expectation, anxiety, sorrow, suffering, fear, contemplation, pleasure, all of which could not be grasped if there were not a primary sensation of "real," or "ontological," time. Different composers stress different combinations of "real" and "psychological" time—in Haydn, Mozart, and Stravinsky, the music is what Suvchinsky calls "chronometric," since the sense of time is equivalent to the musical process of the work. Musical time is equivalent to ontological time, while the music of the Romantics, particularly that of Wagner, is "chrono-ametric," since it has an unstable relationship between the time of the music and the psychological time it evokes. Such thinking (which I am not sure I agree with) led me to the idea of the opening of the *Cello Sonata* of 1948, in which the piano, so to speak, presents "chronometric" time, while the cello simultaneously plays in "chrono-ametric" time.

With my *Cello Sonata*, a whole collection of rhythmic practices began to be developed. Ultimately these were to expand the basic divisions and groupings of regular pulses to include polyrhythmic patterns and rubato, shaped into several methods of continuous change. One, which first found its way into the *Cello Sonata*, has been called "metric modulation." The technique is illustrated in a passage from the "Canaries" (Ex. 2), one of the pieces for timpani. To the listener, this passage should sound as if the left hand keeps up a steady beat throughout the passage, not participating in the modulations and playing the lower notes B and E at the slow speed of metronome (M. 64), while the right-hand part, made up of F-natural and C-sharp—goes through a series of metric modulations, increasing its speed a little at each change. Starting with the same speed as the left hand—64 to the dotted quarter—the right hand substitutes regular quarters (M. 96) for them in the next measure, and in the third measure these quarters are

Ex. 2. "Canaries" from Eight Pieces for Four Timpani (one
player) (1949/1966), p. 19.
Copyright 1968 by Associated Music Publishers, Inc.

accented in pairs, and then triplets (M. 144) are substituted for the two
previous quarters. The notation is then changed at the double bar so that the
previous triplet quarter equals the new quarter, which then in its turn is
accented in pairs for which, once again, triplets are substituted (these are
now at M. 216). The whole process is then repeated on this new level,
bringing the value of the quarters in the twelfth measure to M. 324—with
the left hand still continuing its beat of M. 64, now notated in durations of
eighty-one sixty-fourth notes. The maintaining of two layers of rhythm, in
this case one retaining a steady beat while the other changes its speed step by
step, is characteristic of many passages written since that time. Obviously,
too, in music built, as this is, on four pitches, the matter of the formation of
ideas with such minimal material was a constant preoccupation, as were the
various ways of opposing as well as linking these ideas into phrases and
larger shapes.

The preoccupation with reduction of musical ideas to their simplest terms
became a general formal trend in some works. For instance, the *Adagio* of
my *First String Quartet*, with its strong opposition between the soft, muted
music of the two high violins and the loud, vigorous recitative of the viola

and cello, is the presentation in their simplest terms of the oppositions of rhythm, theme, and character that are characteristic of the entire work, while the *Allegro scorrevole* is a reduction of the typically diversified texture to a stream of sixteenth notes with a seven-note theme, fragmented into diversified bits that form a constantly changing mosaic (Ex. 3). This section itself has as one of its characteristics a tendency to be interrupted and then to return. One of the interruptions is formed by the relaxing break usually placed between two movements.

What preoccupied me through the fifties was a desire to find a new flow of musical thought and expression—a tendency to which the previous efforts seemed to be leading. This tendency was not a very pronounced one during the earlier part of the twentieth century, although Debussy expressed dissatisfaction with the conventional methods of "thematic development" of his time. This led him to explore static as opposed to sequential repetition and to reduce thematic material, especially in his last works, to elemental forms containing motives that formed the basis for a spinning out of coherent, ever-changing continuities, a procedure probably derived from the study of plainsong as taught at the Parisian Schola Cantorum in the 1890s. Stravinsky was to adopt this nonsequential development after 1913, as were many outside central Europe, such as, for instance, Edgard Varèse. However, by the mid-1940s the excessive use of ostinatos and the rather limited uses of plainsong continuity began to seem outworn, especially since the serial technique seemed to provide other possibilities. There was, as is well known, at the end of the Second World War a sudden interest in Europe in all the forms of modernism previously banned, which once more brought back in music the earlier concern with special sounds, irregular divisions of time, and groupings of these according to the serialization of their physical parameters, with only a very elementary concern for their possible interpretation by the listener. This return to old-fashioned avant-gardism was, of course, stimulating, because it put so many things into question—but only peripherally, since it side-stepped the fundamental issues of music from the point of view I am describing here. In effect, none of this was really "experimental" or advanced, as intended, since its approach to "musical" or even "virtual" time was as routined as the regimes of the patients in Thomas Mann's *The Magic Mountain*.[11] It was, on the contrary, an effort to find a more significant temporal thought, such as Hans Castorp (who never had his broken watch repaired) sought in Mann's novel, that directed my own development in the fifties and sixties.[12]

It was with such an aim that the *Second String Quartet* and the *Double*

Ex. 3. String Quartet No. 1 (1951), mm.356–67.
Copyright 1955, 1956 by Associated Music Publishers, Inc.

Concerto for Piano and Harpsichord with Two Chamber Orchestras (written at the same time in 1959–1960) were planned. The primary questions were: How are events presented, carried on, and accompanied? What kind of changes can previously presented events undergo while maintaining some element of identity? and, How can all this be used to express compelling aspects of experience to the listener? In both works, the purely instrumental sound material—the four stringed instruments in the *Quartet* and the harpsichord and piano and their associated chamber orchestras in the *Double Concerto*, each with their unique expressive and sound capacities—was sufficient, and I saw no reason to extend beyond the usual methods of playing. In the *Quartet*, each of the four instruments has a repertory of musical characters of its own, while contributing to the total effect in many different capacities, sometimes following, sometimes opposing the leader, usually according to its own capabilities—that is, according to the repertory of expression, continuity, interval, and rhythmic patterns assigned to it. Each is treated as an "individual," usually making an effort to cooperate, especially when this seems helpful in carrying on the musical enterprise. The work begins and concludes (Ex. 4) with each instument contributing—sometimes the briefest fragments, each characterized in its own fashion—to a mosaic that joins these into one large, audible pattern, a concentrated version of the pattern of the entire work.

While the *Second String Quartet* deals with the separation of four instruments of more or less similar tone color, expressive qualities, dynamic capabilities, and performing techniques, the *Double Concerto* uses soloists of such different capacities that an entirely different approach seemed necessary. The problem in the *Quartet*, given the kind of concept behind it, was to differentiate instruments of similar character, while the problem in the *Double Concerto*, as I saw it, was to join together instruments of very different basic characteristics. The harpsichord, as is obvious, is dynamically much softer than the piano when both are playing their loudest; its attack is much more incisive, however, while its response to the fingers is more mechanical. Dynamic shadings, which are the basis of a pianist's technique, are almost unobtainable by touch on the harpsichord, which has, to compensate, at least on some models, a vast number of possible mechanical-registrational color changes. The idea, therefore, of contrasting two worlds of musical expression and sound had to be carried out quite differently. It should be obvious that the idea of allowing four (as in the case of the *Quartet*) or two (as in the *Double Concerto*) different streams of music to be heard together in any one of the possible uncoordinated ways that have been

Ex. 4. String Quartet No. 2 (1959), Conclusion, mm.599–607.
Copyright 1961 by Associated Music Publishers, Inc.

used either by Ives or by others in recent years will, from the point of view I am describing here, produce a form of entropy, a degrading of the possibilities of communication, which to me have ever to be revitalized and sharpened. Furthermore, while such works as mine do not always receive performances that present clearly all the materials, their relationships and expressive intentions, still, these are there in the score, and performers and listeners can gradually come to recognize them after successive performances. If they were to be played quite differently every time, as is the intention of most aleatory scores, there would be little possibility of learning to hear and interpret more and more of what is in the scores.

So, to join the piano and harpsichord into one world of music that could have many inner contrasts, I chose two small orchestras, each with two percussion players, and, since this was to be an antiphonal piece, the two orchestras contained instruments that would underline the qualities of the soloist they were associated with and, in the case of the harpsichord, add dynamic volume to supplement its lack of dynamic range. It might be objected that the harpsichord could be amplified to make up for this, but I have always preferred to hear instruments, as well as people, present themselves in their own individual way without mechanical amplification, which gets in the way of direct contact, the whole point of a live concert. Under good acoustical and well-rehearsed conditions the harpsichord is perfectly audible and balanced in the way I consider effective for this piece. Because this work, as I got into it, took on the character of a percussion piece, with the soloists acting as mediators between unpitched percussion and pitched instruments, composing for percussion suggested certain ideas that do, indeed, have a rather "clock time" oriented attitude. This is especially true in the coda, which starts with a crash on the largest tam-tam and then is organized as a dying away over many measures of this crash, using the possible patterns of fading in and out of various partials in different phases of the sound-shape of the music, with each different phase filled with various character patterns recalling ideas from the whole work. Indeed, this piece, even more than the *Second String Quartet*, depends for its material on the sound of intervals, combined with various tone colors. Any figurative material that exists is directly derived from the intervallic sounds associated with each group and each section of the piece.

These works, as well as those previously mentioned, depend on a special dimension of time, that of "multiple perspective," in which various contrasting characters are presented simultaneously—as was occasionally done in opera, for example, in the ballroom scene from *Don Giovanni*, or in the finale of *Aïda*. Double and sometimes manifold character simultaneities, of course, present, as our human experience often does, certain emotionally charged events as seen in the context of others, producing often a kind of irony, which I am particularly interested in. In doing this so frequently, and by leading into and away from such moments in what seemed to me telling ways, I have, I think, been trying to make moments of music as rich in reference as I could and to do something that can be done only in music and yet that has rarely been achieved except in opera.

The concept of the *Second String Quartet* and the *Double Concerto* had this dimension built into them, as does my *Piano Concerto*, which pits the "crowd" of the orchestra against the piano's "individual," mediated by a concertino of seven soloists. Here, the conflict was conceived as one of orchestral music that becomes more and more insistent and brutal as the work continues, while the piano makes more and more of a case for variety, sensitivity, and imagination. Over a very long stretch of time in the second of the two movements, the orchestral strings build up more and more dense, softly held chords, which form a kind of suffocating blanket of sound, while at the same time the rest of the orchestra plays patterns of strict, regular beats that increase in forcefulness and are layered into more and more different speeds. Against all this, the piano and instrumental soloists play much expressive, varied music, which near the end of the passage finally becomes more insistent, with the piano crowded into repeating one note, the one note missing in the middle of an aggregate of eighty-one other notes (Ex. 5).

Of course, in these works, all kinds of uses were made of metric modulation, both as a mode of proceeding smoothly or abruptly from one speed to another and as a formal device to isolate one section from another. Generally, these work together, for very often a new section with a different speed and character starts while another layer continues in the same speed. In the course of exploring metric modulation, the idea of dealing with accelerandos and ritardandos intrigued me. The first notational solution of an accelerando, which speeds up regularly from beginning to end of a piece, occurred in the sixth variation of my *Variations for Orchestra* (1954), in which a scheme of six measures in 3/4 time speeds up during its course to three times its original pace, at which point there is a switch of notation, and a part previously playing quarter notes is written in triplets of eighths, while in other parts dotted quarters become eighths, dotted halves become quarters, and eighths become sextuplets of sixteenths. Yet, while each of these notational systems sounds as if it were continuing a regular acceleration, the beat has returned to the speed of that of the first beat of the six-measure scheme (Ex. 6). The entire variation is projected onto this scheme, which repeats itself over and over. Its usefulness here proved to be that the canonic theme could be brought in at different places in the scheme, so that successive entrances, if brought in sooner (for example, as a dotted half-note in its fourth measure), would sound slower, or, if brought in later, would sound faster. A whole pattern of total acceleration was thus achieved, for one of the final entrances occurs with the first note of the theme lasting the full six measures; the second note lasting the first three measures; the third note lasting the last three measures; the fourth to eighth notes lasting dotted halves; the next eighteen notes lasting quarters, and so forth. Similarly, the place at which the triplets of the theme are stopped comes later and later in the six-measure scheme, so that faster and faster notes are heard, until triplets finally invade the very last measure, sounding the fastest note-values heard thus far. The matter of projecting regular beats against such a pattern interested me, too. In this variation, the harp gives the impression of playing in slow, regular time the notes of one of the ritornellos against the music just described. Sometimes, systems of accelerations, ritardations, and regular beating have been combined, as in the slow section of the *Double Concerto* (measures 314–466) and in many short stretches of the *Piano Concerto*.

The *Concerto for Orchestra* of 1969 carries out the idea of waves of sound, used briefly in the coda of the *Double Concerto*, over a duration of more than twenty minutes. With this intention in mind, I started work, developing an overall dramatic and expressive plan and choosing the musical materials and form. After these had been clearly formulated, I came across the long poem *Vents* by the French poet who calls himself St. John Perse.[13] His Whitmanesque description of the United States swept by the winds of change seemed to revolve, as did the music I was writing, around four main ideas in the poem: (1) the drying up of autumn, suggesting the dryness and death of a previous time—men of straw in a year of straw; (2) the swiftness and freshness of the winds that blow away the old and bring in the new; (3) the exhortation of a shaman-poet calling for a rebirth and a destruction of worn-out things; and, finally, (4) the return of spring and life. These ideas are brought together in many different contexts, blended and mixed as the poet constantly stresses the motions of the wind. The music, too, has four main characters, and, while hints of all four are being referred to constantly, the concerto picks out one facet after another to dwell on at some length, subordinating the others. Thus, while there can be said to be four movements, these are almost constantly heard in combination. The

Solo
Pno.

Ex. 5. Concerto for Piano and Orchestra (1965), two-piano
score (reduction by the composer) pp.79, 80.
Copyright 1967 by Associated Music Publishers, Inc.

Ex. 6. Variations for Orchestra (1955), mm.289–99.
Copyright 1957, 1958 by Associated Music Publishers, Inc.

orchestra itself can be seated, when there is enough space, in such a way that the four strands of music are separated stereophonically as well as in timbre, material, and expression. The wind itself was thought of as being a composite of many elements, and the concerto treats the orchestra as groups of soloists, dividing each of the bodies of strings into five or more soloists that form the basis of each of the four sections: the celli, combined with harp, piano, wood percussion, and middle-register winds, are related to the autumnal rattling of pods and straw; the violins with flutes and metallic percussion, to the freshness of the wind; the basses, combined with tuba, timpani, and sometimes trombones, to the poet's invocations; and the violas, trumpets, upper-middle winds, and snare drums, to the reawakening.

Technically, the piece is constructed on a use of all the thirty-eight possible five-note chords (ten of which are symmetrical and twenty-eight invertible) that are distributed among the four movements, as shown in spacings typical of their movements in Ex. 7. Also shown is how the eleven two-note intervals, the twelve three-note chords, and the twenty-nine four-note chords, considered as components of the five-note chords, are distributed. (The inversions of the five-note chords and the seven-note chords, sometimes used, are omitted in the example.) Rhythmically, each movement has its general tendency: movement I is formed of groups of retarding phrases, each starting a little faster than the previous (see Ex. 7); movement II starts very fast and gets slower throughout the entire work with each successive appearance; movement III is made up of accelerating phrases, each starting at a slower point (as in Ex. 7); while movement IV gets faster from beginning to end.

The work starts with an introduction, "These were very great winds over all the faces of this world," [14] in which a twelve-tone chord is presented in four groups (or chords) of three notes (Ex. 8). Each of these groups forms the basis of one of the movements (as numbered), and "places" that movement in character in orchestration, tessitura, and general rhythmic behavior. Then, after a clamorous outburst, based still on a combination of the four basic materials, the other three movements subside and allow the dry rattling of the first movement to predominate (measures 24–140). During this section, music from movement II makes several brief appearances, the most extended of which is at measures 42–47. The same is true of fragments of movement III, as at measures 117–120, and of IV, as at 79–80. After a brief tutti, movement II proper starts (141–285), which suggests the freshness of the wind. Here, too, are occasional incursions of bits of other movements. This leads to a four-layered tutti that subsides into the recitative

Movement I

(a)   (b)   (c)   (d)

(e) Rhythmic basis: groups of retarding phrases, each starting a little faster than the previous.

Movement II

(a)   (b)   (c)   (d)
8va sempre

8va sempre

(e) Rhythmic basis: starts very fast and gets slower throughout the entire work with each successive
appearance.

Movement III

(a)   (b)   (c)   (d)

8 - ⌐

(e) Rhythmic basis: accelerating phrases, each starting at a slower point.

Movement IV

(a)
8va sempre

8va sempre
(b)   (c)   (d)

(e) Rhythmic basis: gets faster from beginning to end.

of the third movement. Finally, the fourth movement occupies most of measures 420–532. This movement made its vestigial appearance in measure 30 at a slow speed that increased at each reappearance until its real emergence following measure 420, after which its speed continues to increase. The coda, from 532 to the end, is multilayered, alternating rapidly between the four sets of materials, which, at times, change their characteristic tessituras. The work finally dies away, sounding fewer and fewer notes of the characteristic chords of each movement.

The musical material of this is entirely built of similar and contrasting items of sound. Intervals and chords are the characterized immediacies, or "nows," out of which motions of constantly changing shapes flow. It is a work fundamentally organized to produce the "virtual image" of "passage" discussed above. As such, it has to do, at least to me, with an image of internal time-consciousness of which Edmund Husserl says:

> The sensible nucleus ... is "now" and has just been and has been still earlier, and so on. In this now there is also retention of the past now of all levels of duration of which we are now conscious. . . . The stream of lived experience with its phases and intervals is itself a unity which is identifiable through reminiscence with a line of sight on what is flowing: impressions and retentions, sudden appearance and regular transformation, and disappearance and obscuration. This unity is originally constituted through the fact of flux itself; that is, its true essence is not to be, in general, but to be a unity of lived experience.[15]

It should be obvious that the general approach to music, rather fragmentarily presented here, could be susceptible of exploration in many directions—that what I have done seems, even to me, like just a beginning both technically and artistically, although the works are meant to be considered primarily in themselves. It has cost considerable imaginative effort, since the artistic horizon of the American composer is not expanded by life in a society that is unable to furnish him with artistic and intellectual ideas and critiques of sufficient depth, clarity, and quality to be of much use. In fact, to have indulged in the foregoing explanations and to be faced with the prospect of their being used as a substitute for listening to the music itself and fed into the general hopper of American educational, artistic statements—later to be ground up and to come out as undifferentiated fodder to

Ex. 7. Concerto for Orchestra (1969). Technical aspects: a. five-note chords; b. four-note chords; c. three-note chords; d. two-note intervals; and e. general retarding or accelerating tendencies associated with each of the four movements.

Ex. 8. Concerto for Orchestra. Compositional basis of each movement: three-note chords that together constitute the twelve-note chord.

be forcibly fed to the young and permanently regurgitated at exams—is apparently the terrible fate of such efforts as these and the disheartening result of America's ambivalence toward the arts. Yet a composer cannot but be grateful for an opportunity to express verbally ideas important to him (for otherwise who would?) in the hope that they may be really helpful to a few others.

Perhaps the only consolation is that any such descriptive discussion as this has really consistently, although not intentionally, evaded the issues and visions most important and significant during the act of composing. For what is discussed here (as should be obvious, but never seems to be) is the outer shell, the wrapping of the music. The reason for writing it—for developing it in the way described, for weighing every note, chord, rhythm in the light of their expressive intention and their living, spontaneous interrelationships, and the judging of it all, almost unconsciously, against a private standard of what gives me genuine sensuous pleasure, of what seems fascinating, interesting, imaginative, moving, and of urgent importance— cannot be put into words. It is, I suppose, what is easily brushed off with words like *involvement* or *commitment* to music, as well as to what St. John Perse somewhat portentously calls "the horror . . . and honor of living." [16]

NOTES

1. Charles Koechlin, "Le Temps et la musique," *La Revue musicale*, January 1926, pp.45–62 (my translation).

2. Suzanne Langer, *Feeling and Form* (New York: Scribner Library, 1953), p.114.

3. I use this expression "human (*Dasein*)" exactly as it is used in Martin Heidegger, *On Time and Being*, trans. Joan Stambaugh (New York: Harper & Row, 1972), pp.1–24. It refers not only to existence or presence, but also to the cognitive activities associated with this.

4. S. Langer, *Feeling and Form*, p.111.

5. Ibid., p.113.

6. Ibid., pp.112f.

7. Henry Cowell, *New Musical Resources* (New York: Knopf, 1930), pp. 45–108.

8. Joseph Schillinger, *The Schillinger System of Musical Composition* (New York: Carl Fischer, 1946), pp.1–95.

9. Pierre Suvchinsky [Souvtchinsky], "La Notion du temps et la musique," *La Revue musicale*, May–June 1939, pp.70–80.

10. Igor Stravinsky, *La Poétique musicale* (Cambridge: Harvard University Press, 1942), pp.19–24.

11. Thomas Mann, *The Magic Mountain*, trans. H. T. Lowe-Porter (New York: Modern Library, 1932). Contains many passages dealing with various aspects of time, especially the chapter "By the Ocean of Time," pp.683–90.

12. Marcel Proust deals with the subject exhaustively in his *À la recherche du temps perdu*, 10th ed., 15 vols. (Paris: Gallimard, 1927). See especially the last pages of the last book, "Le Temps retrouvé," 15, pp.249–61.

13. St. John Perse, *Vents* ("Winds"), trans. Hugh Chisholm (New York: Pantheon Books, Bollingen Series, no. 34, 1953).

14. Ibid., pp.4–5.

15. Edmund Husserl, *The Phenomenology of Internal Time-Consciousness*, ed. Martin Heidegger, trans. James S. Churchill (Bloomington: Indiana University Press, 1966), pp.149–57.

16. Perse, *Vents*, pp.178–79.

A Symphony of Three Orchestras
(1976)

Program note for the première performance by the New York Philharmonic,
February 1977, Pierre Boulez, conductor.

A *Symphony of Three Orchestras*, begun in June 1976 and completed
in December, was commissioned by the New York Philharmonic under a
commissioning grant to six orchestras (Boston, Chicago, Cleveland, Los
Angeles, New York, and Philadelphia) from the National Endowment for
the Arts, a Federal Agency, in celebration of the U.S. Bicentennial. The score
is dedicated to the New York Philharmonic and Pierre Boulez, its Music
Director.

For this work the whole orchestra is divided into three smaller orchestras,
as in the multiple orchestra works of Mozart. The first orchestra is made up
of brass, strings, and timpani; the second, clarinets, piano vibraphone,
chimes, marimba, solo violins and basses, and a group of cellos; the third,
flutes, oboes, bassoons, horns, violins, violas, basses, and non-pitched percussion.

The opening music, which starts in the highest registers of the three
orchestras and slowly descends as the trumpet announces one of the themes
heard at various times in orchestra I and ends in a series of rapidly plunging
passages, was suggested by the beginning of Hart Crane's "The Bridge,"
which describes New York harbor and the Brooklyn Bridge:

> How many dawns, chill from his rippling rest
> The seagull's wings shall dip and pivot him,
> Shedding white rings of tumult, building high
> Over the chained bay waters Liberty—
>
> Then, with inviolate curve, forsake our eyes
> As apparitional as sails that cross
> Some page of figures to be filed away;
> —Till elevators drop us from our day . . . *

---

* Reprinted from *The Bridge* by Hart Crane with the permission of the publisher, Liveright
Publishing Corporation. Copyright 1933, © 1958, 1970, by Liveright Publishing Corporation.

The opening descent immediately leads to a *Giocoso* theme played by bassoons, the central idea of the first movement of orchestra III, which begins the main section of the score. From here to the coda, twelve differently characterized movements, each with its own related themes, are heard, four played by each orchestra. The four movements of each orchestra, while differing in expression and speed, are related, of course, by spatial location and instrumental color and also characteristic harmonies and rhythms. While no orchestra plays two of its movements at a time, each of the twelve is introduced while another movement of another orchestra is being played, briefly surfaces to be heard alone and then becomes the background for another entrance of another movement. Thus there is a continual overlapping and changing flow of music. The listener, of course, is not meant, on first hearing, to identify the details of this continually shifting web of sound any more than he is to identify the modulations in *Tristan und Isolde*, but rather to hear and grasp the character of this kaleidoscope of musical themes as they are presented in varying contexts.

The main section is brought to a stop by a series of repeated short, loud chords for the full orchestra that shatter the previous flow. The score ends in a coda that recalls fragments of the previous music, alternating repetitive passages and expressive bursts, and finally sinks to the lowest registers of the three orchestras as the beginning is remembered.

Although *A Symphony of Three Orchestras* is not in any sense an attempt to express the poem of Hart Crane in music, many of the musical ideas were suggested by it and other works of his.

ARTICLES NOT INCLUDED IN THIS COLLECTION

"Composers by the Alphabet," *Modern Music*, 19,1 (Nov.–Dec. 1941): 70,71

"New Compositions," *Saturday Review*, 27,4 (Jan. 22, 1944):32,33.

"What's New in Music," *Saturday Review*, 28,3 (Jan. 20, 1945):13, 14, 34.

"The Genial Sage," in Paul Rosenfeld, *Voyager in the Arts*, ed. Jerome Mellquist and Lucie Wiese (New York: Creative Age Press, 1948), pp.163–65.

"Illinois Festival—Enormous and Active," *New York Herald Tribune*, Apr. 5, 1953. Reprinted in *Bulletin of the American Composers Alliance*, 3,2 (Summer 1953):17.

"Music of the Twentieth Century," *Encyclopaedia Britannica* (Chicago, 1953), 16th ed.:16–18.

"La Musique aux États-Unis," *Synthèses* (Brussels), 9,96 (May 1954): 206–11.

Autobiographical sketch for the *25th Anniversary Report of the Harvard Class of 1930* (Cambridge: Harvard University Press, 1955), pp.165–69.

Letter to the editor [reply to Gardner Read concerning notation], *Journal of Music Theory*, 7,2 (Winter 1963):270–73.

"Elliott Carter Objects," *New York Times*, Oct. 20, 1968.

"Conversation with Elliott Carter" by Benjamin Boretz, *Perspectives of New Music*, 8,2 (Spring–Summer 1970):1–22.

Acceptance by Elliott Carter of the Gold Medal for Music, *Proceedings of the American Academy of Arts and Letters and the National Institute of Arts and Letters*, 2d series, no.22 (1972):34.

"Edgard Varèse," written in French and read over transatlantic telephone, Oct. 29, 1975, for broadcast over Radio-France (ORTF) for a Varèse program, unpublished; enlarged English version, also unpublished.

Foreward to *Sonic Design* by Robert Cogan and Pozzi Escot (Englewood Cliffs, N.J.: Prentice-Hall, 1976), p.ix.

"To Think of Milton Babbitt," *Perspectives of New Music*, 14,2/15,1 (double issue, 1976; in press).

"A Mirror on Which to Dwell" [six poems of Elizabeth Bishop, for soprano and instrumental ensemble (1975/76)], program note.

"France-America Ltd.—French Influences on American Musical Life" [published in French], catalogue for the opening of the Centre Pompidou, Jan. 1977.

Index

Dates of birth and, where applicable, death have been supplied for twentieth-century composers, and where identification seemed necessary professions have been given for persons other than composers. In a few instances, dates and opus numbers have been listed for compositions.